CONFLICTING PARADIGMS IN ADULT LITERACY EDUCATION

In Quest of a U.S. Democratic Politics of Literacy

CONFLICTING PARADIGMS IN ADULT LITERACY EDUCATION

In Quest of a U.S. Democratic Politics of Literacy

George Demetrion
*Literacy Volunteers of Greater Hartford
Hartford, CT*

LEA LAWRENCE ERLBAUM ASSOCIATES, PUBLISHERS
2005   Mahwah, New Jersey   London

Lawrence Erlbaum Associates, Inc., Publishers
10 Industrial Avenue
Mahwah, New Jersey 07430

Cover design by Kathryn Houghtaling Lacey

Library of Congress Cataloging-in-Publication Data

Demetrion, George.
  Conflicting paradigms in adult literacy education : in quest of a U.S. democratic politics
of literacy / George Demetrion.
      p. cm.
  Includes bibliographical references and index.
  ISBN 0-8058-4623-9 (cloth : alk. paper) — ISBN 0-8058-4624-7 (pbk.: alk. paper)
    1. Functional literacy—Government policy—United States.   2. Adult education and
state—United States.   3. Progressive education—United States.   I. Title.

LC149.7.D416   2004
374'.012'0973—dc22   2004050677
                                                                           CIP

Books published by Lawrence Erlbaum Associates are printed on acid-free paper,
and their bindings are chosen for strength and durability.

Printed in the United States of America
10 9 8 7 6 5 4 3 2 1

Contents

Preface

This book provides a broad overview of some of the major trends and issues shaping the theories, practices, research traditions, and politics of adult literacy in the United States since the mid-1980s. If anything, these have been diverse, conflicting, and often irreconcilable. Impinging factors—from the global economy to urban poverty, from "functional literacy" to the "pedagogy of the oppressed," from demands for aggregate data analysis to alternative assessment design, from scientific-based educational research to practitioner-based inquiry—have been key prisms through which sharply jarring discourses have played out in this field during these years. The first eight chapters examine these issues through three distinctive interpretive frames: the participatory literacy movement, the New Literacy Studies, and the functional and workforce orientation of federal policy. Chapter 9, Research Traditions, closely parallels these schools of literacy. In these chapters, I adopt a strategy of critical description and historical analysis.

The final chapters explore tentative lines of potential reconcilability. A middle ground pedagogy is used to connect John Dewey's educational philosophy of growth to the New Literacy Studies and to a mode of research that links practitioner-based and scientific approaches through the example of Dewey's experimental logic. This exploratory space is mediated through the prospect of a reconstruction, or more technically put, a hermeneutical retrieval of the nation's founding ideals, flowing from the American Revolution as a basis to situate a contemporary U.S. politics of adult literacy. Problems with this construct are also highlighted.

Conflicting Paradigms in Adult Literacy Education: In Quest of a U.S. Democratic Politics of Literacy seeks to fill several gaps. First, it provides a broad historical overview of the field from the senior Bush administration, through the Clinton years, and into the first years of the junior Bush administration. Second, through the examination of educational practice and theory, assessment and accountability, research traditions, and political culture through distinctive paradigms or discourses, I seek to place in sharp relief some of the most compelling conflicts and challenges that the field has faced in its recent history and current setting. The descriptive chapters, accordingly, are narrated sequentially through the prisms of the aforementioned three schools of literacy.

Third, the book draws extensively on Internet resources and electronic discussion forums, as well as books, articles, and reports to illuminate something of the critical discourse that has shaped the field over the past 15 years or so. The forums (listservs), in particular, represent an ongoing practitioner-based inquiry project in "real time" where the field gets to talk to itself on a wide array of issues. Its primary dynamic is in the immediacy of communication across a wide spectrum of positionality. Generally less appreciated by participants is the value of the forum archives in capturing something of the collective wisdom of the field in dynamic and often tensional discourse in the raising of perplexing and challenging issues. It is these provocative strains and pressure points that I seek to draw out through an analysis of extensive e-mail "threads" in several chapters. A variety of voices of practitioners are heard, including my own, hence the reference to myself in the third person as one of the participants in the forum discussions. My hope is that this effort encourages other researchers to draw abundantly on the rich resources embedded in electronic discussion forum archives that remain sadly understudied and underutilized.

Finally, at least in terms of suggestive hypotheses, I seek to describe some potential avenues through which to establish broad-based common ground on a national level. The enduring reality of pluralism and the heightened paradigmatic conflict over such matters as educational theory, research assumptions, accountability, and political orientation may derail any such effort. Nonetheless, it remains an underlying assumption of this book that if the field is to move toward greater policy and public legitimization particularly in terms of its own intrinsic logics, then there is little choice other than of achieving some powerful convergences that reconcile some of the major tensions that currently perplex it.

OVERVIEW

Chapter 1 provides an in-depth overview of the scope and the flow of the book. Chapter 2 picks up in the midst of several (National Literacy Advocacy) NLA electronic forum threads in April 1997. It highlights literacy practitioners' supportive of participatory literacy education in their poignant quest to preserve the authenticity of their vision in light of intense policy pressures to conform to standardized measures of accountability. From their viewpoint, such measures marginalize that which is most essential about learning. The chapter incorporates academic work from this school and concludes with a discussion of a shift in focus from alternative assessment design to an embrace of the Equipped for the Future (EFF) accountability framework as described by one "reluctant standard bearer."

The next two chapters shift the focus to federal policy and include an analysis of formative influences. Chapter 3 reviews the central reports of the 1980s and early 1990s that in varying ways built on the image of the age of information and the implications of the postindustrial economy on secondary and adult education. This literature is both utopian in the prospects it held for economic and social reconstruction and dire in forecast if the educational system and workplace did not meet the challenges that a shift to a "knowledge society" required. Chapter 4 highlights a shift in policy rhetoric during the 1990s in linking adult literacy to welfare reform through an analysis of, and factors leading to, the Workforce Investment Act and National Reporting System of 1998. A workforce rationale for adult literacy remained pivotal, although the postindustrial imagery of a highly skilled workforce became attenuated in the conservative federal milieu of the mid-1990s. Chapter 5 highlights field responses to the new legislation mostly through posts on the NLA. These veered from the highly critical to the pragmatic need to accept its reality, and of finding ways of working within the new framework, without which public legitimacy would be threatened and federal funding would be eliminated or severely curtailed.

The next three chapters discuss challenges and dilemmas of the standard-based accountability movement in adult basic education during the 1990s. Chapter 6 identifies the enduring conflict between those seeking to base outcomes on the complex presuppositions of functional-context theory, participatory literacy education, and the New Literacy Studies, and those emphasizing standardization, objectivity, and quantifiable measurement as the only feasible basis to establish a viable federal accountability system. The chapter includes a discussion of two substantial reports and an in-depth September 1997 NLA thread titled "Documenting Program Effectiveness."

Chapters 7 and 8 examine the National Institute for Literacy's Equipped for the Future project, the most extensive effort throughout the 1990s to reconcile discordant perspectives in the arenas of pedagogy, best practices, assessment accountability, research, and policy. Chapter 7 provides a historical description of EFF from its inception through the development of all of its key components up to the development of the Content Standards.

Chapter 8 turns the spotlight on the Content Standards, with a central focal point on the "EFF/NRS connection." Built on the intellectual premises of constructivism, the EFF train hit a serious snag with the federal policy embrace of standardized measures that could not be easily squared with the complex array of indicators that underlie the 16 lifelong learning Content Standards. Chapter 8 bears in on this conflict, both in highlighting the efforts of EFF developers to work with the Department of Adult Education and Literacy (DAEL) in coming to some meaningful reconciliation with the NRS and pointing as well to the enduring tensions inherent in the effort.

The dilemmas of EFF became even more strained during George W. Bush's administration because of its embrace of scientific-based educational reform. The corresponding epistemological and methodological shifts that entailed resulted in a skeptical assessment of the practitioner-based inquiry model of research that undergirded much of EFF's development, along with its intellectual underpinnings in the psychology of constructivism. Although each of the two chapters highlights different aspects of the EFF project, the common link is the exploration of both the creative quest for a broad-based national consensus and the persisting realities of the strains that worked against the effort. In this respect, the EFF project viewed historically is a large-scale exemplar of the standards movement in adult literacy education of the 1990s. It is this thread—the quest for creative resolution and the enduring conflicts and snags that have marred the effort—that connects the three chapters already discussed.

In Chapter 9, I draw on Donna C. Mertens' construct as depicted in *Research Methods in Education and Psychology*, which centers on three sharply differentiated paradigms of social science research that broadly parallel the distinctive schools of adult literacy pedagogy discussed in the previous chapters. Specifically, the *positivist/postpositivist* (which I refer to as the neopositivist) paradigm informs much of the intellectual universe that underlies federal policy. The *interpretive/constructivist* framework is broadly analogous to the ethnographic sensibility of the New Literacy Studies, whereas the *emancipatory* paradigm resonates with the key Freirian presuppositions of participatory literacy education. I also draw on another key text, Richard Shavelson and Lisa Towne's influential *Scientific Research in Education* in which the authors identified six key principles of scientific research. I work through four of those principles via Mertens' typology to illustrate how they are reflected somewhat differently in each of the three research traditions identified in the earlier part of chapter 9. I also account for certain problems within the context of each orienting framework as applied to the various principles.

As an analysis of research traditions, chapter 9 is largely descriptive. I do not attempt to resolve the problem of the lack of a mediating mode of research that might lend a sense of coherence to provide an intellectual underpinning to the study of adult literacy education. What I stress, as illustrated in chapter 10, is a loosening of the boundaries of each of the paradigms in the effort to establish a more permeable research climate as a basis to examine a broad range of issues related to educational practice and theory. Although a systematic effort at synthesis is bypassed, in chapter 10 I seek to illustrate such an approach through a research orientation that merges Dewey's experimental mode of inquiry with his educational philosophy of growth. The chapter includes a case study description of a small group tutoring session to give practical application to the theoretical discussion. Links between Dewey's concept of growth and the New Literacy Studies are also made.

My core assumption, that the challenge of situating a national adult literacy policy requires a grappling with values at the level of political culture, is most fully examined in chapter 11. For its work on democratic theory, the chapter draws on the political writings of John Dewey, Robert Bellah and his colleagues, and John Rawls. Dewey and Bellah drew out the importance of cultural democracy and the civic republican ideal of the public good. Rawls made a case for a "realistic utopia" based on core constitutional precepts of the U.S. political culture. I interpret these diverse strands as part and parcel of the nation's core political value system, drawn on at propitious times throughout the nation's history that may again have relevance in the reconstruction of a viable U.S. politics of adult literacy education in our current era.

Interwoven throughout the chapter is a persisting anxiety that the project of political reconstruction is flawed on its face for several key reasons, not the least of which is the ineradicable pluralism reflective of U.S. social and cultural life. When that is combined with the sharp ideological distinctions characteristic of contemporary politics, reinforced by substantial differences in the distribution of wealth and power, anything resembling Rawls' vision of a just society bounded by an underlying common ideal, raises the most profound of skepticism in the mind of the discerning critic. These problems and others are explored, along with the search for a viable public philosophy to ground a national politics of literacy.

An even more perplexing issue is whether any articulated ideal—in this case, the quest for a "more perfect union"—is viable as a potent source of mobilization. Perhaps the more pressing challenge is in the creation of stirring language in the midst of political engagement that cannot be superimposed outside of it. On this latter supposition, theory and practice would conjointly generate that which remains to be birthed, including a political rhetoric that would need to prove its efficacy in the field of application. What role, if any, such founding ideals as a "more perfect union" would have, would remain to be determined, which is not to minimize their relevance as an enduring cultural resource.

Conflicting Paradigms in Adult Literacy Education is designed for a broad readership consisting of reflective practitioners and policy analysts, as well as students and faculty of adult literacy and adult education working within the academic sector. Whereas the book is sharply focused on the U.S. setting, the issues it raises are of sufficient significance to appeal to similar colleagues throughout the English-speaking world. Given the strong emphasis on Dewey's educational philosophy and experimental logic, the book, or at least portions of it, may also be of interest to students of the American pragmatic tradition and its neopragmatic revival. Those interested in U.S. political culture may also find some of the chapters of particular significance. In short, *Conflicting Paradigms of Adult Literacy Education* provides a cultural window on critical aspects of contemporary U.S. public and political life through the study of its particular topic. The book is intended both for those whose primary interest is adult literacy, as well as those who seek to probe into broader cultural themes through this topic.

ACKNOWLEDGMENTS

My work on this book goes back many years, well before I began to write the first draft in March 2001. My thanks are to many, both to those who have reviewed this book and to those who have informed my thinking or have provided outlets for the expression of my ideas. My study of political culture extends back to the early 1980s in my PhD days at the University of Connecticut in the field of U.S. History. Special appreciation goes to Professors Richard O. Curry, who introduced me to the importance of ideas in history, and to Kent Newmeyer for highlighting the role of republican ideology in what one historian has referred to as the intellectual origins of the American Revolution. These influences profoundly shape my current thinking.

It would be difficult to repay my debt to the editor of the *Adult Basic Education* journal, Ken Melichar, who provided an outlet for my ideas on adult literacy pedagogy and political culture. Without *ABE*, I'm not sure my essays would have found another home.

I'm similarly grateful to David Rosen, Internet pioneer and founder of the NLA, for providing another venue for the expression of my ideas, an opportunity of which I have abundantly partaken. This book started through a reading of various threads of topics housed in the NLA archives and grew as I moved from one thread to another.

My thinking has also been richly informed through the scholarship of others in the field of adult literacy, especially Elsa Auerbach, Hanna Fingeret, Susan Lytle, Juliet Merrifield, Cassandra Drennon, Sondra Stein, Allan Quigley, and Tom Sticht. Their voices echo throughout this text in which my own thinking is very much a product of a critically collegial encounter with these authors. Equally important are the various e-mail exchanges, both on- and offline with colleagues, especially Catherine King, Eileen Eckert, Andres Muro, Debbie Yahoo, Nancy Hansen, David Rosen, Robert Bickerton, and Jackie Taylor, as well as with Elsa Auerbach and Tom Sticht.

Special thanks especially to those who have reviewed this book, or portions thereof, throughout the various stages of its development. Tom Sticht, an international consultant in adult education, Sheryl Gowen, Department of Education at George State University, Tom Burke, Department of Philosophy at the University of South Carolina, and Regie Stites, Manager of the Menlo Park Office at the Stanford Research Institute also reviewed this text for Lawrence Erlbaum, and provided important commentary at various critical junctures in the development of this book. On my request, Larry Condelli, Ajit Gopalakrishnan, Catherine King, Eileen Eckert, Debbie Yoho, and Audrey Lapointe have also reviewed and commented on various chapters of the book. All of the reviews have caused me to pause in my various reconstructions of this text, as I have grappled with the commentary through different stages of its evolution. Simply put, without the collective wisdom provided by the reviewers, I would not have known what problems needed to be addressed, and this would be a poorer book, indeed. Errors and omissions are my own.

Naomi Silverman, my editor at LEA, has been very supportive of this project from its inception, and has sensitively led me through pointed criticism and encouragement to press through the hard work required to complete a book. Naomi's assistant, Erica Kica, has also been instrumental in lining up reviewers and facilitating lines of communication between Naomi, the reviewers, and me. LEA book production supervisor Eileen Meehan and her team have also been a pleasure to work with.

To my colleagues at Literacy Volunteers of Greater Hartford, present and past (Susan Roman, Barbara Oles, Yvette Garner, Miriam Lopez, C. J. Hauss, Steve Bender, and Cheryl Johnson), much gratitude for your creative talents in doing what it takes to establish a sustaining environment where adult literacy education can flourish. It has been my privilege to labor with you in this important endeavor, to which I hope this book can make some minor contribution.

To my wife, Susan, thanks for living with this book and for demonstrating over and again that there are many deeper realities and joys than those that exist between the cover of a book. You show me through your daily example that the textuality of life is the more interesting and compelling story, something that this lover of book knowledge often finds hard to accept, even as he knows it is true. Thanks also for critiquing my long-winded writing style and pushing me toward greater simplicity and clarity. That journey has been a slow progression to which you have contributed much.

I dedicate this book to my grandsons, Cameron and Chase, to the students and tutors at Literacy Volunteers of Greater Hartford, and to all who labor in the underappreciated but vital field of adult literacy education in whatever capacities that they serve. May we come to our well-deserved fulfillment!

—George Demetrion
January 3, 2004

Introduction: In Search of Common Ground Amidst Conflicting Paradigms in Adult Literacy Education*

First question: who is speaking? Who among the totality of speaking individuals, is accorded the right to use this sort of language (langage)? Who is qualified to do so? Who derives from it its own special quality, his prestige, and from whom, in return, does he receive if not the assurance, at least the presumption that what he says is true? What is the status of the individuals who—alone—have the right, sanctioned by law or tradition, juridically defined or spontaneously accepted, to proffer such a discourse?

—Foucault (1972, p. 56)

Merrifield (1998) referred to the *Contested Ground* to characterize the field of assessment accountability in adult literacy. Merrifield's study intimated that conflict over this topic is intense because it points to the very definition of literacy, and hence, to its legitimacy. Whatever its merit in providing technical information on what students learn, discourse on this subject possesses figurative capacity as a symbol for how literacy is publicly defined and legitimized. Disputes about what counts, therefore, are more than just technical points of concern to specialists. In their contestability, they are also forms of political discourse in demarcating "rules [that] permit certain statements to be made" (Sarup, 1993, p. 64) and that disallow others.

Cherryholmes (1988) argued that beyond methodology, what needs questioning is "which categories, metaphors, modes of description, expla-

---

*With minor modifications, portions of chapter 1 originally appeared in "Discerning the Contexts of Adult Literacy Education: Theoretical Perspectives and Practical Applications," published by the *Canadian Journal for the Study of Adult Education* in the Special Issue on Literacy, Vol. 15, No. 2, November 2001 (104–127). Permission to use this material is gratefully acknowledged.

nation, and argument are valued and praised; which are excluded and silenced?" More fundamentally, "what social and political arrangements reward and deprive [particular] statements" (p. 107) in the contest over legitimacy in regard to research and policy traditions? Specifically, "Who is authorized to speak? Who listens? What can be said? What remains unspoken? How does one become authorized to speak? What utterances are rewarded? What utterances are penalized?" (p. 107). These questions on how knowledge is constructed through relationships of power are critical to any contemporary discussion on conflicting views of the public purposes and definitions of adult literacy education.

The notion of divergent discourses is not intended to negate the prospect of useful knowledge for educators, policymakers, and researchers in devising workable frameworks to advance the field's development. It is to challenge assertions that these frames of reference can be understood simply at the level of literal application. As Merrifield (1998) put it about "accountability systems," they "are not just technical issues of measurement and testing: they are about what is important to us, what we value, what we aspire to" (p. 16). Moreover, the "we" that comprises the constituency of adult literacy is quite varied in its reflection of divergent, and often conflicting, pedagogical, political, and cultural assumptions. In the United States, there is no generally accepted or even working consensus within the field as to the purposes or the definition of adult literacy education. The challenge proposed by Merrifield and myself is the need to establish common ground amidst conflicting perspectives. This is essential if there is going to be any shift in federal policy "from the margins to the mainstream" (Sticht, 2000) in a manner congruent with valid pedagogy, which Merrifield (1998) and I linked with the New Literacy Studies broadly situated within a democratic political culture.

In seeking to establish a valid, consensus-based federal accountability system, Merrifield emphasized sustained dialogue and negotiation. She premised such discussion on the obligation of mutual responsibility among all the stakeholders that should govern the field by agreed on performances. This is to take place through public discourse, research, and field experience. As she envisioned it, "The process of designing measures will be an iterative one, going back and forth between local, state, and national levels, and involving a variety of stakeholders as well as researchers" (p. 76). The gathering of such information, she hoped, would result in increased system capacity and "mutual accountability relationships" among all sectors of the adult education system, despite divergent and conflicting perspectives.

While agreeing with Merrifield, I place more emphasis on framing discourse on adult literacy within the context of a renewed political culture that begins to shift federal policy from its current focus on "market ideology" (Engel, 2000) toward an embrace of the democratic, constitutional, and republican values reflective of the nation's founding political ideals.

This middle ground politics includes support of a reformist vision of capitalism that draws on President G. W. Bush's call for corporate responsibility, which may be viewed as an aspect of the broader concepts of corporate citizenship and stewardship. This is a viewpoint reflected in contemporary management literature and the moral theory of such neoconservative philosophers as Michael Novak.

In Novak's vision, business is a moral calling that sustains the public good in providing for the material foundations of a just and free society. It does so in the following ways:

> (1) satisfy[ing] customers with goods and services of real value; (2) mak[ing] a reasonable return on the resources entrusted to it by investors; (3) creat[ing] new wealth; (4) creat[ing] new jobs; (5) defeat[ing] envy by generating upward mobility and by demonstrating that talent and hard work will be rewarded; (6) promot[ing] inventiveness and ingenuity; and (7) diversify[ing] the interests of the republic, thus guarding against majoritarian tyranny. (Younkins, 1999, p. 18)

The extent to which the impact of capitalism accomplishes this lofty vision within a democratic political culture is more than a passing concern. Still, the potentially galvanizing power of the stewardship vision to instill civic responsibility within the political economy, a point typically dismissed, or viewed ironically by leftist commentary, is a potential resource for political reconstruction that should not be lightly dismissed. Critique is well warranted to the extent that rhetoric belies the reality and serves to mask it. Yet, what it misses is the argument of Novak and others in noting the impact of capitalism as a heuristic force in bringing something of the reality of what Bellah, Madsen, Sullivan, Swindler, and Tipton (1992) referred to as *the good society* toward closer approximation in any given period of time. However piecemeal, such "meliorism" in a democratic capitalist society is one source of potential reform that can serve as a pragmatic means of pushing the body politic toward a closer approximation between the rhetoric and reality of U.S. founding ideals.

Novak's (1991) emphasis on wealth creation through capitalism based on "a sense of equal opportunity" (p. 15) it engenders, are core aspects of a democratic capitalist ethos. Those working out of this reformed tradition from a more progressive political slant, also embrace this core belief from different frames of reference. Those like Bellah et al. (1992, 1996), Barber, (1998), Rawls (1993, 2001), and Habermas (1998) share Novak's desire "to reconcile the social idea of the common good with the liberal emphasis on the free person" (Younkins, 1999, p. 6), based on a sharply different set of arguments.

Novak may be critiqued for his strong ideological stance in reifying the market and the 18th-century concept of limited government. Critics would argue that he also minimized the importance of a strong federal government as an important sector that plays a potentially powerful role in instilling a moral economy and enhancing the concept of the public good throughout the body politic. Still, Novak's call for "democratic capitalism" is a key strand of thought that can link up to a more progressive civic republican tradition articulated by Bellah et al. (1992) in *The Good Society*, Michael Sandel's (1996) *Democracy's Discontent*, and Gary Hart's (2002) *Restoration of the Republic*. Other scholarship of a liberal persuasion calling for a renewal of a democratic capitalist ethos includes Benjamin Barber's (1998) *A Passion for Democracy*, John Rawls' (1993) *Political Liberalism*, various works by John Dewey, and from the European tradition, Jurgen Habermas' (1998) *Between Facts and Norms: Contributions to a Discourse Theory of Law and Democracy*.

Where those of a more progressive slant differ from Novak is in the maintenance of a substantial role for the government, including a regulatory one, in actively contributing to the promotion of the commonwealth, and not simply in the form of removing restrictions for the freer exercise of political and economic liberty. For progressive proponents of a democratic capitalistic ethos like Barber, Sandel, Habermas, Bellah and his colleagues, and Rawls, unchecked corporate power is viewed as much of a threat to the promotion of the common good as is that of an intrusive state. Neoconservative intellectuals like Novak view the market and the entrepreneurial spirit as inherently more liberating than what they view as the rigid hand of governmental bureaucracy. What both groups hold in common is a quest for civic reform within capitalism as the basis to situate a moral political philosophy consistent with the nation's founding political ideals. It is on this ground that I seek to explore as the space out of which to construct a middle ground politics of adult literacy education. This is further discussed in the last section of this chapter and more fully in chapter 11.

THINKING PARADIGMATICALLY

As part of the process of delineating divergent perspectives on adult literacy education in the United States, both the concepts of *paradigms* and *discourse* are critical to an understanding of the issues that shape this field. Three schools of literacy are laid out in several sections of this chapter. To state it briefly, the first is the participatory literacy movement based on the critical pedagogy of Paulo Freire. The second is the focus of the federal government on functional literacy in linking adult basic education (ABE) with the needs of the postindustrial economy and more recently welfare reform. The third perspective, grounded in the intellectual disciplines of cultural anthropology and Vygotskian social psychology, proposes to mediate between the two by focusing on the literacy practices of adult literacy students. This school is referred to as the New Literacy Studies. There may be nothing intrinsically inherent between these perspectives that points to sharp conflict rather than to creative convergence. Still, as the pedagogy and politics of adult literacy education in the United States have played out since the late 1980s, the persistence of intense disputes among these three schools has been the larger reality. For that reason, it is through the guise of paradigm construction that I frame this book.

Referring to the realm of science, Kuhn (1970) was first to use the term *paradigm* as a characterization of bounded worldviews that emerge from the intellectual work of particular communities. Its core argument is that scientific knowledge is a product of historical development and gives shape to what becomes viewed as objective knowledge. *The Structure of Scientific Revolutions* is both ground breaking and controversial. The book challenged fundamental precepts of positivist epistemology that there is a direct correspondence between rigorous observation and direct knowledge, and it opened up the specter of relativism even in the "objective" field of scientific research.

Kuhn denied the latter, noting that paradigms, which can refer to "small" or "large" (p. 49) matters, are not arbitrarily constructed or deconstructed at will. Rather, as a constellation of new insight, paradigms emerge and sometimes burst forth as a result of considerable exploration and ferment among communities of scholars in the process of resolving some question or exploiting some opportunity. Historically entrenched within influential social, institutional, and intellectual processes and traditions, their constructed nature tends to become obscured. The very achievement of paradigmatic status reflects a new stability that becomes "self-evident" in the ways in which it continues to solve new sets of problems arising in response to the crisis that initially brought forth a particular worldview. In taking on normative status, there is typically an effort to fit ongoing problem resolution processes into the given frame of reference, extending its core assumptions into a complexly articulated evolving framework. Notwithstanding their constructed nature, Kuhn viewed scientific paradigms as relatively stable.

Still, as new questions and issues are explored, "anomalies," or not easily resolvable conflicts, may appear. Although the reigning "paradigm will not be easily surrendered," (p. 65), circumstances may arise from various quarters wherein the given framework may ultimately be challenged. Consequently, fresh ways of looking at things might emerge to challenge, or perhaps even to shatter, reigning frameworks. However, Bernstein (1983) noted that "there is always some overlap between rival paradigms—overlap of observations, concepts, standards, and problems" without which "rational debate and argumentation between proponents of rival paradigms would not be possible" (p. 85).

Bernstein sought to open up spaces in the subtle differences between incommensurability where standards of reason within particular paradigms cannot "be measured against each other point by point" and incompatibility where rival paradigms simply conflict. Like Kuhn, Bernstein pointed to the sharp distinctions within rival paradigmatic frameworks, but his intention is less to demonstrate the intractability of conflicting epistemologies than to "recognize losses and gains" (p. 92). In his quest to tease out creative space "between objectivism and relativism," Bernstein added that there is nothing finally definitive in the articulation of rival paradigms. For Bernstein, even sharply conflicting views have potential validity in opening up to "practical reason" a broader array of perspectives than could be construed only through a singular paradigm.

Paradigms refer to constructed worldviews, whereas social discourse theory points to the relation between social, cultural, and institutional structures of power, and rules of language that "enable and delimit fields of knowledge and inquiry" in "govern[ing] what can be said, thought, and done within those fields" (Lukes, 1999, p. 3). Notwithstanding these important distinctions, for the purpose of this study in examining how social and cultural knowledge is constructed in the field of adult literacy, the broad resemblances are more important. Dreyfus and Rabinow (1983) argued similarly in observing the "striking similarity between Kuhn's account of normal science and Foucault's account of normalizing society" (p. 196). The most fundamental implication of such discourse theory is the postmodern assumption that there is no "truth, practice or phenomena that can be studied outside" (Lukes, 1999, p. 4) of the boundaries of what can be framed within the context of human culture. In the language of Richard Rorty, whatever is constructed is a "metanarrative" (or worldview) "all the way down." The significance of discourse theory is particularly important when competing frames of reference vie for authority and public legitimacy. This sometimes results in sharply polarized conflict because particular social groups have powerfully invested in certain frames of reference.

Yet, as Bernstein argued, polarization can be mediated if divergent perspectives become viewed instead as part of a broader inquiry process in the effort to realize a more satisfactory resolution of enduring problems. In this case, an emergent pluralism can attenuate, even if not resolve, sharp ideological divisions. This type of pragmatic adjustment represents neither an escape from history nor a denial of the inevitability of discursive frameworks, but instead a process of ongoing construction in quest of a more satisfactory resolution. How viable such constructions may be are a matter that can only be determined within the context of historical experience.

Accepting the basic assumption of Freire (1970) and Foucault (1972) that power and knowledge are invariably connected, I seek to explore the conflicting frameworks of adult literacy education as they have played out historically over the last 15 years. The tentative praxis that I offer in the last two chapters is grounded within a pragmatic epistemology (Burke, 1994; Dewey, 1938/1991), which "attempts to bridge where we are with where we might end up" (Cherryholmes, 1999, p. 3). The effort is not designed to deny the force of ideology. Its intent is to reconstruct ideology along lines more congruent with the nation's democratic, constitutional, and republican values as a fundamental grounding point of this culture's political core. Drawing on the collective insights of Dewey, Barber, Bellah and his colleagues, Rawls, and others, I propose a middle ground politics of literacy based on a vision of democratic reform within capitalism.

FREIRIAN PERSPECTIVES ON ADULT LITERACY EDUCATION

In the field of adult literacy education, Freire's (1970) *Pedagogy of the Oppressed* represented a powerful discourse, a paradigm-shattering phenomenon. Before its publication, a dominant view of adult literacy prevailed linked to first world efforts of modernizing third world countries promoted by the United Nations and advanced countries in North America and Western Europe. Referring to one U.N. study that linked adult literacy to modernization, Graff (1987) observed that, from this perspective, "literacy was related to liberty, initiation of social and economic change, national destiny, social justice, the transformation of mentalities and the 'awakening of autonomous, critical, constructive minds, capable of changing man's relationship with nature' " (quoted portion from 1975 Persepolis Symposium, cited in Graff, 1987, p. 55).

This viewpoint assumed that a universal evolution toward modernization was desirable that could be achieved by crossing various thresholds within "underdeveloped" nations through increases in economic productivity, and in attaining critical indices of health and education. Although precise correlations between adult literacy rates and modernization were seldom made, it was assumed that raising the literacy rates of the adult population represented one of the critical sources of progress in a nation's march to modernization.

The singular genius of *Pedagogy of the Oppressed* is that this text shattered the self-evident presuppositions of this prevailing viewpoint. It offered an alternative frame of reference that linked literacy to political engagement among the oppressed in the articulation of their own voices: first, in naming what Freire referred to as the sources of their domination, and second, in collectively organizing to effect change in the socioeconomic, political order through cultural and nonviolent political revolution.

Instead of one dominant view of literacy, now there were two, reflecting sharply different ideologies. One, clearly more dominant, was based on the democratic technocratic capitalism of both the U.N. campaigns and the New Frontier and Great Society of the Kennedy–Johnson administration in the United States. The other, based on Freirian ideas of politics and pedagogy, had a substantial grounding in a neo-Marxist vision, buttressed by a radical Christian theology of oppressed social groups, which was supported by left-wing intellectuals throughout the world and in the United States. Rather than the poor passively receiving the benefits of the enlightened state or the international agency in bringing what critics viewed as the false promise of democracy, industrialization, and rational thinking, in Freire's vision, illiterate adults act as agents in their own humanization. Through education, oppressed social groups read the word in order to read the world. The poor have the ability to define the sociopolitical-economic order, at least in part, on their own terms and the capacity to progressively reconstruct it based on their own collective organization. However minimal such change might be in the concrete—and Freire held out for the prospect of cultural and political revolution as a utopian possibility based in social reality—the elevation of critical consciousness, in itself, represented an important form of liberation in transforming the poor from passive recipients to active agents in the process of historical construction.

Coming out amidst worldwide protests against U.S. involvement in Vietnam, *Pedagogy of the Oppressed* was well received in progressive and radical sectors in the United States. Advocates established programs on the participatory model of literacy that Freire described, where nonreading adults were viewed as "searchers . . . [in] their ontological vocation." Freire referred to this as "humanization" (p. 61). For Freire, "both humanization and dehumanization are possible, [but] only the first is man's vocation" (p. 28). The impetus unleashed was an active seeking of the just society where formerly oppressed and oppressors would be unified, ultimately through the power of *agape* love.

Based on this calling, oppressed illiterate social groups would define their primary pedagogical task as political engagement in the quest for revolutionary justice and democracy. This would result in the self-recreation of the poor, who would become active agents in the ongoing process of historical reconstruction, the opposite of the "fated" condition that Freire viewed as characteristic of the pre-liberated thinking of the oppressed. From the vantage point of Freire's "dialogical" pedagogy, the focus of adult literacy programs would be "constituted and organized by the students' view of the world" (p. 101). However piecemeal, this shift in consciousness would emerge in the very process of collectively working toward an emancipatory sociopolitical ethic, stimulating new energies and new perceptions in the very definition of the possible.

Freire understood his vision as clearly utopian in positing an ideal that can only manifest itself partially within history, as there was no end point to what he meant by "humanization." Given the ontological status of "man as an uncompleted being conscious of his incompletion" (p. 27), the function of any ideal is to direct the trajectory of human action. Of fundamental importance to Freire were the processes unleashed along the way toward the direction of a liberated humanity. The determination of the authenticity of these trajectories necessitated critical historical analysis among participants. This required discriminating judgment. The task called for discerning the extent to which such movements were genuinely congruent with the emergence of the emancipatory change, or a manifestation of false generosity by reigning elites (p. 46). Critical, but empathetic, dialogue between students and educators played a pivotal role in the making of such determinations in which "men . . . [search] together to learn more than they know now" (Freire, 1970, p. 79).

Thus, for Freire (1985), utopian thought was the essential ingredient of a liberated vision unleashed in any given historical setting in the transformation of historical reality. It was utopian hope, he argued, that loosened among the oppressed the desire to "engage in [the] denunciation and annunciation" needed to begin the arduous work of transforming the world. As Freire put it, "The announced reality is already present in the [very] act of denunciation and annunciation" (p. 57) that "emerges from concrete existential situations" (p. 59) made problematic through a critical pedagogy in which the oppressed are embedded in any historical moment. For Freire, the power of the oppressed resided in the unleashing of collective consciousness through the active exercise of hope in the desired future. Such liberation of thinking in itself serves as a historically powerful force that helps to stimulate the utopian vision needed to transform the world in which "men" become progressively free (p. 59).

As discussed further in chapter 2, the politics of literacy from a Freirian perspective in the United States is invariably progressive, but its extent depends on which branch of the participatory movement advocates embrace. Auerbach (1992a, 1992b, 1993) drew out the importance of the social context of student lives as the primary source of critical reflection. Her participatory model had a specifically radical overtone in challenging the operative assumptions of the dominant sociopolitical order in fostering the conditions that marginalize poor and minority adults. From this perspective, it is not the individual that should change, but the social order that needs to become more responsive to the voices and concerns of those who suffer most from conditions perpetuated by the dominant power structure.

Fingeret, Jurmo, and Lytle also drew heavily on Freire's participatory framework even while relying extensively as well on the ethnographic literature on literacy of the 1980s, which laid the basis for what Merrifield (1998) referred to as the New Literacy Studies. These more reform-oriented researchers lay more emphasis on validating learner perception as the baseline of an empowering student-centered curriculum and program focus, even if the result is an embrace of normative social and cultural values (Fingeret & Drennon, 1997; Fingeret & Jurmo, 1989; Lytle, 1991).

The politics in this branch of the U.S. Freirian movement are more characteristic of the U.S. Progressive Reform Movement of the early 20th century as expressed in Jane Addams' Hull House experiment and Dewey's (1916) pragmatic pedagogy of growth, rather than radical in the Freirian sense. Its focus in assisting students to achieve their own goals, which mostly centers on the quest for greater inclusion into the prevailing mores and institutions of mainstream social life, is largely assimilationist rather than reflective of a sharp oppositional stance to the dominant sociopolitical order.

Whether centering on politics or on the intricate context of the lives of students, both branches of the Freirian school have become increasingly marginalized throughout the U.S. body politic since the late 1980s. Several factors have contributed to its erosion in the 1990s, including an emphasis on exacting standards stemming from the Government and Performance and Results Act of 1993, the neoliberal workforce impetus of the Clinton era, and the neoconservative emphasis placed on reading, phonemic awareness, and scientific research of the junior Bush administration. The struggle for legitimacy among those espousing a Freirian pedagogy in a political culture that has militated against its operative assumptions, even in its more tempered reformist manifestations, was especially acute over issues of assessment and accountability and research traditions that undergirds this school of thought.

FUNCTIONAL LITERACY AND NATIONAL ECONOMIC IMPERATIVES

As described by Cook (1977), in the 1960s a strong emphasis was placed on the concept of "functional literacy" linked especially to employment. This has remained a preeminent focus within policy sectors ever since. In his review of that important decade, Quigley (1997) added a critical twist in his discussion of the emergent field of adult basic education (ABE), wherein adult literacy became "policy disenfranchised" with the passage of the Manpower Development and Training Act (MDTA) of 1962. The result was that "the issue of illiteracy was discovered anew. However, it was not illiteracy but adult basic education that was now prescribed for those who fell below requisite [employment] training levels" (p. 86). By subsuming ABE as a form of human capital development, Quigley noted that "humanistic responses to learner needs have [had] little role in serious policy formulation" (p. 88). Beder (1991) similarly observed that "human capital development theory has become the dominant rationale for all public subsidy of adult education, including adult literacy" (p. 107).

This functional response was reinforced in the 1970s with the adult performance level (APL) study that played a major role in focusing adult basic education on "basic requirements for adult living" (Northcutt, 1975, p. 1).

In specific terms, the APL study linked adult basic education to the mastery of basic survival skills of "(1) consumer economics, (2) occupational (or occupationally-related) knowledge, (3) community resources, (4) health, and (5) government and law" (p. 2).

In moving beyond "literacy" as then commonly defined through a grade school analogy, the APL researchers sought to clarify the extent to which adult functioning in a complex, print-based society was a national problem. If, according to the research, "approximately one in five Americans is incompetent or functions with difficulty and that about half of the adult population is merely functional and not at all proficient in necessary skills and knowledges" (p. 12), then this indeed posed a serious problem. On the assumption that "education is properly a function of the state," the APL researchers noted that ABE as a field had the "opportunity to take the leadership in providing comprehensive programs dealing with basic education for life" (p. 13). Given the new competency, paradigm proponents argued that the field could now deliberately move from a traditional school-based model to a functional model of adult basic education.

With the rise of information over physical production as a primary resource created in the workplace and the impetus of the competitive nature of the global economy, a tighter focus between capital human resource development and ABE/adult literacy in governmental sectors became prevalent throughout the 1980s and 1990s. Such studies as *Workforce 2000* and *Jump Start* focused on key demographic factors shaping the contours of the modern workplace that pointed to a less educated, older, and increasingly minority-based workforce, ill-equipped to meet the changing needs of the knowledge economy. Unless the nation was prepared to meet the challenges imposed by what Chisman referred to as "demographic destiny," various prognosticators argued that there was little likelihood of the U.S. economy thriving in the 21st century.

Workforce 2000 and *Jump Start* discussed broad trends and the need for policy restructuring. The actual content of the skills and knowledge needed in the modern workplace was the focus of the 1991 and 1992 *Secretary's Commission on Achieving Necessary Skills* (SCANS) reports, published by the U.S. Department of Labor. The SCANS report laid out an array of foundational skills and workplace competencies allied to the needs of the knowledge economy. Although designed specifically as a means of restructuring K–12 public education, it was widely used by adult educators throughout the decade to give specific shape to workplace literacy programs. Through the impetus of the National Literacy Act of 1991 and the establishment of the National Institute for Literacy (NIFL) in 1992, countervailing pressures were operative through the early 1990s to keep open a fluid and pluralistic policy orientation. Notwithstanding efforts to promote a broader understanding of the public value of adult literacy stemming from field energies and policies and institutions emerging from the National Literacy Act, the influence of a workforce rationale remained central, especially in state and federal governmental sectors.

Congressional pressure to make adult education a subset of workforce education was pervasive throughout the second half of the decade. Although more extreme proposals debated in Congress from 1995 to 1997 did not become enacted into law, Congress passed the Workforce Investment Act in 1998. In its final amended form, this included Title II, the *Adult Education and Family Literacy Act.* This, policy advocates argued, "safeguarded the integrity of adult education as a program which not only contributes to workforce development but also contributes to more responsible citizenship and to the intergenerational transfer of literacy skills" (Bowling, NLA, March 23, 1998). The policy sector also maintained that Title II opened up new opportunities for the field that included an "equal access" clause. This, in principle, made funding available to all qualified programs and set a more rigorous set of criteria that would lead to greater professionalism and effectiveness of service delivery.

The Adult Basic Education (ABE) policy leadership viewed the 1998 legislation as the best possible deal the field could have obtained, but critics were more skeptical. From their perspective, the difficult-to-meet standards set in the National Reporting System (NRS) made the concept of "equal access" nil for most community-based volunteer literacy programs. Equally, if not more problematic, Title II placed a set of criteria and a framework on the field that rubbed against the core tenets of many community-based programs. This was particularly the case both among those assuming a strong participatory stance that embraced the concept of the "emergent curriculum" (Auerbach, 1992b) and those advocating for the constructivist standards of NIFL's Equipped for the Future (EFF) project. As discussed in chapter 5, the new legislation was hotly debated in adult literacy and ABE circles throughout the United States.

Other rationales persisted. Yet, as discussed in chapters 3 and 4, by the end of the 1990s, the dominant and most compelling purpose of adult literacy education as defined by the federal government was its role in meeting the human resource needs of the postindustrial economy and welfare reform. At the end of the decade, the contrast between the Freirian perspective of adult literacy education, as well as that of the more reformist-based New Literacy Studies could not have been starker.

MEDIATING PERSPECTIVES: THE NEW LITERACY STUDIES

In their sharp divergences, Freirian and functional visions represent important cultural markers in the iconography of the politics of adult literacy in the United States. Although the polarity provides certain clarity over the critical issues of pedagogical focus and political power, any rigid dichotomy between these perspectives is a profound oversimplification of the complex dynamics that characterize the diverse field of adult literacy education. For example, Jurmo (1990), who has been instrumental in the participatory literacy movement, is also a major practitioner and researcher of workplace literacy programs. Throughout his career, Jurmo has sought approaches to adult literacy education that are simultaneously functional, contextual, and participatory.

Sticht's (1997a) research both in the fields of military and workplace literacy should be viewed in a similar light. His functional-context theory blends the psychological insights of a mediated behaviorism and a Vygotskian perspective of social constructivism (Demetrion, 2001a). Sticht (1997a) drew on a view of cognitive science that includes psychology, anthropology, sociology, linguistics, and philosophy (p. 38). In addition, he took a developmental perspective in the recognition that knowledge emerges through the life span as individuals interact with the social environment in highly particular ways. In focusing on "informational processing," Sticht's cognitive psychology remains somewhat mentalistic. Nonetheless, Sticht recognized that society and culture provide the "symbols and symbol system, such as the natural language and conceptual . . . knowledge, which constitute the primary means for the transmission of cognitive abilities" (p. 42).

Sticht's research project is highly normative in its intent of enabling individuals and institutions to attain a better fit between personal learning and proscribed social needs. This was particularly the case in his early research on literacy in the military and workplace. Sticht now applies his concept to any content areas that adult literacy students find meaningful. Consequently, his pedagogy might be viewed as liberating in providing adult literacy learners with the skills and knowledge base that they themselves seek in order to better meet their own personal goals in many areas, including the spiritual realm.

As described by Lytle and Wolfe (1989), the research of Jurmo and Sticht should be viewed as part of a more complex interpretation of functional literacy that has become pervasive since the 1975 APL study. This more subtle view of functional literacy moves well beyond the philosophy of positivism and the psychology of behaviorism, particularly in contrast to a Freirian-based critical literacy (Lankshear, 1993). In emphasizing deficiencies over strengths, the pejorative interpretation of functional literacy draws heavily on the 1975 APL study as a discourse that "mimimalizes human beings" (p. 91). By contrast, Lytle and Wolfe discussed the evolution and changing definitions of functional literacy through the late 1980s. Acknowledging that early definitions of functional literacy are based on the attainment of particular competencies linked to the alleged mastery of predefined daily tasks, the authors point to other definitions that are "more relativistic. Ideological in nature, these definitions situate functional literacy within the needs and characteristics of different groups and cultures" (p. 8). For example, Hunter and Harman (1985) defined functional literacy as "the possession of skills *perceived as necessary by particular persons and groups* to fulfill their own self-determined objectives as family and community members, citizens, consumers, job-holders, and members of social, religious, or other associations of their choosing" (p. 7, italics in original).

Moving beyond any stimulus–response behaviorism, the complex functionalism Lytle and Wolfe (1989) sought "to capture [is] the thinking required in the interaction among reader, task, and specific types of text" (p. 9). It is this more complex understanding on which Sticht's (1997a) functional-context theory is based in drawing on "to the extent possible, learning contexts, tasks, materials, and procedures taken from the future situation in which the learner will be functioning" (p. 3).

Such shifting definitions led Levine (1982) to question the "extreme elasticity" of the term *functional literacy* (cited in Lytle & Wolfe, 1989, p. 9). The difference between this more complex interpretation and the concept of literacy as a set of sociocultural practices characteristic of the New Literacy Studies reflects more of a continuum than a sharp contrast, although there are dissimilarities. That is, even this version of functional literacy is more focused on task attainment within a more or less self-evident social environment. The literacy-as-practices perspective more subtly draws out the sociocultural context that enshrouds literacy events within particular behaviors, attitudes, and mores within a complex web of interaction where literacy tasks are not so sharply delineated (Barton, 1994b; Demetrion, 2001a; Merrifield, 1998).

The school of thought on which the literacy as practices concept is based, the New Literacy Studies (NLS), has its roots in the ethnographic literature of literacy in the 1980s. Particularly influential were Heath's (1983) *Way with Words* that examined the reading practices of three diverse southern communities, Street's (1988) study of literacy practices in an Iranian village, and Scribner and Cole's (1981) study of the cognitive skills of illiterate Russian peasants. What unites this literature is a rejection of what Street (1988) referred to as the "autonomous" view of literacy as an intrinsically higher source of cognitive development than oral discourse. For NLS advocates, what is more important than the abstract mastery of print literacy, is its relation to desired knowledge, which can only be discerned within specific sociocultural settings. From this vantage point, there is nothing fundamental about literacy per se. Depending on the context, it can serve as a compelling interdependent variable or merely one resource among others in meeting particular objectives.

Scribner (1988) drew on this perspective to critique any radical polarity between the functional and critical perspective in what she identified respectively as *literacy as adaptation* and *literacy as power*. Scribner argued that "the multiple meanings and varieties of literacy [call] for a diversity of educational approaches ... that are responsive to [an array of] perceived needs, whether for functional skills, social power, or self improvement" (p. 81). As Lytle and Wolfe (1989) also described it, the "social meanings of literacy differ from group to group within a society as well as from society to society" (p. 10).

For Scribner (1988), the concept of functional literacy "has a strong common sense appeal" (p. 73) in helping adults in the realm of work, daily living, and in assuming the basic rights and responsibilities of citizenship. Although Scribner acknowledged that the functional approach is an important aspect of literacy, she was aware of how problematic it is "to try to specify some uniform set of skills as constituting functional literacy for all adults" (p. 73). In contrasting functional to critical literacy, she pointed to the influence of Freire for bringing out the importance of "a critical consciousness through which a community can analyze its conditions of social existence and engage in effective action for a just society" (p. 75). From this viewpoint, "the expansion of literacy skills is often viewed as a means for poor and politically powerless groups to claim their place in the world" (p. 75).

Despite its evident appeal among those critical to mainstream ideology, Scribner (1988) also viewed the literacy-as-power position as problematic. Given her understanding that "literacy has different meanings for members of different social groups" (p. 76), she challenged the supposition of an all-embracing dichotomy between functional and critical perspectives. Literacy is best understood, she argued, as a set of practices embedded within the context of particular cultures rather than that of a single movement of "the oppressed" in search of liberation or simply an uncritical adaptation of the status quo. Grounded in the academic discipline of cultural anthropology and ethnographic studies, Scribner focused on the importance of gaining a discerning understanding of the various social contexts that might pertain in any given setting. Scribner provided a judicious critique of the limitations and strengths of functional and critical literacy when viewed as opposite discourses. This enabled her to lay the groundwork for a more nuanced, third school in which literacy practices are shaped by the specific contexts in which they are embedded. As she described it, "As ethnographic research and practical experience demonstrate, effective literacy programs are those that are responsive to perceived needs, whether for functional skills, social power, or self-improvement" (p. 81).

Given the context in which mainstream U.S. ABE programs and community-based literacy agencies are embedded, Scribner's interpretation provides the basis for a multifaceted response to the prevailing social, political, cultural, and economic milieu that draws on various degrees of adaptation and resistance to dominant societal norms. As students, instructors, and program staff work out of the premises of this third way, they may experience considerable ambivalence at various axial points between the continuums of functional and critical literacy as depicted by Scribner.

Merrifield (1998) synthesized a broad array of research in providing a more detailed definition of literacy as a set of social and cultural practices. She references this school of thought to the "New Literacy Studies [ethnographic] research [tradition, which] explores how literacy is used within social groups" (p. 29). This she contrasted to "the one-dimensional scale that holds sway in public policy" (p. 30). From an NLS viewpoint, "*Reading* [italics in original] has no meaning unless we say who is reading what, in what setting, and for what purpose." That determination requires a clear delineation of "the medium (text) from the message (meaning)" (p. 30) in order to grasp the subtle contexts that shape the various dimensions of what comprise literacy as social and cultural practices in any specific situation. Merrifield further broke these down into the concepts of *literacy practices, literacy events,* and *domains.*

Quoting Barton (1994b, p. 5), Merrifield (1998) equated *literacy practices* with " 'general cultural ways of utilizing literacy' that people draw upon in the varied contexts in which they live their lives." These practices "include not only behavior but also meanings, values, and social relationships" (p. 31). From the perspective of Merrifield and others who argued similarly, the definition of literacy practices is highly interpretive. It is not easily discernible through discretely measurable factors that sharply separate the "literacy" function from related behaviors, attitudes, beliefs, and various social and cultural influences that interact and invariably shape individual perception.

Quoting Barton (1994b, p. 5) again, Merrifield (1998) identified *literacy events* as " 'the particular activities in which literacy has a role,' " which "draw[s] on general literacy practice[s] in that domain, but are directly observable," such as "reading a newspaper, writing a grocery list . . . reading a company memo . . . writing an accident report . . . [or] writing a term paper" (p. 31). Merrifield defined *domains* as "the broad contexts of life in which we operate," such as the family, the workplace, church, school, the market, or the social club. These are "shaped in turn by the broader culture and by class, gender, ethnicity, and regional variation" (p. 31). It is these variations, which Merrifield associated with "the concept of *multi-literacies*" (p. 31, italics in original), that provide the specific contexts through which literacy practices are defined and, logically, assessed.

For Merrifield, the NLS research establishes an intricate understanding of the relation between literacy and the lives of adults in the particular and diverse contexts in which such *events* as reading the newspaper are embedded. For this reason, it is among the most important work in the field. Viewed from this vantage point, literacy is an intervening variable, one factor among others, as applied to a broad array of sociocultural *domains*. As Merrifield put it, "The aim is not simply skill acquisition, but making meaning and critical understanding of how literacy is used in [diverse] social contexts" (p. 32).

The National Institute for Literacy's Equipped for the Future (EFF) project, developed during the mid-1990s, can be broadly construed as reform movement congruent with the precepts of democratic capitalism. Its pedagogy complexly weaves Sticht's functional-context theory, participatory literacy education, and NLS operative assumptions. In addition, EFF represents the closest approximation realized in practice on a large scale to the position advocated for in this book in identifying the nation's constitutional, democratic, and republican traditions as the baseline by which to establish a liberal politics of adult literacy premised on a literacy as practices pedagogical model.

The relation between pedagogy and politics in the EFF's consensually striven national vision is evident, although its development in the conservative policy arena of the last decade was anything but straightforward and unambiguous. The NIFL project was founded in a congressional mandate to assess the impact of the national adult basic education and literacy system in achieving National Educational Goal 6. In calling for the equipping of "every adult American [with] . . . the knowledge and skills to compete in a global economy and [with the capacity to] exercise the rights and responsibilities of citizenship," project designers sought to wed a neoliberal postindustrial vision of the learning society with active citizenry engagement in the political process. On a more technical front, designers have attempted to create a comprehensive framework through which to establish accountability standards by merging a student-centered pedagogy based on the philosophical tenets of constructivism with plausible policy orientations linked to workplace readiness, family literacy, and civic participation. As is discussed in chapters 7 and 8, the structure is not without profound contradictions based on the very effort to integrate a progressive pedagogy with a mainstream, and increasingly conservative, social policy. Chapter 6, which more broadly explores the tensions within the ABE standards movement of the 1990s, is also relevant to the discussion on EFF.

Implicit within EFF, but never formally articulated, is a public philosophy of active citizenry engagement in the strengthening of mediating structures and institutions, primarily at the local level, that certain political philosophers have linked with the precepts of a constitutional democratic republic (Bellah et al., 1996; Hart, 2002; Sandel, 1996). This politics is considerably more moderate than proposed by Freire in *Pedagogy of the Op-*

pressed, but profoundly more idealistic and comprehensive than prevailing assumptions of functional literacy that have had a direct impact on policy formation (Chisman, 1989; Johnston & Packer, 1987).

Within EFF, it is this dynamic of active citizenry engagement within the predominant mediating institutions of public life that holds one of the potential keys in helping to shift the value system from economics to the strengthening of democracy. The working hypothesis that I am constructing in this book is premised on the assumption that this shift in values is essential as a way of framing a coherent politics of adult literacy in the United States. In making this argument I accept the importance of economic motivations as an enduring feature of public policy. In so doing, I build on the EFF model of civic capitalism as articulated in its Worker Role Map, supported also in a broad stream of contemporary management literature, as the means of strengthening both economic institutions and empowering the lives of employees, who in this function serve as responsible corporate citizens in their organizations. The broader vision of all of the EFF Role Maps, those related to family and community as well as work, is premised on the image of the active citizen collaborating with others, in the strengthening of an array of local institutions. This viewpoint is supported by an impressive corpus of political philosophy as discussed in chapter 11.

Whether EFF ever achieves the consensus vision that has inspired its designers is a matter of no minor significance, and it is less likely now that NIFL has ended its sponsorship of this initiative. As I write, a new NIFL Advisory Board has been appointed that reflects the Bush-Paige neo-conservative educational vision, and by the time this book is published, a permanent director for the agency will have been hired, likely reflecting a similar outlook. The Bush-Paige administration has brought a strong focus on reading, with phonemic awareness as its foundational source of mastery. It also supports a view of scientific educational research based on neo-positivist philosophical premises, casting a skeptical eye on the interactive learning assumptions inherent within constructivism, a key intellectual underpinning of the EFF framework. With the ending of NIFL sponsorship in 2004, management and technical support for EFF is now in the hands of an interstate group of partners and the Center for Literacy Studies in Tennessee. Its impact will now depend on the viability of EFF as a grass-roots movement and longer-range political climate shifting in Washington, D.C.

If nothing else, EFF's failure to substantially move toward its objective of realizing a viable national consensus through its mediating pedagogy and its political vision serves as an important case study on the limitations inherent in the practical arena of contemporary national politics. It may also illustrate the result of keeping the EFF public philosophy muted and implicit rather than firmly articulated and visible as a galvanizing intellectual and political center through which to ground the sought-for consensus. However EFF may evolve is beyond the focus of this book. In addition to providing a historical overview of the project, my focus is on the framework's pedagogical value and implicit public philosophy based on the twin purposes of preparing people to compete effectively in a global economy and to exercise the rights and responsibilities of citizenship.

INITIAL REFLECTIONS ON THE POLITICS ADULT LITERACY

For those working at the direct program level (students, instructors, and program directors), as well as scholars in the academic traditions of ethnography and critical pedagogy, what matters is what happens at and beneath the surface of the immediate learning situation and environment. Its illumination requires "thick description" and discerning sociopolitical as well as discriminating pedagogical analysis. Those maintaining these perspectives seek policy orientations that support educational practices, research traditions, and accountability frameworks congruent with sound pedagogy based on the interpretive frameworks to which they adhere. For those supportive of the NLS or Freirian principles, the impact of adult literacy education on the lives of individuals remains limited unless social issues related to poverty, racism, and long-seated discriminatory practices are simultaneously addressed in national policy formulations. As characterized by Merrifield, Bingman, Hemphill, and Bennett deMarrais (1997):

> Our profiles put literacy in its place as only one of the factors affecting people's lives. It is not clear for most of these people that a gain in literacy skills alone would make a substantial difference in their lives. Perhaps it would help them get a better job and thus enable them to move out of poverty. That is most likely true for Les, if gains in literacy skills enabled him to get an electrician's license and command higher wages. But without some major changes on a national level (for example, national health insurance and a minimum wage that is a living wage), they would most likely simply move from one sector of the working poor to another. (p. 98)

In short, many practitioners and researchers view as indispensable the need to link adult literacy to a broader set of policy concerns than current mandates supported by the federal government based on the Workforce Investment Act and the Adult Education and Family Literacy Act.

Proponents of a Freirian-inspired critical pedagogy challenge the fundamental precepts of the basic political and epistemological assumptions of current policy and related mainstream perspectives. Their analysis contains a sustained critique against capitalism, per se (Auerbach, 1993; McLaren & Leonard, 1993). As critique, such work points to profound contradictions in the body politic between professed democratic values in a nation of wealth, and the persistence of substantial economic disparity, exacerbated by the enduring presence of racial, ethnic, and gender discrimination. Whether or not this type of critical analysis can result in an effective praxis to alter federal policy is another matter. There is little evidence available to indicate that this is likely in the foreseeable future and a good deal to suggest that it is not very probable.

Others, also critical of federal policy, argue from the generally more reformist NLS perspective. From this point of view, current policy fails to take into account the many ways that adults do benefit from literacy programs that close ethnographic evidence illuminates (Demetrion, 1998, 2001a, 2001b; Fingeret & Drennon, 1997; Merrifield et al., 1997). Advocates of this viewpoint acknowledge the insights of critical pedagogy. Yet, they also maintain that the primary objectives of most adult literacy students are those of seeking the skills and knowledge to better enable them to fit into main currents of society on terms they define through the exercise of their own personal agency (Demetrion, 1998, 2001b; Fingeret & Drennon, 1997). What is needed from this perspective is a student-centered focus as the basis for measuring performance accountability based on the literacy practices they enact in meeting some of their life goals. This would be supported by a renewed policy orientation based on a liberal reform movement within capitalism. As expressed by Merrifield et al. (1997):

> While the people we profile are concerned about their individual skills and advancement, society would also clearly benefit by providing them appropriate literacy education. They are an untapped resource, currently largely wasted. They are competent, thoughtful, hardworking, with strong values. They need literacy programs that recognize and build on their strengths. Such literacy programs would enable them to move out of the margins and turn to other purposes the energy they now use for survival. We would all benefit from investing in people we have come to know in this study, enabling them to become full citizens in the broadest sense of the word. (p. 196)

This reform orientation does not obviate the analysis of critical pedagogy, which provides a compelling boundary in defining social justice and an emancipatory pedagogy as a utopian possibility (Freire, 1970; Giroux, 1983) for a politics of literacy. The radical impulse, which I place on the outer edge of the U.S. political culture (Demetrion, 2001c), can influence the dominant culture at pivotal historical moments, particularly through the impact of powerful rhetoric and political mobilization. At key periods in U.S. history, this influence has resulted in greater inclusiveness of marginalized groups into the prevailing mores and institutions of social, political, and economic life, and has sometimes changed the evolving contours of a democratic capitalist society.

Still, as a pragmatic strategy, the radical impulse remains limited, although not without significance, in the effort to reconstruct the political culture within a manner that has a viable prospect of influencing federal policy and galvanizing a broad-based national consensus on the public purposes and value of adult literacy education. Whether the "middle ground" reformist impetus, which works toward modest progressive change can provide a more viable political context to enact a federal reconstruction of adult literacy policy remains to be determined. My tempered hope is that it can, but if history is prologue to the future, then an overly optimistic prognosis is not warranted. As a reasoned conjecture (Miller, 1985), I draw on this "third way" between functional and critical literacy to probe into the feasibility of a reconstruction of the pedagogy politics of literacy in the United States, a topic taken up in chapters 10 and 11. In doing so, I extend the implicit public philosophy partially articulated within the EFF project.

HERMENEUTICS OF HOPE IN THE AMERICAN GRAIN

The position I support draws on the nation's democratic, constitutional, and republican principles stemming from its 18th-century founding political framework. This grounding point provides an invaluable, often-untapped resource in working for reform congruent with fundamental principles of the main currents of the U.S. political culture. In more technical terms, this is an argument of *hermeneutical retrieval* that builds on the potency of a living tradition as a viable resource for contemporary political renewal.

This is far from an uncritical embrace of a given tradition in which the "truth" resides within the text, in this case the core documents of late 18th-century U.S. political culture. A hermeneutical retrieval, rather, refers to what Gadamar (2002) described as a "fusion of horizons" that requires a profound dialogue in which the interpreter critically appropriates from a text or a tradition insight that applies to a contemporary situation. Gadamar defined a horizon as a boundary that within its "range of vision . . . includes everything that can be seen from a particular vantagepoint" (p. 302). Less a limitation, a horizon provides the starting place for the fuller realization of the tradition's meaning within the context of emergent historical unfolding. It is a continuous, and sometimes contentious, working out of its significance as variously interpreted within history—that is, *a living* tradition, which intersects with an ongoing present.

Such critical appropriation of insight is not automatic process. It calls for "acquiring the right horizon of inquiry for the questions evoked by the encounter with tradition" (p. 302). This necessitates a corresponding willingness to probe critically back and forth from the text or tradition to the current situation, toward the creation of a fresh interpretation that could be deemed viable in the contemporary setting. The text plays a vital role in providing a frame of reference for identifying a set of values that may not be self-evident within contemporary experience alone. It represents an important resource from which authority springs, yet an authority that can only be selectively drawn on in order to speak cogently to the exigencies of the present. It is also an acknowledgment that the encounter could spawn a variety of divergent and even contestable responses, which invariably calls for interpretation. Notwithstanding the inevitable divergences of interpretation, the fusion of horizons has the potential of stimulating rich new encounters, the value of which can only be determined by the ways in which the present is opened up through them. Bernstein (1986) described the variability of this dynamic:

> Because all understanding involves a dialogical encounter between the text or the tradition that we seek to understand and our hermeneutical situation, we will always understand the "same thing" differently. We always understand from our situation and horizon, but what we seek to accomplish is to enlarge our horizon. (p. 63)

Gadamar did not view the initial meanings of a text or tradition, such as the "original intent" of the founding fathers, as foundational in providing the direction for contemporary political action. For Gadamar (2002), the text is a lever for appropriation within a given contemporary context, compatible with the tradition. Its linkage is in the "continuity of memory" (p. 390) the new situation evokes. The vital factor is that the fusion opens new visualizations that bring and often extend various meanings embedded within the tradition into the present through rigorous dialogical encounter. In Gadamar's words, "Reconstructing the question to which the text is presumed to be the answer itself takes place within a process of questioning through which we try to answer the question that the text asks us" (p. 374) in the present. This necessitates, as Bernstein (1983) expressed it, that "we must participate or share in them [texts and traditions], listen to them, open ourselves to what they are saying and to the claims of truth that they make upon us." This "we can accomplish . . . only because of the forestructures and prejudgments that are constitutive of our being" (p. 137). As Bernstein more fully explained:

> We are always understanding and interpreting in light of our anticipatory prejudgments and prejudices, which are themselves changing in the course of history. This is why Gadamer tells us that to understand is to understand *differently* [italics in original]. But this does not mean that our interpretations are arbitrary or distortive. We should always aim (if informed by an "authentic hermeneutical attitude") at a correct understanding of what the "things themselves" [texts or traditions] say. But what the things themselves say will

be different in light of our changing horizons and the different questions that we learn to ask. Such an analysis of the ongoing and open character of all understanding and interpretation can be construed as distortive only if we assume that a text possesses some meaning in itself that can be isolated from our prejudgments. But this is precisely what Gadamar is denying, and this play between the "things themselves" and our prejudgments helps us to comprehend why understanding must be conceived as part of the process of the coming into being of meaning. Meaning is always *coming into being* [italics in original] through the "happening" of understanding. (p. 139)

Although emergent interpretations need to be authentic both to the tradition (or the text) and the present, they cannot become absolutely definitive as history, consequently, the continuous fusions of horizons remain perpetually open. This does not call for a simple embrace of relativism as certain interpretations gain more or less stable forms of legitimacy. Yet, even more settled narratives remain susceptible to possible reconstruction or even deconstruction. What Bernstein wanted us to imagine is "an ongoing and open dialogue or conversation" (p. 144) between a given tradition and the current setting, mediated through diverse and often contestable interpretations, where neither the past nor the present is privileged in isolation. At least at times, the result may be that "our own horizon is enlarged and enriched" (p. 143).

An example was Lincoln's appropriation in 1863 of the Declaration of Independence to render judgment on slavery, which he ultimately viewed as an unequivocal violation of core principles of the republican and democratic values at the heart of the ethos of the American Revolution. A related case in point was Martin Luther King Jr.'s ability, a century later, to draw imaginatively from the language of Jefferson and Lincoln to condemn segregation based on the same set of principles, even as such application moved beyond the literal intent of either Jefferson or Lincoln. What the tradition of 1776 provides is a core value of radical egalitarianism that then can be drawn on in different historical situations to extend the boundaries of human freedom implicit within the meaning of the text, even if not literally reflecting the authorial intent of the writer. As put by Rawls (1993), "It is a matter of understanding what earlier principles refine under changed circumstances and of insisting that they be honored in existing institutions" (p. xxxi). This appropriation requires subtle negotiation, as meaning is always open and neither fully inherent within the text nor in the current situation. Rather, in Gadamar's language, meaning is an event that happens within history, itself through encounter and active interpretation, for example, in the abolition of slavery through the passage of the 13th Amendment to the U.S. Constitution.

The political discourse stemming from the ethos of the American Revolution, drawn on in different periods by Lincoln and King, provides an important staging ground for the reconstruction of the politics of literacy in the contemporary setting. The appropriation is broad. It builds on the various strands of thought comprising democratic, republican, and constitutional principles in providing frames of reference for the development of a coherent politics of literacy in the current era. Given the gaps between its inherent idealism and actual appropriation within any given era, there is clearly a utopian dimension to any vision that draws on the nation's founding political tradition. Such encounters have resulted in the best of periods, in fragmentary fulfillments, and in the worst of times they have been marked by profound contradictions and hypocrisies. Nonetheless, the appropriation I envision is a reform impetus that draws on the belief that the "American experiment" is renewable. It operates despite, and sometimes through, the many constraints that act against it, which when appropriately tapped evoke an aesthetic sensibility that stirs the imagination.

This vision, the American Dream, if you will, in its various materialistic and idealistic incarnations, tempered by the prospect of gradual improvement in an imperfect world, is based on reformist sensibilities that have the capacity to inspire national renewal. It is within this context, through a drawing out of the nation's founding political tradition, that a core belief in radical egalitarianism, gains life as a potentially viable reconstructive force in the current setting. On this vision, everyone has an equal chance to participate in the main currents of American life, even if only as an operative ideal. This notion of radical egalitarianism has played a powerful role in the abolitionist, labor, civil rights, and women's movements of the 19th and 20th century that has sometimes led to reform movements, allowing for greater inclusion for marginalized groups within the nation's political, social, economic, and legal institutions. This democratic ideal in which I seek to situate the politics of literacy is supplemented by a republican sensibility based on a commonwealth tradition of citizen engagement in quest of the public good. These principles are embedded in a constitutional framework of governmental stability through the authority of just law wedded to the doctrine of popular sovereignty.

In grappling with such a project, I seek to ground within a reconstructed politics of literacy the core values of equality, liberty, justice, opportunity, the vocation of active citizenry engagement in the political culture, and the just rule of law, all of which are resident within the nation's political ideals. Even as there is much within political practice, past and present, which belies these ideals, I draw on them as providing support for an underlying vision on which to base public and policy support for adult literacy. I do so on the assumption that they hold the potential of tapping into the collective imagination of the American people, as a potentially viable reconstructive force. A reconstruction of the politics of literacy within the United States based on these values would go a long way to broadening the perceived purposes of adult literacy beyond a somewhat narrow economic calculus that informs current policy.

There are valuable reasons to pursue such a reconstruction, particularly the need to establish a strong public/policy legitimization for the field, despite the difficulties. Still, the problematic nature of such a project remains daunting, including the seeming intractability of divergent and often conflicting perspectives on the pedagogy and politics of adult literacy education that are currently pervasive. Focusing specifically on adult literacy accountability, Merrifield (1998) spoke about "the maelstrom of confusion about how to measure learning." She placed her hope in the viability of "new research [that] could break through the barriers of an approach [standardized testing] that is widely disliked and create new forms of assessment that are firmly based in new understandings of the nature of literacy and cognitive learning" (p. 55). By this, she was evidently referring to the New Literacy Studies.

Neither the advocates of participatory literacy education nor the NLS have been able to convince policymakers of their grounding premises. The likelihood of this is even more improbable in the current neoconservatism of the Bush administration, whose educational policy is based on a repudiation of progressive practice and ideas, which in different ways shape these "alternative" schools of thought. Thus, the field has not established a sufficiently persuasive politics of literacy to cut a discerning path between the radical critique of critical pedagogy and the structural functionalism of current policy largely determined by the marketplace. No third way has gained firm ground and there is little in the short-term horizon that points in its direction.

Much of this book consists of a descriptive analysis of this dilemma. Still, it remains the tempered hope of this book that resources can be erected from the operative assumptions of the NLS and the public philosophy implicit within EFF. If this is not necessarily viable in the short-term, then perhaps it has potentiality in the longer term. This "middle ground," or "third way," would stem from a hermeneutical retrieval of the nation's founding political values as a reconstructive dynamic currently lacking within the field. Its far from easy enactment would require considerable imagination, a high level of focus, broad consensual agreement, and substantial permeability and mediation among the prevailing perspectives to allow fresh constructions to emerge. The purpose of this book is to probe into the issues that tend to divide, and more briefly, to seek through them plausible construals that could lead to new constructions toward a more desirable future without discounting the difficulties.

Adult Literacy and the Quality of Life

> *At 04:54 PM 9/4/97 Regie Stites wrote:*
> *The issue of what the direct and indirect outcomes of adult literacy are or should*
> *be is really a policy issue and thus theory and research can inform the definition*
> *of these outcomes but will not ultimately decide the issue.*
> *Why?*
> *Paul Clay*
> *Well, Paul I loved the question, but I know you are familiar with these realities*
> *that shape the answer:*
>> *funding*
>> *bureaucracy*
>> *public opinion*
>
> —Peggy Lewis (NLA, March 7, 1997)

We enter into the fray through a series of descriptions of the various ways in which certain problems over participatory literacy education and alternative assessment played out in the 1990s. The repartee between Paul Clay and Peggy Lewis over Regie Stite's assumption that outcomes for adult literacy are driven by policy rather than research highlights a continuing dialogue on assessment and accountability that has taken place on the National Literacy Advocacy (NLA) electronic list discussion from 1997 to the present.

David Rosen, former director of the Adult Literacy Resource Center in Boston, established and moderated the NLA from 1994–2003. It is now housed under the American Association of Adult and Continuing Education (AAACE), moderated by David Collings. The NLA has been and is a major forum for a wide exchange of views related to the formation and advocacy of federal policy on adult literacy. Discursive threads range from tactical lobbying strategies to substantive philosophical discussions that undergird policy issues. Between 600 and 700 members subscribe to the list. They include a select group of adult literacy students, practitioners, administrators of local, regional, and national adult literacy agencies, state directors of adult education and their staffs, adult education staff from the U.S. Department of Education, research institute members, and graduate students, professors, and authors in the field of adult education and literacy.

The most contentious topics stem around the politics of literacy. These include specific analyses of literacy policy, particularly the Workforce Investment Act and accompanying National Reporting System, as well as various national initiatives, particularly the EFF project, the Literacy Summit of 2000, and an Action Agenda for Literacy. The entire subject matter of assessment and accountability has aroused considerable controversy on the NLA. With the advent of the junior Bush administration, contentious discussion has centered on such topics as scientific-based educational research, reading theory, the composition of the new NIFL advisory board, and the direction to be established for the agency under the Bush administration.

The current chapter focuses on two interrelated discussions that took place in April 1997. A related thread that same month, although focused on family literacy, was based on the same set of political conflicts that has underlain issues over assessment accountability. The two interrelated threads were titled "Quality of Life" and "Metaphors of Literacy." In those discussions, participants sought to work through the tension of documenting the subtle nuances of learning as experienced at the ground of the student–teacher relationship, with the equally compelling need to draw meaningful inferences and information from a collection of data that could be usefully applied at a system-wide level.

Most of the program practitioners focused on the tensions between these perspectives. Those concentrating on policy and administration sought mediation largely through "performance-based" outcome assessment, which these proponents hoped could satisfy both interests. A certain degree of probing back and forth between alternative and standard-based assessment was a characteristic element in the search to work through these issues. Yet, when advocates pushed assumptions of purpose and methodology to underlying assumptions, fundamental tensions surfaced. For example, Beder (1999) maintained that "because self-report measures are susceptible to response bias in many cases, objective measures are usually preferable, and outcome studies that rely extensively or exclusively on self-report must be regarded with a degree of suspicion" (p. 14). Arguing to the contrary, McGrail (1994, vol. 6) focused on the "need to figure out ways to bring the learners into our conversation. We need to hear their voices. We need to know if our new conceptual frameworks have merit, if our attempts to capture their gains [are] meaningful" (p. 10).

The critical issue revolved around the extent to which the effort would progress through an ethnographic methodology that stemmed from, but included more than, "self-report" based on the interpretive science of cultural anthropology. It would be rich in context, but it would not be (nor was it designed to be) statistically rigorous, as is the case in a more positivist scientific tradition. For the latter, evidence grounded in norms of objectivity and standardization can provide useful information at a statistically based aggregate level. Without such measures, advocates argue, there is little prospect of accessing *comparable data* across programs, agencies, states, and regions, the collection of which was viewed as indispensable from a policy perspective. For proponents of participatory literacy education, the exclusionary, or even primary focus on uniform, statistical data provides little insight into the complex dynamics of adult literacy learning. The methodology of standardized data collection as largely an end in itself seemed to require sacrificing the rich webs of significance and meaning of the learning process that participatory advocates view as the only conceivable starting point on which any valid assessment system could be based. Wagner (1991) characterized the differences between these perspectives as an "emic–etic" distinction" (p. 13). As he stated it, "What is particularly crucial in the emic–etic distinction is that the emic skills be those which can only be adequately understood within a given cultural framework, and were not created for historical convenience by those who desire a common or universal [i.e., an etic] system of measurement" (p. 13).

Wagner noted the usefulness of both types of measurement. He pointed out that by design, the etic "tradition of measurement purposefully ignores most of the process and context features of literacy which affect its acquisition and use" (p. 13). Under persistent outside pressure throughout the 1990s, the Adult Basic Education (ABE) policy leadership focused on developing an accountability system based on etic information that could pass muster with the federal government even while linked to student goals. Advocates of alternative assessment remained more skeptical.

This core tension between emic and etic perspectives and mediating efforts as variously linked to theory, practice, and policy, is depicted throughout this chapter. In the following section and throughout the chapter, the central issue participants struggled with was whether legitimacy should be driven by policy mandates or from field and scholarly perspectives based on the premises of participatory literacy education and alternative assessment design. It might be reasonably argued that legitimacy should be based on an integration of these perspectives. Yet for various political and epistemological reasons linked to the distribution of social knowledge and power, the participatory ideal as a policy potential has seldom moved beyond a marginalized positionality.

The following encounter over how definitions of family literacy were mediated through the politics of literacy paralleled the conflict over assessment accountability. What makes this episode particularly instructive is that the divergent views were articulated by two of the most prominent spokespersons in the field. The first was Robert Bickerton, director of Adult Education in Massachusetts, who played a strong leadership role in adult literacy federal policy formation in the 1990s. Her interlocutor was Elsa Auerbach, professor of English at the University of Massachusetts, a leading advocate of a Freirian-inspired participatory model of education.

ADULT BASIC EDUCATION FOR THE 21ST-CENTURY ACT

Between 1995 and 1998, the field's policy leadership under the direction of the National Coalition for Literacy (NCL) and the state directors of adult education attempted to squeeze out creative space between the constraints of limited funding and opportunities available to give a broader shape to policy than its preeminent focus on economic development. This included the effort to establish an expansive, although realistically based, policy agenda around a broad array of contexts, including, but not limited to, the economic realm.

This comprehensive vision was incorporated into a proposed $1 billion per year funded Adult Basic Education for the 21st Century Act, "carefully negotiated" under the auspices of the NCL (Bickerton, NLA, April 24, 1997). Participant groups consisted of the field's leading national agencies and organizations. Key areas in this omnibus proposal included preparing workers for "success in a global marketplace," supporting "adults on public assistance [who] lack a strong educational foundation," and a focus on the need "to break intergenerational cycles of illiteracy and undereducation . . . [in order to] make parents full partners in their child's education." It factored in "incarcerated adults [who] lack a strong educational foundation at twice the rate of our nation's law abiding population" and the importance of English instruction for the millions of immigrants who "have contributed to our communities and our economy." The relation between education and voting and broader "participat[ion] in civic affairs" was also included.

The 21st Century Act was designed as a consensus-driven position paper. Not likely to be "submitted [as federal legislation] in its own right," it was intended as a framework that "all advocates for ABE/ESOL (etc.) . . . [could]

rally around [in support of] its provisions and underlying philosophy." As a touchstone, the 21st Century Act provided a structure designed to rally the field to help "push the bills emerging from [Congress] . . . as far in its direction as possible" (Bickerton, NLA, April 24, 1997). It required "speak[ing] with one common voice."

With its exclusive focus on parents and their young children, Rosen wondered whether the definition in the 21st Century Act on " 'family literacy services' is too narrow." Rosen thought that a statement on family literacy, including "other adults in the family" along with "children through adolescence" (Rosen, NLA, April 27, 1997), would strengthen the family services provision of this omnibus bill (referred to henceforth, the Act).

Rosen's query sparked an illuminating exchange on whether a more restrictive or expansive definition of family literacy should hold sway for purposes of federal funding. Bickerton supported "collaborative services that reach the whole family." He noted that the Act would support "any of the approaches discussed on this list," but "some just wouldn't be defined as 'family literacy.' " Bickerton answered the question, "Why THIS definition?":

> Well, it's one of two suggested by the National Center for Family Literacy (NCFL) [a highly influential member of the NCL]—we choose the less restrictive of the two, but NCFL convinced the House Education and the Workforce Committee to adopt the more proscriptive one. . . . In order to rally all ABE/Literacy/ESOL (+) constituencies around a single piece of legislation, we need to build a coalition approach which means a lot of compromises we can live with; the family literacy definition is one of these compromises. (Bickerton, NLA, May 1, 1997)

Auerbach wondered "who . . . the we" was that "chose the less restrictive of the two" definitions. She cautioned that such a compromise required by political necessity "contradicts and undermines the direction of so much of current research and practice." In a statement that has parallel implications for assessment accountability, Auerbach noted that "the narrow definition may be politically advantageous (especially to those who promote this model, thus ensuring funding for their models and programs), but an increasingly broad base of researchers and practitioners take issue with it." She pointed to the 1994 draft of an International Declaration of Family Literacy, which "specifically and explicitly rejected narrow definitions like that of the NCFL based on years of ethnographic research and practice in a range of culturally diverse contexts." Auerbach argued that the field would be better grounded by rallying around the "inclusive and ethical set of principles" (Auerbach, NLA, May 8, 1997) issued by the Declaration (Taylor, 1997).

Bickerton pointed to the critical work of the NCL, which he described as "a relatively loosely knit organization that attempts to bring together any/

every national group or organization working on behalf of under-educated and LEP [limited English proficiency] students." Its purpose is in "creat[ing] the best opportunity I'm aware of to conduct the kind of dialogue that builds, nurtures and strengthens a broad coalition across the many different perspectives/voices/forces in our 'field.' " Bickerton explained that the Act was crafted through a carefully negotiated process among the NCL's constituencies as a pragmatic consensus document that necessarily entailed considerable compromise.

Bickerton reiterated the need for consensus as the price to pay for becoming policy effective. As he argued, the field "lacks traditional political clout that it can more than make up for in numbers, passion, and grass roots impact." These means, "however, CAN ONLY BE SUCCESSFUL when they are highly coordinated and we 'SING' (a.k.a., 'shout') WITH ONE VOICE." Bickerton spoke of the need to use "the same key words" without which "leads at best, to confusion among members of Congress and their staff, or at worst, exploitation of real or illusory differences" by oppositional congressional forces.

Bickerton's approach required consummate realism and the capacity to engage in intricate gamesmanship of which he was a highly skilled practitioner. In addition to his national focus in seeking a proper niche for ABE in the conservative congressional era of the mid-1990s, as director of adult education in Massachusetts, one of the most politically progressive states in the field, Bickerton was highly seasoned as a tactical strategist. Bickerton insisted that the definition of family literacy that the Act adopted was the most viable compromise with political reality from a long-term policy perspective. This the field could reject only at the peril of becoming further marginalized.

Bickerton focused on how coalition politics are played, specifically, "how do people who have not moved their own priorities forward in the public policy arena get into this mix?" His answer was "by influencing the organization(s) they are already part of and/or closest to that are participating on the Coalition and/or by going to the organization with the most momentum for its position." On this premise, the most likely strategy for Auerbach would be to seek to influence the NCFL, which carried the biggest clout with the NCL and Congress in establishing a consensus-driven definition of family literacy. This would inevitably involve compromise, argued Bickerton, yet it would provide the compensatory prospect of becoming policy effective and, therefore, realistic.

The inevitable trade-off was that such a stance has a tendency to mute alternative perspectives for the sake of consensus even those based, arguably, on sound research traditions. This was one of Auerbach's major arguments. Moreover, her scholarship was premised on a more inclusive interpretation of family literacy than that proposed by the NCFL (Auerbach, 1989). For

Auerbach to accept what she viewed as the more restrictive version of family literacy would have required compromising with the primary intellectual presuppositions, politics, and supporting program practices that grounded her work. What for Bickerton was the compromise that "we can live with," for Auerbach screened out and marginalized the basic presuppositions that provided the coherence for her work and those of her colleagues.

The conflicting sources of legitimization over competing definitions of family literacy pointed to similar sources of tension over assessment accountability. There was a limited fluidity between 1995 and 1997 in possible policy responses to congressional pressure, but the need for *comparability* through standardized, uniform, and measurable data seemed a clear directive that could not be ignored. The enactment into law in 1998 of the Workforce Investment Act and accompanying National Reporting System, supported by the NCL, the state directors of adult education, and NIFL, became the compromise "we can live with," the necessary price to pay, proponents argued, of achieving public, policy, and political legitimization. This nonnegotiable compromise raised a firestorm throughout the field, as the legislation violated the key assumptions of both the Freirian-based participatory literacy movements and those of the New Literacy Studies. Auerbach's description of the *emergent curriculum* is instructive in highlighting these sharply conflicting perspectives.

THE EMERGENT CURRICULUM

Auerbach and Rutger's professor of adult education, Hal Beder, share a similar outlook even as there is a fundamental difference in their viewpoints. Interpreted through the stance of Auerbach's critical pedagogy, Beder's dismissal of that which advocates of the participatory school maintain as most essential can be viewed as an ironic consequence of normative logic. Beder granted that what may be most important in adult literacy is not easily captured through methodologies that focus on the collection of large-scale aggregate data abstracted from the particularity of lived experience:

> The problem with using learners' goals as an outcome measure is that if we are doing our job as adult literacy educators, learners perspectives, and hence their goals, will presumably change during the course of instruction. In fact, whether (and how) learners' goals change may be a better marker of success than whether they achieve the goals they started with. (Beder, NLA, September 8, 1997)

To resolve the conflict, Beder made a sharp distinction between *outcomes* directly related to the mastery of reading, writing, and computation that can be measured in some objective way, and *impacts*, which cannot be so easily measured. Beder accepted the subtle intervening nature of literacy in conjunction with other factors in enhancing the array of skills and knowledge that individuals draw on in application to the diversity of contexts of their lives. Although noting the significance of these elusive impacts, Beder worried that they are too imprecise to serve as a form of measurement at a national level.

This concern, along with his quest for "objective" data, minimizes for Beder the significance of ethnography as a major research methodology to be utilized as a central means through which to narrate the story of adult literacy on a broad-based societal scale. He noted that ethnographic studies have value on their own terms that might subtly get at impact in a manner inaccessible through quantitative methodologies. Yet, because ethnographic studies cannot be readily generalized from one context to the next, Beder (1999) argued that this form of research cannot serve as the basis to establish federal policy, although it can have supplemental value.

What for Beder is problematic represents the basis on which Auerbach (1992b) constructed her thesis of the *emergent curriculum*. Her reasoning is based, in part, on the assumption "that people learn best when learning starts with what they already know, builds on their strengths, engages them in the learning process, and enables them to accomplish something they want to accomplish" (p. 9). Auerbach sharply distinguished the emergent curriculum from "a more traditional, ends–means approach," although she acknowledged that this establishes "the danger of setting up such a contrast that it creates a kind of polarization that may not correspond to the lived experience of practitioners" (p. 11). Noting that her model is overly simple, Auerbach viewed the contrast "not so much as a system for categorizing or labeling programs, but rather as a tool for framing thinking about possibilities and situating programs along a continuum" (p. 11) that expands perceptual boundaries of the possible. By linking the tenets of the emergent curriculum through a sharply defined neo-Freirian vision of "participatory literacy education," Auerbach provided a theoretical model countercultural to the mainstream, in program emphasis, political culture, and modes of accountability. This provides at least *conceptual* legitimacy for a perspective that could easily be erased through dominance of more normative interpretations of adult literacy.

For Auerbach, an emergent curriculum "has to be built on the particular conditions, concerns, and contributions of specific groups of participants at a particular point in time." This requires that "a host of [highly variable] factors ... be taken into account" (p. 13). Elsewhere put (Auerbach & Wallerstein, 1987), "Learners enter into the process of learning not by acquiring facts (skills, competencies) but by constructing their reality in social exchange with others" (p. 1). Such a sensibility "radically transforms their relation to education, making them subjects of their own learning; at the same time because literacy becomes a tool for addressing problems, it transforms their relation to the world, making them subjects of their own history. Education thus is part of a liberating process rather than a domesticating one" (Auerbach, 1992b, p. 17).

Both Auerbach's ethnographically sensitive critical pedagogy and her approach to assessment in alternative design need to be grasped within her broader politics of literacy, which challenges the assimilationist assumptions of both the New Literacy Studies and the mainstream adult literacy/ABE establishment. From Auerbach's perspective, both of these viewpoints have a tendency to fit students into their lower class status, thereby strengthening the normative assumptions of the prevailing status quo (Auerbach, 1992a, 1993).

Drawing on Street (1988), Heath (1983), and Gee (1986), Auerbach (1992b) built her model on a social-constructivist interpretation of reading that also underlies the New Literacy Studies. As Auerbach (1992b) described it, the acquisition of literacy "in different settings have revealed that the ways people read and write vary according to the task, the situation, the purpose, and the relationship between the reader, writer, and setting" (p. 14). Such practices and beliefs, also identified by Lytle (1991), Fingeret (1992), and Merrifield (1998), "depend on a range of cultural, social, and political factors" (p. 14), including those of race, class, ethnicity, gender, and geographical region. In drawing out what she viewed as the intrinsic politics of literacy that support any pedagogy, Auerbach defined the "status" of literacy "not from its inherent features, but from its relation to the social order, because of who owns and has access to it" (Auerbach, 1992b, p. 15). Auerbach, Fingeret, Merrifield, and Lytle drew somewhat different implications of what an emancipatory politics of literacy might consist. Yet, they all adopted this basic social-constructivist perspective of literacy from a participatory framework and interpreted the pedagogical as political by definition.

Auerbach discussed the key components of the emergent curriculum in terms of *curriculum development process, needs assessment, content, teacher's role,* and *outcomes.* In the participatory model, the curriculum emerges from the "students [who] are assumed to be experts on their own reality and very much involved in researching that reality with teachers." Consequently, "the instructional process . . . [moves] *from the students to the curriculum* rather than *from the curriculum to the students*" (p. 19, italics in italics). In this model, "evaluation is done in students' interests rather than only to meet funders' needs." To the extent that students "participate in choosing or designing evaluation tools and evaluating themselves" they "become subjects rather than objects of evaluation" (p. 114).

In the emergent curriculum, needs assessment is an ongoing process rather than determined ahead of time. Students are engaged "in examining their own contexts, identifying factors that shape their environment [through 'problem-posing' teaching] so they can begin to change it" (p. 19). It follows that:

> Outcomes cannot be predicted if content and processes are genuinely student-centered. The unpredictability of outcomes is valued in that it indicates that participants have genuinely been involved in determining their objectives for themselves. Qualitative change is given as much if not more weight than quantitative change. . . . Whereas measurable changes in skill or grade levels are valued in an ends–means approach, the diversification of uses of literacy and the ability to make meaningful changes in everyday life are valued in a participatory approach. The changes are not easily measurable and may have no clearly observable behavioral manifestations. Progress is seen as *cumulative* and *cyclical* [italics in original] rather than occurring in discrete linear steps. (pp. 20–21)

In *Making Meaning Making Change*, Auerbach provided the broad contours of an integrated vision. To rule its qualitative and ethnographic methods of assessment out of court as the basis to at least influence the development of a national accountability system on the grounds that its tenets lack *generalizability* is to place restrictive boundaries on the epistemological and political criteria on which legitimacy is based. It is to rule out serious public discourse, what Geertz referred to as the "thick description" of ethnographic research, which is "designed to describe and analyze practices and beliefs of cultures and communities" (Mertens, 1998, p. 165) where "multiple realities exist that are time and context dependent" (p. 161). That is not to argue that those advocating a more central role for qualitative modes of assessment are not required to correlate their findings across programs, agencies, and regions. This is essential in order to show impact on a nation-wide level, which well-constructed bibliographic review essays can at least begin to get at.

The basic issue turns on the validity of representational knowledge (even if not a scientific sample) gained through ethnography, critical theory, and various qualitative methodologies. The question is whether information gleaned from the ethnographic research tradition can serve as an alternative foundation to the ideal of uniform data collection, theoretically on every student or even a uniformly based "scientific" sample supported through what some question as an anything but a value-free, rigorous scientific methodology. The challenge is not to delegitimize what Mertens (1998) referred to as the positivist/postpositivist research tradition, but to place it in a supplementary role in providing useful information that can add important context to reports based on thick narrative description and critical analysis. Discerning these different modalities of research requires probing the relation between different social science paradigms in their varied influence on what gets defined as legitimate research both from policy and pedagogical perspectives (chap. 9).

CONFLICTING TENSIONS IN ALTERNATIVE ASSESSMENT DESIGN

As reflected both in Wagner's emic–etic distinction and in the conflicting perspectives underlying the Bickerton–Auerbach exchange, the challenges stemming around assessment accountability are not merely those of appropriate design from a technical standpoint. Also in play are the ways in which methodological issues are linked to pedagogical schools, policy pressures, and the broader social, political, and intellectual contexts that lend status to specific assessment systems. In the baldest of terms, from the policy perspective of the WIA/NRS, adult literacy students are viewed as clients of the state, whereas proponents of participatory literacy education consider them equal partners in the learning process and co-creators of the curriculum. As put by Fingeret (1989):

> It is important to recognize that nonreading adults are creators of their own social lives, as imperfect as those lives may appear by middle-class standards. They participate in the ongoing creation and maintenance of the social world in which they live. Their inherent dignity is at the heart of the belief that they are not only able but that it is their right to participate in creating programs that are supposed to serve their interests. (p. 9)

In the former view, assessment is an observational process designed to monitor student progress in light of predetermined policy-driven objectives in the form of exacting measurement. From the participatory viewpoint, assessment is ongoing and coterminous with instruction. Moreover, goals, and more broadly, sources of motivation, emerge throughout the evolution of the learning process. They are not always susceptible to discrete forms of measurement. In contrast to the policy orientation based on the mathematical metaphor of quantification, alternative assessment is based on storied metaphors of qualitative narrative description in which "we cannot separate the setting from our literacy behaviors" (Fingeret, 1992, p. 6).

In the qualitative research tradition, subjective interpretation is as ines-capable as it is invariably contestable. Plausibility, rather than certainty is the objective of scholarship based on this tradition, a view reinforced by the recognition that multiple interpretations of the same phenomenon are in-evitable given the constructive nature of human consciousness. The narra-tive challenge of a qualitative research focus on adult literacy is to relate the story in sufficiently satisfying ways to the field's major constituents, from students, teachers, and program staff, to administrators, funders, legisla-tors, and the general public in quest of legitimacy and resources. Research based on these objectives requires the utilization of academic methods and valid forms of evidence, but those appropriate for discerning the various contexts of "multiple social constructions of meaning and knowledge" (Mertens, 1998, p. 11). In this tradition, the researcher is the "primary in-strument for collecting [and ordering] data" (p. 175), whose biases and in-terests invariably shape the direction of the research project. Methodol-ogies are more fluid than those in the positivist research tradition, which depend on dispassionate objectivity, the search for causal and direct correlational analysis through favored methodologies of random sampling, and experimental and quasi-experimental design.

In the qualitative research tradition, methods are "softer," as they are in the humanities, with interpretation based on a triangularity of evidence such as interviews, direct observation, and document analysis. Given the na-ture of qualitative research, which seeks to get at complex psychological, so-cial, and cultural meaning, interpretation is open to divergent perspectives. This is not a nihilistic rejection of standards. Scholarly legitimacy in the hu-manities, and in the sciences for that matter, is determined by the canoni-cal traditions of the various academic disciplines that comprise a particular study, as well as the overall plausibility of a given interpretation and the range and type of evidence drawn on in any specific argument. Both quanti-tative and qualitative traditions are viewed as legitimate forms of educa-tional research. The object is not so much to strike a balance between the two, but to draw on whatever research traditions and methodologies that are appropriate to any question or issue at hand. Whereas the scholarly community determines the canon, academic legitimacy does not necessar-ily transfer to the policy sector.

The apprehension among the advocates of qualitative assessment in the 1997 NLA discussion had less to do with the notion that both forms of meas-urement have their place. Rather, as the trend was clearly moving, the ex-pressed concern was that the quantitative emphasis on etic data could dom-inate public discourse about literacy. Practitioners worried that the policy emphasis on quantification reinforced a "deficit" interpretation through an erasure of the qualitative significance of literacy that they felt could never "be quantified into some statistical report" (Clay, NLA, March 31, 1997).

In arguing for a "quality of life" orientation, proponents acknowledged the need for policy legitimacy. This would require at least some inference or generalization from the data obtained through student-centered methodologies such as case study analysis, portfolio assessment, and student writing samples, beyond the specific students of a single classroom or study. Some of the discussants wanted to remain focused on the alternative design that prioritizes subjectivity, values, and emotion, as much as (if not more than) overt behavior, because from their point of view the latter could only be contextually grasped when situated in the former. Lytle (1991) discussed four dimensions through which literacy behavior emerges: *beliefs, practices, processes,* and *plans.* She suggested that although "these developmental processes appear to be reciprocal and recursive, there is evidence that beliefs may be a primary source or anchor for other dimensions of growth" (p. 121). For many within the alternative assessment camp, any shift away from grounding assessment on these basic characteristics of human meaning making violates core principles of student-centered and participatory pedagogy. Schneider and Clarke (1999) articulated this view:

> Participatory education . . . [is] a term that principally means democracy in the classroom. Participatory means that both students and teachers are active in negotiating the direction of the class and their respective roles in it. Participatory education models the democratic process of being heard, negotiating needs and creating solutions. Curriculum becomes a word to describe the process where students ask and answer questions about their own lives. (p. viii)

Learning based on these premises is inherently collaborative and evaluative. It is not readily susceptible to precise or discrete analysis that can be easily quantified in an aggregate manner that vitiates the "thick description" of context that alternative assessment seeks to disclose. It requires sensitivity to an array of social and emotional factors that interplay in the lives of students.

McGrail (1994, vol. 6) laid out the implications of this view in establishing six principles of participatory assessment (as quoted):

1. It must be program-based and learner-centered.
2. It should help the learners achieve their goals.
3. It must build on learner strengths and not deficits.
4. It should be part of the learning experience.
5. It should not be a single procedure but a variety of procedures.
6. It should provide feedback that will lead to better instruction. (p. 5)

While acknowledging these principles, other practitioners were willing to make a more conversionist shift from alternative assessment design toward performance-based accountability that relies for evidence on direct outcomes rather than on perceptions or beliefs. The distinction between the two perspectives remained fluid, although Carabell's (1999) description of his own odyssey, discussed later in this chapter, is instructive. Those participating in the NLA discussion focusing more on policy and administration, yet who also sought to keep literacy linked to the "improved life," wanted to make sure that whatever means drawn on to document such growth could be measurable through some form of data aggregation. As put by Tracy-Mumford of the Delaware Department of Public Instruction:

> If Ken Blanchard (*One Minute Manager*) can quantify "friendliness" in a meaningful way to senior execs in the Banking Industry, surely we can designate meaningful outcomes that convey understanding to policymakers (who want to show that they are good custodians of public funds) and at the same time, produce outcomes that are truly meaningful to our students. (Tracy-Mumford, NLA, April 7, 1997)

The various messages on assessment and accountability in April (this chapter) and September 1997 (chap. 6) on the NLA reflected an array of subtle nuance. There was considerable tension among the exchanges in the effort to work through emic–etic, policy, field, and research issues toward developing "authentic" approaches to assessment that also could begin to meet the need for data comparability. The strains between these perspectives were far from resolved in the 1997 NLA discourses. Nonetheless, the exchanges surfaced many significant issues in the effort to make sense of the underlying epistemology and politics that could give shape both to the meaning of literacy and the sources of legitimacy in the neoliberal era of the Clinton administration.

"THAT CAN'T BE QUANTIFIED INTO SOME STATISTICAL REPORT"

It is difficult to discern precisely when electronic mailing list threads start and end, but in an early NLA message on adult literacy and the "improved life," Paul Clay referred to "a Samoan man . . . who was ecstatic when we went to the library and got him a card. It was a whole world that opened up for him" (Clay, NLA, March 31, 1997). Without further documentation, it would be impossible to derive a sense of what the experience meant for the man. One might speculate that such a "world" had enabled him to see beyond the immediacy of his village experience in a manner that might have been life transforming or at least a significant marker event of a powerful border crossing in self-understanding. As put by a former Nigerian village dweller for whom a whole world did open up, "my ability to read and write had transformed me beyond my immediate environment" (Akinnaso, 1991, p. 84), in this case, into the academic world of European and U.S. scholarship.

Akinnaso briefly discussed the scholarly debate on whether or not literacy is a "*causal* agent" that in itself opens up new ways of thinking not available through oral discourse (greater rationalism, enhanced individual consciousness) or whether it is "a *facilitating* agent [italics in original], promoting the deployment of preexisting cognitive capacities into certain channels that are socially and ideologically sanctioned by the user group." From this latter perspective, the position of the author, "while literacy facilitates the acquisition of certain cognitive skills and operations, it does not, in itself, engender novel cognitive capacities as the 'causative' argument would have us believe." Akinnaso's more important point is that "neither group denies the fact that literacy alters the world we live in and the way we perceive and talk about that world" (p. 75). Something along these lines, I assume, was Clay's point in relating the anecdote of the Samoan man to his colleagues on the NLA.

Some description of the changing consciousness of this individual and how it played out in his life would have been needed if Clay was going to make an informed argument from this example. That was not Clay's purpose. Its use was rhetorical in the sharing of a "self-evident" affinity with other list practitioners in their shared excitement that students and teachers sometimes experience at key moments in their work. What Clay captured was the sentiment, shared by the other NLA practitioners, "that [new learning, insight, and seemingly spontaneous breakthroughs in self-perception] can't be quantified into some statistical report that lends itself to policy making" (Clay, NLA, March 31, 1997). As put by another participant, "The voices of our learners provide ample measure of quality gains—do we want to weigh the value of joy?" Acknowledging the importance of corroborating sources of verification, this practitioner also discussed efforts to document "quality of life" gains through the "unwieldy" process of portfolio assessment and "the growing rich collections of learner writing" (Gabb, NLA, April 4, 1997).

In order to extend the pool of qualitative documentation beyond individual learners or programs, Beth Riley of World Education in Cambridge, Massachusetts, suggested that a "collection of success stories" from many programs be placed on the Internet. That would "make a strong case for lots of purposes" (Riley, NLA, April 7, 1997). George Demetrion, then director of materials development at LVA, Inc., argued that without more substantive change in the manner in which assessment is perceived, evidence from student writing would be viewed as "merely anecdotal" from a policy perspective. He noted, "while there is a need for a both/and approach (quantitative and qualitative), still, the primary metaphors upon which we assess or evaluate the growth of literacy students and the effectiveness of programs may have to change so that the metaphor of narration, itself, takes on a more legitimized role than that of quantification without denying the validity of statistical information in shedding *some* light" (Demetrion, NLA, April 7, 1997, italics added).

Marguerite Lukes, from Literacy Partners, Inc., in New York City, who "completed two primarily ethnographic studies of change of adult learners in school-based parent involvement programs," argued that " 'real-life' data . . . was by no means 'soft,' as many so-called empirical researchers who know little about qualitative research methods generally claim." Those interested in "quality of life" issues should

> stop worrying about the potential criticism we may generate from using such authentic or alternative methods to measure gains in our programs. Or whether such methods will produce data that is understandable or meaningful. They will. Instead, we should use these methods to engage in a reflective process with learners and practitioners and see what our programs are doing right. Then, we can present our findings, which will be much more powerful than we as practitioners may have ever acknowledged.

Still, Lukes noted the dilemma of "find[ing] the long hours needed to talk to learners and engage with them in the kind of participatory research needed to cull out the essence of what impact these programs make" (Lukes, NLA, April 8, 1997).

In a related discussion on "measuring outcomes and/or impacts," reviewed in chapter 6, John Comings, director of the National Center for the Study of Adult Learning and Literacy (NCSALL), favored sampling and collecting in-depth information on a representative group of students. This would allow for a coming to terms both with the quality of life issue and a need to provide a broad representation of relevant data. More provocatively, Comings (1992, in McGrail & Purdom, vol. 3) also emphasized the importance of "keeping assessment out of program accountability." As he argued, "Using student assessment as the measure of effectiveness for program accountability, no matter how good the assessment tool, will always make the test result the focus of programs rather than the needs of students" (p. 43). Comings recommended an accreditation process: "If a program has all of the elements of good practice and service, then students who enter and remain in the program should be doing about as well as they can" (p. 44). Comings' proposal was not echoed on the 1997 NLA listserv discussion. Taking a lead from Lukes' message, participants on the "quality of life" thread, participants began to focus on ways through which qualitative information could be organized and synthesized.

Sharing an affinity with Lytle (1991), McGrail pointed to the interconnection of "beliefs, attitudes, and behavior" that should be taken into account in any assessment process geared to measuring the quality of life. She also emphasized the need to "look at change from a community level not just an individual level" (McGrail, NLA, April 7, 1997). Isserlis echoed this concern in the companion discussion on "metaphors and analogies in adult literacy education." In particular, Isserlis questioned the "deficit" connotation she felt implicit in the major metaphors of literacy as laid out by San Diego-based literacy researcher, Tom Sticht (Isserlis, NLA, April 6, 1997).

Sticht's five metaphors included the *Business Metaphor* where the "Merchant is to the Customer as the Adult Literacy Educator is to the Student"; the *Medical Metaphor* where the "Doctor is to the Patient as the Adult Literacy Educator is to the Student"; and the *Public School Metaphor* where the "Public Schools are to Children as Adult Literacy providers are to Adults." Sticht also identified the *Revolutionary Metaphor* where "The Revolutionary Leader (Liberator) is to the Oppressed as the Adult Literacy Educator is to the Learners," and the *Psychotherapy Metaphor* where "The Psychotherapist is to the Depressed Client as the Adult Literacy Educator is to the Low Self Esteem Adult Learner" (Erickson c/o Sticht, NLA, April 4, 1997). Isserlis, director of the Brown University-based Swearer Institute for Literacy Resources in Rhode Island, wondered whether "somewhere is there not a larger view that encompasses learning communities, where various members within each community has strengths AND needs?" She also "wonder[ed] how rating each metaphor separately informs a larger analysis?" (Isserlis, NLA, April 6, 1997). Along similar lines, McGrail sought to probe into the basic suppositions that underlie the dominant metaphors that shape the field. As she explained it, "By not examining our assumption that it is *capital* [italics added] that is sought for in the end, it doesn't quite matter which metaphor we go by." McGrail further thought that

> it would be interesting to see how one's view of literacy or education matches up with which metaphor you are most drawn to. In other words, if you believe literacy is primarily about learning skills and performing tasks (preset or otherwise), then you are probably drawn to metaphor. . . . If you believe literacy is about critical reflection and action then you would be drawn to. . . . (McGrail, NLA, April 7, 1997)

The proposed inquiry into underlying assumptions would help to flesh out the relation between assessment and the various definitions of literacy in circulation. In Foucauldian terms, this knowledge would better connect such discourses to the various sources of power that legitimize them. In effect, the question posed by McGrail is "who is speaking?":

> Who among the totality of individuals, is accorded the right to use this sort of language . . . [as contained in the various metaphors]. Who is qualified to do so? Who derives from it his own special quality, his prestige, and from whom, in return, does he receive, if not the assurance, at least the presumption that what he says is true? What is the status of the individuals who—alone—have the right, sanctioned by law or tradition, juridically defined or spontaneously accepted, to proffer such a discourse? (Foucault, 1972, p. 50)

McGrail was one of the authors of the participatory ESL curriculum guide, *Talking Shop* (Nash, Carson, Rhum, McGrail, & Gomez-Sanford, 1992) and the editor of the collection of monographs on alternative assessment, *Adventures in Assessment: Learner-Centered Approaches to Assessment and Evaluation in Adult Literacy* (1991–1994). In 1997, she was the executive director of one of the most progressive outposts for adult literacy education in the United States, *Literacy South*, previously directed by Hanna Fingeret. For McGrail, the very legitimacy of the progressive literacy philosophy was at risk in the 1990s. As she put it in her opening volume of *Adventures of Assessment* (1991, vol. 1), "Assessment in adult literacy is a central issue with high stakes" (p. 1). They were weighty, argued McGrail, because the forms of assessment selected by policy and many funding sources, typically standardized tests, determine the basis of program legitimacy in ways that contradict the basic tenets of participatory literacy education. The chief problem with this type of assessment is that it "ignores other legitimate criteria for evaluating a literacy program like the quality of the curriculum, teaching, or its connection to significant social issues relevant to students [sic] lives and interests, and . . . fails to recognize that increases in reading scores have little to do with the way adults live and use literacy in the real world" (p. 2).

According to the advocates of the alternative assessment and participatory education movement, the dominant policy social constructions that gained legitimacy by the late 1990s placed adult literacy students in the undesirable social category of "other," as marginalized "client" of the welfare state. Advocates argued that what was needed was a more enlightened social policy that better corresponded to the politics of a Freirian sensibility. This also required an instructional focus and modes of assessment supported by the new ethnographic research on literacy based on the collective scholarship of Brian Street, Silvia Scribner, and Shirley Brice Heath.

In terms of broad general discourse, no sharp lines had yet been drawn between the New Literacy Studies and critical pedagogy, although Auerbach (1992a) commented incisively on the distinction some years earlier.

Regardless of significant distinctions between the two schools of thought, they share a close affinity at least at the level of methodology on the importance of participatory literacy education and alternative modes of assessment in emphasizing the qualitative nature of the learning dynamic. That convergence could not compensate for the lack of a social policy to support these assumptions.

What is missing, McGrail argued, is "the fact that funders lack good information about the qualitative effects of programs on learners' lives" (p. 4). To even begin to overcome this deficiency would require "wider participation in the conversation about alternative assessment," which advocates hoped the NLA discussion would help to stimulate.

What McGrail desired was daunting. At the least, it would have required something akin to a source of influence where "participatory advocates . . . [would] pull together all their allies—learners, practitioners, community members, and others—to create a power block—a critical mass—of learner-centered activists" (Jurmo, 1989). Through a willingness to compromise in shaping a commonality of purpose (not a strong characteristic of the participatory literacy movement), Jurmo envisioned a "resulting solidarity" that could "serve as a stick that advocates . . . can use to convince unsupportive institutions of the power that these approaches represent" (p. 84). The participants of the NLA discussion were far from unaware of the relation between pedagogy, legitimizing modes of assessment and political power. However, 1997 was a different social milieu than 1989, the year that Fingeret and Jurmo wrote their influential text, *Participatory Literacy Education*. Prospects of such a paradigmatic shift may have seemed plausible to some in 1990. By the latter years of the decade, advocates of participatory literacy education were in a more defensive mode.

MEASURING STUDENT GOALS: PROSPECTS AND PROBLEMATICS

As the April 1997 NLA discussion progressed, the topic subtly shifted from identifying quality of life issues to means of measuring them, which required different epistemologies and methodologies than that which grounds the "objectivist" approach of measuring discrete outcomes. Although not able to recommend a comprehensive ethnographic framework, list participants did provide suggestive clues on which this could consist.

JoAnn Martin, then director of the Texas Literacy Resource Center, referred to a "student intake and management" project that she and her colleagues had worked on for 3 years. This included an "instrument that could be used to measure the goals of adults and quantify the type of information" under discussion in the NLA thread. Martin noted that "this could be done on the computer and . . . with the click of the mouse [students] could . . . check in the appropriate box" to report a variety of accomplishments like "read notes from school." Ruefully, Martin surmised that the project "will probably not get funded to be completed and used in the field." The other problem was whether the funding source, which Martin characterized as a "bureaucratic establishment," would support a data collection system based on self-report (Martin, NLA, April 17, 1997).

Taylor Willingham, director of the reading program at the Santa Clara County Library in California, pushed on the other horn of the dilemma, where contradictions abounded between a "statistically sound . . . research perspective and results that a funder would like to see." Willingham argued here that Martin's "simple statistical checklist" of isolated tasks provides little information of broader policy objectives that interest funders. As Willingham put it: "If person A came in with Goal 1 and achieved Goal 1, then you have statistical proof of the effectiveness of your program. But a policy-maker will still ask, 'Does that mean they go off welfare, their children learned to read, etc' " (Willingham, NLA, April 18, 1997).

These were persisting problems that those seeking to verify quality of life impact faced in depending on metaphors of assessment that ultimately relied on some form of counting (data aggregation). There was the problem with "response bias" that seemed to undercut any reporting system based primarily on self-report. Then there was the matter of what might be verified statistically that might not be easily squared with policy objectives, even if one accepted the validity of self-report. Finally, given the reality that "goals" often change and are not easily segmented into discrete tasks that can be neatly analyzed, developing an accountability system to measure quality of life impact was far from a simple matter. There was no easy solution that could square impact based on what was experienced at the ground of the learning/teaching dynamic with traditional mandates for aggregate accountability design.

Robert Bickerton reported that Massachusetts ABE administrators were "trying to make the correlation between student articulated goals and the results achieved the cornerstone of our accountability system." He noted that funders are, in fact, very interested in "the kinds of results/outcomes that are most important to our students." While viewing "the vast majority of student articulated goals [as] . . . a wonderful match with the educational, family community and economic priorities of policy and legislative leaders," he also stressed the need "to find the ways to clearly and concisely articulate the relationship." Bickerton pointed to the " 'statistically sound' question because there are some who will question the reliability of self-reported data." He noted that it was possible "in some cases . . . to establish links between databases to get very hard data/results." Still, he was troubled by the inevitable intrusiveness, particularly in the lives of those "not receiving a cash benefit [from the State] which is often used to justify such intrusive data collection."

Bickerton realized that "no databases exist[ed] to verify the vast majority of . . . goals our students strive to achieve." As a way to work through such quandaries, he suggested the field "may need to become adept at structured sampling approaches in order to verify the reliability of self-reported data" (NLA, April 18, 1997). The accountability system Bickerton envisioned still needed to be developed. His point was there was something of value to build on in that the kinds of specific goal attainments reported by students that could be reasonably correlated to the expectations of funders and legislators. For Bickerton, this was a critical basis on which to construct a sound accountability system, however difficult the actual task. In a related discussion several months later, he provided an overview of efforts in his state to establish a curriculum and corresponding assessment accountability system congruent with student goals and policy mandates. As he explained it:

> In Massachusetts, we are working on ABE curriculum frameworks. In them we hope to clarify the universe of content our students need to know and be able to do as well as how we can engage students in participatory learning so that such content standards enhance, rather than diminish the breadth and richness of their experience. The "next steps," include "defining" how learning can/should be assessed and associated student and instruction/"school" performance standards will come next—ensuring that assessment is closely aligned with curriculum! (Bickerton, NLA, September 8, 1997).

The tension Bickerton sought to resolve was the need, on the one hand, for standardized, uniform, and measurable data to satisfy governmental reporting mandates, with the vision of those espousing participatory literacy education and alternative assessment methodologies in a state where Freirian pedagogy flourished. This was a formidable task, as Bickerton well realized. This became even more difficult in 1998 with the passage of the NRS, a system that this national policy leader helped to create.

IN SEARCH OF AN ETHNOGRAPHIC METHODOLOGY

Given a general policy bias against the "merely" anecdotal, advocates of alternative assessment acknowledged that broader representation of student learning was required than simply some accounting of the unique learning/teaching moment of individual or very small groups of students. A more comprehensive framework was needed through which to assess "changes in self-concept, attitudes, or conceptions of literacy, diversification of reading and writing practices in everyday life, actions resulting from program participation as well as totally unexpected, unpredictable changes." Auerbach (1992b) added that *"what really counts can't be quantified"* (p. 112, italics in original).

To achieve legitimacy, proponents of qualitative assessment would need to develop a viable ethnographic methodology. Rejecting the goal of attaining uniform (and quite limited) data on every student that could be aggregated into a standardized report, those advocating alternative assessment pointed to case study analysis. This would require a "looking . . . in-depth [at smaller numbers of students] with assessment and evaluation tools that could uncover a wide range of impacts and outcomes" (Comings, NLA, September 20, 1999). Conceivably, proponents would establish a representational framework on the categories identified by Auerbach (described earlier) or on Lytle's (1991) four dimensional model of "beliefs, practices, processes, and plans" of adult literacy learners or on some related structure. A framework based on qualitative factors could draw on disciplines like phenomenology, critical theory, and cultural anthropology for intellectual buttressing (Merriam, 2001, p. 10). This would serve as a countermodel to the more "objectivist" approach premised on a positivist philosophy that underlies standardized testing, in which "words and pictures rather than numbers are used to convey what the researcher has learned about a phenomenon" (p. 8).

According to Merriam (1988), "In a qualitative approach to research the paramount objective is to understand the *meaning* [italics in original] of an experience" particularly in the contestable quest "to understand how all the parts work together to form a whole" (p. 16) within a given context. This contrasts with the positivist approach that "takes apart a phenomenon to examine component parts" (p. 16), based on research traditions that tends to evaluate "interpretive" social science as insufficiently "rigorous." As Merriam further described it:

> Qualitative research assumes that there are multiple realities—that the world is not an objective thing out there but a function of personal interaction and perception. It is a highly subjective phenomenon in need of interpreting rather than measuring. Beliefs rather than facts form the basis of perception. Research is exploratory, inductive, and emphasizes processes rather than ends. In this paradigm, there are no predetermined hypotheses, no treatments, and no restrictions on the end product. One does not manipulate variables or administer a treatment. What one *does* do is observe, intuit, sense what is occurring in a natural setting—hence the term *naturalistic* inquiry (p. 17, italics in original)

In short, the qualitative researcher seeks plausibility rather than certainty, coherence rather than strict correlation, reasonable interpretation rather than incontrovertible proof, avenues for further exploration and continuous inquiry rather than closure.

Dewey (1938/1991) referred to the knowledge that emerges from inquiry as a "warranted assertability," a relatively durable, but tentative conclusion as opposed to certitude even as an ideal. This type of research "involve[s] recognition that all special conclusions of special inquiries are parts of an enterprise that is continually renewed, or is a [*sic*] ongoing concern" (pp. 16–17). Problems and solutions progressively identified are intricately connected to a variety of factors in a growing awareness of the contexts that give shape to a field of inquiry.

This viewpoint is compatible with the participatory vision grounded in the intricacies of the rich interaction between students and instructors in the quest of "*understanding the meaning people have constructed*" (Merriam, 2001, p. 6, italics in original) in and through the learning process. The multidimensional aspects of such knowledge require qualitative research, which, by its very nature, can only be partially and imperfectly known. Depth and complexity of understanding rather than precise analysis of causal variables is the object of research based on a qualitative design. Although only in the most skeletal of forms, a useful discussion toward such an approach to assessment accountability ensued on the NLA.

Frances Tracy-Mumford (NLA, April 7, 1997) suggested the "need to use a page from Complexity Theory and explain through 'webbing' the interrelationship between education–work–community–family in a way that policy makers buy into and understand." Levinson (NLA, April 8, 1997) pointed to the National Institute's Equipped for the Future (EFF) project's wedding of student-centered goals with national policy objectives, but noted that work on assessment based on EFF standards had not, at that time, been developed.

Jaye Norris, from North Carolina, discussed the importance of "identifying outcomes." She suggested, "ironically," that the alternative assessment movement take a leaf from the playbook of "workforce development studies" such as SCANS (see chap. 3). Norris pointed out that employers seek to develop " 'higher order thinking skills' in their employees." These could be drawn on as a standard to measure quality learning in adult literacy. Norris also referred to a "New York study [that] talked about dimensions, from simple to complex, from routine to variable, from concrete to abstract, from structured to unstructured, from recall of knowledge to evaluation of knowledge, from directed to independent, from conventional to innovative." Norris offered the tantalizing thought that "perhaps what sometimes seems to be the opposite of what interests us in literacy (e.g., all the emphasis on workforce and none on self improvement and quality of life and development of one's voice) can also be our friend" (Norris, NLA, April 7, 1997).

Sally Gabb, then an ESOL instructor at the Genesis Program in Providence, Rhode Island, agreed that of "those cognitive/learning spheres"

Norris mentioned, "quality of life at work is a primary goal for many in our programs." Still, she viewed as more fundamental "the theme of learner voice—the definition of 'workforce development' by workers." Although "all of us know many learners whose thinking is 'complex, variable, and abstract,' . . . [many] are unable to provide 'test' evidence of such capabilities." The challenge

> is in entering into dialogue with our learners to unlock these capabilities so that we can "measure"—i.e., enable our learners to express these capabilities and/or to redefine the playing field. When conditions at the workplace are oppressive and limiting—including work overload, discriminatory practices, lack of support for literacy and other training—the so-called "workforce development" is a one sided conversation. The measurable cognitive categories are not invalid, but must be tools for possibility, not exclusion. (Gabb, NLA, April 8, 1997)

On the same day as Gabb's posting, Paul Clay echoed McGrail's call to focus on "beliefs, attitudes, and behavior." Discerning these interrelations might require "a longitudinal study to see if these beliefs and attitudes [whatever they may be for any particular student] are still present as an indicator that behaviors changed." Clay's point was that beliefs and attitudes are critically important factors in the expression of new behavior, and therefore should be manifest in its emergence. Clay, who was developing a curriculum for his "life skills program" in South Carolina, viewed the linkage of these factors as a potentially viable format for establishing an assessment framework consistent with "quality of life" issues. Even still, there was a depressing tone to his suggestion in the realization that the broader system needed in support of a "quality of life" accountability system was not, nor likely to become, in place any time soon. Clay wondered whether "other locations [experienced] . . . a similar feeling of impending doom" (Clay, NLA, April 8, 1997).

Gabb drew sustenance from the various recommendations proffered in support of specific methodologies for the implementation of qualitative assessment. These were needed in order to offer more than merely the impressionistic insight of the immediate learning/teaching episode, which, on her account and others, still represented the underlying basis for the legitimization of alternative assessment modes of assessment. As expressed by Gabb's colleague, McGrail (1993, vol. 4), paying attention to "the way learners actually talk about their own learning process is a baseline for me by which we measure all that we say and do" (p. 4). In order to extend this baseline, Gabb viewed the "participatory case study methodology" suggested by Marguerite Lukes, "as a model many of us could follow, work with, and dialogue around."

Gabb spoke of a project she was planning with a student in which they were "going to journal about his goals, in terms of quality of life on/off workplace." She noted that he was "already . . . excited beyond words about learning—creating his 'codes'—thinking about the power of his workplace strategies without literacy, and how to enhance these with literacy" Gabb (NLA, April 9, 1997) agreed with Lukes in claiming, "quality is measurable—perhaps in 'multiple' ways a la [Howard] Gardner." She, along with her colleagues, sought some visible hooks through which to make this case.

As they struggled with various issues related to establishing a coherent framework, the practitioners on the April 1997 threads to a person, shared Clay's sentiment that the richness of such learning as previously described and what they experienced in their own classrooms "can't be quantified into some statistical report." Developing a coherent framework that captured something of the subtlety, complexity, and richness of the qualitative aspects of the learning process, which was simultaneously useful to students and instructors and reportable on a large-scale basis, proved more problematic.

A RELUCTANT STANDARD-BEARER

With Auerbach and McGrail as leading lights, the Bay State was one of the most progressive outposts for participatory literacy education in the United States. The desire among participatory educators in Massachusetts to maintain a distinctive "alternative assessment" philosophy grounded in the framework laid out by Auerbach and McGrail would not be easily squared with a performance accountability system based on "the universe of content adults need to know and be able to do" (Bickerton, NLA, September 8, 1997).

Carabell (1999), from neighboring Vermont, was also seeking to mesh student goals with outcomes that could achieve a degree of policy legitimacy. A convert from a strictly adhered to alternative assessment philosophy, where "each teacher and student relationship developed its [own] measures of quality," Caraball became a "reluctant standard-bearer." Previously Carabell had

> viewed standards as a bureaucratic construct devised to restrain creative teaching, foisted upon teachers in the field in the name of greater program accountability. Standards implied a uniformity and universality borne out of the K–12 mainstream (the model that failed learners in the first place). Adults in our programs were telling us they were succeeding precisely because we offered an alternative to that model. (p. 15)

Eventually, Carabell's "discordant tone regarding standards-based education found a new key" (p. 15). The shift began in the early 1990s while

Carabell was participating in a "study circle" with colleagues who were work-ing through key texts on alternative assessment. The group met "to rethink our approach to assessment" in response to "impending changes in state and national policy." There was much to consider in the arena of educa-tional philosophy and political culture on who or what would be served in any rethinking. Whatever changes might be needed to restructure alterna-tive assessment in order to be policy congruent in the emerging climate of state and national politics, the group "wanted assessment to . . . [remain] a collaborative activity, done with rather than to the learner" (p. 16). This, along with the need to ensure that assessment remained useful for students and teachers, were key tenets in which there could be no compromise, with-out placing in peril the core beliefs of the participatory school. In this, the study circle shared McGrail's (1994, vol. 6) sensibility that "to engage in truly alternative assessment, we need to include learners as active partici-pants at the center of the process of measurements" (p. 5).

Carabell was in full empathy with this, but was troubled by the disjunc-ture between the "soft" methodologies advocated and standards that the state of Vermont would accept that "continued to view adult students through the lens of a sequential, competency-based K–12 model" (Cara-bell, 1999, p. 17). Modes of assessment based on these assumptions erased the rich contextuality that Carabell and others wanted to illuminate. This was deemed essential in order to highlight strengths rather than deficits and to guide attention to the rich learning processes experienced in the uniqueness of "learning/teaching moment." This, they felt compelled to preserve, even as Carabell and others identified a need for significant changes in order to gain policy legitimacy. As Carabell ruefully put it, "Nothing we did in the field by way of alternative assessment would matter" (p. 17) in shifting policy beyond standardized modes of accountability.

Given its rooting in the ineffable learning/teaching moment, the diffi-culty of establishing comprehensive and systematic approaches to assessment accountability intrinsic to the precepts of participatory education, was no mi-nor problem. Beyond the internal problems, the evident lack of policy legiti-macy for supportive methodologies that might be based on these premises had an erosive effect in limiting investments of time, talent, and funding needed for developing them in an ample and thorough manner. Its creation, logically, would have required some common field agreement on a set of frameworks that could be applied across programs in order to meet account-ability needs to funders. There was material available in Lytle's four concepts and work based on the New Literacy Studies, as summarized by Auerbach (1992b) and Merrifield (1998). Still, any variation of what Lytle, Auerbach, or Merrifield outlined would have required considerable fleshing out and re-finement in order to serve as a viable framework to unify and bring policy le-gitimacy to alternative assessment design. Whether such a prospect was ultimately feasible, the possibility remained untested. Assuming the internal problems among advocates could have been resolved, the felt sense of impracticality in fundamentally altering the trajectory of federal policy inhibited serious efforts from forming in the first place.

Whether in principle such a set of standards could have emerged on alternative assessment premises, an attempted integration between a "bottom-up" and "top-down" framework did appear with EFF in the call for performance-based accountability. EFF developers drew on scholarship that undergirded alternative assessment design as well as on research that supported a normed-based accountability system. The synthesis project designers sought was the creation of standards that "authentically" stemmed from student goals and interests, yet resonated with policy mandates that could be projected from National Educational Goal 6. EFF appealed to Carabell because it held the prospect of resolving the practitioner–policy polarization he experienced in his own state. He also found EFF satisfying in that it provided him with a framework for better tapping into student needs than the more intuitive approach to which he was accustomed based on his understanding of the participatory literacy model.

For practitioners like Carabell, EFF was a federally sponsored and well-coordinated effort. It was buttressed by a coherent student-centered framework based on a set of Content Standards, plausibly acceptable to the policy sector. This provided Carabell and like-minded colleagues with what they deemed a reasonable way of working through the tensions that historically led to a climate of polar opposition between participatory practitioners and policymakers. For Carabell and others who made the conversion to EFF, prospects of achieving broad-based public and policy legitimacy in the 1990s through a purified allegiance to alternative assessment design no longer seemed credible. A case study description of where he utilized the EFF framework with his own student confirmed for Carabell the intellectual integrity of the framework in its capacity to stimulate student-centered instruction. Noting an inevitable "tension between the specific student and the general rule" in any standards approach to assessment, Carabell came to believe that standards "work when they codify our own internal values and respect our individuality" (p. 18).

Nonetheless, as is discussed in chapters 7 and 8, problems with EFF for the advocates of participatory literacy education and the New Literacy Studies abound, particularly over the issues that Carabell identified, the relation between standards, modes of measurement, and student-centered instruction. This became increasingly problematic as EFF developers sought to make their performance standards compatible with the standardized reporting requirements of NRS levels.

Notwithstanding these dilemmas, the plausible prospect for system integration as it appeared to him in 1999, spoke much to Carabell's decision to embrace EFF as a way of resolving the seemingly enduring conflicts that had perplexed him for years. Whether EFF ultimately provides the consensus and synthesis its developers seek (a prospect that as of this writing is exceedingly doubtful), or further masks political and epistemological tensions embedded in the U.S. adult literacy system, requires further probing.

CONCLUDING REMARKS

Chapter 2 explicates the core assumptions of participatory literacy education and its accompanying viewpoint on alternative assessment. It highlights challenges faced by proponents in the effort to attain legitimacy in an increasingly conservative political climate. These challenges were several-fold. Historically, broad-based accountability at the state and federal level has required some form of aggregate documentation. Those holding this view consider some form of data uniformity essential in order to address the issue of comparability and the related issue of data objectivity. The ethnographic research framework and the philosophical-political tenets that richly informs alternative assessment assumptions, are not easily squared with the quantitative metaphor that underlies the etic perspective on which policy accountability systems are based.

Also problematic was the matter of leadership and coalition building for the purpose of gaining policy and public legitimacy for adult literacy. The state directors and the NCL sought to sway Congress largely through "interest politics" through a "return on investment" rationale. They laid out a related agenda broader than what the current policy supported, should political conditions open up for a more expansive appreciation of the public value of adult literacy.

Those within the participatory literacy camp held to a more radical political vision that moved beyond the "return on investment" metaphor. As noted by Jurmo (1989), any effort to change the dominant political culture bearing on adult literacy would require sustained grassroots effort. It would also call for compromise among its constituents in establishing a common framework to structure alternative assessment principles that could address the issue of public accountability through some type of comparability, not necessarily quantitative or standardized, across programs, agencies, and regions.

Inklings for such a movement percolated in the late 1980s and early 1990s largely on the east coast. Such efforts did not translate into a coordinated political movement or even a generally agreed on field-driven framework that would allow the elusive "teaching moment" to be translated into forms that would meet the reporting needs of funders and legislators. As indicated by Comings, a coordinated shift in addressing accountability issues did not necessarily require uniform statistical information on every student. Yet, unless the matter of accountability for funding were removed as a funding issue, for which Comings argued, it would then require a coherent alternative, based on some combination of sampling, the utilization of multimeasures to demonstrate impact, and thick narrative description through case study analysis and well-constructed written reports. However technically feasible the construction of such a framework might have been, this would have necessitated substantial political advocacy to have changed the dominant culture in the 1990s, at least as it related to adult literacy.

The advocates of the participatory literacy and the alternative assessment movements were largely convinced of the validity of their insights based on their own practice, corroboration with colleagues, and the theory and research base on which they drew. Yet, they also experienced considerable dissonance in wrestling with the intractable dilemmas they faced. These included both the need of establishing a common framework among advocates that did not dilute the ineffability of the existential teaching moment and the orchestration of a concerted effort in challenging the dominant political culture. Without coming to terms with these matters, along with the ongoing effort of further refining underlying relations between practice, theory, and empirical research, the public and political legitimacy of their position remained precarious. This was the reality regardless of the internal logic that advocates insisted underlays their principles and their practices.

A sustained effort to establish a coherent coordinated, and generally acceptable, framework would have required greater resource allocation. There was little within the prevailing political culture in the early 1990s to have sustained such an effort. If a revitalization movement were going to occur based on participatory premises, then it would have had to spring forth via an extensive grassroots mobilization effort. Notwithstanding the considerable creative work that shaped the participatory movement of the early 1990s, there was little on the horizon of a sufficiently organized manner to energize the mobilization needed to counterbalance the ongoing policy trajectory that ultimately resulted in the WIA/NRS. Neither the progressive literacy community nor the more mainstream policy leadership was able to offset this policy trend, although in the halcyon days immediately after the passage of the National Literacy Act of 1991 and the establishment of NIFL, hope blossomed in a variety of directions. Still, there was little prospect of broad-based public and policy support for the collective perspective of Auerbach, Fingeret, Lytle, and McGrail during the 1990s.

As a way of resolving the chaos of grounding assessment on the unique particularity of the hard-to-define teaching moment, more than a few followed along the path of Carabell (1999) in migrating to performance accountability through EFF. This provided a way of linking a student-centered philosophy within a coherent framework that helped students and instructors to sharpen learning goals, while also holding the prospect of becoming policy legitimate.

Others within the progressive camp remained skeptical. In providing a sense of clarity through performance-based outcomes, some expressed concern that equal attention would no longer be placed on emotional, perceptual, and socially contextual dimensions, particularly on the strong emphasis Lytle (1991) gave to the centrality of beliefs. There was also concern among some within the progressive literacy camp that policy pressures would push accountability demands for standardization and uniformity that would override the participatory impetus that Carabell and others identified as resident within the EFF. Unless assessment was "authentically" based on what advocates viewed as developing student interests and needs discerned through the *emergent curriculum*, some feared that EFF would minimize the most important aspects of learning. Yet, unless advocates of alternative assessment could address policy concerns, their views had little prospect of being supported through public resources. Whatever limitations certain members of the progressive camp held about EFF, it had at least the prospect of becoming policy legitimized—a prospect critics noted that came with certain price tags.

Workforce Readiness in the Information Age

> *Education and training are the primary systems by which the human capital of a nation is preserved and increased. The speed and efficiency with which these educational systems transmit knowledge govern the rate at which human capital can be developed. Even more than such closely-watched indicators as the rate of investment in plant and equipment, human capital formation plays a direct role in how fast the economy can grow.*
>
> —Johnston & Packer (1987, p. 116)

Chapter 1 provided a brief overview of the 40-year linkage between federal policy and adult literacy. The current chapter focuses on trends since the late 1980s. It highlights three influential reports, *Workforce 2000, Jump Start*, and SCANS that cumulatively had a major impact in shaping adult literacy policy during the 1990s. Chapter 3 begins with a discussion of postindustrial discourse in the 1970s and 1980s and a highly influential educational report, *A Nation at Risk*. The confluence of a radically perceived new socioeconomic order founded on information, knowledge, and technology, with an educational report pointing to a failing U.S. educational system, resulted in a peculiar combination of alarm and expectation, sometimes of utopian proportions, in the nation's capacity to meet the needs of an increasingly competitive marketplace. The convergence between the postindustrial scenario and the challenges of a failing educational system resulted in a focus for policy-driven adult literacy/ABE initiatives on which nothing less than the national interest depended (Chisman, 1989).

THE COMING OF THE POSTINDUSTRIAL SOCIETY

In the prognostications of the year 2000, futurology became a cottage industry as early as the 1960s. Technology and planning in business and governmental sectors in the post-World War II setting played an important role in undergirding the activity of forecasting that the millennial year held out as an attractive target (Kumar, 1978, pp. 185–192). In that decade, Bell (1967) sketched out the notion of a "post-industrial society," a concept he elaborated on in the next decade in a major work titled, *The Coming of the Post-Industrial society: A Venture in Social Forecasting* (Bell, 1973). In Bell's vision, the postindustrial and the industrial era are sharply contrasted in the shift from goods to services, from blue-collar to white-collar work, and from assembly-line mechanization to the emergence of the knowledge worker. Bell characterized the concept of the postindustrial society as an "analytic construct" (cited in Steinfels, 1980, p. 163) to describe more or less inevitable tendencies given then current social and economic trajectories of Western society (Steinfels, 1980). Toffler's *Future Shock* (1970) and the *Third Wave* (1981) provided a more popular version of the ideas articulated in Bell's academic treatise.

Commenting on these early scenarios, Kumar (1978) noted that the shifts identified by Bell and others represented significant developments of long-range trends based on 150 years of capitalist-based industrialization. Kumar questioned whether the newly emerging changes pointed "to a new social order, with a new set of problems, [and] a new social framework within which to resolve them" (p. 199). Where Bell and others, like Drucker (1969) noted substantial changes, Kumar (1978) pointed to "massive *continuities* within the basic system of the developing industrial society" (p. 232, italics in original). The changes were important, noted Kumar, but they were "extrapolations, intensifications, and clarifications of tendencies which were apparent from the very birth of industrialism." Notwithstanding important shifts in emphasis, the service and knowledge sectors also are marked "by the continuing processes of mechanization, rationalization, and specialization" (p. 232), the very characteristics of mass industrial organization.

Kumar noted, for example, that in the shift from blue- to white-collar work, "the vast majority of . . . workers are clerks; mostly female, and mostly involved in routine, unskilled duties" (p. 209). For Kumar, that fact, and other continuities with the industrial society, undercut Bell's (1973) "axial principle" of not merely knowledge, but "theory" as the primary engine as the driving force of the emerging postindustrial society (p. 112). Kumar (1978) was deeply skeptical about the utopian implications of the postindustrial vision particularly with its linkage to futurologist predictions, noting in passing that Bell was chairman of the Commission of the Year 2000 (p. 186).

Notwithstanding Kumar's skepticism, forecasting, based on the imagery of a radically discontinuous postindustrial society, became widely prevalent in the 1980s. Naisbitt's (1984) best-selling *Megatrends,* which drew heavily from Bell's work, set the stage for the new thinking in business, government, and educational sectors for a decade. Naisbitt pointed to the central role such factors as information, technology, globalization, decentralization, networks, and participatory democracy in the workplace and throughout society would play in the postindustrial era. In his description of these developments, he was particularly utopian in contrasting the old and new order and the fundamentally novel opportunities opened up in the markedly shifting trends in the latter. The computer, Naisbitt noted, would be the instrument that "actually smashes the hierarchical pyramid" (p. 281) of bureaucratic entrenchment in the unleashing of fresh entrepreneurial energies of the informational era.

At the center of Naisbitt's vision was knowledge, the key cultural capital of the postindustrial society. The principal shift was not so much from goods to services, but more fundamentally, "in the creation, processing, and distribution of information" (p. 4). Naisbitt pointed out that the largest occupational category in 1979 was that growth of the white-collar clerk who was replacing the blue-collar worker for the primary spot in the labor market, a trend that would continue apace for the rest of the century. Naisbitt also noted the rise of middle-class professional occupations from 1960 to 1981. In 1960, 7.5 million employees served in those ranks, or 11% of the workforce. By 1981, the figure jumped to 16.4 million knowledge workers, representing almost 17% of all employees (pp. 5–6), a trend that prognosticators argued would only continue into the millennial future. What empowered the economy in the new society was "*not money in the hands of the few but information in the hands of the many*" (p. 7, italics in original). The result, claimed Naisbitt, was a transformation from Marx's theory of labor to a knowledge theory of value (p. 8).

Naisbitt maintained that speed, entrepreneurship, local decision making, and future orientation would be the hallmarks of the new society. Information, or more fundamentally, knowledge—the right kind, the right amount, at the right time—would become the fundamental commodity, that is, the central glue of the postindustrial vision. That placed a premium on education throughout all social sectors. Naisbett spoke of the need, in this "literacy-intensive society" for improvement in basic literacy in the workplace and throughout the culture in order to overcome "an increasingly inferior product" (p. 11), the cumulative impact of a substandard public educational system. At a time when knowledge was needed more than ever, Naisbett sounded the alarm bell that "*the generation graduating from high school today is the first generation in American history to graduate less skilled than its parents*" (p. 25, italics in original).

For Naisbitt, the gap between the challenges of thriving in the postindustrial future and the inadequacy of public secondary schooling was startling. Referencing a contemporary Carnegie Study, he noted that "about one-third of our youth are ill-educated, ill-employed, and ill-equipped to make their way in American society" (cited in Naisbitt, pp. 25–26). At the bottom of the rung were a high number of adult "functional illiterates," ranging from 18 to 64 million, depending on definition. Based on the influential 1975 adult performance level (APL) study, this group had difficulty even in the post-World War II manufacturing era with basic functional tasks in the areas of employment, consumer education, health awareness, and accessing community resources. Functionally illiterate adults would be even harder pressed when knowledge became the basic skill needed in the postindustrial society.

In short, the pressing problems of inadequate schooling were now amplified with the fundamental societal, economic, and cultural changes forecasted in the new era. Reflecting the energetic tone that the postindustrial image was meant to signify, Naisbitt was largely optimistic. Keeping focused on "the bright side," he envisioned new entrepreneurial opportunities in "a growing market for educational consulting services in the new information society" where the problem "of what to do with the surplus of teachers generated by the baby-boom kids" (p. 26) would be met. "My God, what a fantastic time to be alive!" (p. 283) exclaimed Naisbitt, at the conclusion of his book.

A NATION AT RISK

The imagery of the postindustrial society played a major role in policy thinking about the relation between economic development and adult literacy in the 1980s and 1990s. Closely related in impact was the 1983 report, commissioned by U.S. Secretary of Education Terence Bell, *A Nation at Risk: The Imperative for Educational Reform*. The concern that sparked the report, "the widespread public perception that something is seriously remiss about our educational system" (National Commission on Excellence, NCE, 1983, p. 4), had its roots in post-Sputnik educational policy in the call for academic rigor, particularly in math and the sciences. The critique within *A Nation at Risk* was aimed against what the report viewed as the standards-slack relativism of the progressive educational movement of the 1960s. This resulted in "a rising tide of mediocrity" (p. 6) that threatened the very fabric of the nation. This revival of progressive education was damaging on every front, but most emphatically in the state losing its competitive edge, where other nations began to match and even surpass the educational achievements of students in the United States.

Thus, the shift toward rigorous academic work that stemmed from an all-too-brief post-Sputnik interlude (Kliebard, 1995) against what critics viewed as the "feel-good" life adjustment curriculum focus of the 1940s and the 1950s, was short-lived. The result was a squandering of gains made in that brief era from 1957 through the much of the next decade. As put in the report, the relativistic standards of the late 1960s represented "an act of unthinking, unilateral disarmament." Drawing on additional cold war imagery, the report associated the progressive intrusion to "an unfriendly foreign power" imposing on the nation's schools a mediocrity analogous to "an act of war" (NCE, 1983, p. 6).

Critics argued that the changes after the immediate post-Sputnik era, reflecting the collective impact of multiculturalism, disenchantment with the Vietnam War, and the pervasive influence of the counterculture, were startling. The comparison years were 1964–1969 and 1976–1981 with a markedly downhill shift. By the latter years, the school curriculum became "homogenized, diluted, and diffused" due to a "cafeteria style curriculum in which the appetizers and desserts can easily be mistaken for the main course." The startling growth of elective courses resulted in a "smorgasbord" curriculum that further contributed to the erosion of academic standards.

Although traditional academic courses accompanied by rigorous measures of performance were still offered, the percentage of students taking them rapidly dwindled. As the report noted, whereas courses in calculus were available in many schools, only 6% of students successfully completed them (p. 15). Of similar concern, students who were enrolled in the general track high school received one quarter of their credits "in physical and health education, work experience outside the school, remedial English and mathematics, and personal service and development courses" (p. 16). The result of such a diluted curriculum was that "many students opt for less demanding personal service courses, such as bachelor living" (pp. 16–17). The report also noted "deficiencies" in terms of grades, high school graduation requirements, grade inflation, and the lack of "rigorous examinations." The attack on the progressive education movement of the late 1960s and 1970s could not have been sharper.

The perceived failure of the nation's educational system would have been viewed as a significant problem on any account. What made it a crisis was the demands that an emergent global and increasingly competitive economy was placing on the nation's workforce, and, therefore, on its school system. As the report noted, "History is not kind to idlers." With the "global village" a daunting reality, the United States was no longer in a position where it could develop its economy largely on home products and vast internal markets.

The manufacturing sector, which historically could depend on large numbers of non- and semi-skilled employees to handle most of the routine work would be largely replaced by the modern office that would increasingly depend on "knowledge, learning, information, and skilled intelligence" not just of a technocratic and managerial elite, but of the many. This would require capabilities in the knowledge realms throughout the workforce (the "raw materials of international commerce"), in which the nation's competitors were well skilled. Because "learning," . . . [was] the indispensable investment required for success in the 'information age' " (p. 7), it was incumbent on the secondary schools to prepare students to face that world.

The viability of the U.S. marketplace was an important focus of *A Nation at Risk*. Also significant was the concern for the future of American civilization. As expressed in the report, a "high level of shared education is essential to a free, democratic society and to the fostering of a common culture, especially in a country that prides itself on pluralism and individual freedom" (p. 8). Equipping the population with the skills and knowledge that would matter in the knowledge society was perceived as crucial for the nation's competitive marketability. It was also viewed as the pathway for the realization of the American Dream "regardless of race or class or economic status" (p. 8). It was focus that was needed in gearing the schools to retool based on these clear national priorities.

NATIONAL EDUCATIONAL GOALS PANEL

Key segments of the corporate sector, conservative interest groups, the National Governors Association (NGA), and the senior Bush administration drew both on the imagery of the "age of information," and the problems inherent in a failing national school system to establish a major national policy initiative on education, referred to as *America 2000*. At its center was a well-focused emphasis on academics, the adoption of "world class" standards, and a call to accountability of students, teachers, and schools to produce results, with real-world consequences for failure. President George W. H. Bush convened the Educational Summit of 1989, attended by the 50 governors.

The summit resulted in the formation of six National Educational Goals in 1990 (ultimately eight) and the creation of a National Educational Goals Panel charged with the mandate of issuing annual reports on the nation's progress in meeting them. The goals, appended by the phrase, "By the year 2000," were broad. They included elements of the Great Society's emphasis on preschool and parental education. Goal 3 focused on academic competency in the core subject areas. These "new basics" included English and civics, as well as science, mathematics, and foreign language study. Panel members viewed these subjects as essential for gaining the skills and knowledge needed "for responsible citizenship, further learning, and productive employment in our Nation's economy" (National Educational Goals Panel, Goal 3). Mathematics and science, prominently featured, had their own goal statement in Goal 5.

For the purposes of this book, Goal 6, the Adult Literacy and Lifelong Learning Goal, is of particular importance. Goal 6 states:

> *By the year 2000, every adult American will be literate and will possess the knowledge and skills necessary to compete in a global economy and exercise the rights and responsibilities of citizenship.* (italics in original)

Notwithstanding the dual focus on economic development and citizenship, the stated objectives for Goal 6 placed a clear priority in the vocational realm. Citizenship was not highlighted per se, although it was assumed that greater economic and vocational opportunity would better enable individuals to participate in the fruits of U.S. democracy and civilization. The negative was also implicit. Those who do not attain the required level of education will suffer, economically, socially, politically, and culturally. These assumptions, which laid the basis for federal policy on adult literacy education in the 1990s, were more thoroughly articulated in the major reports of the era, to which we now turn.

WORKFORCE 2000

In the mid-1980s, the Reagan administration commissioned the Hudson Institute to study factors that needed to be addressed to meet the emerging challenges of the workplace in light of the competitive and knowledge demands of a global and postindustrial economy. *Workforce 2000* (Johnston & Packer, 1987) was not designed "to provide policy prescriptions" in an overly precise sense. Academic and popular studies of the postindustrial society were available, which the authors of the Hudson study liberally drew on. *Workforce 2000* provided a particular niche in the postindustrial literature by linking anticipated trends to broad range economic and educational policy implications.

Workforce 2000 situated the new challenges within three intersecting contexts. The first was the increasing globalization of the economy and the need for the U.S. to maintain and expand vigorous export markets. The second was the shift from goods to services with an increasing focus on information, knowledge, and technology for all major sectors of the economy. The third was the rapidly changing dynamics of the U.S. workforce based on projections that by the year 2000, the nation's employees will be increasingly older, female, minority-based, and less educated than the then current workforce. *Workforce 2000* concluded that a highly focused invest-ment in workforce training was essential both to enhance the lives of indi-vidual employees and to assure the viability of the nation's economic pros-perity.

Globalization

According to *Workforce 2000*, international trade was playing an increasingly dominant role both in the world and in the U.S. economy. Between 1973 and 1984, according to the authors, growth in industrial home markets in-creased 2.4% annually on an average rate. By contrast, exports within eco-nomically advanced countries increased from 12% to 18% from 1965 to 1983 (p. 2). The growth of world trade pointed less to the need for cut-throat competition than policies, particularly among the wealthier nations to help assure the economic development of the poorer nation. The fate of the United States and the world's economy were inextricably linked. What the United States faced was the challenge of "increase[ing] its own produc-tivity while stimulating maximum world growth—not to capture economic activity from other nations" (p. 6). The authors anticipated that by 2000 the United States would profitably trade with India, China, and Latin America and thereby expand the outlets for its own goods and services (p. 7).

Maximizing opportunities that a global trade economy offered would re-quire considerable repositioning of the U.S. economy. The barriers of over-coming the twin factors of economic isolationism and a sharply competi-tive, winner-take-all capitalistic ethic were formidable. The point was not to uproot competitiveness as a core value, but to re-channel it in light of changing world economic conditions. What the authors were seeking to define was a more subtle competitive environment linked to the nation's overall productivity that a more cooperative world economic order would stimulate in the promotion of world trade. Even so, "the erosion of the competitive position of steel, automobiles, textiles, consumer electronics, and other U.S. manufacturing industries" (p. 13) posed persisting prob-lems. Major economic and psychological changes would have to take place before the new economic view envisioned by the authors would gain maxi-mal influence in the U.S. policy and business sectors.

From Goods to Services

The authors projected that goods more than services would continue be the primary commodity of U.S. exports in the years leading to 2000, but that services would play an increasingly critical role even in the nation's manufacturing sector. This was reflected in the increasing importance of "services that occur upstream of the plant, such as product and market research, design, engineering, and tooling and by downstream activities such as transportation, retailing, and advertising" (p. 26). These trends would combine with increasing automation within the plant that would require fewer factory laborers, on the one hand, and higher skilled employees within the plant, on the other hand, with technology playing a greater role within the productive process.

The fundamental point of *Workforce 2000* was that the general shift in the U.S. economy from goods to services was an inevitable historical trend. The report noted that the nation had little choice but to restructure economic and social policy to allow for maximal growth as well as expansion of economic opportunities throughout society in a manner that maintained the viability of the free enterprise system. According to the Hudson Institute study, that required increasing deregulation of industry and privatization of governmental services to allow full vent for entrepreneurial energies to respond without fetters to the challenges of transforming the economy in a manner that would keep profitability, overall stability, and reasonable wage distribution intact.

The authors of *Workforce 2000* projected that the manufacturing sector would continue to grow. Yet, on a comparative basis, it would become less critical to the U.S. economy "than changes in productivity and economic patterns in the service industries" (p. 20). The authors noted that services have been stereotyped "as low-productivity, low-wage industries" (p. 22). They acknowledged the relatively low-wage retail trade in the largest growing service sector. Yet, they also pointed to the more skill intensive educational, health care, governmental, and finance industries also experienced significant growth.

Notwithstanding the critique leveled against the loss of industrial jobs, the authors pointed out that this was part of an economic transformation that would turn out to be increasingly irrelevant "as manufacturing plants become less and less the places where economic value is created" (p. 28). Upstreaming, downstreaming, and automation would facilitate the productive capacity of plants and create new industries that would be part of a changed socioeconomic landscape based on a postindustrial form of organization. Deindustrialization was "not a threat to society's wealth-producing potential, it . . . [was] a reflection of it; it represent[ed] a shift in the economic challenge to new sectors: retailing, health care, education, government, food service, and other industries." The more pressing point was the authors' argument that "the nation's economic future will be written by these industries, not by the revival of manufacturing" (p. 29).

The question of wage equity, on whether service jobs were, or eventually would be, as well paying as manufacturing jobs, remained an open issue that the authors carefully probed. They noted that in the mid-1980s, wages in service jobs "were less equitably distributed than those in manufacturing or government" (p. 29). This declension was partially offset by enhanced benefits, which, from 1973 to 1985, rose about 4% per year (p. 32). The other factor was slow economic growth, particularly after the oil crisis of 1973, which affected both industrial and service sectors. Although industry continued to accelerate at a modest rate (2.9% per year), service output dropped from 1.4% to −0.2% from 1970 to 1985 (p. 38). Part of the problem was in the nature of measuring service-oriented productivity, particularly in the areas of health, education, government, and even many business services, because the rates did not capture information that could not be strictly quantified. Even still, the authors projected that the disparity between industrial and service output would continue to widen throughout the 1990s.

More important than the status of the then contemporary economy, was the manner in which future trends would shape conditions of the year 2000 and beyond. In this, the authors were guardedly optimistic that technological advances would play a major role in establishing a more dynamic economy. This was not viewed as a foregone conclusion, but would require the most discerning entrepreneurial and policy-oriented acumen to usher in and sustain. The authors pointed to major growth industries in information storage and processing with the advent of microcomputers and microchips, and in communications in which by "2000, the nation will be blanketed by a digital telecommunications network that will connect most businesses and many homes" (p. 34).

Technology and change were key factors in overcoming the logjams in productivity in the transition from a manufacturing to a service economy, although the authors noted that future direction remained uncertain. What seemed clear was the omnipresence of technology in "introduc[ing] change and turbulence into every industry and every job." This infusion necessitated "constant learning and constant adaptation by workers" as well as organizations. The authors based their guarded optimism on the expectation that the creativity unleashed would stimulate "a certain outgrowth of technological innovation" (p. 37) that would spur the needed changes required to restructure the American economy on new grounds. They noted that this potential was far from inevitable. It would require a growth orientation to stimulate "accelerating investment in human and physical capital" in order to eliminate "institutional barriers to productivity enhancements in services." Informed risk taking could result in "huge dividends" (p. 73) toward the creation of a service-oriented economy of the first order. Its attainment would require the discriminating shrewdness of a high caliber.

Workforce Readiness in the Postindustrial Era

Whether the workforce would be up to the challenge was a critical issue the authors raised as they pointed to the demographic trends that would shape it in 2000. What seemed clear was how different it would be from the workforce of the 1960s and 1970s. Key factors included a slower growth rate in population, an aging workforce, and one dominated by more women, minorities, and immigrants. The authors noted that most of the jobs then currently in place would still exist in 2000 and two thirds of the workforce of the millennial year would include employees who held jobs in the mid-1980s. The demographic changes would be particularly significant for new additions to the labor force and in the new jobs created in the post-industrial sector that would be increasingly dependent on information, knowledge, and technology.

The authors were particularly concerned about a growing gap between the middle class and poor, between those with advanced marketable skills and those lacking them in a "rapidly upscale" economy in which most of the new jobs would require "more education and higher levels of language, math, and reasoning skills" (p. 96). The authors noted that of the new jobs to be created between 1984 and 2000, more than one half would require some form of postsecondary schooling as compared to the 22% that required a college education in the mid-1980s. Of the new jobs to be created by 2000, only 4% would be filled with those possessing the lowest of skills, as compared to 9% of jobs among that grouping in the economy of the mid-1980s. The authors noted that regardless of job category, a generally higher level of educational aptitude would be required. For midlevel skilled employment in marketing, sales, retail, and administration, where the vast majority of new jobs would be created, "workers will be expected to read and understand directions, add and subtract, and be able to speak and think clearly" (p. 100).

The authors noted that the transition to the new economy would be especially difficult for Black and Hispanic youth, who "will hold a *declining* [italics in original] fraction of all jobs if they simply retain existing shares of various occupations." Given the changing demands of an ever-increasingly skilled workplace, the problem of "structural unemployment" was likely to become even more pervasive (p. 101) among low-skilled, minimally educated minority groups unless counteractive processes, in short, "radical changes," in job training, education, and urban job creation were intentionally put in place (Wilson, 1996).

Required was a combination of re-socialization and "on-the-job training and basic skills remediation" (Johnston & Packer, 1987, p. 115). Reflecting a personal responsibility ethos, the authors of *Workforce 2000* pointed to problems they believed were historically endemic to inner-city poverty. Thus, "before minority unemployment can be significantly reduced, there must be a change in cultural values that make it seem more attractive to sell drugs or get pregnant than to do well in school and work at McDonald's" (p. 115).

At the structural level, the authors looked to the creative energies of the corporate sector to mitigate the problem of minority dislocation through the implementation of effective on-the-job training design. If there were to be a solution to integrate low-skilled minority youth into the new economy, then it would be provided by business through the design and implementation of "cost-effective and technology based" (p. 115) programs, rather than through the largely failed governmental programs like the Job Training Partnership Act (JPTA). The authors thought that, given the right set of circumstances, the U.S. economy could be successfully reconstructed on postindustrial premises, but were far from sanguine about the prospect of adequately integrating the poor in a manner that lessened rather than aggravated economic disparities. They did, however, hold hope and provided what they thought was a roadmap to the desired destination.

JUMP START

Basic Skills Development for Workforce Readiness

The challenge of linking adult literacy to the strengthening of the rapidly emerging postindustrial economy was more fully developed in the highly influential policy studies of Chisman (1989; Chisman & Associates, 1990). Chisman drew on the Hudson Institute report to inform his analysis, but *Jump Start* differed from *Workforce 2000* in placing leadership responsibility on the federal government rather than the corporate sector.

Chisman identified two problems. First, adult literacy education was not appropriately focused on the most pressing national priority, that of preparing undereducated workers for the demands of an information-age economy. Second, the field as a delivery system was too fragmented and required a focused direction set by the federal government. These were obviously related:

> The twenty million-plus are adults who simply have not mastered basic skills very well. They can read, but often not well enough to use a reference book or understand much of what is in a daily newspaper. They can write, but often not well enough to compose a business letter or fill out an application form. They can compute, but often not well enough to balance a checkbook or prepare an invoice. Their problems can be described in many different ways, and each person has a different set of problems. But they have this much in common: they lack the skills to function effectively in an increasingly demanding social and economic environment. (Chisman, 1989, p. 2)

Chisman identified several reasons for "caring," although the primary one was the need to assure the solvency of the nation's economy. Chisman was particularly concerned about "a demographic deadline" around the year 2010 "when members of the baby boom generation will begin to retire"

(p. 2). This was especially pressing because of changing demographics that were placing increasing numbers of undereducated minority groups and women into the workforce who were unprepared to meet the demands of the new economy.

To prevent this, Chisman argued that the nation must galvanize its resources and provide direction "to ensure that the twenty-million plus adults who are seriously deficient in basic skills become fully productive workers and citizens well before the rendezvous [with 'demographic destiny'] occurs" (p. 3). It was on this challenge, Chisman claimed, that the material well-being of the United States resided. "Without their best efforts over the next twenty years, there is little hope for the economic and social future of this country" (p. 3). Given these stakes, to focus adult literacy policy on anything else would not only be foolhardy. It would be a dereliction of civic responsibility.

Chisman viewed the nation's "basic skills" problem as one that could be substantially mitigated with a relatively minor investment of only a few billion dollars. Such a commitment would greatly enhance current scarce resources where, on average (circa 1989), only approximately $200 was allocated per year for each student participating in federally funded adult education programs. This would require focus in a field that Chisman believed was intellectually, institutionally, and politically fragmented. The problem was that "there is no clearly stated goal or plan and no mechanism for developing one. There is no federal spokesman for literacy—no place where the buck stops in Washington" (p. 9). For Chisman, it was only from the nation's capitol that ultimate leadership and direction could stem, although he sought to inspire a nationwide consensus around the goals developed through a DC-based leadership.

The Need for Governmental Leadership

To assure focus, Chisman recommended that "*the president should clearly establish the enhancement of adult basic skills as a major national priority and workforce literacy as a major priority of his (sic) administration*" (p. 19, italics in original). This mandate should lead the president to "establish a high-level task force on adult basic skills, with a six-month deadline to: 1) evaluate present federal activities and the overall national effort; 2) develop a statement of national goals and set of objectives for the federal government that will contribute to meeting them; 3) propose a process for coordinating federal activities; and 4) suggest new federal initiatives" (p. 20, italics in original).

A "*Cabinet Council on adult literacy*" should also be appointed charged with the primary task of developing and overseeing "*new government initiatives in workforce literacy*" (p. 20, italics in original). An annual report measuring progress would be issued to the president and Congress.

For its part, Congress would need to pass supportive legislation, particularly an omnibus *Adult Basic Skills Act* that would "combine new initiatives with amendments to . . . existing federal programs" (p. 20). This proposal would provide a singular focus within government, which would also serve as "a rallying point for the political forces outside Washington that are ready to be mobilized for a greater national effort to upgrade adult basic skills" (p. 21). Chisman estimated that the federal cost would be approximately $550 million annually, a mere 3% increase in spending on education and training.

Chisman's proposed legislation contained a number of key points, which filtered into the National Literacy Act of 1991 and the formation of the National Institute for Literacy (NIFL). The latter was foreshadowed in "*national center of excellence*" as a "*not-for-profit quasi-governmental corporation*" (italics in original). The proposed center would focus on research, development, and information dissemination and would operate under a board consisting of the secretaries of Labor, Commerce, Education, Health and Human Services, and the director of the Office of Personnel Management. The board would also include representatives of state and local government, business, labor, voluntary groups, and the research community (p. 25). In calling for "a family of assessment tools that will meet the varying needs of policymakers, program designers, teachers, employers, and learners, themselves," Chisman placed the setting of standards for learning gains and program accountability as "*the first and highest priority of the* [proposed] *Center*" (p. 25, italics in original). The center would also focus on "basic and applied research," provide technical assistance and training to the field, engage in policy analysis, and monitor progress toward achieving the nation's adult basic skills goals through reports, statistical analysis of assessment data, and making policy recommendations to "federal, state, and local governments" (p. 24). Chisman viewed the development of the center as "*the highest priority for federal legislative action*" (p. 24).

Chisman also issued a call to federalism as a means to strengthen the capacity of the states to respond to the nation's need for a revitalization of adult basic skills. This included a reorientation of federal legislation to allow for increased autonomy and flexibility in the delivery of services in the states. Chisman also recommended matching grants to develop state resource centers. The centers would provide staff development and "cooperation and coordination among professionals," for the purpose of "establish[ing] new programs." The centers would participate in research, and "aid policy-makers in the development, implementation and monitoring of state plans and other initiatives" (p. 28).

Reform of existing federal legislation to strengthen current basic skills initiatives, especially those focused on workforce development, was also crucial. This included "more flexible use of funds . . . and encouraging the development of delivery systems that are more results-oriented, account-able, and designed to produce large learning gains" (p. 29). Emphasizing the long-term development of the U.S. workforce, Chisman recommended the reform of the Job Training Partnership Act (JPTA) away from its focus on placing individuals in jobs within a period of a year or less, and "in-vest[ing] resources" among those "who need extended periods of time . . . [for] basic skills training, whether employed or not" (p. 29). Also recom-mended was an expanded 4-year, $100 million-per-year funded project "*de-voted to large scale demonstration projects in workforce literacy*" (p. 30, italics in original) as a critical research project.

In addition, he called for reform of Carl D. Perkins Vocational Educa-tion Act, with a sharper focus on basic skills development rather than "job-specific training." Because of the importance most employers placed on basic skills for entry-level positions, Chisman argued that the Adult Basic Education (ABE) Act also needed revamping, primarily in the area of much-expanded funding. Given the large numbers of students it serves and its basic skills focus, Chisman insisted that municipal-based and state-sup-ported ABE programs should no longer be consigned "to a position of low visibility within the Office of Vocational Education of the Department of Education" (p. 31).

A Plan and Call to Action

Chisman's vision consisted of several interlocking foci. The first prioritized the educational needs of the "current workforce." For Chisman, this did "not mean that we should abandon or de-emphasize our other efforts in any way." Neither should "upgrading our workforce . . . be the exclusive goal of basic skills programs" (p. 14). However, *Jump Start* did stress the need to mitigate this clear neglect on the grounds "that the employed are far more likely to benefit immediately from basic skills instruction than any other group" for the simple reason that "workers with deficient basic skills can readily see the payoff in doing something about their difficulties" (p. 14).

Second, Chisman pointed to the necessity of substantially strengthening basic skills training among the undereducated and not "be content with the attitude that any gain is a good gain in most cases." In "demand[ing] large gains," a likely initial result might be that of "serv[ing] fewer people with more intensive program" (p. 15). Impact would be measured through well-developed assessment and accountability standards that would provide the field with needed information in how basic skills programs could be best or-ganized to maximize results.

Third, with a clarified national focus and a plan of action in place, Chisman called for the mounting of a nationwide effort for its effective real-ization. Advocacy for "the [nation's] basic skills problem [was] politically weak only because no one . . . [had] taken the trouble to mobilize the enormous political forces that might be brought to bear on its behalf" (p. 15). Chisman called for a mutual effort among the business and the "public-policy community" at local, state, regional, and federal levels. This would be supported by a "popular constituency" that, combined with business and policy-driven support, could result in sufficient political mobilization to achieve the restructuring of national priorities in the manner laid out in *Jump Start.* The mobilization effort would include "the twenty-million plus themselves," along with "the many millions of people who have been sensitized to the basic skills problem" (p. 17).

SCANS

Background

Jump Start identified mastery of basic skills in reading, writing, and computation as "*a primary goal of vocational education.*" To meet this need, Chisman recommended that the educational and labor departments collaboratively "*develop measures of the level of basic skills competency required by employers today and likely to be required in the years to come*" (p. 31, italics in original). Two of the National Educational Goals centered on preparing a well-equipped workforce to face the new challenges of the postindustrial future. Goal 3 stated that "*American students will . . . learn to use their minds well, so they may be prepared for responsible citizenship and productive employment in our modern economy.*" Goal 6, which focused on adults, similarly emphasized "*the knowledge and skills necessary to compete in a global economy*" (emphasis added in the original goal in the SCANS Report, 1991, p. xii). The National Literacy Act of 1991 established the National Workforce Literacy Assistance Collaborative in the U.S. Department of Labor to help marginally unemployed out-of-school youth and adults to develop job skills. The U.S. Department of Education established a National Workforce Literacy Strategies grants program "to fund projects that develop, test, and replicate cost-effective successful workforce strategies for the nation" (Spangenburg, NLA, February 5, 2001).

With the National Educational Goals established, the Department of Labor under Secretary Elizabeth Dole, appointed the Secretary's Commission on Achieving Necessary Skills (SCANS) "to determine the skills our young people need to succeed in the world of work" (Academic Innovations, 2000, p. 1). The Commission was charged to (as quoted):

- Define the skills needed for employment;
- Propose acceptable levels of proficiency;

- Suggest effective ways to assess proficiency, and
- Develop a dissemination strategy for the nation's schools, businesses, and homes. (SCANS, 1991, p. viii)

The commission was quick to point out that the workforce focus, although critical, was only one purpose of U.S. public education. It was quite important, however, if not central, in light of the changing needs of the "new" economy that called for a substantial re-focusing of the public school curriculum, especially at the secondary level. "Comprehensive instruction in history, literature, geography, and theoretical science and mathematics" (p. 2) would also be stressed, but the commission viewed preparing youth for the postindustrial workplace, a high order responsibility. As described by the commission:

> As the Secretary of Education has said "America 2000 is not a program but a crusade." If the crusade is to succeed, education must effectively be linked to work. Employers and labor leaders, therefore, must participate in decisions about what the future American schools will look like, what kinds of skills and knowledge they will teach, and what kinds of certificates of competence will accompany the high school diploma. (SCANS, 1991, p. 26)

In more dramatic language, "President Bush has encouraged all of us to be revolutionaries in the cause of education" (p. 26). Through the imagery of "high performance organizations . . . relentlessly committed to producing skilled graduates as the norm, not the exception" (p. ii), the school as an institution became the focal point of reform, not merely its instructional focus.

The commission instructed mothers and fathers "to display the SCANS skills prominently in [their] . . . home and discuss them, often, with [their] children." In addition, energized parents were encouraged to meet directly with school officials with SCANS list in hand to "find out where and how the school is equipping your child with these skills" (p. iii).

Given the reality that "nine out of ten [businesses] are operating on yesterday's workplace assumptions" (p. iv), the SCANS initiative also called for corporate responsibility. The charge was for business to establish the learning organization as the foundation for a renewed corporate culture. Otherwise, "students [will keep on] understand[ing] intuitively, often correctly, that what they are doing in the school today [will continue to] bear . . . little resemblance to what they will be expected to do in the workplace tomorrow" (p. 5).

In the SCANS vision, each sector would play its role in "support [of] the President of the United States in his effort to put World Class Standards—incorporating the SCANS vision—into American schools and workplaces."

This broad consensus on national purposes would call educators to exercise the moral responsibility to "inject the competencies and the foundation" of SCANS "into every nook and cranny of the school curriculum" (p. iv).

SCANS was established primarily as a guide to restructure the public education among youth rather than adult education programs. Yet, because of its focus on skills and knowledge needed in the new economy, it had been widely drawn on in workplace literacy settings for adults.

This connection was facilitated by the conceptual grounding of SCANS in the adult literacy educator's, Sticht's functional-context theory of education. The key point was Sticht's fundamental concept that relevant workplace knowledge could not simply be "picked up," but has a specific content that needs to be systematically learned. Both functional-context theory and the broader constructive-based cognitive science on which it was premised became highly influential in the early thinking of SCANS staff (Sticht, 1997a, p. 1). As summarized in the SCANS (1991) Mission Statement: "Skills are best learned in context and especially in the context of realistic workplace problems. Thus the teaching of functional skills will require the most radical change in educational content since the beginning of the century!"

Sticht accepted the importance Chisman placed on the mastery of the "basic skills." Yet, he had a stronger appreciation for the relevance of content both in expanding specific knowledge of workplace dynamics as well as its facilitation role in basic skills development. Drawing on research that informs whole language reading theory, Sticht (1997b) argued that the more knowledge one possesses about a given content area, the more complex level of text an individual can master about that topic. Conversely, the less one knows about the content, the more one is required to rely on the text rather than background knowledge, which calls for simpler reading material to compensate for the gap.

The intellectual edifice supporting SCANS integrated basic skills mastery, contextual learning, and knowledge transference capacity. Its underlying constructivism allowed SCANS skills to be highly abstract in enabling workers to assimilate a great deal of information, skills, and knowledge applicable to a wide array of specific contexts.

Foundational Skills and Workplace Competencies

SCANS identified two general types of skills that the "high-performance workplace requires [of] workers." The first was "*a solid foundation* [italics in original] in the basic literacy and computational skills, in the thinking skills necessary to put knowledge to work, and in the personal qualities that make workers dedicated and trustworthy." The second area focused on other competencies needed in an information-driven workplace, namely "the ability to manage resources, to work amicably and productively with others, to acquire and use information, to master complex systems, and to work with a variety of technologies" (Academic Innovations, 2000, p. 1).

Basic skills include interpreting "manuals, graphs, and schedules," technical vocabulary, and discerning "the accuracy, appropriateness, style, and plausibility of reports, proposals, or theories of other writers." The basics require the ability to communicate "thoughts, ideas, information, and messages in writing; record[ing] information completely and accurately," and "compos[ing] and creat[ing] documents such as letters, directions, manuals, reports, proposals, graphs, flow charts," as well as attention to "form, grammar, spelling, and punctuation." Mathematics basics include drawing on "quantitative data to construct logical explanations for real world situations" and "understand[ing] the role of chance in the occurrence and prediction of events." Speaking basics take into account not only verbal adroitness, but also "body language appropriate in style, tone, and level of complexity to the audience and occasion" (Academic Innovations, 2000, p. 4).

Thinking skills require using "imagination freely, combin[ing] ideas or information in new ways, mak[ing] connections between seemingly unrelated ideas, and reshap[ing] goals in new ways that reveal new possibilities." Also important is the capacity to "generate alternatives" and making informed risk assessments. *Seeing things in the mind's eye* was another critical attribute. Knowing *how to learn* incorporates "being aware of . . . personal learning styles (visual, aural, etc.), formal learning strategies (note taking or clustering items that share some characteristics), and informal learning strategies (awareness of unidentified false assumptions that may lead to faulty conclusions)." *Reasoning* consists of "[d]iscover[ing] a rule or principle underlying the relationship between two or more objects and apply[ing] it in solving a problem" (Academic Innovations, 2000, pp. 4–5).

Personal qualities include "setting high standards, paying attention to details, working well, and displaying a high level concentration even when assigned an unpleasant task." Related skills consist of "punctuality, enthusiasm, vitality, and optimism in approaching and completing tasks." *Self-esteem* factors are those of "self-worth," awareness "of impact on others," and capacity to recognize and address one's own emotional needs. *Self-mastery* is defined as the capacity to set "well-defined and realistic personal goals," track "progress toward goal attainment" and exert self-motivation through "goal achievement." This necessitates "self-control," the capacity to assimilate "feedback unemotionally and nondefensively," and to be a "self-starter" (pp. 5-6). Summarizing the three-part foundation, the SCANS commissioners maintained the following:

> Effective performance in today's workplace absolutely requires high levels of performance in all three parts of the foundation. There is no point in belaboring the obvious. People who cannot read cannot be trusted in a transcrip-

tion service. The rude salesman who alienates customers will not make sales. The cashier with a hand in the till cheats the business and ultimately the customers. The electrician who cannot solve technical problems threatens the production line. And restaurant owners who cannot creatively approach problems will probably not be in business for long. (SCANS, 1991, p. 15)

The foundational skills are critical, but need to be integrated within the workplace competencies of *resource* management, *interpersonal acuity*, processing and using *information*, understanding the complexities of *systems*, and using *technology* effectively. *Resources* consist of time, money, material and facilities, and human resources. Goal setting, prioritizing, using and/or preparing budgets and linking them to organizational objectives, storing and allocating material and/or space efficiently, and evaluating employee performance are also critical to effective resource management allocation (SCANS, 1991, p. 10).

The *interpersonal* realm takes into account team membership, teaching new skills to others, serving clients or customers, exercising leadership, effective negotiation skills, and the capacity to work in a culturally diverse workplace. *Information* includes acquiring, evaluating, organizing, and maintaining relevant data, and using quantitative and qualitative means for interpreting and communicating information through oral and print formats.

Systems consists of grasping multiple systems that affect work, acuity in "diagnos[ing] deviation in systems' performance and correct malfunctions," proposing "modifications to existing systems" and creating "new or alternative systems to improve performance" (Academic Innovations, 2000, p. 3). "Workers should understand their own jobs in the context of the work around them; . . . how parts of systems are connected, anticipate consequences, and monitor and correct their own problems." This sensibility enables employees to "identify trends and anomalies in system performance, integrate multiple displays of data, and link symbols (e.g., displays on a computer screen) with real phenomena (e.g., machine performance)" (SCANS, 1991, p. 11).

Technology includes choosing appropriate procedures or equipment to meet any particular work task, including mastery of "overall intent and proper procedures for setup and operation of equipment" (Academic Innovations, 2000, p. 3) and equipment maintenance and troubleshooting capacity. Proficiency also consists of "high levels of competence in selecting and using appropriate technology, visualizing operations, using technology to monitor tasks, and maintaining and troubleshooting complex equipment" (SCANS, 1991, p. 11).

The SCANS commissioners sought a fundamental transformation of public schooling that would "change life-long learning from a slogan to a reality for all" (p. 20). They wanted to remove the stigma of "vocational education" for special track students and infuse SCANS skills throughout the curriculum, especially "the five core subjects (history, geography, science, English, and mathematics)" (p. 16), and even into extracurricular activities. SCANS was premised on the following "principles of cognitive science":

> Students do not need to learn the basic skills before they learn problem-solving skills. The two go together. They are not sequential but mutually reinforcing.
>
> Learning should be reoriented away from mere mastery of information and toward encouraging students to recognize and solve problems; and
>
> Real know-how—foundation and competencies—cannot be taught in isolation; students need practice in the application of these skills. (p. 16)

These principles apply to a wide array of learning tasks and curriculum objectives (Duffy & Jonassen, 1992; Fosnot, 1996). What distinguishes SCANS skills and competencies is their sharp focus on preparing individuals for the social, psychological, and technical expectations of meeting the needs of the postindustrial economy as described through the prescriptive literature of certain management theorists (Senge, 1990). At the same time, without a strong commitment to SCANS by the corporate sector, reforming the schools would prove of little avail. Such concepts as self-management, problem solving, and "ownership" would be illusory unless the power to enact them is delegated to those on the front lines in businesses and there is clear reward in doing so. Whether the SCANS competencies would come to represent the intellectual capital of the postindustrial workplace of the new economy *in fact*, and not merely as a form of rhetoric, was a matter of no minor significance as the commissioners recognized. On their considered view, the viability of the proposed educational reform movement in preparing workers with the requisite knowledge to meet needs of the new economy, would be determined, in part, by the extent to which a high level of civic corporate responsibility would come to inform business ethics.

COMMENTARY

The policy reports and broader literature on the workforce needs of the new economy reinforced the long-term tendency to link federal policy on adult literacy education with employment readiness. *Workforce 2000* was an influential text. *Jump Start* was widely disseminated. The Business Council for Effective Literacy (BCEL, 1991) newsletter provided a summary review of Carnevale's (1991) influential *America and the New Economy*. The nation's growing workplace literacy programs drew on such texts as *Bottom Line: Basic Skills in the Workplace* (U.S. Department of Labor and the U.S. Department of Education, 1988) and the SCANS report.

With the passage of the National Literacy Act of 1991 and the formation of NIFL, the federal government recognized other reasons to support adult literacy, especially family literacy, but a postindustrial workforce orientation remained the critical underpinning of national policy. The prospect of resolving the country's human resource needs through training and education stimulated an aura of optimism and hope throughout certain sectors of the field. Its applicability to adult literacy learners, especially the millions not likely to attain a GED, was more critically received among the more skeptical.

Applicability to the Twenty-Million Plus

In *Jump Start*, Chisman pointed to the skill enhancement of the "twenty-million plus" as a fulcrum point to assure U.S. competitiveness in a global economy. *Workforce 2000* took a less stark view in not making as pointed a link between economic buoyancy and the skill enhancement among the nation's least educated sectors. Yet, that report, too, was couched in imagery of demographic destiny in the potential collision between the increasing knowledge demands of the emerging economy and the nation's underclass, especially those residing in the urban sector among African American and Hispanic minorities.

The point of this analysis is not to question "the growing importance of information technology, even an information revolution" (Kumar, 1995, p. 17) in the shifting nature of work over the past 25 years. Kumar, who stressed continuities with the longer term industrial capitalism, accepted the reality of a general shift to services and information as forecast by Bell, Drucker, Toffler, and Naisbitt, while pointing to the persistence of large numbers of low-skilled jobs in janitorial maintenance, food service, manufacturing, retail, and health care. Thus, Kumar rejected any notion "of a new industrial revolution, a new kind of society, a new kind of age" (p. 17) forecasted by the early prognosticators of the postindustrial society. Kumar also commented on the enduring problems of maldistribution of wealth, "de-skilling," and the continuation of Taylorite principles of "scientific management" in postindustrial jobs, along with the persistence of vastly unequal relations of power and wealth between the lower and upper echelons of the office-driven workplace. The increasing democratization of work touted by Naisbitt and a good deal of contemporary management literature was a reality that Kumar and other critics viewed as best as an illusion, and more suspiciously as a manifestation of "false-consciousness."

The 1990 National Adult Literacy Survey (NALS) (Kirsch, Jungleblut, Jenkins, & Kolstad, 1993) examined literacy capacities of adults in three categories: prose literacy, document literacy, and quantitative literacy. The researchers identified five levels of mastery throughout the U.S. population. Based on NALS measurements, those employed as knowledge workers primarily fall into the highest three levels of the five-scaled survey, essentially those possessing high school to postgraduate levels of education.

The linkage between the postindustrial needs of the information economy is even more problematic when applied to adults identified at NALS Level I. The authors estimate that this group represented approximately 20% to 23% of the adult population in 1990 (over 40 million people), with significantly higher rates in urban centers. There are gradations of skills and aptitudes in each category. Moreover, it is problematic to draw direct correlations between literacy measurements and daily life functioning (Sticht, 2001). Still, as rough indices, NALS provides some broad barometers in assessing wide-scale literacy attainment. Based on the NALS, one may reasonably conclude that the "twenty-million plus" to which Chisman referred are not, nor are they likely to be, the knowledge workers of the new economy, nor are they those individuals most likely to embody the values and complex work skills set out in SCANS.

Workforce 2000 pointed out that "the economy of the future will not produce or sustain . . . high-wage, low-skill jobs" (Johnston & Packer, 1987, p. 103). This poses a major problem for the nation's impoverished urban and rural sectors that might require a different configuration of economic, social, and educational resources than that discussed in the postindustrial literature. The reality remains that for millions of adults whose literacy skills stay substantially below a high school equivalency, their entry into occupations that require fluent reading, writing, computational, and information-processing skills, even of a most basic sort for successful employment in the postindustrial office, is not likely, even after years of study in adult literacy programs.

Needed Skills Set

A related issue is whether the SCANS skill set in the mastery of "generic skills," is what is most needed among adults with lower levels of formal education and literacy attainment, rather than training in a more "job specific" (Lewis, 1998, p. 4) focus. The key SCANS-based skill is the capacity to apply cross-functional skills in a wide array of contexts. Given the impact of SCANS on workplace literacy rhetoric, if not practice, Lewis noted that employee training no longer focuses on "traditional content knowledge." The *new* " 'basics,' like 'rithmetic and reading, working in teams, problem solving, and facility with technology" (p. 5), represents content, Lewis argued, that has limited applicability among those not seeking employment in the "informational" sector.

Lewis maintained that the motivation for this shift is not dissimilar from the old vocationalism of the industrial era based on "the dictates of the employer class." On Lewis' reading, "policymakers, schools, and the vocational curriculum were falling in line" (p. 5) with the new vocationalism as set out in SCANS. The irresolvable tension is the conflict between "high status knowledge and the elite or white-collar class on the one hand, and low-status knowledge and the blue-collar class on the other hand" (p. 7). SCANS blurs this distinction, argued Lewis, by characterizing high status knowledge work as the norm for all significant employment in the contemporary economy.

Lewis also questioned unequivocal correlations between the nation's competitiveness in a global economy and the need for a highly skilled workforce at all levels of organizational functioning. Lewis did not dismiss the need for skills upgrading at least in certain occupations, even among those of relatively low status. Still, he challenged the notion of the learning organization as a central model of postindustrial restructuring and pointed to a trend toward "lean production," or de-skilling, and a corresponding "reliance on lower-pay, less skilled workers" (p. 16) at various echelons in the postindustrial economy. Kumar (1995) concurred, noting the growth in credentialism, the transference of knowledge from people to machines in increasingly automated stores, banks, and offices, the rise in jobs in low tech services and retail in the "lower levels of the tertiary economy" (p. 26), and the de-skilling of even large numbers of middle managers and professionals. Lewis (1998) speculated that new vocationalism "rhetoric notwithstanding, high skill might not necessarily be a concomitant of successful companies in today's global economy" (p. 16).

Lewis pointed to evidence "that the most common skills in lean production are behavioral ones (such as working in teams and ability to communicate), not technical ones" (p. 17). Thus, on Lewis' account, there may be more than a little socialization at work in the new vocationalism where employees are expected to accept low skilled, low pay employment while simultaneously embracing the work ethic of the managerial, professional, and technical classes.

The Enduring Impact of Racism and Urban Poverty

A more perplexing problem is the disappearance of work among those whom Wilson (1996) referred to as "the new urban poor." With fewer full-time jobs of any sort available in inner-city neighborhoods, matters of limited education and training are compounded, making the attainment of even marginal employment, especially among Black men, more problematic than for previous generations. A close correlation between poverty and urban residency among minority groups has existed throughout the 20th century, but the disappearance of urban jobs was a relatively new phenomenon that Wilson (focusing on the case study of Chicago) attributes to socioeconomic changes beginning around 1970.

Wilson pointed to several factors, one being rapid urban depopulation between 1970 and 1990. The shift to the suburbs among Whites and middle-class Blacks resulted in an "increasing [concentration of] poverty and joblessness" (p. 16) among those who remained in the inner city. This was compounded by the transition from a manufacturing to a service-based economy, which had a particularly severe effect in lessening opportunities for full-time employment among uneducated minority groups, particularly African Americans residing in urban centers. The occupational transfer had an especially adverse effect on Black males, who were less likely than their female counterparts to enter into low level retail or service sectors. Wilson noted during the 1970s that "two-thirds of prime-age workers with less than a high school education worked full-time, year-round, in eight out of ten years" (p. 26). By the 1980s that figure dropped to 50 percent. The decline was even more precipitous among black males in the inner city.

These factors point to the complex interplay between problems of limited education, accessibility to jobs, and the enduring influence of poverty and institutional racism. Of Chicago males born in the late 1950s, 52% had worked in manufacturing and construction trades in 1978, a figure that dropped to 28% by 1987 (p. 30). Joblessness and downward mobility, especially among Black urban males, became a persisting reality for city residents by the end of the 20th century.

The combined impact of the "outmigration of nonpoor families" (p. 43) and the increasing concentration of the jobless poor within the urban sector not only impacted employment and income. It also contributed to the relative breakdown of inner-city institutional life and community networks. It is these local resources that Wilson viewed as essential in facilitating the search among residents to find work and in meeting other social and personal needs not easily accessible through more impersonal city and state bureaucratic social service and job placement institutions. "Neighborhoods that offer few legitimate employment opportunities, inadequate job information networks, and poor schools lead to the disappearance of work" (p. 52). A cycle of institutional erosion follows consisting "of young people . . . [who] may grow up in an environment that lacks the idea of work as a central experience in adult life" (p. 52).

Wilson noted that this characterization can reinforce a "culture of poverty" image of inner-city life that bolsters conservative social policy in its emphasis on "personal responsibility" over the need for structural reform. While rejecting notions of "pathology," Wilson also repudiated depictions that focus too readily on the intrinsic strengths of urban communities. For

Wilson, this creates an opposite mythology that ignores the reality of enduring inner-city problems.

The issue simply stated, but exceedingly complex in implementation, is that the focus of adult literacy education particularly in the urban sector, needs to take into account these sociological realities. The extent to which its programmatic focus should be based on a workplace scenario of assisting adults to become prepared for postindustrial jobs, as claimed in the proscriptive literature, needs to factor in the broader opportunity structures accessible to individuals within the actual exigencies of their daily lives.

Reductionism

One additional critique that I focus on is that of reductionism. This is particularly evident in *Jump Start*, which although acknowledging other purposes, placed workforce readiness at the center of a national call to revitalize the "basic skills" of the "undereducated" and "underclass." Whether there is a direct correlation between adult basic education and employment readiness is a contestable matter. Even if that case could be made, it remains a questionable proposition that adult literacy alone leads to the attainment of upward mobility (Graff, 1979) as implied in Chisman's call to strengthen the capacity of the "twenty-million plus" to attain entry-level jobs in banking, finance, and other high tech, information-processing sectors.

Jump Start mirrored and powerfully reinforced prevailing assumptions about ABE/adult literacy in its commonsense linkage to the assumed human resource needs of the nation's global economy. This was the basis of its influence in undergirding policy directives and public perceptions throughout the 1990s. My primary critique is not that Chisman's focus was unimportant. It is, however, overstated and marginalizes other aspects of adult literacy education as reflected, for example, in the ethnographic literature that details a more complex story (Bossort, Cottinghan, & Gardner, 1994; Demetrion, 1998, 2001b; Fingeret & Drennon, 1997; Merrifield et al., 1997; Royce & Gacka, 2001).

Of note is a broadening of Chisman's (2002) focus in linking adult literacy to the vitality of the nation's democratic ethos. As he stated it:

> Adequate education is essential to the economic prospects, the social standing, the civic participation, the personal safety, and the self-esteem of every person. Central to American democratic values is the equal worth of each and every man and woman. To deprive these Americans adequate education is to diminish their worth—in their own eyes, and in very practical ways, in the eyes of the nation. This would be a grave violation of one of this country's most important founding principles. (p. 11)

This represents a substantial shift in Chisman's earlier argument and a broadening of the many values of adult basic education based on "an irrevocable national commitment to equal educational opportunities for all adults" (p. 13). By drawing out the importance of "American principles and the American experience" (p. 1) and linking these to the ethos of "American democratic values" (p. 11), Chisman is helping to ground a public philosophy on adult literacy within a context congruent with the political culture of the nation's founding political ideals. In bringing this political rationale to formal public articulation, Chisman's essay *Adult Literacy and the American Dream* may help to expand the dialogue on the nature, purpose, and value of adult literacy education to the public good. The shift in Chisman's thinking from an economic rationale to a principled position in political culture, in a merger of self-interest and idealism, is a fundamental one of no minor significance, a central point taken up in chapter 11.

Workforce Investment Act/National Reporting System (WIA/NRS)

> *Senator Kassenbaum's bill, the Workforce Development Act, has not yet been released publicly, but a major feature is likely to be combining vocational education with adult education—without separate funding for each. It is also likely to establish evaluation standards based on the percentage of participants entering the workforce, rather than purely educational outcomes like improving reading skills, obtaining a GED, or learning to read to one's child. If Senator Kassenbaum's bill becomes law, it would force adult education and literacy programs into competition for scarce funds with vocational and job training programs, and the scales would be strongly tipped toward job training.*
> —OLRC (May 25, 1995, p. 2)

With the National Literacy Act of 1991 and the creation of the National Institute for Literacy (NIFL) in 1992, the early 1990s might be viewed as the high tide of adult literacy in the United States. Based on the recommendation of *Jump Start* and the new legislation, state and regional literacy resource centers were established across the country. EFF had its origins in this period. Influential nongovernmental institutes like Literacy South in Raleigh/Durham, North Carolina, the Center for Literacy Studies in Knoxville, Tennessee, and the National Center for Family Literacy in Louisville, Kentucky, were set up in the early 1990s. In the participatory literacy movement, important work had been conducted in practitioner-based inquiry (Cochran-Smith & Lytle, 1993), participatory-based ESL instruction (Auerbach, 1992b; Nash et al., 1992), and alternative assessment (McGrail, 1991–1994). As required by the National Literacy Act, states developed quality indicators as the basis to evaluate local programs (Condelli, 1996). Literacy

Volunteers of America (LVA) revised its basic tutor training text to reflect the insights of whole language reading theory, process writing, and collaborative learning (Cheatham, Colvin, & Laminack, 1993). Anthologies of learner narratives and student support and advocacy groups peppered programs across the nation.

Policy analysts at LVA and Laubach Literacy Action (LLA) took an active role on Capitol Hill in coordination with the state directors of adult education in the effort to influence federal policy. The National Coalition for Literacy was established during this period to develop common strategies among major organizations seeking to effect national legislation. Barbara Bush played a major role in publicizing the importance of family literacy, helping to reinforce a pluralistic appreciation of the value of adult literacy.

Notwithstanding the expanded focus, the workforce impetus as primary source of justification maintained a steady hold in the policy sector throughout this period. This was reflected both in the high skills quest in preparing knowledge workers for the "new" economy, and in the lower skills focus of welfare reform, in the placing of marginally educated adults with little work history into whatever realms of employment that were available. The conversion of these two economic rationales, accordingly made "employment . . . ever more explicitly the primary purpose of education" (Merrifield, 1998, p. 5) both in K–12 schooling and adult education. The National Governors Association (NGA), a major advocacy group for the ABE workforce emphasis, reinforced this tendency.

The National Literacy Act extended well beyond a workforce focus. It included a broad definition of literacy "as an individual's ability to read, write, and speak English, and compute and solve problems at levels of proficiency necessary to function on the job and in society, to achieve one's goals, and to develop one's knowledge and potential" (National Literacy Act, 1991, p. 2). Nonetheless, a workplace focus remained central as business metaphors like "customer" abounded in the discussion of adult education, as did phrases such as "return on investment, "the bottom line," "efficiency," and "outcome-based performance." As argued by Merrifield (1998), "Even in 'general' adult basic education, the skills needed for work have come to dominate" (p. 13).

Through the National Literacy Act, a Workforce Literacy Assistance Collaborative was established in the Department of Labor to:

> improve the basic skills of individuals, especially those individuals who are marginally employed or unemployed with low basic skills and limited opportunity for long-term employment and advancement, by assisting small- and medium-sized businesses, business associations that represent small- and medium-sized businesses, and labor organizations to develop and implement literacy programs tailored to the needs of the workforce. (National Literacy Act, 1991, p. 8)

In short, a strong connection between ABE and job training persisted un-abated, even though the 1991 legislation contained a considerably broader focus.

A CONSERVATIVE REVOLUTION

The political climate remained fluid in the halcyon period of the early 1990s. Mid-decade national politics would place adult basic education in a more constrictive domain, although even after the massive congressional Republican victory of 1994, the direction for the field was not cast in stone. Despite a sharp congressional shift to the Right, the ABE/adult literacy pol-icy sector continued in their diligent efforts to identify achievable strategies that might place the field in the best possible light. Still, the limitations were inescapable in acknowledging the force of the "Contract with Amer-ica," which cast a suspicious eye on governmentally funded social programs and the "welfare state."

In the second wave of the Reagan Revolution, the 104th Congress, under the leadership of House Speaker Newt Gingrich, focused on "balanced budgets, welfare reform . . . [and] massive government cutbacks" (Johnson & Broder, 1997, p. 547) in an unstinting critique of "command bureaucra-cies" (p. 545). This point of view was based on the conservative *bête-noir*, the welfare liberal state. The legacy of the New Deal and the New Frontier and Great Society of the 1960s continued to typify the liberal wing of the Demo-cratic party in the 1990s. Arguably, such liberalism characterized much of the first 2 years of the Clinton administration, particularly in the failed ef-fort to overhaul the nation's health care system, vilified by various conserva-tive groups as a dangerous governmental intrusion into the ordinary lives of citizens (Johnson & Broder, 1997).

The 1994 midterm elections consisted of a massive Republican victory in every respect. "Not a single Republican seeking reelection [for the House, Senate, or governorships] lost" (p. 554). Republicans broke into traditional democratic strongholds in the industrial north and with organized labor. "Antigovernmental ads and rhetoric . . . resonated" with the voters, while " 'trust in government' hit an all time low in 1994" (p. 555). As character-ized by Johnson and Broder, "The Gingrich-era Republicans who came to power in 1994 . . . truly believed themselves to be the vanguard of the revo-lution and approached their role of disbanding the liberal social programs with passion, conviction, and a relentless determination not to be diverted" (p. 563).

Clinton would learn well from this massive Democratic defeat. In the 1996 presidential race he successfully co-opted significant aspects of the conservative agenda on issues of a balanced budget and welfare reform. It was these political realities with which the marginalized field of ABE/adult literacy was forced to come to terms that put a crest to the field's high tide fueled by the passage of the National Literacy Act, the creation of NIFL, and the setting up of state and regional literacy resource centers.

In a series of brief reports formerly archived at the Ohio Literacy Resource Center (OLRC) and NIFL *Policy Updates,* the field's policy analysts scrutinized the trends as they were taking place in Congress through which to devise a series of best possible and worst case scenarios in a challenging political climate.

As early as December 1994, the field was being advised about a "Workforce Development proposal" that would "streamline 14 different adult education programs into a unified adult education and literacy system." Its focus would remain pluralistic in the emphasis on "basic skills [adults] needed to be productive workers, effective parents, and involved citizens." Yet, the fact that the proposal fell under the rubric of a workforce agenda was telling, as was the emphasis on "One-stop Career centers . . . [that] would . . . assist in the transition from adult education to job training and employment" (OLRC, December 19, 1994, p. 2). This proposal would "consolidate" the various separate programs under the Perkins Act and JPTA and thereby bring efficiencies to the governmental bureaucracies that spawned them and avoid unnecessary duplications. Such language would characterize various congressional proposals that culminated in the Workforce Investment Act of 1998.

In response to the new realities, the National Council of State Directors of Adult Education's Legislative Committee put out a plaintive memo to the state directors on "The Way We Were" and "The Way We Are." During the early 1990s, the memo noted, the legislative committee had impressed on the U.S. Department of Education the importance of reauthorizing the Adult Education Act (AEA) in keeping it "separate from employment and training . . . to be joined instead to library literacy and Even Start in a single piece of legislation." Prior to this lobbying effort, the memo noted, the "Secretary of Education was seriously considering blocking literacy education in with employment and training and turning *our* [italics added] Act over [to] the Department of Labor" (OLRC, February 1995, p. 1). The memo implied that this conserving effort gained through persistent advocacy was a notable victory in terms of "The Way We Were."

The 1994 "Congressional and Gubernatorial elections changed everything . . . [casting] a totally different [political] environment." Among other matters, the memo noted that the 104th Congress "is likely to pay little heed to Administration initiatives." Advocates argued on the need "to keep faith with the department for having recognized and supporting us as a distinct identity" (p. 2), but that entity was no longer the central source of reliability. In the post-1994 political climate, reauthorization of the AEA would likely be opposed "in favor of block grants," which will "allow [Congress] . . . to decide how much money, if any, will be used for each of the eligible activities supported by the block grant."

The memo also pointed to the shift in congressional power from "committee and subcommittee chairs" to "increased power in the speaker of the House [Gingrich] and the Majority Leader in the Senate" (Bob Dole) to better assure party discipline and ideological conformity to the mandate of the Contract with America. It was becoming clear that "increased emphasis . . . on performance outcomes [would be] . . . the quid pro quo for the receipt of federal funds." Such standards would be based on traditional quantitative measures produced by standardized testing, rather than those gleaned from alternative methodologies or the constructivist principles that underlay the slowly emerging EFF standards. The memo also stated that given the desire to roll back federal funding, even "some successful programs which are deemed nonessential will be slated for termination" (p. 2). In short, survival would go to the fittest.

The legislative committee laid out three best case to worse case scenarios in encouraging the state directors to prepare for any eventuality. The committee clearly favored reauthorization of the Adult Education Act that would best guarantee the distinctive identity of the field, although the memo stressed the "need to keep . . . expectation levels realistic" given Congress's "momentum" for block grant funding. A fallback position was a support of block grant funding as recommended by Congressman Goodling, which would include a strong focus on ABE, ESOL, and family literacy. Strategically, this required the ABE lobby "to craft a streamlined version of the Adult Education Act" consistent with Goodling's plan for block grant funding just in case "reauthorization [should] get 'derailed.' " Least desirable was Senator Nancy Kassenbaum's proposal "of a single, broad employment and training block grant." The memo stated that every effort should be made to convince Kassenbaum and the Senate Labor and Human Resource Committee that she chaired to support reauthorization of the AEA. Should the committee remain unconvinced, there was little choice but to attempt to find an accommodation by identifying "ABE/ literacy/ ESOL related OUTCOMES" (p. 3) as a component of training and employment.

The legislative committee of the ABE directors faced troubled times in the 104th Congress. Congressman Tom Sawyer (D-Ohio), a major supporter of adult literacy, made an impassioned protest against the House-sponsored Omnibus Rescissions and Disaster Supplemental Appropriations bill. That bill would cut back $17.1 billion in human services "that had previously been acted into law" in the 1995 federal budget. The proposed cuts in ABE included the elimination of funding for state literacy resource centers and NIFL; in short, the progress made by the field as a result of the National Literacy Act of 1991. Sawyer accused "the Republican leadership

. . . [of] trying to amend the Constitution of the United States for the second time in 100 days" in denying the "60 million Americans [who] can't read or write beyond the eighth grade level" the opportunity "to read and understand the Constitution" (OLRC, March 16, 1995, p. 3). Although the state and regional resource centers and NIFL survived elimination, difficult times lay ahead as the ABE Legislative Committee sought to navigate the troubled waters the best it could.

ABE/adult literacy related legislation was debated in Congress throughout spring 1995. Despite notable differences between various House and Senate, as well as Republican and Democratic, versions, all of the proposals accepted the major tenets of the Contract with America on the need to balance the budget, streamline programs, reduce bureaucracy, reform welfare, and link ABE with job training and vocational education. In an Action Alert from LLA, policy analyst Bill Raleigh reported that programs slated for elimination in a "$26.4 billion budget rescission of funding already appropriated for FY 95," included "the State Literacy Resources and the literacy program for the homeless." "The workplace literacy program would be cut by 68%" (OLRC, May 25, 1995, p. 1).

Prospects for 1996 appeared even worse, with a potential "33% cut in education programs" in the Senate and even larger cuts slated for the House. The House proposal under consideration would have "eliminate[d] the U.S. Department of Education . . . and Americorps . . . (including VISTA) that provides many volunteers to many community service agencies and literacy organizations." Raleigh also alerted the LLA network that the "funding for the state-administered ABE program" was in jeopardy, as well as the existence of NIFL "and the prison literacy . . . program" (p. 1). The president's veto was always looming against more extreme versions of dismantling ABE funding, and House–Senate reconciliation efforts typically had a moderating effect. Nonetheless, the conservative call for substantial slashing of the educational budget along with welfare reform and reducing ABE to workforce education had an enduring impact on state and federal government policy in the mid-1990s.

DEVELOPING A NATIONAL OUTCOME REPORTING SYSTEM FOR THE ADULT EDUCATION

Overview

The effort of the state directors to be prepared took a variety of responses. In addition to paying close attention to emerging nuances of congressional policy, as discussed in chapter 2, the policy community had taken a more proactive stance through the development of the omnibus *21st Century Act*.

Given the emphasis on accountability stemming from the Government Performance and Result Act and the competitive pressure to demonstrate high quality easy-to-measure performance in the aftermath of the 104th Congress, the state directors, working within the general guidelines of the law, also sought to exert an element of control in this arena, before federal mandates were imposed.

In 1995, staff from the Office of Vocational and Adult Education (OVAE) met with a dozen state directors of adult education at their request "to discuss improving the data currently collected for program accountability" (Condelli & Kutner, 1997, p. 1). The state directors sought from OVAE an accountability system "compatible with similar efforts from other agencies, that would provide meaningful measures for program and policy use at the Federal, state, and local levels" (p. 1). A follow-up meeting was held in 1996 where "state directors identified outcome measures to assess" program impact consistent with accountability systems "of other programs and agencies" (p. 1). The result was a resolution recommending a study to review, analyze, and synthesize national and state developed accountability systems already in place that could provide the basis for a new framework in response to an unformulated, but emerging, direction of the federal government.

In response, OVAE created the *National Outcome Reporting System Project* to begin the process of designing a field-driven, policy-compatible accountability system to document student outcomes in federally funded adult education programs. In order to help shape the impending report, state directors met in 1997 "to make initial goals of the reporting system [and to decide which] measures to include and methodologies to pursue" (p. 1). This resulted in the publication of *Developing a National Outcome Reporting System for the Adult Education Program* (DNORSAEP), which reviewed "existing and planned accountability systems" and pointed to "many of the major issues that must be resolved in establishing an outcomes-based reporting system" (p. 1).

The direction for such a reporting system was far from set in this preliminary study. It was designed as more of an exploratory study to examine accountability issues stemming from a range of *possible* outcome areas that plausibly could become embodied in a national ABE program. However provisional the document's findings were in terms of the content of possible outcome areas, it stressed the importance of standardized measurability as a general accountability norm. This view stemmed from the combined pressures to legitimize ABE accountability in conformance with the reporting system of other federal agencies as required by the Government Performance and Results Act, the conservative impact of the 104th Congress, and President Clinton's cooptation of the conservative agenda from 1996 onward. Based on categories to be discussed, the Condelli and Kutner (1997) document identified accountability measures for an array of outcome areas that reflected the desire of the state directors to broaden the basis of federal policy within a discourse and framework that Congress might deem credible.

Preparing to Meet the Challenge

At their March 1996 meeting, the state directors identified "seven categories of outcome measures for adult education that *could* be used to demonstrate the program's effectiveness to a broad audience" (p. 2, italics added). These were (as quoted, with original italics):

- *Economic impact*—measures that reflect a change in a participant's employment or economic status, such as obtaining a job or going off public assistance.
- *Credentials*—measures that reflect attainment of a diploma, a skill certificate or other formal acknowledgement of completion of a program or study of training.
- *Learning gains*—measures that demonstrate that the participant acquired reading, writing, functional or employment-related skills, numeracy, or English speaking and listening skills.
- *Family impact*—measures that reflected improved literacy-related activities with family members, such as reading to children, or greater involvement in children's school-related activities.
- *Further education and training*—measures of a participant's continuation or training program after leaving the adult education program.
- *Community impact*—measures of improved community or civic involvement, such as voting, achieving citizenship or increased community activism.
- *Customer satisfaction*—measures demonstrating the degree of a participant's satisfaction with adult education instruction and whether services helped participants achieve their goals. (pp. 2–3)

These outcomes were similar to those identified by Beder and Valentine (1990) at the beginning of the decade in a study on adult basic education in Iowa that summarized students goals as the following: "(a) self improvement; (b) family responsibilities; (c) diversion; (d) literacy development; (e) community/church involvement; (f) job advancement; (g) launching; (h) economic need; (i) educational advancement" (p. 78).

The categories of outcomes also shared similarities with the EFF project, particularly the Worker, Parent/Family, and Citizen/Community Member Role Maps (Stein, 2000). Yet, they were not likely to be informed by the constructivist assumptions that underlay the then still emerging EFF Content Standards.

Although the content focus of the emerging reporting system remained open in 1996, Condelli and Kutner (1997) stated that because "the reporting system is envisioned as a *national system* [italics in original] . . . all states will need to report a uniform set of quantitative measures using an individual record system at the local level." Under this format, states could still "collect additional measures for their own reporting purposes," but the uniform data for national reporting would be mandatory. The authors noted that "policy goals . . . are typically decided prior to the development of measures" (p. 3), but regardless of specific direction in which policy would unfold, based on the Government Performance and Results Act, accountability systems needed to be based on objective, uniform, and quantitative measures. Given the operative political realities of the late 1990s, it would have been highly difficult to have constructed a federal accountability system on anything other than a statistical model of quantification.

Despite the political limitations that constrained the hands of the state directors, Condelli and Kutner proposed that their research would lend clarity to "the system's purpose and . . . define it more precisely" (p. 3) once a policy was firmly established in law. The immediate focus of the study was to critically examine issues concerning various measures and methodologies related to outcome-based assessment in the seven categories as possible foci for a federally driven accountability system. Notwithstanding the limitations of political reality, Condelli and Kutner had cast a discerning eye on subtle measurement and methodological issues. In 1996 and 1997, there was substantial pressure, but no inevitability about the path that ultimately ensued when the National Reporting System became wedded to the Workforce Investment Act in 1998. The 1997 study was designed to enable the field to address and influence accountability issues from a research base once a specific policy direction, the general tenors of which seemed evident, although far from cast in stone, emerged.

Findings

The Condelli and Kutner document accepted standardization and comparability as the sine qua non of accounting for learning gains in a national reporting system, but noted that without a highly specific content-based evaluative framework, measurement would remain problematic. The resolution required that "functioning levels [of learning] . . . be defined with specific skills and competencies associated with each level," however levels were to be defined. To be valid at a highly technical level, this would necessitate correlation of "test and skill levels used by local programs . . . into a single, national standard" through "skill level equivalencies" calibrated from various assessment instruments.

To solve the complex tensions between assessing learning that takes place in specific educational environments, and not only that of standardization, but that of data uniformity across assessment instruments for the purpose of gaining a valid national picture, would require a technical solution of a highly sophisticated sort (Beder, 1999). To move forward in this manner would have necessitated sustained focus, political will, and resources for which a budget-cutting Congress and the Clinton administration had little inclination. Yet, unless critically attended to, it was likely that framing a national reporting system on uniform levels measurement, without rigorously attending to correlative issues, would result merely in data aggregation over already aggregated data (standardized tests), thus exacerbating the tension between etic and emic forms of measurement.

In a general sense, a levels framework, even one not rigorously proficient in a technical sense, can provide useful, although not strictly reliable, information. Sticht (1990) pointed out, "Nationally standardized tests, properly administered, can provide information about broad growth in literacy or mathematics skills" (p. 28). In a review of quantitative testing in the United States throughout the 20th century in adult literacy, Sticht and Armstrong (1994) concluded that various tests "indicate that, on average, adults achieve about one half to one-and-a-half 'years' [grade school equivalency] of gain in a wide variety of programs" (p. 22). Based on this general assumption, translating various standardized instruments into uniform levels could have some validity (in an informal sense) in demonstrating program efficacy, although the result would be considerably less from what scientific-oriented educational researchers would view as evidence based. This level of aggregation information might be useful for a variety of reasons, including the political, but as Sticht (1990) argued, even "nationally standardized and normed tests [never mind their aggregation into uniform levels] are not sensitive enough to the specifics of what is being taught" (p. 11) at the programmatic level.

Sticht also pointed out that evaluation of learning gains in any comprehensive sense requires "multiple assessments [that] can contribute multiple types of information" (p. 28). On Sticht's interpretation, such measures are not ranked as *primary* and *secondary*, the categories that emerged in the 1998 National Reporting System, but are viewed as useful for various insights that they shed on the learning process. For Sticht, both standardized testing of various types and alternative methods of assessment have their strengths and weaknesses and can contribute to a comprehensive picture of what students have learned. Yet, because the pressure for comparability was pervasive in federal accountability designs by 1997, the gap between the quest for etic information based on a uniform framework, and the need to link assessment to concrete learning environments reflected an ineradicable tension that neither the state directors nor Condelli and Kutner were able to resolve.

Condelli and Kutner pointed to various data collection issues in linking a national reporting system to each of the specific impact areas identified by the state directors beyond learning (or to be more specific, reading) gains. For example, employment goals would only be relevant to students who identified them or to programs that had a specific workplace focus. An overly tight focus seeking to articulate connections between literacy and jobs would result in a too-restrictive definition of adult education. It could also result in measuring what was not being learned, or in failing to measure what was actually learned.

A similar argument was made in linking assessment to removing clients from welfare, which should only be applied to programs with such a purpose. Otherwise, programs will fail to be evaluated based on their intended focus. One difficulty the researchers identified with linking literacy education to obtaining credentials like the GED is "that program impact may not be readily apparent" for the several years that it may take to achieve such goals. Condelli and Kutner made a similar argument with family and community impacts as a goal. Also, without an instructional focus on such goals, an assessment system based on them fails to link what is being evaluated with what is being learned.

Condelli and Kutner's review surveyed a broad array of approaches and issues that would need to be worked through in developing a national reporting system where the specific direction of policy was not yet clear. The study provided an array of options based on possible policy outcomes. However, in pointing to various dilemmas over reliability and validity, the authors identified a range of problems that any scientifically rigorous accountability system based on quantification, measurability, and comparability would encounter and need to resolve. The study provided grist for considerable reflection on key matters underlying assessment/accountability issues and the nature of federal policy, although it did not resolve the dilemmas it identified in developing an accountability system that was both scientifically sound and politically expedient.

Rather, external events were to have a more pronounced impact on the future of federal policy as the third, least desirable scenario of subsuming adult education into a workforce training and educational model became a reality in 1998 during the 104th Congress. The full brunt of this workforce direction was modified through the influence of the Condelli and Kutner study and the intensive lobbying of the state directors of adult education in salvaging what they could for the preservation of the integrity of the federal adult education and literacy system.

THE WORKFORCE INVESTMENT ACT

Condelli and Kutner (1997) observed:

> Recently, the U.S. Congress through the *Careers* bill and other legislative ini-
> tiatives, sought to redefine adult education as a component of a workforce de-
> velopment system. Several states are also moving in this direction. This view of
> the program would make adult education employment-focused, requiring an
> emphasis on economic impact and employment measures. Adult educators,
> however, have consistently fought to keep adult education an *education* [italics
> in original] program, which would make learning gain measures most appro-
> priate for assessing the program's performance. Adult educators appear to
> have been successful in defining the goal of the program as educational, and
> the current Congress is not moving toward workforce consolidation. How-
> ever, the close link between adult education and employment programs
> makes it likely that any outcome-based reporting system will need to include
> both types of measures. (p. 54)

Streamlining Bureaucracy

With the passage of the Workforce Investment Act (WIA) one year later, such
a greater consolidation took place, although the state directors successfully
lobbied to gain inclusion of learning gains and family literacy in Title II of
the WIA, referred to as "The Adult Education and Family Literacy Act." The
legislation also included the grafting on of a National Reporting System.

Herman (1998), then Secretary of Labor, characterized the Workforce
Investment Act as "the first major reform of the nation's job training system
in over 15 years." Its stated purpose is to provide "workers with the information, advice, job search assistance, and training they need to get and keep
good jobs." The WIA also aims to provide "employers with skilled workers"
(p. 2). As part of its consolidation, the WIA replaced the Adult Education
Act of 1969 and the National Literacy Act of 1991.

Secretary Herman argued that the consolidation of job training programs and services to the un- and underemployed would be facilitated by
the elimination of "many of the administrative regulatory barriers that have
previously existed" (p. 2). For the secretary, the problem stemmed from the
"patchwork of Federal job training programs that has taken shape over the
last six decades, [with] each element responding to a particular concern at
a specific time, but never fully brought into alignment with the other components of the 'system' " (p. 3). One of problems Herman identified in previous job training programs was *limited choice*, in which "men and women
seeking new opportunities . . . ha[d] available rather than being permitted
to search the market to select the job training program that is right for
them" (p. 3). The secretary also pointed to problems that plagued work-

force training initiatives for years, lack of *quality information* on available work, lack of emphasis on skills required for such employment, and little information on accessing the most effective programs designed to meet the training needs of clients. Herman pointed out that w*eak strategies* in "deploying Federal resources, or for effectively integrating Federal efforts with one another" (p. 3) have, historically, impeded the capacity of state and local communities in providing support to the unemployed and underemployed. "By integrating numerous Federal education, training and employment programs into a comprehensive, streamlined system, the Workforce Investment Act strives to overcome these and other shortcomings of the nation's job training system" (p. 3).

The "One-Stop delivery system" (p. 3) was the mechanism that would facilitate this consolidation by "unify[ing] numerous training, education and employment programs into a single, customer-friendly system" and "provid[ing] a full menu of job training, education and employment services" (p. 5). Clients "receive skills assessment services, information on employment and training opportunities, unemployment services, job search and placement assistance, and any up-to-date information on job vacancies—all at one center specifically tailored to meet the needs of the community it serves" (p. 1). Each of the states would "use a common intake and case management systems in order to take full advantage of the One-Stop's potential for efficiency and effectiveness" in coordinating the roles of "numerous partners that will provide [the] core services" (p. 5).

The WIA would streamline services and empower clients by "enabling eligible participants to choose the qualified training program that best meets their needs." The efficiency of the system would be determined by monitoring, in which "states, localities and training providers will be held accountable for their performance," as measured by "core indicators of performance—including job placement rates, earnings, retention in employment, skill gains, and credentials earned" (p. 3). Herman noted that "failure to meet goals will lead to sanctions, while exceeding the levels could lead to the receipt of incentive funds" (pp. 3–4). Such a system would also reinforce localism and efficiency with "business-led local Boards relieved from 'nitty-gritty' operational details" in order "to focus on strategic planning, policy development and oversight of the local system" (p. 4).

The cumulative impact of the legislation was designed to improve the workforce by providing a supply of sufficient numbers of qualified employees "to sustain America's economic growth" and better prepare the workforce for the knowledge demands of the postindustrial economy. The WIA was also designed to reduce welfare dependency in providing job resources to "the hardest to serve." In "integrat[ing] TANF and other programs that serve the welfare customer" (p. 4), the needs of this group received priority for "intensive and training services."

Service Delivery Through the One-Stop Centers

The WIA "provides for three levels of services: core services, intensive services, and training . . . to be accessed sequentially." Access to the more extensive services is available only after "the individual is unable to obtain employment with the more basic services" (p. 6). One-Stop services are open not only to the unemployed but also to the underemployed, such as "former welfare recipients who are placed in a job through the Welfare-to-Work Initiative" (p. 7) who seek to improve their vocational prospects.

The One-Stop Centers are open to "all Americans . . . as a community resource" that can be accessed "throughout their lifetime to enhance their job skills as they move up the career ladder" (p. 7). This is particularly so with the first level of support, *core services* that provide access to information about the job market and training providers. Core services also include "job search and placement assistance and career counseling," assistance in filling out unemployment eligibility forms and "eligibility for Welfare-to-Work and financial aid assistance" (p. 7). Less clear is the extent of the follow-through of the core services because under the WIA local boards cannot provide direct services unless determined by special arrangement of local and state officials.

Intensive services are available to the unemployed and to those who have exhausted their resources in obtaining employment through core services, as determined by the One-Stop operator. This second level is also available to "dislocated workers who are employed, but . . . in need of intensive services in order to obtain or retain employment that allows for self-sufficiency" (p. 8). Intensive services include (as quoted):

- Comprehensive and specialized assessments of skill levels (i.e. diagnostic testing);
- Development of an individual employment plan;
- Group counseling;
- Individual counseling and career planning;
- Case management;
- Short-term prevocational counseling. (p. 8)

The One-Stop Centers would provide intensive services in some instances, although mostly through local contracted providers. Intensive services are technically available to any adult who has exhausted the core services. However, in areas where there is a shortage of funds for these services, the local board and state governor can direct the One-Stop operator to prioritize "intensive services to welfare recipients and other low-income individuals" (p. 8).

Training services would be available only after individuals failed to gain employment through the support of intensive services. A determination would be required to evaluate not only whether potentially qualified individuals were in need of those services, but also whether clients "possess the skills and qualifications needed to participate successfully in the training program in which they express an interest" (p. 8). Any training provided would have to "be directly linked to occupations that are in demand in the local area" (p. 8), unless the individual is willing to relocate to where there is market demand for the occupation for which the person seeks training. Herman described the "underlying principle" of these services as driven by "customer choice," in which those who qualify for training are given information about the various agencies that could provide such support that they might access. The result is "a market-based system" for these services and a " 'level-playing field' " among the providers, both those "large and small, public and private." The intended result was to require providers to compete in the marketplace and "meet the test private businesses meet every day" in "deliver[ing] value to their customers, or risk losing them" (p. 8). Training services would be provided through Individual Training Accounts (ITAs), which basically make up a voucher system that enables individuals to purchase specific services from training agencies on an individual basis.

Critical Perspectives

A U.S. General Accounting Office (GAO, 2001) report pointed to a variety of technical problems needing resolution for the One-Stop Centers to function with maximum efficiency. Difficulties included burdensome reporting requirements leading to the unintended consequences of a reduction of services provided by participating agencies. Agencies were also apprehensive that WIA requirements would impinge on the quality, mode, and type of services they provided, which were not always related to immediate job placement, especially when proof of efficacy needed to be measured within the context of a one-year calendar as mandated by the legislation. Participating agencies also questioned both the feasibility and desirability of "full integration" of "all partner programs coordinated and administered under one management and accounting system, offering joint delivery of program services from combined resources" (p. 9).

Other analyses pointed to more perplexing political, social, and economic problems. For example, the WIA allows for contracted services if "the local board determines that there is a training program of demonstrated effectiveness offered in the local area by a community-based organization or another private organization to serve special participant populations that face multiple barriers to employment" (Herman, 1998, p. 9).

Many smaller, community-based organizations that work with low income adults with limited formal education might qualify for the exceptional contracts the system allows. However, there may not be enough of an exact match between direct employment services called for in the legislation and what the agencies provide in terms of supportive and related services of education, counseling, and prevocational skills.

An effective response to the gap may require what Savner (1999) referred to as a *generous* interpretation of the legislation in which the impact of obtaining employment may not be direct, for example, in community-centered adult literacy programs that tailor instruction to a broad array of student needs and interests, including employment. However, as noted by Herman (1998), such "exceptions are meant to be limited" (p. 9), in that the intent of the legislation is to maximize efficient system delivery in moving people into unsubsidized employment. Still, without this more generous interpretation, "failure . . . to implement the exception for community-based providers is likely to have the perverse result of decreasing rather than increasing consumer choices, exactly the opposite result from that intended under the Act" (Savner, 1999, p. 8).

D'Amico (1997) raised similar issues in shedding light on the relationship between people leaving welfare and the attainment of unsubsidized employment among low skilled, low educated populations. For example, D'Amico found that "low cost job search work experience programs (a labor force attachment approach) produced larger earning gains and welfare savings than programs that emphasized higher cost components, such as education and training (a human capital investment approach)" (p. 3). Yet, as she argued, "these gains do not usually result in higher incomes for public assistance recipients or improved prospects for long term self sufficiency" (p. 3). As she noted, certain policy trade-offs were implicit in the welfare reform legislation of the late 1990 in that "*providing mandatory job search will maximize welfare savings and job holding, but by itself usually will not get people better paying jobs or benefit the most disadvantaged. Providing higher cost more intensive services to a selected population can get people jobs with somewhat higher earnings, but will produce lower benefit savings per dollar invested*" (p. 3, italics in original).

D'Amico identified several problems with the current delivery system, including insufficient class time in programs, limited funding for programs, and lack of clear vision among teachers and programs of relevant educational focusing related to long-term employability (p. 3). D'Amico also critiqued "*the design of welfare to work programs, and research that evaluates them[, which] tends to isolate outcomes of welfare to work programs from the context of participants lives*" (p. 4, italics in original). Related issues are ignored such as "mental and physical health problems, lack of child care, transportation issues and for some, discrimination by race and gender in the workplace" (p. 4). Elsewhere, D'Amico (1999) pointed to additional factors that im-

peded the effective job attainment of socially and educationally marginalized groups, "includ[ing] the state of the local job market, racial and gender segmentation indicative of employment in the United States, and
access to social networks that can provide entry to employment" (pp. 2–3).
Critics noted that these barriers that can "stand between participants and
work" (D'Amico, 1997, p. 4) are not often factored into the design of welfare-to-work programs. The problem in most welfare-to-work programs is
that "participants do not, by and large, acquire full-time jobs at wages that
can support families. This means that they continue to receive public assistance, albeit less of it, and that they are likely to cycle, as has long been characteristic of the majority on public assistance, between low paid, unstable
work and welfare" (p. 15).

D'Amico identified current research that still requires greater longitudinal study to more definitively assess the correlation between full-time, livable wage, benefit-supported employment, and extensive training and education among low income, low educated adults. She noted that this
provisional research shows greater long-term impact "for the human capital
development approach" (p. 14) that would enable welfare clients to allocate sufficient time and sustained effort to obtain the needed skills and education to qualify for more permanent, stable, and better paying work. In
summarizing the findings of a study on which she favorably comments,
D'Amico argued that "*a more holistic understanding of work, learning, and the
lives of welfare recipients demands a holistic response to education and training, one
that individuals can take advantage of regardless of their levels of literacy or education and whether they are working or not*" (p. 34, italics in original).

As D'Amico more succinctly put it, "*Training should become more like adult
education, and developing pedagogies that are contextualized, student centered, active and project or activity based*" (p. 35, italics in original). Whether such "substantial investment" (p. 17) of money and resources is feasible in a sharply
defined, cost-benefits utilitarian value system maximizing "efficiency" is another matter. The WIA indicators (as quoted) more narrowly focused on:

1. Entry into unsubsidized employment;
2. Retention in unsubsidized employment 6 months after entry into employment;
3. Earnings received in unsubsidized employment 6 months after entry
   into the employment; and
4. Attainment of a recognized credential relating to achievement of educational or occupational skills for individuals who enter employment. (Herman, 1998, p. 11)

The WIA's consolidation of the "patchwork" of programs into a coordinated workforce direction was a logical culmination of a four-decade his-

tory of federal policy. The U.S. trajectory resembled the modernization model of post-World War II U.N. campaigns, in which literacy was viewed as one of the critical thresholds that "underdeveloped" nations needed to achieve as a perquisite of entering into the modern industrial era. The analogy is that this modernization imagery was reconstructed for the post-industrial era in preparing the workforce to meet the increasing knowledge demands of the information-based competitive environment of the global economy. That has been one consistent strand in workforce literacy initiatives and rhetoric since the 1980s, a position that has been embodied and reinforced in the WIA.

At least as powerful was a pervasive school-to-work ideology linked to the more minimal demands of the low tech service economy, particularly for the "twenty-million plus" identified by Chisman. It is this latter focus on low tech service employment that seems to be the primary emphasis in the WIA, as only the unemployed and largely unskilled are most likely to utilize the secondary and tertiary services provided through the One-Stop Centers. The rhetoric of efficiency, coordination, streamlining, consolidation, accountability, and reinventing government embodied in the language of the WIA face the enduring reality of urban poverty and joblessness (Wilson, 1996). Former Vice President Gore's vision of *reinventing government* also invariably encounters traditional logjams of bureaucratic entanglements and political turf guarding, which critical skeptics of the political Left have identified as the functional equivalence of reinforcing the social and economic status quo (Bowles & Gintis, 1976).

Surfacing within and throughout the new legislation is the haunting question of whether or not the civil polity of the United States is able to substantially confront the pressing issue of social and economic justice for all of its citizens. Without a coming to terms with the underlying structural, political, and ethical issues that impede this quest, it is at least questionable whether the matter of jobs among those citizens and residents most in need can be addressed through a governmental system based on efficiency and welfare reform. The related matter of reducing adult literacy to a subsystem of workforce readiness training through a cost-benefits utilitarian value system also troubled critics.

WORKFORCE INVESTMENT ACT—TITLE II: ADULT EDUCATION AND FAMILY LITERACY ACT

Overview

The adult education policy sector lobbied diligently to expand the initial focus of the Workforce Investment Act beyond the emphasis on employment to include three of the original seven outcome areas that the state directors identified in Columbia, Maryland, in 1996: *learning gains, family impact,* and *credentials.* The outcomes identified in Title II were designed to:

> (1) assist adults to become literate and obtain the knowledge and skills necessary for employment and self-sufficiency; (2) assist adults who are parents to obtain the knowledge and skills necessary to become full partners in the educational development of their children; and (3) assist adults in the completion of a secondary school education. (Workforce Investment Act—Title II, 1998, p. 2)

Through Title II, the WIA funds agencies that provide instruction to adults below the secondary level who do not have a high school diploma or "recognized equivalent" and "lack sufficient mastery of basic educational skills to enable the individuals to function effectively in society" (p. 3). The self-evident definition of functionality was left undefined, with literacy viewed as directly correlated.

Title II defines *family literacy* as "services that are of sufficient intensity in terms of hours, and of sufficient duration, to make sustainable changes in a family, and that integrates all of the following activities":

(A) Interactive literacy activities between parents and their children.

(B) Training for parents regarding how to be the primary teacher for their children and full partners in the education of their children.

(C) Parent literacy training that leads to economic self-sufficiency.

(D) An age appropriate education to prepare children for success in school and life experiences. (Workforce Investment Act—Title II, 1998, p. 3)

By definition, family literacy, as described in Title II, precluded other aspects of intergenerational activities beyond a school-based focus, as reflected, for example, in the EFF Parent/Family Role Map (Stein, 2000).

In line with the workforce focus of the new legislation, the funding formula "include[d] only adults age 16–61." States could use federal funds in support of participating students over the age limit, but the new regulation "change[d] how state allotments are allocated." The result was that "states with a large population over 61 may receive smaller percentages of the Adult Education Grants next year" (NIFL Policy Update, September 21, 1998, p. 2).

In accordance with the National Reporting System (see next section), each state would be required to have a uniform assessment system based on "objective and measurable" criteria. States would also be required to demonstrate their "effectiveness in achieving continuous improvement of adult education and literacy activities" based on levels of performance negotiated with the U.S. Secretary of Education. With the passage of the legislation, the states would be required to submit an annual report to the Secretary and to Congress as a basis for making future decisions about adult education and literacy funding.

The driving force underlying the standardized accountability system was the potential of enabling states to "make a compelling case that money invested in adult education and literacy is paying off in terms of student gains." With appropriate evidence to back up the claim, NIFL argued that funding could increase "substantially" (NIFL Policy Update, November 18, 1998, p. 2). Specific performance indicators (*primary outcomes*) based on Title II are (as quoted):

1. Demonstrated improvements in literacy skill levels in reading, writing, and speaking in the English language, numeracy, problem-solving, English language acquisition and other literacy skills.

2. Placement, retention, or completion of postsecondary education, training, unsubsidized employment, or career advancement.

3. Receipt of a high school diploma or its equivalent.

4. Other objective, quantifiable measures, as identified by the state agency. (NIFL Policy Update, September 21, 1998, p. 4)

In addition, states could add additional, *secondary outcomes*, such as the then developing EFF Content Standards, as well as other forms of evidence to demonstrate the impact of adult education "related to strengthening families, increasing community involvement, or other goals that are not necessarily tied to work" (NIFL Policy Update, November 18, 1998, p. 3). The secondary measures would not count for official statistical purposes, but would provide additional evidence of influence that could be drawn on to help sway congressional decision making over funding. The state directors and the NCL leadership placed considerable emphasis on the secondary measures in the belief that they provided the field with a potential source of legitimization within the law to make the case for the public value of adult basic education beyond a workforce focus.

The new legislation required each state to develop a Five Year State Plan "for improving adult education and family literacy activities in the state[s]" (NIFL Policy Update, September 21, 1998, p. 4). This included the setting of statistical goals for the first 3 years. States would be evaluated on the extent to which they met the goals, which had a conservative tendency on standard setting to assure that the state ABE programs would meet the targets.

Each state director of adult education would provide leadership for establishing the state plan, which then "must route it to the Governor for review and comment before sending it to the [U.S.] Secretary of Education" (NIFL Policy Update, November 18, 1998, p. 1). The development of the state plans would be undertaken with the collaboration and consultation of "literacy providers within the state" (NIFL, September 21, 1998, p. 4). These other providers could have input in setting levels of student achievement, particularly in terms of establishing secondary measures.

THE NATIONAL REPORTING SYSTEM

Political Factors Leading to the NRS

The National Reporting System Implementation Guidelines (U.S. Department of Education, 2001) was a product of a more general call for "accountability of Federal programs" that pervaded policy discourse in the 1990s. The text pointed to the Government Performance and Results Act of 1993, which requires "all Federal agencies to develop strategic plans to ensure that services were delivered efficiently and in a manner that best suits client needs, and to develop indicators of performance to demonstrate their agency's impact." The authors identified an imminent political threat to the ABE/adult literacy sector when the U.S. Congress in 1995 "considered eliminating adult education as a separate delivery system by integrating the program into a general system of workforce development." This required "strong and convincing data on the impact of adult education at the state and federal levels . . . in order to demonstrate its importance as a separate educational program" (p. 1) as preserved in Title II.

This impetus sparked the meetings among state directors, OVAE staff, and others and the outcomes study (Condelli & Kutner, 1997), discussed earlier. However, the effort of the state directors to take the initiative hit a serious snag when "the proposed voluntary nature of the [emerging] NRS changed in August 1998" when "the Adult Education and Family Literacy Act . . . became law." The result was that "the NRS mandate was then expanded to establish the measures and methods to conform to the Workforce Investment requirements" (U.S. Department of Education, 2001, p. 1).

The NRS identified specific "measures for national reporting," along with corresponding definitions and "methodologies for data collection" (p. 2). Although clearly focused on the workforce goals of Title I of the WIA, NRS developers also considered "the need to *accommodate the diversity* of the adult education delivery system and to assure *compatibility* . . . with related adult education and training programs" (p. 3, italics in original). A major challenge consisted of a need "for outcome measures [to] be broad enough to accommodate these differences, yet concrete and standardized sufficiently to allow the NRS to establish a uniform national data base" (p. 3). Not considered were other measures beyond standardized statistical data as *primary measures*, such as sampling, multimeasures, and "thick [ethno-

TABLE 4.1
The Six Levels for Literacy

Level	CASAS Score Range
Beginning ABE/Literacy	200 and below
Beginning Basic Education	201–210
Low Intermediate Basic Education	211–220
High Intermediate Basic Education	221–235
Low Adult Secondary Education	236–245
High Adult Secondary Education	246 and higher

Adapted from U.S. Department of Education, 2001, pp. 14–16.

graphic] description" of programs in a manner that could become com-
piled into narrative state reports based on agreed on methodologies of
qualitative research design (Merriam, 1988).

Requirements

The NRS reporting requirements consist of mandatory *core measures* and
voluntary *secondary measures*. Core measures consist of three types. *Outcome
measures* focus on educational gain, employment, and attainment of secondary school diploma or equivalency, or placement in postsecondary education or training. These are the *primary measures* of the NRS. *Descriptive measures* include student demographics, reasons for attending, and student
status. *Participation measures* consist of contact hours and enrollment in instructional programs for special populations or programs such as family or
workplace literacy (U.S. Department of Education, 2001, p. 3). The NRS
also includes *secondary measures*, which are based on "employment, family
and community [objectives] that adult education stakeholders believe are
important to understanding and evaluating adult education programs," although "*states are not required to report on* [italics in original] [them] . . . and
there are no performance standards tied to them" (p. 3).

Core outcome measures designed to assess educational gains are based
on "educational functioning levels in reading, writing, speaking and listening and functional areas" (p. 4). The outcome requirement is that the
"*learner completes or advances one or more educational functioning levels from starting level measures on entry into the program*" (p. 13, italics in original). The determinations of the "level descriptors" are based on "a uniform, standardized assessment procedure approved by the state, [which] . . . may be a
standardized test or a performance assessment with standardized protocols" (p. 13). These would have to meet the guidelines set forth in the NRS.
In order to assure comparability and aggregation of data that then would
be reported upward at the national level, each state would need to use a single "assessment procedure." The legislation required that students be post-

tested at least once at the end of class or program year. "An 'advance' or 'completion' is recorded if, according to a subsequent assessment, the student has entry level skills corresponding to one or more levels higher than the incoming level in the areas initially used for placement" (p. 19). No longer would criteria be based simply on reporting gains. Only level completion counted.

The NRS identified CASAS, Adult Basic Learning Examination (ABLE), Adult Measure of Educational Skills (AMES), Student Performance Levels (SPL), and the Basic English Skills Test (Best) as among the approved assessments for NRS measures and established level benchmarks for them (p. 19). I illustrate the six levels for literacy through the example of CASAS (pp. 14–16): Each level contains a level descriptor based on reading and writing, numeracy skills, and functional and workplace skills. Juxtaposing the first three levels for basic reading and writing provides a sense of them and clues as to the assumptions upon which they are based.

Beginning ABE Literacy Level (200 and below on CASAS):

Individual has no or minimal reading and writing skill. May have little or no comprehension of how print corresponds to the spoken language and may have difficulty using a writing instrument. At the upper range of this level, individual can recognize, read and write letters and numbers, but has a limited understanding of connected prose and may need frequent re-reading. Can write a limited number of basic sight words and familiar words and phrases; may also be able to write simple sentences or phrases, including very simple messages. Can write basic personal information. Narrative writing is disorganized and unclear; inconsistently uses simple punctuation (e.g., periods, commas, question marks); contains frequent errors in spelling (p. 14)

Beginning Basic Education (201–210 on CASAS)

Individual can read simple material on familiar subjects and comprehend simple and compound sentences in single or linked paragraphs containing a familiar vocabulary; can write simple notes and messages on familiar situations, but lacks clarity and focus. Sentence structure lacks variety, but shows some control of basic grammar (e.g., present and past tense), and consistent use of punctuation (e.g., periods, capitalization). (p. 14)

Basic Reading and Writing (211–220 on CASAS)

Individual can read text on familiar subjects that have a simple and clear underlying structure (e.g., clear main idea, chronological order); can use context to determine meaning; can interpret actions required in specific written directions, can write simple paragraphs with main idea and supporting detail on familiar topics (e.g., daily activities, personal issues) by recombining learned vocabulary and structures; can self and peer edit for spelling and punctuation errors. (p. 15)

The *NRS Implementation Guidelines* document does not specify how or on what basis these level descriptors were made. It simply states that "the functional level descriptors describe what a learner entering that level can do in the areas of reading and writing, numeracy, speaking and listening and/or functional or workplace skills" (p. 13). The specific assessment instrument was left to the states, although the selected choice required approval by OVAE. States would be evaluated based on the "total number of learners who complete a level during the program," as well as by "the number who fail to complete a level and leave the program and the number who remain in the same level" (p. 19).

Discrepancies in the reported data can be significant. For example, in Connecticut's Annual Performance Report for 2000–2001, the targeted percentage of students that would progress to the Beginning Basic Literacy Level was 39% on CASAS. Based on the total numbers of enrollees, the state failed to reach its target, as only 17% reached the goal. Students, who left the program before a follow-up test could be administered, were an important variable in accounting for these low figures. Yet, based on "matched pairs," for students who remained in the program sufficiently long to take a posttest, the actual attainment for the same category was 71%. Although OVAE included an option for reporting matched pairs, its primary focus of measurement was total students based on initial enrollments. This had a conservative tendency for states to make purposely low target goals. Also, by placing the beginning level category of CASAS at 200, it made it exceedingly unlikely that students with pretests in the 170–190 ranges (many of the students in the NALS Level 1 category and those participating in community-based literacy programs) would make satisfactory progress based on the NRS standards. That put additional pressures on the states that used this assessment to keep goals low and to limit the number of the most basic beginning level students.

The NRS was designed to track outcomes of adult education students across a wide array of programs and agencies and to bring a sense of cohesiveness to the data consistent with the direction of national policy. Its stated purpose was "to establish . . . the measures, methods and reporting requirements, to ensure valid and reliable data, provide assistance to states in understanding these requirements, monitor the system to ensure that it is producing valid and reliable measures, report the data to federal agencies and decide on state incentive awards based on NRS data" (U.S. Department of Education, 2001, p. 31). Under its provisions, it was the responsibility of the states to implement federal guidelines and to provide resources, training, and ongoing support to local programs for data collection, and to provide funding and monitoring of programs. It was also the responsibility of the states to promote a continuous improvement process into state plans, based, in part, on student and program performance on the NRS measures. Local programs "are responsible for allocating sufficient resources to collect the NRS measures and reporting them according to state requirements" (p. 31).

Additional Components

In addition to assessing learning gains through prescribed levels, the NRS also seeks to measure self-identified student goals. Most goals are linked to the outcome areas defined by the NRS such as learning gains, employment, and obtaining a GED. Other goals, the *secondary measures*, are related to citizenship and personal achievements. In their totality, the stipulated goal categories reflect many of the seven outcome areas identified by the state directors of adult education in 1996 and the Condelli and Kutner (1997) study. The challenge for programs lies both in the time-consuming work of tracking goals, which include direct report, surveys, or phone calls of students who have left the program, and in facing the reality that goals may change or perhaps are not realizable within the annual time frame of the reporting system. Because, according to the regulations, it is incumbent to identify at least one goal accomplished within the program year, there may be a certain reluctance among program staff to check off more than the basic goal of *improve basic literacy skills* as discerned through standardized forms of measurement.

Within the restrictive milieu of the WIA/NRS, the ABE policy leadership was able to add increased focus on learning gains and family literacy through Title II. Without the initiative of the state directors, the NRS as developed likely would not have been enacted. However, given the temper of the times, the issue of performance-based accountability premised on the quest for comparability through measurable, uniform, and objective standards would have proven difficult, if not impossible to dodge. In accepting the post-1994 political reality of a conservative Congress, policy advocates argued that they preserved the adult education and literacy system, which, without their intense lobbying, quite likely would have been eliminated and subsumed within a workforce paradigm. Nonetheless, the reception of the WIA/NRS among the field, as discussed in chapter 5, was not particularly welcoming.

NLA Polemics: Criticism and Counterarguments

The role of performance-based accountability standards in mediating the tension between alternative assessment design and the quest for comparability through data aggregation is discussed in the next three chapters. Chapter 5 reviews field critiques of the NRS leveled largely by participants subscribed to the National Literacy Advocacy (NLA) electronic discussion list. The following discussion on direct and equitable access, literacy "levels," and the "power/knowledge nexus," gives a flavor of the range of field-based concerns that was aroused in response to the NRS.

DIRECT AND EQUITABLE ACCESS

Immediate Aftermath of the NRS

A major field concern was that the requirements of the NRS were so stringent that despite the language of "free and equitable access," the result was the effective elimination of large numbers of volunteer-driven community-based programs from participation in the federally funded program. Leslie McGinnis, who operated a volunteer tutoring program in Oakland, California, observed that none of her colleagues intended to apply for funding given the stipulations of the new legislation. Noting that she and her colleagues worked with adult students mostly at below fourth grade reading levels, the "hardest to serve," she argued that it was unrealistic to expect that they could demonstrate the expected gains of moving from one level to another on the NRS scales based on the state-mandated CASAS instrument (McGinnis, NLA, April 16, 1999).

McGinnis' colleague, Ruth Kohan, from San Jose, also noted that the new legislation would likely result in the exclusion of "most library and community-based literacy programs." Kohan explained that the 2 hours per week of instruction provided for students in her volunteer tutoring program did not provide sufficient instructional time to enable students to make the level of progress mandated by the legislation. In addition, Kohan pointed to the onerous nature of having to oversee such requirements with limited staff and volunteer tutors (Kohan, NLA, April 16, 1999). The capacity to administer pre- and posttesting to every student in the program for decentralized one-to-one tutoring programs was a major dilemma that faced both the LVA and LLA networks.

George Demetrion, at the time, an executive director to a small LVA affiliate in East Hartford, Connecticut, raised additional issues, challenging the assumption that "testing and outcome documentation" was needed on every student in order to determine *program* effectiveness. He pointed to an alternative framework in "multidimensional assessment processes," including the use of narrative information, and challenged the value of "micro-statistical analysis of insufficiently staffed and funded programs." The result, he argued, could only lead to "negative self-fulfilling prophecies" of program failure that NRS statistics were likely to confirm. Calling for a broader value system than "cost–benefit utilitarian analysis of social efficacy," Demetrion advocated for a policy orientation that connects literacy to the capacity of individuals to contribute to the strengthening of "mediating institutions" of the family, the workplace, and the community. This was where community-based adult literacy programs had their most significant current and potential impact, he argued, rather than with the "reductive" outcomes highlighted in the new legislation that "further marginalizes programs which work with lower-level readers" (Demetrion, NLA, April 19, 1999).

Kevin Smith, executive director of Literacy Volunteers of America–New York State, maintained that the most viable response to the legislation was not for volunteer literacy programs not to apply, but to submit an application and "honestly" identify the difficulties to the state funding agency in meeting the requirements. Even if the result was failure to achieve funding in any given cycle, by participating in the process, volunteer-based programs would be better positioned later "to negotiate changes" with the state funding agency, which would be more reflective of their needs. Smith pointed to the difference between forever being beyond the capacity of staff in volunteer literacy programs to collect all the data required by the legislation and difficulties merely due to lack of resources. Smith pointed to the reality that, regardless of the complexities, the volunteer literacy sector had no choice but to meet the requirements of the legislation if it was to survive at all in the new fiscal and political climate (Smith, NLA, April 19, 1999).

Then president of Literacy Volunteers of America Inc., Marsha Tait explained that "the Direct and Equitable Access provision" of the WIA/NRS legislation referred only to the "equalization of the *process*" (italics added) of funding accessibility for volunteer literacy programs. As Tait explained, "Congress intended to encourage, but not necessarily to compel, inclusive funding." Previous federal legislation had excluded, whether "deliberately or systematically" by design, the free-flowing participation of the volunteer literacy sector. She and her colleague Peter Waite, Tait's counterpart at Literacy Laubach Action, and others had worked diligently with the National Coalition of Literacy and the state directors of adult education to lobby for inclusive language in support of all ABE and adult literacy programs. Achieving even "the small victory" of having the Direct and Equitable clause inserted into the legislation was a major accomplishment that Tait insisted should not be taken lightly by the field. The new legislation both "encourages inclusive funding" and "imposes requirements for accountability and reporting that many programs may have difficulty meeting." Despite the problems, Tait encouraged programs that were "serious about delivering quality instruction through sound management and practices" and have the capacity to "prove it," to apply for federal funding.

Under Tait, Waite, Jon Randall, and others, the adult literacy leadership has labored persistently for years to achieve a degree of equity with the state directors of education. The result was inclusive language built into the new legislation along with increased credibility for the adult literacy sector. The challenge now, as Tait and Smith envisioned it, was for local programs to work within the existing framework and seek partnership with the state director of adult education. This included "ask[ing] for funding to build the infrastructure of a viable accountability system." As part of long-term relationship cementing, Tait also encouraged local program staff of volunteer literacy programs to "participate in the state's four or five year plan . . . participate on committees and participate in statewide efforts to advocate on behalf of literacy providers." In short, adult literacy programs were encouraged to seek the role of active partner with the ABE sector, working within the constraints and opportunities of the precarious, but hopefully emergent status of legitimacy the new situation offered. In the meantime, she and her colleagues would "keep hammering away in Washington on . . . [the] behalf" (Tait, NLA, April 25, 1999) of the adult literacy sector.

More Recent Discussions

For volunteer and community-based adult literacy programs that work with students below the GED preparation level, there has been no easy resolution of the issues highlighted in the April 1999 NLA discussion on direct and equitable access. The topic has continued to percolate on the list. For example, Nancy Hansen, of the Sioux Falls Area Literacy Council, in South Dakota, who works with low level reading adults, largely in one-to-one settings through volunteer tutors, noted that in a technical sense, her program was not barred from participating in the federally funded program. However, her agency had chosen not to participate because the required test for South Dakota, TABE, was not viewed as an adequate indicator of their students' learning progress.

Accountability, itself, was not the issue for Hansen, whose agency used other measures when reporting to other funders. Of concern was the requirement for all programs in the state to use TABE when their program had used Slossen and Dolch scores, which Hansen viewed as a more adequate measure of the progress of students in her agency. Of particular concern to Hansen about TABE was "the trauma of subjecting adult learners to a [timed] paper and pencil standardized test" (Hansen, NLA, February 25, 2003), which on her account emphasized student deficiencies rather than strengths. As Hansen viewed it, the required test was not only an inaccurate indicator of student progress. It adversely impacted on the self-esteem of students. Because Hansen and her director believed the requirements of the law violated the basic tenets of their program, the Sioux Falls Area Literacy Council viewed itself as effectively eliminated from participating in the federal program, notwithstanding the direct and equitable clause.

Not all practitioners agreed with Hansen's assessment. Steve Gerard, director of program services at Vermont Adult Learning located in East Montpelier, explained how his program was able to work within the framework of the law. Gerard was on the hot seat as the staff person required to implement the NRS mandated tests. Gerard's agency consists of six sites with instruction provided in one-to-one settings with full-time teachers and some volunteers. Most of the teachers embraced the participatory philosophy of adult literacy education and alternative modes of assessment that draw on narrative and self-report. Gerard noted that before the federal mandate, the agency lacked a standard way of measuring the efficacy of their various sites and the caliber of instruction provided by their teachers. "Discussions of best practices often became duels of the most moving anecdote" with argumentation particularly heated "when the state department of education was mentioned." In the new system, teachers were still able to use whatever measurement instruments they desired, but they also had to use the required instrument, TABE.

Gerard took an organized approach in implementing the mandate that included a "committee of teachers to monitor and direct the implementation of standardized testing." Gerard noted that teachers discovered that students were "not harmed or tortured" by the standardized testing. They were also surprised to learn that many students actually enjoy taking the tests and were interested in the results. Gerard did not seek to defend the scientific validity of standardized tests, although neither did he reject their utility as a diagnostic tool. Accepting political reality, he made a pragmatic adjustment that helped to secure funding and an effective site-based utilization of the required instrument. As Gerard explained:

> I am convinced that the TABE is just a tool, like a hammer or a structured exercise. A hammer can be used to kill and it can be used to build, but it is just a tool. When teachers use the TABE badly, students are hurt. When they use it well, students are strengthened. I think that early on, out of their frustration, anger and resentment, some of our teachers may have used the tests badly. However, they are professional enough that when they saw that using it badly hurt students, they quickly demanded that we show them how to use it better. Today, with the TABE being used with over 2000 students in our organization, I don't think students are being hurt or abused with the test. Mostly, they are being given more detailed information about their academic strengths and needs.

As Gerard concluded about the agency-wide implementation of TABE, "It's not nirvana, but it's not Armageddon either" (Gerard, NLA, February 26, 2003).

The appropriation of TABE by Gerard's agency represents a type of middle ground that program realists worked with in diverse ways, although not necessarily with the degree of subtlety that he described. Even so, the problems of implementation and the matter of whether to work within the new framework, or to opt out among community-based adult literacy providers, has remained a pressing issue. Although it is too early to evaluate long-term trends of participation in the federally funded ABE program, first year (FYI 2001) implementation statistics document that 2,673,692 students were enrolled, which compared to 2,891,895 for 2000. More significant is the declining trend for the preceding years from 2000 back to 1996 (see Table 5.1). The decline in the years 2001 and 2000 from the few previous years in California (Table 5.2) in ABE and ESL was especially dramatic in programs like those of McGinnis and Kohan, which provide community-based literacy and ESL services through the state's library system, where resistance to the NRS was particularly sharp.

The pre- and postfigures for the implementation of the NRS are subject to a variety of interpretations, including the possibility that the last 2 years are more accurate portrayals resulting from a more rigorous accountability system that the legislation demanded. The statistical data require a substantive analysis in their own right, and even with that, it would take more than 1 or 2 years of data of NRS implementation to document a trend.

At the least, they provide additional impressionistic evidence lending weight to the concern of critics that notwithstanding the direct and equita-

TABLE 5.1
Federally Administered Adult Education Enrollment

Year	Total Enrollment	ABE Enrollment	ESL Enrollment	ASE Enrollment
2001–2002	2,673,692	998,152	1,119,685	555,855
2000–2001	2,673,391	997,971	1,119,589	555,831
1999–2000	2,891,895	1,065,771	1,102,261	723,863
1998–1999	3,616,391	1,171,834	1,695,516	749,041
1997–1998	4,020,550	1,287,745	1,927,210	805,595
1996–1997	4,017,272	1,323,176	1,861,125	832,971

Note. Data from U.S. Department of Education, Office of Vocational and Adult Education, Division Of Adult Education and Literacy, March and June 2002.

TABLE 5.2
California-Administered Adult Education Enrollment

Year	Total Enrollment	ABE Enrollment	ESL Enrollment	ASE Enrollment
2001–2002	729,976	55,334	492,709	181,933
2000–2001	592,403	46,912	401,502	143,989
1999–2000	512,780	39,469	347,893	125,418
1998–1999	1,181,563	129,422	1,018,084	34,037
1997–1998	1,435,341	161,364	1,220,594	53,383

Note. Data from California Department of Education, Office of Adult Education. Retrieved from http://www.cde.ca.gov/adulteducation

ble clause, the requirements of the NRS contributed to declining, or at best, a stabilizing rather than expanding enrollment. The statistics markedly contrast with the number of adults in the United States identified as possessing relatively low levels of functional literacy, a figure that one influential study asserted hovers around 90 million (Kirsch, Jungleblut, Jenkins, & Kolstad, 1993).

The difficulties identified particularly among community-based adult literacy agencies in meeting the requirements of the NRS are several-fold. There are pragmatic problems of implementing a rigorous accountability system with limited fiscal and human resources and of administering pre- and postassessments of every student, especially in decentralized one-to-one tutoring programs. Other issues include the perceived inappropriateness of the assessment instrument both in terms of relevance to the focus of the instructional program and reliance on a scale of measurement that is not sufficiently calibrated to adequately determine small gains in progress.

Seeking system reform, Bingman (2000) observed, "Increased flexibility on the part of state and federal policy makers is needed so that locally developed processes of a wide variety of outcomes can count as measures for program accountability." Bingman noted that "while the national legislation focuses on the economic outcomes of adult education, learners have a variety of goals." Staff, therefore, would need to "have the ability to focus on these goals as well as the national mandate" (p. 6) and base selection of outcomes and modes of assessment that reflected the self-identified needs of the students. Such a shift would also have required a change in the law. Bingman and her colleagues at the Center for Literacy Studies, looked to EFF as a potentially workable framework to integrate students and policy sector needs at a system-wide level. However, given the political reality of the late 1990s, profound chasms remained as no general embrace of EFF was on the horizon.

NO LEVELS OUT THERE

Theoretical Overview

With his studies on literacy and the military and workplace, Sticht has been at the forefront of contextual-based approaches to adult literacy since the 1960s. In more recent times, he has linked contextual learning to any selected areas where students apply basic skill mastery to acquiring knowledge and information that they deem important. Sticht (1997a) built on this understanding in support of his *functional-context* thesis, wherein "literacy is developed while it is being applied" (p. 2). Cognitive advancement, on Sticht's interpretation, stems from an interactive learning process between social and cultural "symbols and symbol systems" (p. 2) and an internal processing system "inside the head" (p. 3). On Sticht's version of cultural assimilation, learning takes place through "information-processing" activities as the individual internalizes key social and cultural symbols and symbol systems deemed by the learner and some important segment of the social order as worthy of knowing.

Sticht pointed out the centrality of "*context* [italics in original] in learning new information and in transferring information already learned to new and different problems and situations" (p. 3). This capacity, according to Sticht, is the activity of learning itself. Notwithstanding his lineage to behaviorist psychology, Sticht took a constructivist approach to learning even as it is wedded to a stimulus–organism–response model through the imagery of an information-processing metaphor (Demetrion, 2001a). In demonstrating his lineage to the neo-Vygotskian school of psycho-socio mediation, Sticht (1997a) connected his functional-context thesis to such "concepts . . . as the social basis of cognition and literacy, constructivism, situated cognition, situated practice, contextual learning, anchored instruction, problem-based learning, cooperative learning, multiliteracies, and multiple modes of representation" (p. 7). From these theoretical premises, Sticht drew the following principles of learning (as quoted):

- Explain what students are to learn and why in such a way that they can always understand both the immediate and long term usefulness of the course content.
- Consider the old knowledge that students bring with them to the course, and build new knowledge on the basis of this old knowledge.
- Integrate instruction in reading, writing, arithmetic, and problem solving into academic or technical training programs as the content for the course poses requirements for information processing using these skills that many potential students may not possess; avoid decontextualized basic skills "remedial" programs.
- Derive objectives from careful analysis of the explicit and tacit knowledge and skill needed at home, community, academic, technical training, or employment context for which the learner is preparing.
- Use, to the extent possible, learning contexts, tasks, materials, and procedures taken from the future situation in which the learner will be functioning. (p. 3)

In short, Sticht did not separate mastering the basic language skills with their utilization in real-life contexts, although he recognized that those adults at the lower levels of reading proficiency require more attention to the former.

Sticht (1997b) further explained his theory in a *Focus on Basics* article. He argued that cognitive psychologists "have found that what people know about what they are reading greatly influences their ability to comprehend and learn from texts" (p. 7). Citing previous research, Sticht found that "young adults in a remedial reading program required 11th grade 'general reading' ability to comprehend with 70% accuracy if they lacked much knowledge relevant to what they were reading." Reversing this, "those with high amounts of knowledge about what they were reading were able to comprehend with 70% accuracy, with only sixth grade 'general reading' ability" (p. 7). On Sticht's interpretation, "general reading" levels neither correlate with knowledge that students gain through reading, nor with the ability of students to draw on print of various levels, based on their familiarity or lack thereof of the specific contexts of such materials.

Elsewhere, Sticht interpreted literacy "as a psychological construct," which "cannot be directly 'described'" (Sticht, NLA, November 15, 1999) in general terms, but only within the context of its specific uses. This did not rule out quantitative modes of assessment based on standardized testing scores, but did require that such instruments be tightly calibrated to the content of instruction in order to be scientifically valid. Even the broader problem of data correlation of large numbers of students, programs, and diverse assessment instruments was not ruled out as scientifically valid in principle, but the matter of correlation posed severe problems that in practice have not been resolved in the arena of adult literacy accountability instrumentalities. These issues were at the core of Sticht's critique of the NRS, which he communicated in some highly polemical formats on the NLA.

Pressing the Envelope on the NLA

In a message titled *Levels Metaphor*, Sticht (NLA, November 14, 1999) pointed to the widespread use of levels as a metaphor "in all education, including adult literacy." In this message, he specifically referred to the National and International Adult Literacy Surveys (NALS/IALS) in observing that the five levels of competency identified in the surveys represented a synthetic correlation of prose, document, and quantitative scales. People were assigned specific levels in which "it was strongly implied that the person could not perform tasks [of a general nature] above the assigned level." Sticht rejected this assumption on the grounds that people learn in highly specific ways that the NALS/ IALS scales did not adequately take into account.

As Sticht explained, "The fact [is] . . . that on the NALS Document scale, a person who scored at the average for literacy Level 1 could perform almost half the tasks at Level 2, a quarter of the tasks at Level 3, one out of five at Level 4 and even one in six at the highest level, Level 5." These adults, observed Sticht, "might not take well to the idea that their literacy level was fixed at some static, 'lower level.' " According to Sticht's research, many individuals can function quite well at tasks clearly above their assumed reading level when the content is based on what they do know. Although limits are obviously evident, interest, need, and motivation play important roles in the capacity of adults to work with texts of various levels of reading difficulty. On Sticht's interpretation, to be scientifically valid, a quantitative metaphor based on numbered score scale would somehow have to account for these personal variations.

The dilemma over levels, at least as characterized in the NALS/IALS scales and the NRS levels, raised for Sticht the issue "of just how literacy ability should be represented." As he put it, is literacy:

> well represented as "levels," like an onion with a core and successive layers of growth out to some current "level?" Or perhaps as "levels" in geological strata? Or would it be more useful to think in terms of networks of specialized domains of knowledge interrelated by the use of common vocabulary words . . . and a limited set of syntactical rules for selecting and sequencing parts of

words into new words . . . or words into sentences. In this type of representation, growth in any amount in any direction in the knowledge network would count as improvement for accountability purposes.

Here, Sticht was making a strong case that the "levels metaphor" is skewed in its capacity as an instrument of measurement because (a) literacy is a construct comprised of various definitions, and (b) the complexity of personal variables in any practical sense confounds the likelihood of devising accurate scales.

In a follow-up posting titled *No Levels Out There*, Sticht (NLA, November 15, 1999) continued to press against the levels metaphor, arguing that "there are no 'literacy levels' to be 'described.'" Instead, and in accordance with the assumptions that ground the alternative assessment movement as well as his functional-context theory, Sticht claimed that "there are various ways of conceptualizing the nature of literacy and different procedures of measurement that can lead to the construction of alternative representations of adult literacy in society." The problem with such scales as NALS or assessment instruments like CASAS is that they conflate "everyday literacy tasks" with "other abilities, such as problem solving, reasoning, language comprehension, vocabulary knowledge, management of test-taking anxiety, interpersonal skills, or some complex, interactive combination of all these or whatever." Underlying this conflation is a lack "of a clearly specified theory of 'literacy' as a psychological construct" that should, on Sticht's interpretation, ground any assessment process that seeks to be valid. Without a commonly agreed definition, designing accurate scales was beside the point. As Sticht put it in his critique of the NRS:

> If government contracting agencies cannot inform adult literacy education programs with some degree of precision about what it is they should be teaching based on the types of measurements the government develops or otherwise promotes to construct particular representations of adults' literacy abilities, should these same government agencies then turn around and use performance on such measures to give or withhold funding for programs that fail to teach and improve whatever it is that the tests measure? (Sticht, NLA, November 15, 1999)

Sticht and other critics argued that the general levels constructed in NRS that allow reporting from a variety of approved standardized tests are not sufficiently correlated with each other to demonstrate "comparability." One matter is that the approved instruments measure different things. For example, CASAS is a competency-based assessment designed to measure life skills and is not designed as a tight measurement of literacy levels. Whereas TABE measures reading levels, its content is not necessarily calibrated to the contextual focus of programs that utilize this instrument.

Moreover, in "translating" both to NRS levels, the federal government had not undertaken the work of calibrating CASAS and TABE to each other in the formation of a common scale system. In short, Sticht and others argued that the goal of correlation that drove federal policy had not been achieved by the NRS.

A final note is Sticht's (NLA, June 3, 2000) "informal research" in which he asked "state directors, program administrators and teachers in many states" to comment on the utility of "using a common set of outcome measures and a uniform data collection system [as the basis to] . . . measure and document learner outcomes." As Sticht described it, those with whom he spoke did not have "a clue about what this is supposed to mean with respect to what is being taught in classes." In pointing to "a [widespread] lack of understanding of what these tests measure," Sticht reasoned that the field was as similarly confused as he was about the stated purposes of the NRS. By articulating the problems he and others observed about the NRS through the medium of the NLA, Sticht sought a public forum to give voice to a wide set of concerns as expressed by practitioners, administrators, and researchers. Referring to the political realities of the federal legislation, Sticht observed that "despite all these negative feelings about the assessment of learning outcomes in the NRS, states are moving right along and mostly arbitrarily using whatever tests they choose to report learning, even when they know tests are not valid indicators of what students are learning."

In his survey, Sticht noted that no ABE personnel at the state divisions of adult education had any inkling of how the U.S. Department of Adult Education and Literacy (DAEL) would "combine [the highly disparate] state data into a national database [in] describing [uniform] outcomes for adult education." Flawed in its capacity to achieve its stated purpose of data comparability, Sticht questioned the validity of the NRS that was only able to rely on a "patchwork of measures . . . for indicating national advancements in adult education and literacy." In his field survey, he found "no one [who] was able to state what the goals for the federal department of OVAE/DAEL are." He concluded that "the state goals are whatever the states submit that the federal government will accept." Sticht also wondered what mechanisms were set up, if any, to assess whether "OVAE/DAEL is reaching its goals and is doing its job well or not." In short, Sticht questioned whether the NRS was based on sound research, theory, and practice. He concluded that the evidence pointed to the negative and ended his message with the following caustic observation:

> In general, then, in the various states where I have been, it seems like people are simply rolling over and going along with whatever the NRS says to do, not because they think this will help them serve their students better, but because they hope to keep their funding by going along with the reporting requirements. Some states have asked for money to do the assessments. Some states

appear to be setting their yearly goals under the five year planning at very conservative levels compared to what they seem to be accomplishing up to now. The federal government seems to be working interactively with states to get a five year plan that can satisfy the mandates of the WIA and allow OVAE/DAEL to show that it is meeting its performance goals under the Government Performance and Results Act. Like the rest of the AELS, federal agencies want to keep their funding, too! (Sticht, NLA, June 3, 2000)

Through both his formal publications and more populist NLA postings, Sticht mounted a substantial critique of the NRS on the grounds that it was not appropriately designed to accomplish its stated purposes. The result, he reasoned, has had a deleterious effect on the U.S. adult education and literacy (AELS) system. In principle, Sticht did not dismiss the value of standardization and the possibility of comparability on scientific grounds if the means are appropriately developed that can stand up to rigorous design. Nonetheless his stronger point in relation to the NRS is that there are no current models available to draw on and little on the near-term horizon in the development of appropriate instruments that would adequately resolve the issue of adult literacy assessment accountability on rigorous scientific grounds that could meet the standard of comparability.

PROBING THE POWER/KNOWLEDGE NEXUS

An Overview

Between September and December 1999, the NRS was hotly debated on the NLA. The first two of Sticht's posts, identified in the previous section, were part of those broader discussions. Additional criticism of the NRS ranged widely. Some pointed to the ironic effect of fostering greater "equal access" by imposing unmanageable requirements on understaffed, underfunded programs. Many agencies that previously obtained federal grants did not even apply for funding under the NRS mandate. Others reflected on the narrow, pedagogical focus fostered by the NRS. And, others still emphasized the limited epistemological perspectives based in what they perceived as the behaviorist and positivist theoretical precepts implicit in the NRS.

Those who supported the NRS did so primarily on pragmatic grounds. They argued that the U.S. Congress was on the verge of eliminating adult education as a distinctive, funded entity. Although such consolidation with workforce training did in fact take place with the WIA, as a result of Title II, the ABE/adult literacy policy leadership was able to maintain at least some focus on adult education as a distinctive entity in its own right.

As explained by Massachusetts State Director Robert Bickerton (NLA, September 8, 1999):

> with much encouragement and prodding by many in the field, they [Congress] have created a second "optional" list of measures that restore the depth and breadth of our work, including measures related to family, community and life long learning related purposes/goals. OUR challenge is to get as many states as possible to meaningfully sign on to these broader purposes—giving them EQUAL WEIGHT as those referred to as "core measures."

As defenders argued, without an accountability system in sync with the Government Performance and Results Act, any prospects of ongoing policy legitimization and stable funding streams at the federal level would be put in jeopardy. By having the opportunity to report *secondary outcomes* through the NRS, the field had additional opportunities to publicly identify and legitimize their work for policy purposes. Critics countered, arguing that there was little point to secondary measures if they do not count for reporting purposes. Hard-pressed practitioners argued that they simply added an extra burden to their already overloaded plates.

The objective of this section is to review how practitioners grappled with what they viewed as the conflicting paradigms of power and knowledge construction embedded within the already constructed policy as reflected in the debates over the NRS. At its center was a defense and critique of "positivism." As explained by Mertens (1998), "The underlying assumptions of positivism include the belief that the social world can be studied in the same way as the natural world, that there is a method for studying the social world that is value-free, and that explanations of a causal nature can be provided" (p. 7). Mertens noted that this early view of positivism was replaced by a more sophisticated neopositivism. This latter school exhibits a common adherence to the earlier assumption that objective reality exists, but in the second view, there is more of an acknowledgment that "it can be known only imperfectly," which can only be discovered "within a certain realm of probability" (p. 9).

In broad terms, both positivism and neopositivism represent a common outlook based on the quest for sure knowledge, the attainment of objectivity unclouded by human interpretation at least as an ideal, dispassionate neutrality, and reliance on quantitative data as the primary source of valid information. As Mertens noted, this research tradition sharply contrasts with other perspectives that emphasize the social construction of knowledge, the inescapability of interpretation based on varying points of reference, and qualitative sources and analysis of data. A discussion of these divergent research traditions takes place in chapter 9. The focus in the following argument is on the symbolization of the term *positivism* as a reflection of political discourse of a highly contentious nature as perceived by the participants.

The discussion had its roots in a posting by Sticht, in which he reprised his 1997 message on metaphors. There, he described the revolutionary metaphor in which "the Revolutionary Leader (Liberator) is to the Oppressed as the Adult Literacy Educator is to the Learners" (Sticht, NLA, October 2, 1999).

Coleman Versus Muro

Preston Coleman (NLA, October 18, 1999), a conservative from the University of Georgia, acknowledged the "rich tradition linking adult education with the Left," although he challenged the Revolutionary Metaphor as not particularly useful among "those who take public money." He compared Left-oriented educators "who would use the classroom as a rostrum from which to air their political views" as on the same par as those who use their podiums to espouse religious views. On Coleman's view, the publicly supported classroom should not be the "battlefield on which to fight cultural wars" as educators should stick to the more commonplace task of teaching.

In that same message, Colemen defended the "quaint virtues" of positivism, such as the "humble striving towards objectivity, even in the face of the uncertainty that we're incapable of being truly objective." Coleman acknowledged "valid critiques of positivism coming out of the Left," but was concerned with "throw[ing] the baby out with the bathwater." When it came to public funding and accountability, he argued, "positivism is still the dominant paradigm . . . for which the Left ought to be grateful." Coleman challenged Left educators to secure their own funding through "labor unions, liberal churches, or private advocacy groups." That would free them to "use whatever qualitative methods they wished to measure effectiveness." However, "with federal administration comes standardization, consensus, and perhaps mediocrity." Coleman issued a final goading point that "we'll all just have to go on thanking the powers that be for the money they allow to trickle down to adult ed, even as we spend precious bits of scarce resources 'proving' (sort of) that we're doing what we've been doing all along—empowering adults to learn and think for themselves" (Coleman, NLA, October 18, 1999).

Andres Muro, a Freirian attuned ESL educator from El Paso, Texas, challenged Coleman's pitting of positivism "in opposition to the [L]eft," which he viewed as a "false dichotomy." Instead, Muro argued "the Left, the Right and the Center have embraced and rejected positivism at different times in history" (Muro, NLA, October 19, 1999). Muro observed that the Frankfort School of Social Research critiqued the positivist tradition of classical Marxist scholarship in its ascribing direct correlations between economics, social organization, and power distribution. Muro also noted that "popular education movements have challenged traditional Marxism for its rigidity in examining culture in a historical context." On the other side of the coin, Muro identified the Religious Right as drawing on epistemologies that are far from rigorously empirical in the positivistic sense. According to the crux of Muro's (NLA, October 19, 1999) argument, "There is no apolitical educational model. The purpose of an educational system is to transmit culture from one generation to another. This is a very political act. Those in power determine what is transmitted and there is always a contest for power. Philosophies, such as positivism, have been used to defend or challenge political ideologies throughout history." Coleman agreed with much of Muro's argument, but each drew fundamentally different implications for educational praxis and the sources of political legitimacy.

Coleman Versus King

Catherine King (NLA, October 20, 1999), a civic republican constitutionalist from California, also took issue with Coleman. First, she challenged the notion that even as an ideal, positivism's association with the " 'blank slate' " vision of " 'scientific' purity," wherein the observer does not affect that which is observed, is flawed. The critical task of education is "in finding out what those presuppositions are and choosing which one[s] make sense to us, and answer the most questions for us." Hence, interpretation and value judgment are inescapable.

For King, positivism as a self-evident epistemology, at least as embedded within the operative assumptions of the NRS, had the adverse impact of "de-centering . . . the fullness of the student–teacher relationship," in what she depicted as "an over-emphasis on flat accountability, in meaningless quantification, and in naïve, indiscriminate standardization [which] . . . ignore[s] in principle the things that keep a culture sane." Like Coleman, King was opposed to the educational goals of the Religious Right in its tendency to impose theocracy on the body politic. Nonetheless, she favorably viewed its critique of positivist reductionism, as "rightly responding to . . . [the] desiccation of a full education on moral grounds." On this, she sought to turn Coleman's argument on its head in linking public education to the realm of values.

King also critiqued Coleman for his conflation of a critical perspective with the Revolutionary Metaphor. Like Muro, King assumed an ineradicable connection between education and political culture. Unlike Muro's affinity to the "oppositional" viewpoint, King sought to ground public education in the *civic republican* principles of the U.S. political tradition. A fuller discussion of King's views on democracy follows in chapter 11. Her argument is that the most fundamental root for a politics of literacy stems nei-

ther from Coleman's structural-functional legitimization of the status quo,
nor in Muro's call for a pedagogy of the oppressed, which according to
King's view may be the *fruit* of democracy but not its branch. For her, the
primary purpose of public schooling at any level is to educate citizens in order to strengthen the nation's democratic heritage based on its underlying
taproot in popular sovereignty and representative government.

King drew on this understanding of the politics of literacy both from the
general principles of democracy inherent within the political culture of the
United States and the specific "writings surrounding our Constitution." Her
criticism of positivism stemmed, in part, from the barriers it inhibits in allowing such a value-laden understanding of education to flourish. As she
expressed it, "How is a democracy's educational institution NOT in violation of the democratic mandate when" federal policy is focused "on anything less, even if we cannot get full 'accountability' by 'bean counters?' "
King argued the federal government would be better oriented in "developing policies to promote" the expansion of the democratic potency of citizens "instead of throwing up barriers to it." Reconstructing Coleman's position, King argued that it is for such purposes that "public money" should be
allocated, not as a hand-out, but in service to the public good. As King argued, that is because the strength of the republic depended in no small
measure on the civic and moral education of the nation's adult citizens.

The third critique issued by King centered on the importance of "remote" development, where "people learn much more and deeper than
merely the topical or 'proximate' thing at issue." In contributing both to
the lives of individual students and to the long-range vitality of the republic
in the education of citizens, King noted that such distal learning is a critically overlooked factor in the current policy orientation and "grates against
the reality of what adult education is and means" (King, NLA, October 20,
1999). "Neither standardization nor accountability ... are intrinsically
wrong," she noted. It is when they block out other modalities of evaluating
learning that they become problematic. It was concerns such as these that
King leveled at Coleman's support of the "quaint virtues" of positivism.

Coleman Versus Demetrion

George Demetrion (NLA, October 19, 1999) resonated with the viewpoints
of Muro and King. He critiqued Coleman for only making a passing reference to the Leftist intellectuals from the Frankfort School of Social Research
without an accounting of the substance of their critique of capitalism.
Whereas Coleman referred to "social science," Demetrion pointed to "social
philosophy" as a broader intellectual framework to ground educational
scholarship, in contrasting the "positivistic mindset" that his interlocutor defended. Demetrion pointed to the ideological function of critical theory in

defining the status quo as "socially constructed rather than naturally given," and therefore susceptible to radical critique and potential reconstruction. Drawing on the social scientist Polkinghorne (1983), Demetrion identified a number of social theories such as hermeneutics, pragmatism, phenomenology, and narratology, grounded in the *interpretive sciences*. These theoretical perspectives, he argued, and other schools of thought (e.g., feminism, critical theory, multiculturalism, and postmodernism) provide intellectual, cultural, and sociopolitical resources for interpreting social reality differently from frames of references embodied in the positivist research tradition (Giroux, 1995; Sica, 1998).

Demetrion (NLA, October 19, 1999) drew on Coleman's "baby and bathwater" analogy in challenging the positivist pathway as the surest means of moving toward the *ideal* of "objectivity." Coleman claimed that the "baby" was the quest for objectivity. Demetrion argued that the "baby" was "critical thought . . . struggled for through a range of discourses and paradigmatic assumptions that need to be contested through the fabric of our society, culture, and politics."

Demetrion also responded to Coleman's political argument, claiming adherence to the pragmatic tradition of John Dewey, which he contrasted with the critical pedagogy of Freire and Henry Giroux. Demetrion argued "that liberal democratic capitalism" represented what Freire referred to as the "limit-situation" of the political culture of the United States through which adult literacy would have to locate itself. On this point, both he and Coleman acknowledged democratic capitalism as the only viable grounding point to situate a U.S.-based politics of literacy. Yet, each drew different implications over the potential impact of reformist energies that could be unleashed from this common reference point. Demetrion argued that the boundaries of such a limit-situation are more porous than what Coleman intimated and contain emancipatory potential of an undetermined order. Although both democracy and capitalism are active forces striving for hegemony in the political culture, Demetrion maintained that, in principle, there is nothing predetermined that necessarily puts capitalism in the lead position.

Coleman (NLA, October 21, 1999) reiterated his main point that public money demands accountability and that for such "public accountability, there is no substitute for empirical, quantitative, as-close-as-we-can-get-to-objective methods." Colemen also objected to "theory for theories sake, especially when it masks as revolutionary activity," noting the " 'Revolutionary metaphor' " was "a bit too Romantic to be useful in this debate." Coleman closed by describing himself "as a conservative walking target in the left-dominated academy."

In a follow-up, Demetrion (NLA, October 23, 1999) contended that the issues identified in this debate went "to the heart of what literacy and democracy are about at the dawn of the new millennium." He found it interesting that Colemen acknowledged the legitimacy of qualitative methods and pointed out that beyond methodology, epistemology is the more fundamental issue. Also "disconcerting" was Coleman's "cloister[ing of] such thought to the university," which divorces theoretical analysis from "policy formation and governing." For Demetrion, this established a schism "between the life of the mind and the world of action," a false polarity that has a legitimizing function of reifying the status quo through the tenets of positivism linked to a "commonsense" interpretation of "reality" that marginalizes other perceptions.

Demetrion pushed on what he viewed as the ideological precepts that underlay the hegemony of positivism when it serves as a universal discourse underlying policy. Specifically, he challenged Coleman's assumption that positivism provides the closest means possible of moving toward "objective" truth. Demetrion also refuted the notion that more qualitative approaches to knowledge construction lead to anarchy, revolution, or subjectivity. Instead, he made the case for a Deweyan (1938/1991; Burke, 1994; Demetrion, 2000c) sense of logic based on " 'warrantable assertions' that emerge in moving from problems identified to problems resolved, worked out within the context of the community of inquirers involved in any particular issue or problem." Demetrion argued that Dewey, as well as the positivists, "embraced a scientific methodology." But, Dewey's logic was linked "to an existential understanding of human experience" that requires a naturalistic form of inquiry.

Demetrion pressed on what he viewed as Coleman's conflation of "critical literacy" with revolutionary rhetoric. He pointed to the "various definitions" of critical literacy and the preeminent figure of Freire, as well as of Giroux and Ira Shor, all of whom embrace the value of "reading the word in order to read the world." Demetrion acknowledged the "political connotations associated with 'critical literacy,' " but pointed out as well that prevailing notions of functional literacy were also socially constructed on "the normative acceptance of the basic social, cultural, economic, and political patterns of our society." He concluded by calling for an approach to assessment that draws on "in-depth ethnographic insight," which would necessitate an acceptance of sampling and multimeasures for which John Comings, director of the National Center for the Study of Adult Learning and Literacy (NCSALL), advocated. Underlying the necessity for "a broader diversity of methodologies" is a need for:

> a more pluralistic embrace of diverse epistemologies to better depict the broad range of experience and knowledge that adult learners both possess and what they attain by participating in adult literacy programs. [Beyond methodology, s]uch diversity is at the heart of establishing a more enlight-

ened democratic political culture, which if not an objective of Washington, D.C. certainly should be. (Demetrion, NLA, October 23, 1999)

Demetrion argued that any reform impetus to substantially change federal policy for the purposes of adult literacy and corresponding methodologies of assessment have "to come from the field." However, such efforts would need to seem sufficiently plausible in order to move beyond the "howling in the wilderness" that would appeal to only a few. Demetrion hoped, but doubted, that the "D.C. crowd" was paying attention and such discourse from the margins would not be dismissed as idle " 'chatter' and 'complaints' from the [L]eft that don't really count in the 'hard' policy perspective of federal funding."

CONCLUDING REMARKS

The three issues brought out in this chapter at the ground of practice, technical research, and politico-educational theory, span a wide range of concerns in their critique of the WIA/NRS legislation. It is not my intent here to provide a systematic analysis of these or other criticisms of the NRS. My purpose is historical in illuminating something of the politics of adult literacy as played out in the United States at the end of the 20th century. Chapters 4 and 5 together seek to underline the divergent perspectives through which the policy sector and a significant aspect of the field differed when survival pragmatics and issues of principles were sharply pitted against each other.

What I have attempted to illustrate is the reasoning operating through the various positions held in both of these chapters on the grounds that they are important to an understanding of the politics of literacy in the late 1990s. I am also assuming that substantial resolution of the tensions that give shape to the contested ground toward a field reconstruction of the politics of adult literacy will need to work through the various positions highlighted in these chapters.

As exemplified in Gerard's Vermont agency, as well as the commentary by Smith and Tait on direct and equitable access, there was considerable attempt throughout the field to find various mediating positions amidst the tensions. Although they brooked no simple resolutions given its status in law, the state and municipal-based ABE programs, in particular, could not ignore the NRS. Still, many community-based adult literacy agencies opted out of the federal funding loop, which exacerbated the cleavage between that sector and their ABE counterparts. Sticht's technical appraisal challenging the validity of the new legislation on the grounds of science, combined with a sharp politico-pedagogical critique of the WIA/NRS, as illustrated in the last section, further heightened the ideological splits between the ABE policy sector and the advocates of the participatory literacy movement and the New Literacy Studies. These matters are revisited in the last three chapters of the book via a focal point on research traditions and political culture. In the next three chapters, I review efforts, pervasive throughout the 1990s, to institute performance-based accountability within the ABE/adult literacy sector as a mediating perspective, which found its capstone in EFF.

Defining Outcomes and Impacts of Adult Literacy Education: Enduring Problems and Conflicting Perspectives

> *Fate is fulfilled in the revelation of conflicting norms against which the identities of the participants shatter, unless they are able to summon up the strength to win back their freedom by shattering the mythical power of fate through the formation of new identities.*
>
> —Habermas (1975, p. 2)

Performance-based accountability in adult basic education had its roots in the K–12 "world class" standards movement, a major reform initiative that grew out of the challenges laid out in *A Nation at Risk*. As Merrifield and others pointed out, those same forces that influenced the governors and the federal government under the senior Bush administration, also gave shape to the standards movement in ABE.

Chapters 1 and 4 provided an overview of the struggle during the 1990s to shape standards by the policy leadership sector in an effort to outflank the workplace emphasis of federal policy while remaining policy realistic. Although they were not the standards envisioned by many within the field, the National Reporting System was a product of outcome-based education. In the 1990s, outcome-based education, reflecting various points of view, was a dominant theme for policy-based educational initiatives.

It is impossible to separate the standards movement in ABE from the development of the National Institute for Literacy's (NIFL) Equipped For the Future (EFF) project, the focus of chapters 7 and 8. Both had their more immediate origins in National Educational Goal 6 in linking adult literacy with the "knowledge and skills necessary to compete in a global economy" and in "exercising the rights and responsibilities of citizenship" (National Educational Goals: Goal 6).

ABE standard bearers at NIFL, under the leadership of Sondra Stein, were driven by a progressive pedagogy and politics of literacy, modulated by the neoliberalism of the early Clinton era. In their mediating vision, they sought to cut a discerning path between the broad and elusive aspirations of the alternative assessment movement and the quest for data comparability based on the aggregation of standardized assessment instruments. In the mediating vision, what counted were outcomes (rather than beliefs or perceptions) subject to quantification and precise measurability, but grounded in what adult literacy students sought to learn in terms of basic skills and application to the critical social areas of their lives, at work, home, or the broader community.

The standards movement in ABE received a push in 1993 when Congress instructed NIFL to evaluate the nation's progress toward fulfilling Goal 6 (Merrifield, 2000, p. 5; Stein, 1997, p. 3). The dilemma facing NIFL and the National Educational Goals Panel that jointly responded to the mandate of "arriv[ing] at a measurable definition of this goal" (Stein, 1995, p. 5) was the lack of a common framework regarding the purposes of the adult education system. NIFL researchers viewed Goal 6 as "broad and rhetorical," but not well grounded at the curriculum development and program implementation levels. Without a more specific system or framework in place there was no substantive "agreement [in place] on what achievement of this goal would look like." For Stein (1997), the general aspirations embedded in Goal 6 were an insufficient basis to establish "measurable goals for our public educational system" (p. 3).

This lack of a common framework to shape a coherent federal policy was troubling, observed Stein, given both the importance of adult literacy and persisting problems of funding, resources, and legitimacy. Quandaries included lack of retention among students, consequently, limited learning gains, lack of a coherent curriculum, minimal financial resources, and full-time, professional teachers (p. 4). Stein insisted a "customer-driven vision" was essential in order "to assure that the results the system does produce make a real difference in people's lives" (p. 5). Only on this basis, she argued, could an adequate accountability system be devised, without which it would be impossible to respond to Congress' query.

As is discussed in the next chapter, Merrifield (2000) viewed the EFF project as a possible way out of what she sensed as the hopeless morass of an infinitely fragmented system, already resource-marginalized, that would become even more so if some consensus toward a coherent national purpose could not be found. The critical issue of whether or not a consensus would be satisfactorily negotiated that respects learner's goals and derivative beliefs (Lytle, 1991) and also meets policy needs that is both sufficiently rich to capture the subtleties of learning and sufficiently rigorous to meet data aggregation and correlational needs remained unresolved throughout the 1990s.

STANDARD FOR ADULT LITERACY:
FOCAL POINTS FOR DEBATE

In a National Center on Adult Literacy (NCAL) technical report on standards, Stites, Foley, and Wagner (1995) sought "to create a measure of coherence out of a highly fragmented discourse" (p. 1). The authors pointed to an underlying source of the tension. They noted, on the one hand, that "the general question of whether or not there will be standards for adult literacy will be decided in the political arena." They pressed the notion, on the other hand, that any resolution "will be fruitful only to the extent that they are guided by a clear vision of the technical issues raised by the design and implementation of various forms of standards" (p. 1). Whereas, in theory, these tensions might be resolvable on the grounds that policy and pedagogy could be closely aligned, the NCAL report pointed to persisting conflict and to the likely continuation of "acrimonious debate" (p. 18) as witnessed, later in the decade, over the development of, and dispute over, the National Reporting System.

By the mid-1990s, the issue was no longer whether or not there would be standards for the federally funded adult education program, but who would set them and for what purposes. Different perceptions about the value and purposes of adult literacy, both among those close to and those more distanced from the immediate field of practice, were at the center of what those seeking policy coherency referred to as fragmentation. The authors of the NCAL report pointed out that business and government represent the dominant constituency pushing the standards movement toward clear, "commonsense" outcomes linked directly to measurable learning gains, credentials, and economic impact.

They pointed to "a need to broaden participation in adult literacy standard setting," including a call "for the inclusion of the voices and interest of adult educators in the standards debate" (p. 2), as well as those of students. Without their participation, the process of standards setting could only be established by the business and political sectors, which viewed adult literacy as a subset to their broader institutional interests. In order to set standards on field-based criteria, adult literacy educators, administrators, and students would need to become directly involved. Yet, in so doing, they would expand potential points of conflict and jeopardize the prospect of broad, consensus-based standards from emerging.

The authors hoped that probing dialogue could serve "as starting points for the development of new forms of standards to suit the particular quality and accountability of the needs of the field" (p. 2). At the same time, they noted the difficulty of establishing consensus in working out the complex issues of defining legitimacy in standards setting that could appeal to practitioners, researchers, and policy advocates. Wide agreement would be needed on the direction of policy formation, a common understanding of the components of sound practice, and an acceptable scholarly framework in setting research paradigms in determining the intellectual legitimacy of the emerging standards. It was not simply a matter of technical proficiency in the development of rigorous standards, but the issue of values clarification and resolution in defining the purpose and meaning of adult literacy education. As the authors understated it, "the extent to which content, performance, OTL [Opportunity-to Learn], or other forms of standards for adult literacy are possible or desirable is not yet clear" (p. 7). More to the point, there was no readily available framework to even begin the arduous work of crafting a unified vision. An examination of the critical tensions embedded in the quest to establish content, performance, and opportunity-to-learn (OTL) standards in adult literacy will illuminate some of the major tensions the field faced in the mid-1990s.

Content Standards

In the quest for technical proficiency, *content* standards set the platform for measuring levels of performance. Determining legitimate knowledge for any field is not necessarily an easy matter as criteria change and canonical traditions invariably influence selection. In addition, the chosen content not only influences the substance of the subject matter, but often the means of measurement. For example, a transactional theory of learning had underlain the pedagogical presuppositions of the *Standards for the Assessment of Reading and Writing* (1994), developed jointly by the International Reading Association (IRA) and National Council of Teachers of English (NCTE). Drawing on disciplines of sociolinguistics, ethnography, and collaborative education theory, the IRA/NCTE standards were premised on an inquiry mode of learning.

On this interpretation of the language arts, the central classroom activity does not reside in the mastery of a given set of texts or preestablished subject matter. The focus is on the quality of engagement between readers and texts, invariably sifted through the social context of the classroom, the school, and the broader sociocultural matrix in which the lives of students and teachers are embedded. Based on this premise, content is a stimulus. In Dewey's (1916) words, content "has the office of a middleman" (p. 188) for engaging students in the exercise of critical investigation. In a curriculum that places inquiry at the center of the learning process, assessment requires a creative synthesis of multidimensional indicators that takes the various contexts that give shape to learning into account. The evaluative process is invariably subjective and susceptible to multiple interpretations, although disciplinary and pedagogical traditions provide a stabilizing factor.

The contrast with a more traditional language arts curriculum is striking, where competence is defined by the attainment of objective knowledge, based on a preestablished curriculum, whether of the basic skills of reading, writing, comprehension, and critical thinking or in the mastery of a selective body or canon of literature. Content viewed from this vantage point can be measured through rigorously designed standardized tests, along with objectively scored essay questions, based on well-constructed rubrics (Mislevy & Knowles, 2002, pp. 36–49).

In such fields as the language arts, history and civics, and even mathematics, the issue of content and means of measurement was a source of significant tension in K–12 standards movement throughout the 1990s. Unless the matter of legitimate content was resolved, either on the grounds of research, pedagogy, best practices, or on the playing field of politics, or through some combination that could lend a reasonable consensus, conflicting perspectives over measurability as well as curricular focus could only be the result.

Stites, Foley, and Wagner noted that determining the content of adult literacy education is particularly difficult, given the many variables that need to be considered. The issue of definition is problematic, the authors argued, even when sifting through various uses of the term *functional literacy*. Those who interpreted this concept broadly in the early 1990s considered it "in terms of the print demands of occupational, civic, community, and personal functioning" (Venesky, 1990, p. 7). Much of the business and policy sector linked the concept of functional literacy more exclusively with the idea of effective workplace functioning. It is not simply that the standards would be different based on these two interpretations of "functional literacy," which a pluralistic system might accommodate. The more pressing issue is that in the struggle over legitimacy and funding, competition amidst these divergent views is a pervasive political reality in the determination of which set of content standards will prevail in the policy sector. Without resolution of the content of adult literacy, the authors argued any application of performance measurements would be invalid on technical grounds.

The authors pointed to another problem: that of drawing on the National Adult Literacy Survey (NALS) as a basis to measure the broad goals of literacy identified in National Educational Goal 6. The problem was in using the criteria of increasing "the percentage of adults aged 16 and over who score at or above Level 3 in prose literacy on the National Adult Literacy Survey" (cited on p. 5), as an indicator to measure progress of adults gaining the capacity "to compete in a global economy and [in] exercis[ing] the rights and responsibilities of citizenship" (National Educational Goal 6). This convergence may have made sense politically in that both NALS and the National Educational Goals were widely visible initiatives on the national scene, but from a technical perspective the indicator was not correlated with what it was purported to measure. Consequently, the standard of measurement was invalid on scientific grounds.

Stites et al. (1995) also noted how different definitions of literacy further added to the complexities of establishing commonly agreed-to content standards. Definitions vary greatly, depending on whether literacy is viewed as a basic skill of "encoding and decoding basic text," a specific functional task, or a set of "communicative practices of a particular community, culture, or social context" that cannot be precisely measured. Although "these different conceptualizations *can be* [italics added] seen as interrelated, they imply rather different directions for the development of content standards for adult literacy" (p. 9). Without a resolution of the content on which to base the measurement of standards, which the authors viewed as exceedingly unlikely, outcome-based education remains problematic on its face.

Performance Standards

Performance standards need to be congruent with the content they are intended to measure. Lack of agreement on the purposes of adult literacy education as reflected in the divergent points of view identified in this book is a fundamental problem. Without such an agreement on the definition, purpose, and content of adult literacy education, efforts at developing a viable performance-based assessment system invariably falter.

The authors of the NCAL report pointed to two related problems. The first is that even if content and performance are aligned, there is often a "lack of appropriate and adequate measures of learning gain to serve the purpose of accountability." In principle, that is a technical matter that could be resolved once definitional problems were settled. The second factor is the marginality, the "weaknesses in the current infrastructure of adult literacy education delivery systems" (p. 11) in terms of staff, expertise, and financial resources to adequately implement a high quality, aligned accountability system. The authors noted that additional resources are required to achieve a technically proficient accountability system. The irony seemed inescapable that funding sources would remain scarce unless programs could provide clear evidence of their effectiveness.

The more fundamental matter is that of aligning accountability with what is taught and learned, a potential problem for any standardized assessment instrument. The problem is compounded, given the need for comparability at the state and national level, which adds another stage of data aggregation that further distances assessment accountability from what is learned within specific programs. The authors argued that this problem was inherent in NALS, which was based on an implicit, or commonsense, perspective not derived "from any theoretical model of functional literacy or component literacy skills" (p. 11). Hence, the effort to obtain accurate literacy rates from increases on the NALS prose indicator is "highly problematic" (p. 11) even as NALS serves as shorthand to demonstrate comparability. In its politically rhetorical purpose, reliance on NALS as a symbolic conveyer of progress exacerbated the cleavages between practice, research, and policy, leaving the issue of reliable measurement confused.

Stites, Foley, and Wagner pointed to research linking "standards to more 'authentic' and more complex measures of student performance" (p. 10). These would include the types of examples identified in chapter 2 that stem from alternative design, although with more emphasis on measuring performance through "hard" indicators rather than on internal changes in attitudes or beliefs. Authentic performance could be organized as "exhibitions, investigations, portfolios of student work, or any other assessments that require learners to make use of prior knowledge, recent learning, and relevant skills in actively solving significant and realistic problems" (Stites, Foley, & Wagner, 1995, p. 10).

A technical description of performance-based, authentic assessment is discussed in Custer, Schell, McAlister, Scott, and Hoepfl (2000). These authors pointed to such theories of learning as "situated cognition," "meta-cognition," and "contextual learning," measured by "student self-assessment," "rubrics," "learning logs and journals," and "projects." Custer (2000) defined "authentic assessments . . . [as] essentially those that embed assessment in real-world contexts . . . in which students are engaged in applying skills and knowledge to solve 'real-world' problems, giving the tasks a sense of authenticity" (p. 3). These forms of assessment are linked to a constructivist theory of learning, in which literacy is viewed as an indirect variable in mastering, mediating, or negotiating the print environments of particular social contexts in the various life domains of work, home, or community settings. The problem, as Merrifield (1998) pointed out, is that policy is not based on the pedagogical premises that underlay authentic assessment. The substantial gap between the constructivist epistemological assumptions on which current models of authentic assessment are premised and the behaviorist and positivist postulations that underlie current standardized testing in ABE/adult literacy is symptomatic of broader conflict over the public values and purposes of adult literacy education.

Opportunity-to-Learn (OTL) Standards

Problems of grounding technical efficacy within a framework of political legitimacy are further evident in the authors' discussion of OTL standards. Whereas there is controversy as to whether OTL standards are legitimate (Manno, 1994), Stites et al. (1995) argued they are indispensable on technical grounds because lack of sufficient resources to meet prescribed standards invariably skew accurate measurement of student learning. Although OTL standards for ABE had not been developed at the time the NCAL report had been published, the authors pointed to various inputs that would help to create a more equitable system, including *program quality indicators* mandated by the National Literacy Act (NLA) of 1991. These refer to the various inputs that provide a baseline in instructional focus, staff development, and student support "to determine whether programs are effective, including whether such programs are successfully recruiting, retaining and improving the literacy skills of individuals served in such programs" (NLA, Section 331[a][2], cited in Stites et al., 1995, p. 13). Given its legal standing based on the 1991 legislation, there was strong focus on program quality indicators in the early 1990s. However, many programs had limited staff and expertise to reach a high quality threshold in the key areas of program planning, curriculum development, student support, and assessment recommended by the quality indicators.

Also in support of OTL standards, Merrifield (1998) argued that "capacity to be accountable means that resources have to be commensurate with accountability expectations" (p. 65). She sited NLA moderator David Rosen's statement on the relation between extent of funding and corresponding levels of accountability in asking "what should funders hold programs accountable for?" Rosen argued that alignment was critical. Consequently:

> A program whose goal is to help people to learn to read and write should not be held accountable for students getting jobs. Nor should job-oriented programs be held accountable for students reading to their children (because, among other reasons, students may not have children in such programs.) This would imply that some programs will need to define their goals more sharply, or at least to specify which goals they agree to be held accountable for. (Rosen, NLA, May 12, 1997)

Rosen also pointed out that programs funded for different amounts should not be held to the same standards. He reasoned that programs funding students at $200 per year should only be "held accountable to keep records of the students served, and how the money was spent." A program funding students at $1,000 per year would be held to a much higher level of accountability. Retention in such programs would be critical, along with the many other indicators of program quality, including "staff and program development," and some reasonable degree of alignment between program focus, the articulation of student goals, and their attainment. For Rosen, it was only with programs that funded students at $5,000 per year or more that should be accountable for reporting learning gains based on "valid and reliable instruments." Programs funded at this level should also be able to link what students are learning in class to outcomes in their lives outside of class. It would take funding at this level, Rosen argued, to begin holding the system accountable in proving that the government's "investment was succeeding" (Rosen, NLA, May 12, 1997).

Regardless as to whether alignment issues related to technical proficiency, policy orientation, and different definitions of literacy could be addressed, for Rosen, Merrifield, and Stites, Foley, and Wagner, the lack of funding alone necessary to realize OTL standards remained a persisting problem. Mandates for performance standards tightened up in the late 1990s, yet resources were not available to build the infrastructure to sustain an effective accountability system, even if there was a consensus among practitioners, researchers, and policymakers on the public purposes of the ABE/adult literacy, which there was not.

Stites et al. (1995) acknowledged the inevitability of persisting conflict in identifying the purposes of adult literacy education, and the unlikelihood of widespread agreement on a generally acceptable set of standards. However, they also viewed the "broad-based discussion" on the topic as "providing rare opportunities for ongoing and critical exchanges of views on questions of vital concern to all who have an interest in improving literacy among adult Americans" (p. 18). Others wondered whether the "acrimonious debate" would have more deleterious effects. As one observer put it, conflicting perceptions over outcome-based education (OBE) are a place "over which many are doing fierce battle across America today" (Manno, 1994, p. 2).

NLA DISCUSSION ON IMPACTS AND OUTCOMES

The dilemmas identified in Stites, Foley, and Wagner were further elaborated in a September 1997 NLA thread titled, "Documenting Program Effectiveness." The following discussion draws on reflections of three researchers: Hal Beder, professor of adult education at Rutgers University in New Jersey; Regie Stites, an educational researcher at the Center for Educational and Human Services at SRI International in California; and Juliet Merrifield, founder of the Center for Literacy Studies in Tennessee. Their scholarly research included, or would then soon include, significant work on performance-based adult education. Stites and Merrifield were, or were soon to be, closely connected to the EFF project. Merrifield (1998) and Beder (1999) would soon write major policy reports for the National Center for the Study of Adult Learning and Literacy (NCSALL) on the prospects and challenges of establishing an outcome-based, ABE/adult literacy system. The discussion includes commentary from Andres Muro, the director of El Paso College/Community Program in Texas. Muro was one of the major NLA listserv contributors in the late 1990s.

Like the NCAL report, *Standards for Adult Literacy: Points for Debate* (Stites et al., 1995), the September 1997 NLA discussion brought out many detailed points on issues surrounding performance-based ABE/adult literacy. This included probing the feasibility of only measuring "direct outcomes"—namely, reading, writing, and computational gains—as opposed to "indirect outcomes," or "impacts," such as the *effects* of literacy learning on the daily lives of adult students. In offering another "critical exchanges of views" (p. 18), the thread raised more issues than it resolved.

Hal Beder

In the September 1997 NLA discussion, Beder referred to his then impending report on "outcomes and impacts of adult literacy education," based on an analysis of "29 studies which have been selected as being the most credible since the late 1960s." Beder noted that "every study yet conducted is seriously flawed in respect to outcome data." He referred to the "lack of generalizability, substantial subject (i.e. learner) attrition, inaccurate data collection, lack of valid and reliable tests, and reliance on self-report data." He also pointed to the lack of "standards that can be used to assess the practical significance of gains noted" (Beder, NLA, September 3, 1997). As Beder (1999) described the dilemma in his then upcoming report, "It is impossible to select a sample that represents the universe of adult literacy programs and clients if one cannot precisely define the universe and its components in operational terms" (p. 24).

Beder also raised the pragmatic issue of what adult literacy programs could realistically measure. He acknowledged that "direct outcomes of instruction—certain skills, knowledge, and changed attitudes" could be reasonably assumed. However, he questioned the extent to which education alone is able "to produce indirect outcomes of instruction." Whatever the impacts were in which literacy contributed as one variable among several, given the minimal resources available for assessment, plus the inherent difficulty of measuring its more elusive impacts, Beder argued for another tact. He maintained that a better course is to concentrate measurement on the more direct outcomes, specifically, reading gains as measured on standardized tests, which requires that the field "first define what adult literacy education is and to reach some sort of consensus on what we expect learners to learn" (Beder, NLA, September 3, 1997).

Andres Muro

In a follow-up, Muro linked the issue of "outcomes" to that of epistemology, or "what we mean by adult literacy." For Muro, what Beder referred to as "indirect outcomes"—such as "obtaining employment, filling a health insurance application, seeking health care, repairing your kitchen, helping children with their homework, [or] writing a note to the night shift supervisor"—represented the very essence of what adult literacy education was about. Muro maintained (although without elaboration), that an accountability system could be established for what he called *direct* outcomes, "contextual literacy behaviors" (Muro, NLA, September 3, 1997), which Beder referred to as *indirect* outcomes, or *impacts.* Beder (1999) explained the difference:

> Outcomes are changes in learners that occur as a result of their participation in adult literacy education [e.g., gains in reading, writing, and comprehension of texts]. Impacts are the changes that occur in the family, community, or larger society as a *consequence* [italics added] of participation (where direct links between instruction and behavior cannot easily be made). (p. 4)

Beder agreed with Muro that "in a functional context . . . it is possible to consider the direct outcomes of instruction to be a set of life-oriented skills." That raised for Beder the need to identify "what skills and whether the skills can be and are applied to the benefit of the learner and society." Questioning a too-metaphorical definition of "multiple literacies," Beder expressed skepticism that attainment of literacy was possible without an extensive focus on the mastery of basic skills. As he put it:

> But where do Message, writing, and computation fit into this? Is it possible to say Message, writing, and computation are fundamental to all conceptions of literacy and represent a core that can be used as a benchmark for all programs? Is it possible to become "literate" without knowing how to read, write, and do basic math? (Beder, NLA, September 4, 1997)

Beder acknowledged the validity of functional literacy, as well as the possibility of measuring its impact, but only when curriculum, instruction, and assessment are tightly correlated. Nonetheless, given the difficulty of developing a national *accountability* structure that is valid and reliable at a high level of comparability, Beder worried that shifting the basic criteria from general reading gains to the context of learning would place any such system in jeopardy. Others felt that without a contextual focus, the relation between instruction and assessment would be invariably skewed on its face.

Regie Stites

Stites weighed in, stating "measures of both skills (literacy and numeracy skills) and social outcomes (jobs, parenting skills, citizenship, etc.) will be included in accountability systems that funders apply to literacy programs." Stites argued that funders held little value for an increase of isolated reading gains, which would likely prove modest in any event. Rather, they will only be persuaded by outcomes linked to specific impacts, especially in the economic realm. Expanding on Beder's point, Stites argued:

> It is possible to say that Message, writing and computation skills are fundamental and can represent benchmarks for all programs. But these should not be the only benchmarks and if they are (as they are likely to be) the core benchmarks, they need to be measured in ways that reflect as accurately as possible the application of these skills in real-life contexts. (Stites, NLA, September 4, 1997)

Stites did not further address the issue of testing, although elsewhere he discussed performance-based accountability through standards that, if well-constructed, could link basic skills and social outcomes into a coherent framework that integrated curriculum, assessment, and policy. The type of assessment/accountability system Stites visualized consists of three types of "validity":

> From a measurement perspective, the central concern is likely to be construct validity—the degree to which an assessment system meets technical criteria for validity and reliability. From a policy perspective, the central concern is likely to be consequential validity—the degree to which the uses of an assessment system lead to fair and equitable outcomes for learners, instructors, programs, and funders. Finally, from a popular perspective, the central concern is likely to be face validity—the degree to which an assessment system is meaningful and understandable to all. (Stites, NIFL-4EFF, October 18, 2000)

For Stites, "all three general types of validity . . . are equally valid" (October 18, 2000) and interrelated. As previously discussed, Stites also identified types of standards—specifically, *content, performance,* and *opportunity-to-learn* (OTL) standards—that would form the basis for an integrated accountability system.

Stites and his colleagues (Stites, Foley, & Wagner, 1995) elsewhere argued that "content standards for adult literacy in the sense of creating a framework for a national literacy curriculum is unlikely and probably unwise" (p. 7). As the preceding section illustrated, that is so because of the widely different approaches, objectives, and assumptions that underlie the diverse constituency that comprises the field. Given this ineradicable pluralism, a national framework might seem like an imposition with its invariable privileging of certain positions over others.

However, Stites (1999) also drew on the EFF framework, which provides an overarching framework in the skills and knowledge needed for lifelong learning in the critical social roles of worker, family, and community member. Whether EFF is ever successful in forging a national consensus, even in its current status outside NIFL, it is at least plausible to argue that if there is going to be any prospect of wedding highly technical and exacting standards that stem from practice and research to social policy, it will take something like the comprehensive effort underlying EFF to bring it to bear. Otherwise, either the pluralism and fragmentation of the current system would render any common policy purposes for adult literacy education hopeless or would likely result in an imposition of standards from the realm of policy that likely would not fit well the exigencies of practice. However problematic any of the proposed solutions for the standards issue seemed, including EFF, either of these other two alternatives could only further marginalize a field already lacking resources and public legitimacy.

According to Stites, there is more at work in the standards movement than the quest for methodological coherency. The underlying factor is that the notion "of what the direct and indirect outcomes of adult literacy are or should be is really a policy issue." As Stites noted, "Theory and research can inform the definition of these outcomes but will not ultimately decide the issue" (Stites, NLA, September 4, 1997). The implication is that whatever scholarship is drawn on to provide the intellectual framework for the establishment of educational standards will not be simply a reasoned reflection of pure science. Rather, as Stites noted, the formation of standards is also part of a political process linked to knowledge construction and resource allocation. As characterized by Cherryholmes (1988), "Constructs and measurements . . . are interpretive from the outset" (p. 125). This does not negate their viability for usable knowledge that assessment and accountability systems are designed to provide. However, it is to situate them in the realm of values in terms of epistemology and political culture.

Stites did not ignore these issues, particularly in his technical work in linking performance accountability with the EFF design. Yet, largely missing from his discussion is the broader matter of how policy is shaped, whose interests it serves, and the theory of knowledge and political culture that it reflects. These concerns were at the heart of the April 1997 NLA thread on the "Quality of Life" discussed in chapter 2, and point to the complex interplay of pedagogy, politics, and culture that underlie the working out of adult literacy education in the United States at the turn of the 21st century.

Muro Revisited

Muro reentered the discussion, highlighting the contextual perspective. He acknowledged the importance of the basic skills, although he insisted that "these skills are often a means to something else and not an end in itself." Muro listed some of the key goals among the ESL students who participated in his program in areas related to employment, communicating with English-only speaking grandchildren, citizenship, and obtaining adequate health care. He critiqued the "current educational system [which] offers mostly G.E.D. and traditional ESL classes." Muro acknowledged that both types of programs "provide some of the skills necessary" for obtaining the highly specific goals his students identified. However, the linkage between these more general programs and the skills and knowledge students sought to attain was not always clear. The result is that "adults [frequently] get frustrated with learning what they consider meaningless and drop out." What would be better, Muro argued, is for basic skills to be developed through instructional content that meshed with the most compelling student interests.

Beyond the search to identify an effective pedagogy, Muro linked the issue of outcomes to the politics of literacy. As he framed it, "for Macedo, literacy is a means to understand how the government controls our lives. For the Dept of Labor language is the means by which workers can become familiar with new technology, in order to improve productivity and strengthen the economy" (Muro, NLA, September 4, 1997). For Muro, the focus in Congress of "increasingly conceiving adult literacy to be part of the nation's workforce readiness system" (Beder, 1999, p. 10) is not necessarily benign because it has the potential of becoming a "domesticating" pedagogy linked to class, race, and gender oppression.

Auerbach (1993) took a similar stance on definitions of literacy "emphasizing individual goal setting without any accompanying social analysis." The result is to strengthen "the specific Western mainstream value system of individualism—that through hard work and individual effort, learners can change the basic conditions of their lives." More strongly put, the "vision of individual self-betterment may be a false promise in a society where race, ethnicity, gender, and the general vicissitudes of the economy play such a dominant role in the distribution of jobs, social status, and income" (p. 544). Auerbach's view is contestable (Demetrion, 2001a), but it raises the thorny issue of the value structure at the level of political culture underlying policy assumptions.

Beder Revisited

Beder acknowledged Muro's point on the importance of contexts, particularly in programs that have a highly specific topical focus. Still, Beder argued that impact remains indirect and difficult to measure, particularly in a performance-based assessment system requiring multiple levels of data aggregation. As Beder (1999) further described the problem, "unless it is known with confidence that participation in adult literacy education caused a particular outcome, such as the achievement of increased income, little is known, and if little is known, how can reasonable policy be made?" (p. 14). Beder was appreciative of in-depth ethnographic studies that may, with reasonable certainty, demonstrate certain correlations between outcomes and impacts in *specific cases*. However, he argued that this type of information is too thin at a national policy level, which requires data aggregation of a more "objective" nature that standardized test scores can provide.

Although Beder was quick to point out the flawed nature of the standardized instruments that currently exist, that does not negate his broader point that, in principle, more exacting measures could be constructed that more closely approximate the ideals of objectivity, standardization, and uniformity based on precepts of the positivist and neopositivist research traditions (Mertens, 1998). Those adhering to an ethnographic research model would maintain that whereas information gleaned from standardized tests can be useful as part of the picture, their *textual* importance lies in the particular story that any data helps to illuminate. Ethnographers argue that narratives are cultural products shaped by history and the various interpretive lenses that participants and observers draw on. "From the perspective provided by this model a discourse is regarded as an apparatus for the production of meaning rather than only as a vehicle for the transmission of information about an extrinsic referent" (White, 1987, p. 42). Those critical of Beder's position argue that discourse practices underlie issues of assessment and accountability. They require, consequently, a probing into their various and sometimes contestable meanings before matters of technical efficiency can be resolved (Cherryholmes, 1988).

In his policy study, Beder (1999) made the important point that the need for an objectively based evaluative system stems from the imperatives of Congress and state legislatures, which have tightly linked adult literacy to the human resource needs of the global economy and welfare reform. Because these "are the bodies that allocate resources . . . the will of these legislative bodies [including methodological design to assess accountability] cannot be ignored" (p. 10). What Beder did not focus on is the contestable nature of the political process, particularly in a democracy where representative bodies both mediate and are influenced by countervailing influences.

The mandates of the legislative branch cannot be ignored, but they can be challenged through the coordinated action of the field in the effort to reconstruct policy from its own premises rather than those set by Congress. That may be difficult and perhaps even unlikely, but erasing the prospect of a vigorous grassroots discourse of democratic participation from the discussion on policy, reifies the power of the law as it *is*, to define and even to "naturalize" reality. At the least, the *critical pedagogy* to which Muro alluded helps to provide another perspective to the more normative political assumptions that grounds Beder's policy framework—more from the philosophical perspective of Deweyan pragmatism, so does Habermas' (1998) *Between Facts and Norms: Contributions to a Discourse Theory of Law and Democracy*.

Habermas characterized tension between democracy and law as more complex than any simple polarity between elite control and ascendancy of popular sovereignty. In "a liberal political sphere, actors can acquire only influence, not [direct] political power" where "public influence is transformed into communicative power only after it passes through the filters of institutionalized *procedures* [italics in original] of democratic opinion- and will-formation and enters through parliamentary debates into legitimate lawmaking" (p. 371). It is:

> not influence per se, but influence transformed into communicative power [that] legitimates political decisions. The popular sovereignty set communicatively aflow [through the press and other channels and networks of collective discussion] cannot make itself felt *solely* [italics in original] in the influence of informal public discourse—not even when these discourses arise from autonomous public spheres. To generate political power, their influence must have an effect on democratically regulated deliberations of democratically elected assemblies and assume an authorized form in decisions. (pp. 371–372)

The imperatives of the legislative bodies cannot be ignored. Still, they can be contested within the context of a "civil society" "in spite of asymmetrical access to expertise and limited problem-solving capacities . . . by mobilizing counterknowledge and drawing on the pertinent forms of expertise to make its *own* [italics in original] translations" (p. 372). No doubt, this is a difficult challenge.

Clearly, for the field to engage in such a sustained level of democratic will formation would require a higher level of political acumen, coordination, and collective commitment for change than is currently in place, the lack of which represents a serious limitation on any potential influence. At the same time, to deny its possibility or practicality tends to subvert any notion of democracy in the strong sense as having viability in the American political culture. Even so, any profound shift in current policy on the purposes of ABE/adult literacy and the means of measuring impact would require a powerfully concerted effort within the field to change the political culture at least in respect to adult literacy education. Notwithstanding the difficulties, what I am suggesting is that the structural-functionalist tendencies implicit in Beder's policy study need to be substantially mediated both by the precepts of critical pedagogy as well as through the more pragmatic reform impulse suggested by Dewey and Habermas. The very openness of the American political culture hangs in the balance, which can only *but* impact the direction of adult literacy at least on a broad-based, national level. Whether the adult literacy community will rise to the challenge of system reconstruction by appropriating the value and imagery of democracy in this Habermasian sense, in order to move beyond the logic of Beder's structural functionalism, is another matter.

Juliet Merrifield

Merrifield pointed to the difficulty of defining "what works" in adult literacy education. The problem, according to Merrifield, is that "we have not said clearly what we want literacy education to do, what is it for." As with Beder and Stites, Merrifield agreed that the effort to determine valid outcomes before this more fundamental task takes place is intellectually incoherent. "Only when we have said what it's for (i.e. what the expected outcomes should be) can we begin to unravel what variations in program design and process are more effective at producing the outcomes."

Merrifield agreed with Beder "that it is much more difficult to say what 'literacy' outcomes should look like (skills, knowledge) than what the other, more indirect (perhaps) outcomes should look like—jobs, income, community involvement, children's success in school, self-esteem." She questioned common efforts to get at such impact through checklists of isolated skills or tasks that "tend to become not only tedious but also 'so what?' " (Merrifield, NLA, September 5, 1997). As an ethnographer (Merrifield, Bingman, Hemphill, & Bennett deMarrais, 1997), Merrifield argued that lists "don't seem to bear much resemblance to what we really care about, which is not only the ability to do well on tests, but the ability to live our lives fully" (Merrifield, NLA, September 5, 1997). As she and her colleagues (Merrifield et al., 1997) described it regarding the literacy and ESOL students from rural Appalachia and urban California:

> They are competent, thoughtful, hardworking, with strong values. They need literacy programs that recognize and build on their strengths, relate to their experiences, and support them to make changes in their lives. Such programs would enable them to move out of the margins and turn to other purposes the energy they now use for survival. [And from a policy perspective, w]e would all benefit from investing in the people we have come to know in this study, enabling them to become full citizens in the broadest sense of the word. (p. 196)

Although the details of such a proposed national focus would need to be spelled out, *Life at the Margins* provides certain clues. Additional ethnographic studies like Fingeret and Drennon's (1997) *Literacy for Life*, and other similar work could help to round out a more comprehensive picture of the various influences of adult literacy education. However, the challenging effort remains that of articulating in sufficiently convincing ways the relation between personal student goals and valued public outcomes, the focus of chapter 11.

In response to the 1997 NLA discussion at hand on outcomes and program effectiveness, Merrifield drew on the research of the *New Literacy Studies* for her interpretation of the impact of literacy. As she put it, "The whole point of literacy is that it is not a neat bundle of skills and knowledge. What matters is how literacy is used, and . . . is shaped by its contexts and its users." Merrifield (NLA, September 5, 1997) referred to her then impending collaborative work, *Life at the Margins*, which "documented the remarkable range of 'literacy strategies' that people who can't read and write very well use to accomplish literacy tasks." Based on the presuppositions of the New Literacy Studies, Merrifield suggested that "we need to change our thinking about the purpose of literacy education":

> Perhaps it should be something like: "literacy equals the ability in everyday life to accomplish literacy tasks, take part in the literacy events that one chooses, and understand the literacy practices common in one's community and culture"—and all these can be documented through a variety of authentic assessment and performance assessment techniques.

This would require a shift in focus "from performing in the context of a classroom test to performing in the highly varied contexts of everyday life." As she further described the challenge:

> We accept [with Muro and Stites] that there is a reason for our difficulty in defining literacy in singular and absolute terms [a tendency implicit in Beder's approach]. But we keep the focus on literacy, rather than the more diffuse outcomes of performing in employment, family and community (which Hal so rightly points out, are subject to the impact of so many other variables).

It is the relative mastery of such literacy *events*, like reading a newspaper or a job manual within the structure of various social contexts that Merrifield suggested could be measured "through a variety of authentic assessment and performance assessment techniques" (Merrifield, NLA, September 5, 1997). What remained unclear is the extent to which a national accountability system would draw on statistical rather than ethnographic indicators of achievement of a more qualitative nature that could not be easily quantified. This is an important consideration as Merrifield's concept of literacy practices stemmed from qualitative insights derived from ethnographic research.

In the quest to work through the *contested ground* to develop a national consensus on adult literacy, Merrifield also skirted the full import of the "multiliteracy issue," which points to a wide diversity of purposes and methodologies to illuminate the various epistemologies that her pluralistic understanding of literacy assumes. As characterized by Muro (NLA, September 4, 1997), "We live in a society that is becoming more multicultural and fragmented. The idea of people getting a universal education [or being evaluated by the same methodology] is becoming a thing of the past." Whether or not national policy would support anything like Muro's pluralism or Merrifield's concept of "multiliteracies" is another matter.

IN SEARCH OF CONSENSUS AMIDST
CONTESTED GROUND

It was amidst this contested ground that Merrifield recommended public dialogue as a way of working toward a common framework to achieve a set of durable standards to link policy, practice, and research in ABE/adult literacy. Like Stites et al. (1995), Merrifield was acutely aware that beneath the issue of establishing a set of technically proficient standards laid the issue of values. Whether or not Merrifield (1998) thought values clarification was practically resolvable in *Contested Ground* is uncertain, although she stressed the importance of "debate and action that addresses both accountability and performance" (p. 56). Performance measurement, she argued, should be based on "what literacy education should achieve, for individuals, for communities, and for society," the settlement of which would require a high level of national consensus among the literacy field, the business sector, and state and federal governments. The challenge was to "develop *mutual* [italics added] accountability relationships at all levels of the system, from local program to national level" (p. 56). Merrifield's vision also required an across-the-board acceptance of the controversial OTL standards that sharply separated progressive and neoconservative policy advocates throughout the 1990s (Hirsch, 1997; Manno, 1994).

Only if these value-oriented concerns could be worked through the body politic, could the more specialized matters be addressed of "design[ing] new technologies to measure performance, report on results, and provide the information tools needed for program improvement" (Merrifield, 1998, p. 56). These latter challenges were crucially important to Merrifield because of the gap between *authentic assessment* and the need for *comparability*, which, however limited, standardized tests are at least symbolically designed to address. Given the current system, Merrifield argued that "standardized tests . . . [will] continue to be used in uneasy partnership with various explorations of portfolios and related methods" (p. 55). She might have added that, in terms of policy acceptability, the former would maintain the preeminent role.

Clearly, Merrifield was uneasy with this arrangement that stemmed from incompatible epistemological frameworks about the nature of adult literacy education. However, she did seek through dialogue fresh "opportunity" *in* "the maelstrom of confusion about how to measure learning" (p. 55). She hoped that through an intense and provocative national dialogue, "new understandings of the nature of literacy and cognitive learning" (p. 55) would break forth that could stabilize a national consensus. However, she did not address the issue of political values, a coming to terms with which is essential for any formation of a vital political culture that could anchor the consensus she and others have sought, in order to mediate the contested ground, which she more clearly depicted.

Although aware of the daunting nature of the quest, Merrifield was in search of an impetus or a series of impetuses that would usher in the needed paradigmatic shift in values that could then lead to the more manageable *technical* development of a sophisticated accountability system. That same quest for system reconstruction is at the center of the praxeological goals of *Conflicting Paradigms in Adult Literacy: In Search of a U.S. Democratic Politics of Literacy*, although I place more emphasis than Merrifield on the need to identify a mediating political framework as an anchor.

Merrifield pointed to the insights of the New Literacy Studies as the basis through which to situate core content for adult literacy education. Its intellectual edifice, she argued, "should stimulate the field to rethink performance in terms of literacy practices rather than [isolated] literacy skills, of application and use rather than classroom achievement" (p. 56). From these assumptions, Merrifield argued that legitimate performance requires an embrace of the concept of "multiliteracies," with the concomitant insight "that there are multiple purposes and uses of literacy and multiple goals and expectations for literacy education" (p. 56). From this vantage point, "accountability could be approached through a concept of 'performances'—multiple purposes and expectations that must be negotiated among multiple players" (p. 57).

In seeking to honor the pluralism characteristic of the system, as well as establishing generally agreed on purposes for a publicly based adult literacy national accountability system, Merrifield underlined both "commonalities as well as differences" (p. 57) without a too-exacting specification of terms. In stressing the three EFF Role Map categories of worker, family member, and community member as examples of where programs might specialize, she suggested a range or a menu of choices "within which most people can place themselves" (p. 57). Accountability would be based on particular "performances" relevant to the specific chosen area(s) that would be "defined neither too tightly or too loosely." The latter danger is the lack of any "shared mission" or purpose that might be tied to some policy objective. On the other hand, if performances were defined too tightly, then the result might prove a "mismatch between system goals and individual goals" (p. 57). Although Merrifield did not highlight EFF in *Contested Ground*, she did argue that "a common framework [like EFF] is needed within which different performances can be nested" (p. 57). Once linked to specific content areas of work, home, or community, "specific performance indicators and measurement" would be developed to "track . . . performance separately" (p. 57).

In her policy paper, Merrifield did not resolve the tension between qualitative and quantitative forms of measurement. She took a somewhat vague, but not unfounded, middle ground, and called for performance indicators that are *specific*, tied to certain particular outcomes, *measurable*, "although not necessarily quantitative," *action-oriented* in focusing indicators on "something that can be controlled" (p. 67), *realistic* based on the resources available, and *timely*, so that such information can be utilized for direct program improvement.

Distinctive "approaches," or "technologies," would be drawn on, such as *research, evaluation*, and *monitoring* in response to specific informational needs, about "correlations and meanings" (p. 68), on whether "programs are meeting their objectives," or "questions about day-to-day operations" (p. 69). In Merrifield's proposal, "each of these accountability technologies shines a flashlight from a different angle to illuminate different aspects of reality" (p. 69). Although stimulating in its imaginative scope, these ideas were only barely sketched in *Contested Ground*. To propose more would have imposed a system of Merrifield's own creation rather than reliance on the national dialogue she believed essential to bring a consensually based accountability system into place. Nonetheless, her understandable vagueness begged potential epistemological and political conflicts that underlie the nature of what is or could be deemed as valid.

Namely, this pluralistic framework would require a level of complexity and sophistication dependent on a broad consensus sustained over time that could satisfy a diverse range of practitioners, researchers, and policymakers. Such a tightly woven system as Merrifield proposed could only be "*negotiated* [italics in original] between the stakeholders in a process that engages all the players in clarifying expectations, designing indicators of success, negotiating information flows, and building capacity." In this framework, OTL standards play a significant role where "each responsibility is matched with an enabling right," where "every player knows clearly and agrees to what is expected of them," including "the capacity [of all] to hold others accountable." In this vision, "efficient and effective information flows" to "all players" (p. 60) and is the glue that holds the system together.

Merrifield was aware that such a system was not then currently in place, although she pointed to the then impending National Literacy Summit, under the sponsorship of NIFL, which took place in 2000 as "the kind of work to be done to ensure stakeholder involvement in deliberations about the future of ABE" (p. 61). Drawing on Deming's business model of quality assurance through "continuous improvement," Merrifield placed much weight on the metaphor of the "learning organization" to describe the way in which a viable national accountability system could come into place. In her vision, "systems that [have the capacity to] learn" (p. 63) would provide the direction to guide the "informational flows" that an emergent multipronged and de-centered accountability structure would require. I argue throughout *Conflicting Paradigms in Adult Literacy* that, whereas such an organizational vision represents an important tactical step, the more fundamental issue requires addressing the political culture at the level of core values.

Assuming the field could agree on some broad content areas on which to base policy through a system of mutual accountability (as well as achieve agreement on the epistemological assumptions of the New Literacy Studies), the testing and piloting alone of developing and using new accountability technologies is, at the least, a daunting task. It would require years of highly intricate social-scientific analysis, to link together practitioners, research-ers, and policymakers in a series of agreed on, multidisciplinary experimen-tal initiatives.

At a minimum, this would require some enduring *raison d'être* as to the public value of adult literacy in order to grapple with the value issue well be-fore any logical system construction or accountability technologies could be fully developed. To put it bluntly, it would necessitate some act of faith amidst a broad and far-from-unified, diverse constituency that the effort would be well worth the investment of fiscal and human resources before all the evidence was in. In a policy-oriented culture dominated by a cost-benefits metaphor based on "return on investment" imagery, this would likely prove exceedingly difficult. Thus, without a shift in values that gives shape to the politics of literacy beyond the mainly economic realm that can span political boundaries of a wide scope, it is not easy to fathom how com-mon ground can come into place in the United States at the dawn of the 21st century. These are thorny matters, as Merrifield well intimated, that will require more than "meetings and taskforces" to resolve.

Merrifield placed the onus on policymakers "to set the stage, harness re-sources, and create a common agenda" (p. 78). Clearly, that is a far-reaching aspiration. It is especially difficult to achieve given the conservative political climate that has dominated the U.S. Congress since 1995. Administration policies such as the National Reporting System and the workforce orienta-tion of the Clinton administration, and under President Bush, the emphasis on scientific-based educational research and phonemic awareness, have fur-ther strengthened conservative policy tendencies. Merrifield's consensual vi-sion as articulated in *Contested Ground*, stands in sharp relief as a progressive one that more than a few policymakers would view as contestable. The prospect of working through the development of a sophisticated, progressive-leaning consensus-based accountability structure in the midst of the neoliberal and neoconservative political ideologies that have dominated the federal government since the Reagan era, was not well grounded in the political realities that any system reconstruction of adult literacy/ABE would have entailed in the late 1990s. An embrace of EFF as a potential way of establishing a national consensus at least seemed plausible both for Merrifield and Stites, who helped lay the foundation for the construction of its Content Standards that began to take shape in the late 1990s.

Beder (1999) also held out prospect that EFF could provide a path for moving forward. As he put it, its "goals are broad-based and comprehensive and have been generated through systematic qualitative research" that conceivably could pass muster with the federal government. Still, Beder wondered "whether [or not] a voluntary system of outcome accountability would satisfy the current pressures for national accountability evident in Congress and state legislatures" (p. 125). It is to EFF and the complex interplay between its pedagogical and policy objectives to which we turn next.

Equipped for the Future:
Building the Infrastructure

Partial conclusions emerge during the course of reflection. They are temporary stopping places, landings of past thought that are stations of departure for subsequent thought. We do not reach the *conclusion at any single jump. At every single landing stage it is useful to retrace the processes gone through and to state to oneself how much and how little of the material previously thought about really bears on the conclusion reached and* how *[italics in original] it bears.*
—Dewey (1933/1989, p. 174)

From its inception, the National Institute for Literacy's (NIFL) Equipped for the Future (EFF) project was constrained by the tensions its developers have sought to mediate between policy, practice, and educational theory for the purpose of establishing a nationwide consensus framework for ABE/adult literacy. The policy impetus stemmed from the performance-based operative assumptions that reflected powerful strands within education, business, and government during the early 1990s. In this climate, the term *accountability* was a watchword of more than a passing symbolic significance. As a governmentally based initiative, there was little alternative, but for EFF to ride this train, and to seek system reform from within its premises.

CONSTRUCTIVISM AS EFF'S INTELLECTUAL NERVE CENTER

From its inception, EFF developers were motivated by a particular view of learning, *constructivism*, which is a theory that knowledge is less mastery of specific facts or preset skills than a series of interactions between particular learners and social environments in quest for and creation of usable knowledge. Constructivism is not based on a denial of the objective world, but views the mastery of facts or tasks "out there" as part of a broader process "in which the learner is building an internal representation of knowledge, a personal [and expanding] interpretation of experience" (Bednar, Cunningham, Duffy, & Perry, 1992, p. 21). As described by Gillespie (2002b), constructivist "learning is . . . a process of activating our prior knowledge related to a topic we want to learn about; questioning, interpreting, analyzing, and processing new information in light of our past experiences" (p. 1).

In this understanding, what is important is not, typically, the mastery of facts or an external canon, but the identification and progressive resolution of perceived problems or issues deemed worthy by students of their sustained time and effort. According to Dewey (1910/1991), whose pragmatic philosophy may be viewed as an early 20th-century precursor of constructivism, "*demand for the solution of perplexity is the steadying and guiding factor in the entire process of reflection*" (p. 11, italics in original). It follows that "ideas are not . . . genuine ideas unless they are tools in a reflective examination which tends to solve a problem" (p. 109). The resolution is a constructive process requiring active work on the part of the learner, mediating self-knowledge and selective information from the environment in an adaptive reorganization of experience. This "purposeful, constructivist approach to learning," rooted "in the context of people's lives," focusing on "application, not just possession, of skills" (Merrifield, 2000, p. 9) was the educational theory that underlay the work of the EFF developers in the iterative building of their framework.

The EFF framework was also premised on "a view of adult development as transformative rather than additive" (Merrifield, 2000, p. 9), which drew from Kegan's (1994) influential text, *In Over Our Heads: The Mental Demands of Modern Life*. Central to Kegan is the transition from a third-order to a fourth-order consciousness, which he viewed as a key characteristic of the demands of modern life. This shift is one from social dependency on the values and mores of the given social order to a sense of "self-authorship." This shift still represents a type of socialization, but one where sense of personal efficacy is profoundly internalized. In short, "the demand for this construction of self—as author, critiquer, and remaker of its experience . . . , is the demand that we be in control of our issues rather than having our issues be in control of us" (p. 134).

Put more formally, Kegan argued that "the mental burdens of modern life may be nothing less than the extraordinary demand that each person, in adulthood, create internally, an order of consciousness comparable to that which would ordinarily only be found at the level of a community's collective intelligence" (p. 134). Facilitating the development of adults toward such a transformation represents one of the key constructivist principles on which EFF is based, particularly the transference of learning from one situation to another (Gillespie, 2002a). EFF framers also drew on Mezirow's (1996) concept of "perspective transformation" in explaining the shift in consciousness that adult leaning can stimulate, linking it to the progressive mastery of the knowledge demands of key social roles. Viewed in this manner, learning is "a process not of acquiring facts and skills but of enhancing one's ability to understand one's situation, make decisions about and act upon knowledge, aimed at transforming how one views the world and acts in it" (Merrifield, 2000, p. 11).

POLICY ASPIRATIONS

It is the intersection of policy as it existed in the mid-1990s with that of a constructivist theory of learning that gave shape to the EFF project. Because EFF developers "need[ed] to work simultaneously at the policy level (on accountability systems) and at the program level (on teaching and learning) [this] meant that the research had both to gather new data and link it with existing policy and tools" (p. 7). This linkage speaks not only to the constraints working on EFF, but also to opportunities it afforded to the ABE/ adult literacy sector in pedagogical and system reconstruction.

This tension can be discerned in the very mandate of NIFL by Congress to evaluate the nation's progress toward achieving the aspirations expressed in National Educational Goal 6. The stated objective was to eliminate illiteracy by the end of the decade and provide "every adult American [with] . . . the knowledge and skills to compete in a global economy and exercise the rights and responsibilities of citizenship" (cited in Stein, 1995, p. 7). There is no need to repeat the issues raised by NIFL staffers as discussed at the beginning of chapter 6 over the perceived fragmentation of the nation's ABE/adult literacy system in the early 1990s. Of significance for this chapter was NIFL's response, reflective of both the constraints and opportunities for system reconstruction that the mandate from Congress opened up.

The challenge was to keep focused on the objectives articulated in Goal 6 in a manner that could ultimately be conceived as policy realistic. This required "breakthrough" change in terms of system reconstruction. To state this more sharply, without transformative change in the federal ABE system, any effort by NIFL to reconstruct the nation's adult education program would not likely overcome the entropic forces of the dominant patterns and values that reinforced the marginality of the adult literacy sector and its absorption with workforce training.

The paths chosen were several-fold. The first was in the response by NIFL that given the diffusiveness of the then current system, only a "coherent vision based on a real-world assessment of the knowledge and skills adults need" (Stein, 1997, p. 5) would fit the bill of placing the nation on its way toward realizing the vision inherent in Goal 6. This was a need NIFL proposed to fill. Second was the decision among NIFL staff to survey adult literacy learners on their understanding of what they require to compete effectively in the global economy and to exercise the rights and responsibilities of citizenship. Wedding the language of participatory literacy education to the metaphors of business, Stein called for a "customer-driven vision . . . to assure the results the system does produce make a real difference in adults' lives" (p. 5).

Third, NIFL gave equal billing to the goals of economic development and citizenship in the effort to restructure Goal 6 away from its primary focus as identified in *Jump Start* and SCANS in meeting the human capital needs of the global economy. In giving equal billing to the place of citizenship, and eventually to family education in the creation of Role Maps, EFF developers broadened the major social contexts in which a policy-driven ABE/adult literacy system could be situated. These Role Maps (discussed later in this chapter) would become defined in the EFF framework as a "publicly-agreed to, explicit, consensus depiction of the adult roles of worker, parent/family member, and citizen/community member" (Stein, 1997, p. 31). This joining of student goals and public policy represented an important effort to achieve an intellectual and social synthesis in the articulation of adult literacy education to the public good.

The EFF project established a central role for the adult literacy learner as actively engaged in realizing the objectives of Goal 6 within the context of the mediating institutions of the workplace, family, and community. According to certain social philosophers, the internalization of these roles is at the center of responsible citizenship. As argued by the authors of *The Good Society* (Bellah, Madsen, Sullivan, Swindler, & Tipton, 1992):

> Freedom cannot mean simply getting away from other people. Freedom must exist within and be guaranteed by institutions, and must include the right to participate in the economic and political decisions that affect our lives. Indeed, the great classic criteria of a good society—peace, prosperity, freedom, justice—all depend today on a new experiment in democracy, a newly extended and enhanced set of democratic institutions, within which we citizens can better discern what we really want and what we ought to want to sustain a good life on this planet for ourselves and the generations to come. (p. 9)

The national consensus EFF has sought supports such a vision via the critical engagement of the participatory citizen to exercise the skills and knowledge needed to strengthen workplaces, families, and community-based organizations. Individual development is nurtured in the process of enhancing the public good. The needed knowledge and skill sets are embodied throughout the EFF components, the 4 Purposes, the 3 Role Maps, the 12 Common Activities, the 6 Knowledge Domains, and the 16 process-oriented Content Standards. It is the interaction of these components in the areas of learning, teaching, curriculum development, assessment, and accountability, which is the heart and soul of EFF's consensus shaping vision.

The underlying factor to consider in NIFL's appropriation of the congressional mandate was in taking the Adult Literacy and Lifelong Learning National Goal 6 as *leverage*, to point out the wide disparity between such a broad-based statement and the given realities of actual practice. This provided the basis for NIFL to justify a system reconstruction that led to the EFF project. There was nothing inevitable about these responses, which posed various constraints, but afforded opportunities as well, for system reconstruction as envisioned in the EFF framework. In short, this initiative was the result of considerable *constructive* effort and *creative* interpretation in the wrestling with complex national issues that framed the discussion on the public value of ABE/adult literacy in the mid-1990s. What emerged was an imaginative effort to achieve a synthesis that could bring together a wide disparity of perspectives of a somewhat fragmented and discordant discourse about a field that had attained, at best, marginal status within the public consciousness and in the policy sector. The success of the NIFL pioneers would be based on the extent to which the EFF developers could reconstruct an alternative vision and place adult education on the cutting edge of the national consciousness in mastering the challenges of an increasingly complex knowledge society of the 21st century.

EFF FOUR PURPOSES—BACKGROUND

Preparatory Work

As part of a process of "arriv[ing] at a measurable definition" (Stein, 1995, p. 4) of National Educational Goal 6, a Work Group consisting of staff from NIFL and the National Educational Goals Panel commissioned a series of reports. Specialists of various sorts and policymakers wrote on such topics as "the relationship between literacy and citizenship, family, welfare, and workforce issues, as well as then current efforts to develop skill standards for occupational clusters" (Merrifield, 2000, p. 8 fn). Student feedback was also sought through an "Open Letter" in January 1994 to programs throughout the country, "to ensure that our customers were active participants in this process" (p. 8).

The Work Group sought two critical sources of information. First, they wanted to find out the level of understanding students possessed about the global economy and the rights and responsibilities of citizenship. Second, in addition to *knowing* about these two topics, the Work Group wanted to learn "what knowledge and skills they [the students] would need to perform effectively according to their definition of each area" (p. 9).

About 6,000 invitation packets were sent to a wide array of programs and agencies. "The goal was to get a broad response from across the country, from different regions and types of programs" (p. 13). By early spring 1994, NIFL received about 1,500 responses from 151 programs in 34 states. The learner responses were substantive and detailed, "with an average student response . . . [of] two paragraphs" (p. 13).

In their NIFL-commissioned *Voices from the Community*, Sticht, Erickson, and Armstrong (1996) questioned the generalizability of the information received based on the relatively small "response rate" from students "considering the thousands of literacy programs and millions of adult learners in the nation." The authors also commented on the failure of the Work Group "to control the number of responses from any one program" and the likelihood "that some few programs may have heavily biased the data base" (p. 4).

Merrifield (2000) acknowledged that the feedback received did not consist of "a representative sample" (p. 13). However, she pointed to "the geographical distribution and breadth of programs and learners" (p. 14) as sufficiently extensive to support a qualitative, although not a statistically reliable, quantitative study. She also pointed to the diversity of *types* of programs, which covered a broad range, as lending further legitimacy to the pool of student feedback received. Stein (1995) argued similarly, but acknowledged the lack of representation from a strictly quantitative model, which would need to be based on random sampling. As she expressed it, "We believe the writings are a significant collection and that they reflect the diversity of adult literacy programs and adult learners" (p. 101).

Clearly, the 1,500 student responses did not match the "rigorous" research design of Beder's (1999) proposed long-term impact study, based on "experimental design and qualitative components" (p. 125), in which "the researcher explores all possible interpretations of causality" (p. 129). However, from a qualitative research tradition, a case for legitimacy could be made. Based on the criteria of "triangulation," the diversity and range of responses did provide considerable feedback in the pragmatic effort of moving the NIFL project forward. The proposed task of establishing a framework for forging a national consensus in real time broadly linked to Goal 6 was no simple matter. This would require subtle and pragmatic working out of a range of tensions and conflicts by blending research, student, practitioner, and policy input into a coherent whole that could stimulate sufficient motivation to move a system.

What emerged was an *interpretive* process, reflecting the interaction of various groups and interests, including the influential perspectives of the EFF development team. Human interpretation is an inescapable aspect of qualitative research (perhaps of all research), and inherently contestable. Based on these premises, what is important is not value-free objectivity, but the cogency and coherency of the interpretation that nonetheless needs to be compatible "*with the data*" (Rescher, 2001, p. 190, italics in original) while acknowledging the viability of other construals even of the same information.

Sifting the Data

Once the student input was returned, NIFL hired Ray Rist, director for the Center of Policy Studies from George Washington University, to help "develop and implement a process for analyzing the data" (Stein, 1995, p. 101). Rist proposed "a systematic content analysis of the adult learner responses" and the utilization of a social science software program capable of ethnographic data storage. Rist developed a team that included assessment expert Gregg Jackson to begin the process of "identifying and refining themes" (p. 101). Four "coder/analysts" were also added, with Stein from NIFL assigned to work with them (Merrifield, 2000, p. 40).

According to Stein (1995), "The team followed stringent qualitative procedures for analyzing and interpreting the data" (p. 102). The texts were coded according to region and type of program. The team reviewed and discussed "a broad cross-section of learner responses in order to identify themes that appeared robust enough to be used as categories for coding" (Merrifield, 2000, p. 14). The work proceeded by their developing a "coding frame." Four initial codes emerged: Personal Development, Family/ Parenting, Job/Compete in Global Economy, and Roles and Responsibilities of Citizenship. Each Coding Category was supported by several subcategories backed up by several sample statements taken from the student feedback.

Merrifield noted that the categories and subcategories were representative of "the kinds of reasons adult learners often give for enrolling in programs." The analytical breakdown of the student input "could have been elaborated . . . into ever more specific and particular categories" (p. 15) resulting in an extensively long list of purposes that would likely have caused the kinds of "proliferation" problems that Sticht and his colleagues identified with Comprehensive Adult Student Assessment System (CASAS) performance indicators. Commenting on this problem, Sticht et al. (1996) observed that "in such 'outcome-based' methodologies for specifying what people should know and be able to do, there is no rationale given for how many sub-areas should be identified." The authors noted that such a process can "get very specific, as in the 5,000 test items that CASAS has for assessing the 317 'competencies' . . . , [in which] each item can be seen as a specific 'competency.' " In contrast, by extracting just a core set of competencies needed in the workplace, SCANS only "specifies a few, very broad categories of knowledge and skill" (p. 22) through which a wide array of information and data can be integrated. Avoidance of this proliferation tendency was a central concern in the thinking of the team, which led to a crucial step of "synthesis" (Merrifield, 2000, p. 15).

From Skills and Tasks to Purposes

In response to the proliferation dilemma, a fundamental restructuring in the analysis of the data eventually took place "that crosscut and linked with the original codes, but created a new way of looking at purposes of learning" (Merrifield, 2000, p. 15). Instead of further subdividing the "dizzying variety of skills," and "an equally impressive array of tasks" based on a literal breakdown of the student input, a more constructivist approach emerged. Thus, the team began to probe beneath the surface to what they perceived as the "*more fundamental purposes that express the social and cultural meaning or significance of these accomplishments for individuals engaged in defining themselves as competent actors in the world*" (Stein, 1995, p. 9, italics in original). Based on the "stringent qualitative procedures for analyzing and interpreting the data" (p. 102), the Four Purposes that emerged might be viewed as a creative leap, an inference from the data to explanation as a result of an imaginative construal, which is more or less inevitable at some point in qualitative research projects.

As discussed in chapter 9, what is important in nonquantitative, nonpositivistic research is a sense of *coherence* between the data and interpretation rather than strict linear correlation (Rescher, 2001). Based on these premises, EFF framers argued that their interpretation was coherent. Even still, they might have acknowledged more directly, that by its very nature, qualitative research is subject to diverse construals and that other interpretations were plausible.

Sticht et al. (1996) questioned the validity of the Four Purposes (Access, Voice, Independent Action, and Bridge to the Future) "induced" by the EFF team. They noted the "extensive subjective coding" of the student feedback, but remained concerned that "no inter-rater reliabilities were obtained and no cross-validation, using independent coding teams was conducted to determine how replicable the research findings were." Sticht and his colleagues also wondered to what "extent the four purposes accurately and reliably captured the statements by the 'customers' or 'clients,' or instead expressed the beliefs and attitudes of the researchers" (p. 4).

In one sense, the authors answered their own concerns by viewing their own research on the NIFL project "as essentially a social, political process" because "no entirely technical means exist to establish what people should know and be able to do to meet their life requirements." Short of an exacting science to get at what are essentially social, cultural, and psychological phenomena, "members of a society, a community, a neighborhood must come together to discuss, debate and render judgments about what the purpose of education is and should be taught in an educational program" (p. 5).

This, it might be argued, is what the NIFL-based research team had done first in sifting through the student feedback, then coding the material through a variety of formats. Ultimately, the research team took an interpretive leap based on the student input in moving beyond the data to its *significance* or underlying purposes as the team finally discerned them. Based on "grounded theory," a type of qualitative research, the goal of such scholarship is not to discern the incontrovertible truth, but to provide reasonable inferences and hypotheses, which remain contestable and subject to further analysis. Merrifield (2000) quoted Glasser and Strauss (1967) to articulate this view:

> *In discovering theory, one generates conceptual categories or their properties from evidence; then the evidence from which the category emerged is used to illustrate the concept. The evidence may not necessarily be accurate beyond a doubt . . . but the concept is undoubtedly a relevant theoretical abstraction about what is going on in the area studied.* (p. 23, cited in Merrifield, 2000, p. 7, italics in original)

In this form, research findings are useful for their heuristic capacity in the avenues of new insight that they open up, that is, they possess a constructive potential. For the research team, the Four Purposes represented an economical way to organize the student data in categories that were integral to, but transcended, the specific content areas identified in the raw input. Their efficacy would be proven in practice as students and teachers drew on the Four Purposes as a baseline in working with the other aspects of the EFF framework as they emerged, to help structure the focus of instruction. As a constructive interpretation of the received student data, the Four Purposes are inherently controvertible. Their legitimacy is based on their fidelity to the initial student input, and also prospectively, on their efficacy as a heuristic in contributing to the quality of instruction on those who draw on them.

SYNOPSIS OF THE FOUR PURPOSES

Access and Orientation

As described by Stein (2000):

> **Learning for access and orientation** includes not only physical or geograph-
> ical orientation—reading maps and signs—but also psychological or social
> orientation—knowing what is going on in the world, understanding institu-
> tions that have an impact on one's life, getting needed information. This pur-
> pose underlies many of the specific goals adults bring to literacy programs—
> for example, understanding the world, helping children with schooling, get-
> ting a job, gaining economic awareness, being an informed citizen. (p. 6)

The capacity to read road signs is an example of a literal application of
this purpose. Stein (1995) argued that the more fundamental "orientation
adults seek from literacy is psychological or social" (p. 11). Fingeret and
Drennon (1997) concurred by pointing to the many skills and sources of
knowledge that non- or low level adult readers possess, and the importance
of oral subcultures to the personal identities of those whom society may define as "illiterate." Still, as they also observed, "in the larger literate society
the inability to read and write fluently defines inequality and incompe-
tence." Consequently, "interactions with the institutions . . . of the larger society often result in adults with minimal literacy abilities feeling hindered
and stigmatized by the limits of their literacy practices" (p. 72). As Stein
(1995) explained, adults want access to relevant information and resources
that will expand their life's potential:

> No matter how elementary or advanced their basic reading and oral compre-
> hension skills, adults are also interested in learning and strengthening the
> skills associated with using information and having an impact on the world.
> They identify the need to develop the problem solving and critical thinking
> skills that have to do with analyzing and reflecting on information in order to
> make good decisions. (p. 24)

Concisely stated, the NIFL-based research team discerned that one of the
underlying purposes that adults seek is increased capacity "to place themselves on the map of daily life roles and responsibilities, to place themselves
in relationship to the world around them" (p. 11).

Voice

> **Learning for voice** embraces all aspects of communication—written and
> oral—needed to present oneself to the world. It goes beyond communication
> skills to the reasons for communicating: to speak and be heard. The writings

about citizenship offered an important arena for voice, but it was also important to adults in other aspects of their lives: to communicate with their children's teachers, to exchange ideas at work, to speak up in their community.
(Stein, 2000, p. 6)

Regardless of specific purposes, Stein (1995) identified *voice*, the desire to
be heard and to be taken seriously, as a central theme that came across in
the student narratives the research team studied. This "include[ed] the
ability to use written and oral language effectively in interpersonal and social situations" (p. 11). This aspiration was reflected in the initial coding
categories and the corresponding subcategories of the student narratives
that the research team worked through, particularly, "feel better about
self," "protection/vulnerability," and be "able to communicate" (Merrifield, 2000, p. 14). This subtle dimension of personal identity enhancement
through the expansion of voice, often opened up by adult literacy education, is pervasive within the student anthologies that abound in programs
across the country, and is linked to the underlying concept of self-esteem.
As expressed by one student with whom I worked:

> You have a lot of ideas to offer. But it takes education to bring all this out. I
> guess what education has done for me is to bring all these things out for me. I
> may have had it from the beginning, but there never was an opportune time
> for it all to be brought out. I had to wait until education came into my life and
> opened up these things to me, to give me more ways to express myself.
> (Smith, Ball, Demetrion, & Michelson, 1993, p. 108)

The EFF research team would also find linkages between the enhancement of self-esteem and the articulation of voice, although Stein (1995)
placed more emphasis on the close connection between voice and citizenship. She quoted one student, who stated that "to me, having the right to
participate in the political process means . . . being able to voice your opinion in many different ways such as voting, letters to editors, speech, and fly-
ers. This is a great way to be heard in government." Another student said,
"Being a citizen with rights and responsibilities makes me feel very important. It tells me that my opinion counts in what happens in my own very
community and I am just as prominent as the next person." Another student linked civic responsibility directly to self-esteem, stating, "When you
vote you have a say-so. You feel good about yourself because your vote does
count and make a difference" (p. 12).

Although some of these responses seem stylized, that was undoubtedly
due to the nature of the writing assignments in a predisposition to draw
out certain connections between student aspirations with citizenship and
the work demands of a postindustrial economy. It is, therefore, not sur-
prising that responses came back reflecting such language and concerns.

Nonetheless, whether the focus is economics, civic participation, or simply personal development, the importance of voice as a major source of student motivation is well supported by a wide array of primary and secondary sources.

This is not to deny the argument by Sticht and his colleagues that another group of researchers might have viewed the evidence from other angles of vision and placed different emphases in other areas. Even still, the categorization of voice that the research team highlighted could be viewed as a reasonable interpretation of the data, which drew support from a considerable body of qualitative research on adult literacy, other student-based evidence, and the premises of constructivist epistemology.

Independent Action

> **Learning for independent action** includes the dual elements of independence and action. Many adults who feel their literacy skills are limited depend on others for help with reading and writing. In statements pointing to this purpose, learners expressed their desire to be able to act for themselves, make informed decisions, and not have to rely on others to tell them what to do. Learners' responses stressed independent action in all aspects of life: supporting their families, achieving economic self-sufficiency, and fulfilling responsibilities in their communities. (Stein, 2000, p. 6)

The desire to achieve independent action spans a broad continuum from the distinctly personal and psychological to the desire for increased capacity to participate in the major social institutions and mores of contemporary life. In support of the former, Stein (1995) provided the following student example: "I never did put myself down because of it . . . but I had an empty spot inside of me, always depending on someone to read things to me" (p. 12). A student in Hartford, Connecticut, stated the following: "I live by myself, so I have to be motivated because I don't have anybody to do anything for me. And I get afraid. I'm ashamed to ask the lady I see to do things for me. So that motivates me. To be able to do things for myself because you're ashamed to ask people to do it for you. That motivates me, I think" (Demetrion & Gruner, 1995, p. 64). Fingeret and Drennon (1997) summarized this need in the following manner:

> The quest for independent literacy practices is a quest to fit in, to do things the way the dominant culture does them, to remove a stigma and to become free of a deep source of shame by changing performance in particular circumstances. Adults who feel powerful in other areas of their lives [or not] seek a resolution to the tension introduced by their limited literacy practices. (p. 73)

This is particularly so in social settings and cultural milieus where print literacy is widely prevalent and reinforced by social expectations of self-worth based on the mastery of functional competency.

Because of the policy focus, Stein (1995) connected independent action to vocational preparedness and the skills and knowledge needed to engage in active citizenship. Given this linkage, it is difficult to make sharp distinctions between the highly correlative purposes of *access and orientation* and *independent action*, which was not the intent of EFF in any event. Rather, the research team delineated the distinctiveness of the Four Purposes for analytical reasons. For purposes of instruction and real-world application, developers emphasized the interrelated nature of all of the components of the EFF framework.

It might be noted here that there is a minimal emphasis on the category of the self, notwithstanding the *coding category* of personal development in the research team's initial analysis of the student feedback. EFF developers would argue that the self is subsumed within the social roles. It is difficult not to conclude that this embedded emphasis of the self was influenced by the policy-oriented mandate to link EFF with worker, citizenship, and family education, what might be viewed as at least a partial skewing of what students actually identified as important. Whereas sharp graduations between the self and the various social roles would reflect a false polarity, in chapter 2 we observed the importance of the self as reflected in the precepts of the student-centered instruction and alternative modes of assessment, a view that is subtly modified with EFF. Although both camps identify these roles as important, a significant issue between the proponents of EFF and alternative assessment design is whether the social roles or the quest for lifelong learning, both within and beyond the roles in the mediation of self-perception, is the more important source of motivation. As put by Stein, closely following Fingeret:

> What we learned from these adult perspectives on Goal 6 is that adult students don't make this separation between literacy for life and literacy for the workplace or for citizenship. While the specific tasks, roles and responsibilities vary from context to context, the four purposes remain the same. Moreover, these purposes of education—what adults need literacy for—drive the acquisition of skills and knowledge both within and across the contexts. Adults seek to develop literacy skills in order to change what they can do, how they are perceived and how they perceive themselves in specific social and cultural contexts. (p. 10, italics in original)

Nonetheless, in privileging one or the other, the social roles or self-understanding, as an ultimate grounding point both for pedagogy and assessment, the manner in which the proponents of EFF and alternative assessment design interpret the quest for independent action *differently*, subtly points to the influence of political culture in shaping these pedagogical distinctions.

Bridge to the Future

Learning as bridge to the future reflects learners' sense that the world is changing. A prime purpose for learning is to be ready for the changes—to learn how to learn and prepare oneself for lifelong learning. Keeping up with change is a necessity, particularly at work, but in personal and family development and citizenship, learners also saw themselves in rapid social transformation. Keeping a job, adjusting to technological change, and improving family circumstances were all reasons to continue learning. (Stein, 2000, p. 6)

One of the participants NIFL surveyed expressed it this way: "Today in 1994 it would not be so easy to get a good job in a big corporation if one cannot read. But back then [in the 1950s] workers were needed and their education level was not as important as it is today. So if you are a person out there who thinks you can get by without learning to read you are wrong" (Stein, 1995, p. 16).

Another student pointed out that "the more skills you know and learn [the] better for you because more companies will hire a person with skills than without them" (p. 18). As indicated by some students, computer training was especially important. Not all identified skills were technical. As one student observed, "to me, having the skills and knowledge to compete . . . means punctuality, responsibility, and courage to progress and to have more work opportunity" (p. 18).

Students in Hartford also pointed to the important link between education and their future. One talked about being an art teacher. "I want to share my knowledge with a younger generation" (Demetrion & Gruner, 1995, p. 49). Another "want[ed] to go up in life." When asked what that meant, she responded, "to the top," which, for her, was to become a nurse (p. 58). Another linked future challenges with the quest to seek out his limits, which literacy education stimulated him to pursue. As he expressed it, "If I get into something that doesn't work right, I move onto the next thing. I think that's where I stand right now. I'm just taking anything I can grab onto and see what I can do with it" (Smith et al., 1993, p. 109).

As Fingeret and Drennon (1997) described it, "Basic self-concepts begin to change as adults begin to view themselves as writers and readers" (p. 84). New possibilities about the future open up, both those seemingly intangible, and those more specific and concrete, linked to employment or other life roles and goals. Whether an enhanced sense of potentiality, or in a concrete attainment of expanded skills and knowledge built into the challenges of everyday living, Dewey's (1916) concept of growth addresses some of the more enduring impact of adult literacy education. According to Dewey, growth "is essentially the ability to learn from experience; the power to retain from one experience something which is of avail in coping with the difficulties of a later situation. This means power to modify actions on the basis of the results of prior experiences, the power to *develop dispositions*" (p. 44, italics in original) of learning.

Fingeret and Drennon (1997) linked this concept to adult literacy:

> When students engage in new literacy practices, they are also engaging in a profound process of reconstructing their definitions of normal and their relationship to the dominant culture. Once the deep sense of shame begins to abate, anxiety over performance changes as well. This facilitates moving across boundaries, from inside to outside the program, from public to private situations, and from practices that seem more flexible to those that feel more standardized. The courage to engage in intensive interaction is essential to this movement. (p. 86)

To put this in formal constructivist terms, what typically happens when students achieve this level of competency and confidence is a growing capacity in their ability to master the challenges and opportunities of the future for themselves.

In linking the Four Purposes to the specific student feedback, however interpolated, project designers sought to ground system reform in a "customer-driven vision." Stein and others hoped that the unfolding effort would provide the framework for a widely accepted, standard-based adult education system that would link enlightened social policy to important adult educational principles and practices. In this first stage of the emerging project, Stein (1995) hoped the "four purposes [would] enable us to maintain a sense of unity to the field, while supporting the development of programs and curricula appropriate to different contexts, including the workplace, the community and the family" (p. 26).

The Four Purposes pointed to "the purposeful side of learning, but not what needs to be learned" (Merrifield, 2000, p. 17). The content of a revitalized ABE/adult literacy national system was envisioned in Goal 6 in the most general of terms. Much work was needed to flesh out the concrete aspects of what became the Three Role Maps, well before the issue of standards could be addressed. The development of the Four Purposes was the first critical step in a decade-long odyssey to fully establish the EFF framework.

CITIZEN/COMMUNITY MEMBER, PARENT/ FAMILY MEMBER, WORKER ROLE MAPS

The very purpose of the NIFL/Goals Panel query was to identify what was needed to link worker and citizenship education to effective pedagogy in order to fulfill the stated goals of national policy. Family education was also added to the then still emerging EFF project because of its place in Even Start legislation, the American Reads initiative (Merrifield, 2000, p. 40), its inclusion as a key area in the National Literacy Act of 1991, and its advocacy by former First Lady Barbara Bush. This focus was confirmed in the student essays that also reflected strong emphasis on family as well as career goals, and improving community life (Merrifield, 2000; Stein, 1995). As noted by Merrifield, the three roles of worker, family member/parent, and community/member/citizen "are not the only adult roles, but are key ones for public policy" (p. 18) consistent with NIFL's objective of developing a national consensus for the purposes of legitimizing public support for adult literacy education.

The first major effort after the student feedback had been assimilated was to award planning grants to eight agencies to further test the Four Purposes and to gain more information on "what adults in each role know and are able to do" (Merrifield, 2000, p. 18). The planning projects included various stakeholders from community organizations, the business sector, and the field of adult education. They all incorporated focus groups to probe into "questions about what adults needed to know and be able to do to fulfill their roles" (p. 19). As Merrifield noted, this latter emphasis on action was an "important shift" in the development of EFF thinking. As she explained it, "The emphasis on what adults do, on broad areas of responsibility and key activities," which would represent the core of the Role Maps in their fully developed form, emerged in this early work.

Each planning project reported its findings on the four questions the NIFL asked the grantees to examine related to identifying the "broad areas of responsibility" and "key activities" of each of the three roles, along with the skills and knowledge needed to carry them out effectively. Separate reports from each project were synthesized for each of the roles. The Citizen/Community Member Role was synthesized by the Knoxville-based Center for Literacy Studies. The Worker Role, which drew on SCANS, O*NET, and other resources, was synthesized by Performance Consulting, Inc. Similar work for the Parent/Family Member Role was handled by the National Center for Family Literacy (p. 41). Merrifield observed that EFF framers viewed the emerging framework as "less a 'foundation' (something static and unchanging) and more a 'core' (a dynamic source of energy and fusion)" (p. 20).

As a result of this research, NIFL created a new publication in early 1997 titled *Equipped for the Future: A Reform Agenda for Adult Literacy and Lifelong Learning* written by Stein, which spelled out EFF's policy goals in the creation of a national consensus based on a 21st-century world-class adult education system. The sense of public legitimacy for the NIFL-based project was telegraphed in the first few pages in the impressive list of national advisors in support of this new venture. In succeeding pages, this publication reviewed EFF's origins in Congress' desire to measure the nation's progress toward the fulfillment of National Educational Goal 6. The publication pointed to the then current failure of the ABE system and the need for a "coherent vision based on a real-world assessment of the knowledge and skills adults need," along with "specific objectives" and "clear criteria for measuring achievement" (Stein, 1997, p. 5).

The text presented a sharp contrast between the fragmented, school-based ABE model and the proposed "21st century" alternative. In the new system, "education *is* [italics in original] action" in that "it happens throughout life, preparing for changing needs and interests." Rather than the traditional view of adult education as "remedial," in the 21st-century system "[adult education] is preparation for the future, enabling people to meet the demands in their life today and in the future." In the proposed system, "adult education focuses on what adults need to know and be able to do as parents, citizens and workers." It "integrates core skills and knowledge with their application across contexts" and enables adults to exercise the role of lifelong learner.

In the new system, the "content of education is customer-driven, shaped by what adults say they need to know to succeed in the world." Rather than mastery of "specific competencies" (p. 9), the recommended system emphasizes "generative skills and knowledge . . . that are core to the performance of a wide range of tasks found in multiple roles that are durable over time in face of changes in technology, work processes, and societal demand" (p. 30). Consequently, "progress is measured in relationship to capacity to organize experience and perform real-world tasks" (p. 9). To summarize, the 1997 NIFL publication spelled out in bold terms sharp differences between what it characterized as the outdated, fragmented, school-based system that needed to be replaced with a dynamic new vision designed to achieve policy legitimacy, national consensus, clear standards, and substantial system reform.

The publication laid out in chart and pictorial form the three Role Maps. Each Role Map had an overall action orientation. Thus, "effective citizens and community members take informed action to make a positive difference in their lives, community and world." For what became the Parent/Family Member Role Map, "effective family members contribute to the building and maintaining a strong family system that promotes growth and development." For the third role, "Effective workers adapt to change and actively participate in meeting the demands of a changing workplace in a changing world" (Stein, 2000, Appendix A, n.p.). In the EFF vision, "Citizenship is not just about voting in elections, for example, but about taking action in many ways to make a positive difference in the world. Parents are seen as creating a vision for the family, and promoting values, ethics, and cultural heritage. Workers not only do the work but pursue work activities that bring personal satisfaction and meaning to them" (Merrifield, 2000, p. 27).

Broad Areas of Responsibility (BAR) and key activities buttress the Role Maps. Broad Areas of Responsibility are "the critical functions that an adult performs within the role to achieve the role's key purpose [its overall definition]. They represent large segments of role performance and provide a high level definition of the critical areas of action found in each role" (Stein, 1997, p. 32). In the final EFF rendition, the BAR for the Worker Role Map are, Do the Work, Work with Others, Work within the Big Picture, and Plan and Direct Personal and Professional Growth.

Each BAR contains several Key Activities, which:

> 1) show how knowledge, skills, and abilities come together in actual practice; 2) can be demonstrated, observed, and assessed; and 3) can be expressed as an outcome. Key activities are NOT areas of knowledge or skill: rather, they show how adults *combine* knowledge, skills, abilities and personal characteristics to perform a particular adult role. They consist of *several* [italics in original] adult tasks, not just one task or a series of steps. (Stein, 1997, p. 32)

In its final rendition, the Key Activities for the BAR Work within the Big Picture are as quoted:

- Work with organizational norms
- Respect organizational goals, performance, and structure to guide work activities
- Balance individual roles and needs with those of the organization
- Guide individual priorities based on industry trends, labor laws, contracts, and competitive practices. (Stein, 2000, Appendix A, n.p.)

Between 1997 and 2000, the Broad Areas of Responsibility and Key Activities underwent various revisions, mostly minor, some more significant. These need not be considered for the purposes of this analysis, except to point out that the changes reflected fine points of constructivist pedagogy as well as in some cases, policy concerns, such as the broadening of the original Parent Role Map to its final iteration as the Parent/Family Role Map. Merrifield (2000) concluded that "as a result of the structured feedback process [through several iterations], there can be some confidence that the broad areas of responsibility and the activities in the role maps represent a credible portrait of the three adult roles, distilled from the experience of a broad sector of the population" (p. 27). Public legitimacy and consensus building were as important to the EFF framework developers as was the technical proficiency that went into the refinement of the Role Maps.

FROM BROAD AREAS OF RESPONSIBILITY AND KEY ACTIVITIES TO SKILLS AND KNOWLEDGE: MOVING TOWARD STANDARDS

Although the Role Maps were designed to include the skills and knowledge needed to carry out their purposes, the 1997 NIFL publication only extended as far as the Broad Areas of Responsibility and the Key Activities. Standard-based reform within an EFF framework would require an analysis of the *skills* and *knowledge* needed to meet the Four Purposes through the Three Role Maps.

In the early era of EFF, there was a certain degree of probing on whether or not the standards should be directly linked to "the various contexts relevant to family, citizenship, and work" (Stein, 1995, p. 26). The emphasis on several "role indicators" (indicators traditionally being a focal point for measurement) for each of the Key Activities, reinforced at least in early EFF thinking, the prospect of developing content standards based on the role maps. However, role indicators like "develop, implement, and evaluate strategies to achieve the family vision" or "reflect upon and support family's common goals and values" for the Key Activity "create a vision for the family and work to achieve it" (Stein, 2000, Appendix A, n.p.), proved cumbersome for economical measurement.

There were two problems in making role indicators the basis for standards. First, their unmanageable number, 229, raised the proliferation specter. Second, "*They usually require multiple skills and knowledge*" (Merrifield, 2000, p. 28, italics in original) and would be difficult to assess in a reasonably logical way. What gradually unfolded was a focus on skills and knowledge that would serve as the basis for developing standards that ultimately emerged, with the role indicators providing feedback in helping to gain a handle on them (p. 33).

To obtain information outside of the immediate feedback loop, the three role consortiums reviewed key literature in their areas to discern skills and knowledge needed for effective performance. Input from these sources was intended to buttress the primary data gleaned from the ongoing EFF research project. These included such key monographs as *Quickening of America: Rebuilding Our Nation, Rethinking Our Lives* (Lappe & Dubois, 1994), *The Seven Habits of Highly Effective Families* (Covey, 1995), and *The Essential Skills Employers Want* (Carnevale, Gainer, & Meltzer, 1990).

Merrifield noted that the "documentary sources were uneven in terms of quality and comprehensiveness." With progress on standards in the realm of employment already achieved as a result of SCANS, O*NET, and the National Skill Standards Board, she noted that the worker literature sources were richer than those for the other two roles. Reflecting on the literature on family and parenting, Merrifield observed that it contains much insight on what might be viewed as normative familial behavior, but that little of it stems from "solid research on the skills and knowledge needed" in becoming effective parents and family members. She also noted that much of the literature the consortium drew on for the citizen's role reflected the traditional K–12 civics concept of knowing about government, but "fails to include the broad domain of practical 'citizenship' identified in EFF's own research" (p. 30).

An initial articulation of skills emerged from the literature surveys. To help bring the literature review under a unified mode, a technical assistance team created "an initial coding guide that made it possible to bring skills and knowledge from each of the documentary sources into a common framework, which then could be linked [back] with the role maps" (Merrifield, 2000, p. 30). This resulted in five broad categories of skills: *Foundation Skills, Extended Literacy Skills, Interpersonal Skills, Personal Development,* and *Knowledge,* supported by 26 subskills. The coding frame was then revised for each role through another iterative process of specialists, practitioners, and EFF staff. "Text items [from the literature survey] within a particular subcategory, such as reading [one of the Foundation Skills], were sorted and re-classified into new 'sub-categories' " (pp. 31–32) applied to the skill or knowledge needs of each of the three roles.

At this point in the quest to identify skills and knowledge that would ultimately lead to standards, "EFF had two independently derived documents about each role" (p. 32); the train of work that led to the Broad Areas of Responsibility, Key Activities, and role indicators, and the skills and knowledge discerned through the literature survey on each role. EFF developers established "linkage meetings" to bring these two disparate sources of information together. Integrative connections were found by matching up the Key Activities of the Role Maps with the skills and knowledge in the "revised coding frame" that stemmed from the literature review at the "sub-subcategory level" (p. 32).

It was at this point that the role indicators provided important linking connections. Thus, the Key Activity, "identify and monitor problems, community needs, strengths and resources" (Stein, 1997, p. 15) under the BAR Become and Stay Informed in the Citizen/Community Member Role Map, would be linked with the sub-subcategory "comprehend what you read" (Merrifield, 2000, p. 32) under the Foundational Skill, Reading. The role indicator, "asks the right questions to get relevant information" (p. 28), would provide additional information in discerning the key skills and knowledge areas needed to fulfill this objective.

What remained uncertain was how far to take the analytical process of further sifting and refining the data before obtaining sufficient information to shift from discrete competencies to comprehensive processes. In principle, the analytical process was infinite. At some point, a creative leap would need to be taken before all the data could ever be amassed in order to make the shift to broader categories in moving toward an economical set of standards. Merrifield observed that "the linkage process reveals how complex the relationships are between skills and activities." As she further explained, "Most of the activities require several skills. Most of the skills could be applied in a number of activities" (p. 33).

EFF developers viewed this analytical process of sifting through the various kinds of field-tested information and expertise insight as essential to assure that the intellectual integrity of the emerging framework would be deliberately built stage-by-stage. The process of engaging various groups, agencies, expert authorities, and diverse sectors of the ABE/adult literacy constituency was also deemed essential in order to achieve the legitimacy and consensus needed to operationalize the framework on a nationwide basis.

For EFF developers, legitimacy needed to stem from sound intellectual premises coherent within a constructivist epistemology while remaining useful to practitioners and students; firmly grounded in federal policy, and comprehensible to a broader interested public in order to garner the required widespread support. The thoroughness of the analytical examination of the various components and subcomponents of the emerging framework represented a wrestling with these not-easily-reconcilable objectives. As Merrifield summarized this stage of the work, there was now for each role "a set of skills and knowledge based on the literature" (p. 33) subject to further refinement through field testing.

Matters could not rest at this level of precise analytical definition and correlation of the framework's various components, which ultimately did not cohere. "As a basis for standards, the separate roles still needed to be linked and brought into one coherent framework" (p. 33). The standards needed to be relatively few in number and grounded in constructivist principles that had the capacity to perform a great deal of work in assisting students to realize the Four Purposes within the Three Role Maps. For assessment and accountability purposes, the standards would need to serve as the vehicle for evaluating significant areas of student learning that could be readily conveyed to students, instructors, program administrators, and policymakers.

For both purposes of achieving philosophical coherence and for system building "there was a need to condense and abstract the three role maps into one, without losing the capacity to draw on the finer details of the individual role maps" (p. 33). The Common Activities, Knowledge Domains, and Generative Skills that resulted were designed to support this bridging between the role maps and the standards. As reviewed next, their pedagogical impact is clearer to discern than the precise role they played in facilitating the transition from role maps to standards.

MOVING TOWARD STANDARDS: COMMON ACTIVITIES, GENERATIVE SKILLS, AND KNOWLEDGE DOMAINS

Common Activities

The development of 12 cross-functional Common Activities provided EFF framers with a way of identifying tasks that students need in order to progressively master the Key Activities of the particular Role Maps that they may be working on. In the coding and sorting process, these "activities were designated as 'common' only if they appeared in all three roles . . . [, although] common activities had different emphases and meanings in the context of each role" (Stein, 2000, p. 14): "For example, the citizen and family member roles were particularly strong on interpretation and communication activities such as 'guide and support others' and 'respect others and value diversity.' The worker role was particularly strong on systems activities like 'work within the big picture' and 'keep pace with change' " (p. 14).

Merrifield (2000) briefly reviewed how the Common Activities were constructed, based on research stemming from the Role Maps. The movement from concrete to more general application required an abstractive process that would not diminish the specific activities reflected in each of the roles. This necessitated careful deliberation because "the three role maps had been constructed separately." Thus, "common activities [within each role] were not necessarily found in the same levels" (p. 33). In some roles, they emerged from Broad Areas of Responsibility. In others, they stemmed from Key Activities that reflected "their importance or frequency in different roles" (p. 34).

Although the "common activities had different emphases and meanings in the context of each role" (Merrifield, 2000, p. 35), EFF framers still found a level of generality within them that applied to all the Role Maps, even if not in a precisely balanced manner. This lack of full system integration reflected a tension inherent within the EFF project at large. As described by Merrifield, this

> tension is between creating the "big picture," a common framework within which everyone can find a space, and honoring and paying attention to the specific social context in which each individual learner lives and the particular purposes for each's learning. The more distilled the framework gets and the further from the role maps, the harder it is to stay in that social and purposeful context. Yet that context is where adults need to act, and it is what learning needs to address. EFF is seeking a different learning guide from the "skills in isolation" approach. The tension is the essence of the approach, but nonetheless hard to manage. (p. 39)

In moving from Role Maps toward Standards it was this quest for increasing abstraction that the EFF developers sought in shifting from what they viewed as the behaviorism that underpinned the competency-based model as reflected in CASAS, for example, to a constructivist framework based on what they interpreted as a more adequate cognitive psychology. In the latter, learning would be measured not through the performance of specific tasks, isolated from the broader literacy practices in which the lives of students are situated, but in developing the metacognitive aptitude in learning how to learn that can be applied to a broad array of situations and specific tasks.

Dewey (1933/1989) referred to this abstractive capacity as the "ability to dig underneath the already known to some unfamiliar property or relation that is intellectually much more significant because it makes possible a more analytic and extensive inference" (p. 277). This was a major pedagogical objective of EFF framers' efforts in the creation of Common Activities. In this respect, the Common Activities played a mediating role in system construction from the Role Maps to the Content Standards. Whereas the precise relation between the Common Activities and the Content Standards is not exactly clear, their educational impact is more thoroughly articulated in the EFF literature.

Stein (2000, Appendix A, n.p.) illustrated the potential educational value of the Common Activities through a grid that links each of the 12 with Key Activities in each of the Role Maps. She also identified particular tasks within each Common Activity that then can be linked to specific Key Activities in the Role Maps. As an example, the general description of the Common Activity "Manage Resources" is as follows: "Find, manage, share and allocate time, money, and material resources in a way that supports your own needs, goals, and priorities and those of your family, community, and workplace." The specific tasks under Manage Resources are:

- Identify those resources you have and those you need
- Determine where they are and how they can be obtained
- Use the resources in an efficient and effective manner
- Balance resources effectively for family, work community, and self. (Appendix A)

This Common Activity applied to the Key Activity of the Parent/Family Role Map, *manage family resources,* may stimulate lessons on monthly budgeting, time management, exploring additional avenues for increasing resources, or enhancing usage of existing resources. This work, in turn, would be part of a larger objective linked to the Broad Area of Responsibility to "meet family needs and responsibilities" within the *key purpose* of the overall Role Map of "building and maintaining a strong family system that promotes growth and development" (Appendix A). Connecting lessons like these to the Four Purposes would help to solidly ground the work in important areas of student motivation linked to the policy objective of enhancing family literacy. Such efficacy provides the Common Activities with considerable heuristic power in probing into various intricacies and nuances of student learning as applied to the various Role Maps, which may emerge through discovery processes as well as from preselective goals.

For practitioners, it is this educational potency that reflects the paramount value of the Common Activities. For policy and public perception purposes, they have an illustrative value in demonstrating the overall integrity, comprehensiveness, and integration of the EFF framework, although they do not appear to possess any precise *system* function in the maintenance or definition of the Content Standards or their properties, what ultimately came to be referred to as "components of performance."

Knowledge Domains

EFF developers define *Knowledge Domains* as "the concepts, procedures, data, information, and perspectives that support the generative skills [discussed later] and [that] are necessary to carry out the common activities in our adult roles" (Merrifield, 2000, p. 36). They emerged through a similar combination of information gathering and coding that informed the development and refinement of the Role Maps. Initially, the relevant knowledge (as distinct from activities and skills) was linked to each role, separated into "academic and practical/experiential" (p. 36) categories. Whereas "it was clear from the coding process that knowledge domains are more context-specific than either skills or activities, [in grounding EFF in constructivist principles, designers sought] . . . a common knowledge base" (p. 36) appropriate to all of the Role Maps.

"The knowledge domains are conceptual rather than detailed; the specifics emerge in relationship to the activities themselves" (p. 36). They supply the broad context that gives shape to particular learning objectives. For example, under the Citizen/Community Member Role Map, one of the Broad Areas of Responsibility is "form and express opinions and ideas." Under this is the Key Activity, "Strengthen and express a sense of self that reflects personal history, values, beliefs, and roles in the larger community" (Stein, 2000, Appendix A, n.p.). A lesson might be drawn on autobiographical experiences of adult literacy learners in a collection of oral histories (Lestz, Demetrion, & Smith, 1994) in which individuals discuss their migration from one place to another. This could be within a given country, such as the migration of African Americans from the south to the north in the early part of the 20th century in the United States, or an external migration from Latin America or the Caribbean.

In the quest to gain deepened understanding of the personal narratives of adult literacy learners, the Knowledge Domains might be drawn on to connect personal stories with broader social, cultural, and historical trends. To do so, the instructor might utilize several of the Knowledge Domains. These could include *how systems work* in terms of government policy on immigration and race, *culture, values, and ethics* in terms of connecting autobiographical experience with more deep-rooted family and community values, and *how the past shapes the world we live in* linking personal narratives to broader historical patterns on race and ethnicity. There is a profusion of personal narrative collections of adult literacy learners to draw on. With few exceptions, these texts seldom include discussion of the wider context that gives shape to individual lives. When the context stems from a reflection on personal experience, it possesses the capacity to make a more powerful impact on the reader than when viewed simply as an external text about other people and events.

As an example, in an interview in our Hartford-based program (Demetrion & Gruner, 1995), we asked one student to comment both on what we referred to as "general history," including Black history in which he was highly interested, and on our collection of oral history texts (Lestz, Demetrion, & Smith, 1994) of adult literacy learners. First we asked, "What relationship do you think there is between general history and your own personal history?" His response was, "General history is everyone's history. My personal history may be similar to the general history, but it isn't written in textbooks" (Demetrion & Gruner, 1995, p. 48). We then asked him what he thought of the Hartford-based oral history collection: "Very interesting. People have to work hard to get where they're at today. Their experience is more complex than someone else's history. You can put yourself in their situation; it's more like my history" (p. 48).

After that, we asked him how he would compare personal oral histories of adult literacy students with traditional types of biographies about African American leaders that he had read. "They each have their history and someone is writing about it. It's kind of a neat way to understand their history." He continued, not making a sharp distinction between traditional biography and the narratives of the adult literacy students: "They have a pattern; like this person had a hard time, the other person may have had good times, but it always comes back to the past" (p. 48).

Throughout his educational program, this particular student combined reflection on personal experience through the prism of race consciousness, a study of African American biography, and an empathetic reading of the narratives of other adult literacy students (Demetrion, 2001b). Consider the following essay this person wrote, titled, *Open Your Mind to a Different Race*, which captures some of these connections:

> Why do the majority of white people think that black people are outspoken when blacks stand up to white people who try to own black people? Some whites don't want the blacks to stand up for their rights. Blacks are tired of hearing, "that's a black problem." Many whites have problems understanding how blacks go through life because they don't know the black race. That's why both races have too much to hate in society.
>
> We all face difficulties about different races and heritages. We lost hope in the American creed of being equal and the respect for goodness of one another. Luxury and material things are taking the place of goodness and equal rights. Each individual should take a step to make peace by trying not to judge one another by their ancestry. (Demetrion, 1995, p. 26)

This essay emerged both from personal experience and a study of African American history, culture, and biography in which personal and public history was fused. Developing an educational plan that made the personal more public and the public more personal enriched this student's educational experience.

In principle, instructors do not need the prompt of the Knowledge Domains to establish linkages between personal and more public histories. However, they can serve as a powerful heuristic by providing a convenient frame of reference through which instructors might incorporate broader systemic and cultural influences to deepen the context of personal experience within a learner-centered milieu. The systemic function of the Knowledge Domains in the development of the Content Standards is undefined, although they took on some underarticulated heuristic purpose in the thinking of EFF framers in the movement from the Role Maps to the Standards.

Generative Skills

EFF defines *Generative Skills* as:

> Skills or knowledge that are core to the performance of a wide range of tasks found in multiple roles and that are durable over time in face of changes in technology, work process, and societal demands. Generative skills are cross-functional and serve as the foundation for effective adaptation to changes in role requirements. (Stein, 1997, p. 30)

The educational function of Generative Skills is to provide the skills and knowledge to support the Common Activities (Stein, 2000, p. 15) of enabling students to progressively master the context of the Role Maps as they relate to specific purposes that learners self-identify as important. In this respect, the Generative Skills might be viewed as a toolbox to be selectively drawn on to better enable students to meet their learning purposes. Although students may draw on various tools to meet particular objectives, enhanced mastery of the Generative Skills expands flexibility of approach and leads to the greater likelihood of progressing toward the achievement of their goals. In short, in the EFF model, the Generative Skills make a substantial contribution in enabling learners to achieve their purposes in and through their primary social roles of parent/family member, community member/citizen, and worker.

The same tendency as marked the early work on the Common Activities toward "proliferation" manifested itself in the initial effort on developing the Generative Skills. In the latter case, a long concrete list "of over 50 skills" was eventually abstracted to 17 skills in the four broad categories of communication, interpersonal, decision making, and lifelong learning (Merrifield, 2000, p. 35). EFF framers viewed these "integrated skill processes" as foundational in "carry[ing] out the common activities identified from the role maps, and many day-to-day tasks" (p. 35).

Each of the four general groups in which the Generative Skills were arranged contained a broad definition linked to the specific skills of each category. Thus, the general category of Lifelong Learning Skills is defined as that which "enable[s] adults to keep learning in order to keep up with change." The four specific skills that fall within this group are:

- Take Responsibility for Learning
- Reflect and Evaluate
- Learn Through Research
- Use Information and Communication Technology (p. 35)

Each Generative Skill includes a number of basic properties. For example, *learn through research* contains the following dimensions, as quoted:

- Pose a question to be answered or make a prediction about objects or events.
- Use multiple lines of inquiry to collect information.
- Organize, valuate, analyze, and interpret findings. (p. 57)

Students and instructors would draw on any and all of these dimensions of this generative skill as relevant to any learning situation.

Many of these Generative Skills imperceptibly emerged with the work on the Common Activities, which were only gradually delineated into specific categories of "activities" and "skills," respectively (p. 35). What they both had in common in their evolving state was a "higher order" abstraction from the concrete specificity of the role maps in the quest for cross-functional, transferable knowledge.

Their underlying constructivist orientation is evident, for example, in the Generative Skill, "Read with Understanding." The definition is as follows: *"To read with understanding adults need to determine the reading purpose; monitor comprehension and adjust reading strategies; analyze the information and reflect on its underlying meaning; integrate it with prior knowledge to address reading purpose"* (p. 35, italics in original). The constructivist implications are expressed in the powerful verbs that characterize this statement: "determine," "monitor," "adjust," "analyze," "reflect," "integrate," "address." As Merrifield explained, " 'Reading with Understanding' is more than a simple additive effect of more specific skills: it requires a critical evaluative stance to reading, a view of reading that is conceptual, not mechanical" (p. 36).

However abstract from the immediacy of concrete objectives, the Generative Skills are designed to feed back into the Role Maps and the Four Purposes in an integrative process of meaning making, critical action, and learning. The Generative Skills are designed to serve as a powerful heuristic in structuring learning in self-defined areas of student learning. They also provided the foundation for the EFF Content Standards, the focus of the next chapter.

EFF Standards: Linking
Pedagogy and Policy in Quest
of a National Consensus

> *By summer 2003 EFF will have developed and validated definitions for perform-*
> *ance for 12 of our standards. These definitions will support the development of*
> *new assessments that hopefully will take us all out of the dismal swamp—and a*
> *little further toward our vision of a system in which teaching and assessment, re-*
> *porting and accountability are aligned with and produce results that matter—to*
> *our students and to the public and private agencies that provide resources for*
> *adult literacy services.*
>
> —Sondra Stein, National Director, Equipped for the Future,
> NLA (November 9, 2001)

> *The mind at every stage of growth has its own logic.*
> —Dewey (1933/1989, p. 181)

The Generative Skills provided the underpinning for the 16 EFF Content
Standards. Each of the skills was succinctly defined in short statements that
emphasized constructive action as well as mastery of relevant knowledge.
For example, the Generative Skill, "Cooperate with Others," is defined as
follows: "Work with others across differences in culture, ethnicity, social
background, belief, or physical ability. Use principles of group dynamics
and consensus-building strategies, building on the strengths of individual
group members including yourself" (Levinson, 1998, p. 13).

As a starting point toward the development of Standards, the Generative
Skills contained the core information and abilities adults would need to
know, particularly in carrying out the Common Activities within the Role
Maps. However, the Generative Skills needed further development in their
transition to standards. In the effort to be useful to the field, manageable
for reporting purposes, and keeping grounded in constructivist learning

179

principles, in its first iteration, EFF's "technical-assistance team" created "an overly complex first standards draft" (Stein, 2000, p. 15). Additional development in the early months of 1998 was facilitated through field testing by 25 local programs.

Participating program staff members were asked at the beginning of the study to identify student goals and to note how they identified them. They were also asked to connect learning activities based on these goals to the EFF framework, and to identify which of its components was most relevant. The instructors were requested to document changes in their initial instructional plans over the course of the project period and to explain the basis for any shifts. Focusing more intentionally on the utilization of specific EFF draft standards, participants were asked to "describe as specifically as you can what evidence you saw/heard, collected that students could use this skill," for whatever learning activity the participants were evaluating. They were also asked to identify specific "performance indicators . . . that were especially helpful . . . in clarifying what counts as evidence" (Stein, 2000, Appendix B, n.p.).

Participants also identified which Common Activities supplied "the context for working on" any given draft standard in the specific learning/ teaching situations that they tracked. In addition, they were instructed to "look at the components of skill performance for this Standard" and "how the components will inform what you plan to do" as a teacher. Each *component* was described as "a critical point in the successful application of the skill." Participants were also asked to describe something about "the level of performance of your students" and write a "separate paragraph to report on each component" (Appendix B, n.p.). Based on criteria outlined in Bransford, Brown, and Cockings (1999), the field testers were reminded of the four dimensions of performance EFF developers wanted to track, "building knowledge base, increasing range, increasing flexibility/automaticity, and increasing independence" (Stein, 2000, Appendix B, n.p.).

The main focus of the field research was to obtain detailed information on the draft standards and levels of student performance. To acquire this, the EFF internal document, *Guidelines for Field Research* (Levinson, 1998), provided an overall orienting question, "How Do You Know When You Are Doing This Well?" for each component of the standard that it sought to analyze. Thus, for the standard, "Read Critically," the components were, "to acquire information, to deepen understanding, to interact with others, and to inform decision-making and action" (pp. 19–20). Each standard description in the packet included the Common Activities most applicable for each Generative Skill under investigation. While concentrating on identifying performance indicators for each draft standard, field researchers were also asked to reflect on how the various combinations of the EFF framework intersected.

The permutations among the different EFF factors were multiplicative, which demonstrated something of the rich heuristic potential of the framework to stimulate instruction. At the same time, the combination of relations of the various factors also highlighted the "proliferation" syndrome that stemmed from the desire to establish an interlocking system in which all of the parts might be related to each other in a tightly integrated structure.

ESTABLISHING THE STANDARDS

The NIFL–4EFF listserv archives for 1998 provide additional information on this initial field research phase of the development of the Content Standards. Whereas EFF's larger purpose in their development was aimed at policy legitimization, the field testing was designed to assure that the standards and the accompanying performance indicators would be grounded in a solid pedagogical basis. In sifting through these not-always-compatible objectives, one participant wondered whether "EFF [is] a philosophy about teaching and learning, or is it an assessment tool, or both" (Attrawick, NIFL–4EFF, March 2, 1998).

Another participant provided what she viewed as a clear illustration of the pedagogical potentiality of EFF. The instructional setting consisted of low level readers with "learning disabilities." The teacher was interested in finding out whether what her students learned in class could be "transfer[red] to their jobs" through the Communication Skill, Listen Actively. To help determine mastery, she asked one student to "describe how you can use on your job the knowledge you learned in this module."

At first, the student did not think there was an application. After further discussion, he had learned that because most of the equipment in his work area consists of metal, in putting out a fire one would use dry foam rather than water. The instructor viewed that as "an incredible leap for him to make," which she was not "sure he would have made it if not asked to think about and apply what he had learned." It was only at that point that the instructor "really [grasped] . . . the benefits of EFF" (Bolte, NIFL–4EFF, March 11, 1998). National EFF Director Sondra Stein noted this example gave her "a sense that the standards [were] . . . useful as a tool for focusing on 'results that matter' " and provided additional information "about *how* [italics in original] teachers are using the standards," which was critical in "mak[ing] them more useful" (Stein, NIFL–4EFF, March 19, 1998).

More systemic issues about the role and development of the draft standards ensued. Andrea Nash, one of the EFF developers at World Education in Cambridge, Massachusetts, reflected on the extent to which various practitioners drew *explicitly* on the EFF framework to structure lessons, or more *implicitly*, to gain a better handle on the learning process, once topics were underway and goals selected. She was particularly interested in exploring "whether or not people were using the standards for validating what they'd already done," as a source of confirmation. The consensus that Nash discerned from the field was that "most felt that their initial planning needed to be in response to student needs, but that once they got going, the standards were helpful for thinking about where you might take the lesson." In addition, Nash reported that most of the field practitioners did not find "the indicators particularly helpful, as written." Many, therefore, wrote "their own" (Nash, NIFL–4EFF, March 18, 1998).

One field participant reported that her "students are a bit flummoxed by the language and number of [standards] components" and viewed the "performance standards . . . difficult to conceive of using as they are" (Bronz, NIFL–4EFF, March 14, 1998). Stein agreed that there were too many, but that she was depending on field "input . . . to . . . hone in on the most important indicators," with the end result of having "fewer for each standard." At this phase of the process, explained Stein, all the EFF developers were attempting to do was to "identify [what] the elements performance should look like for adults at varying levels" while not being overly concerned about measurement issues. Consequently, she was not "surprised to hear that the indicators seem too vague to use for measurement" (Stein, NIFL–4EFF, March 19, 1998). She assured participants that further refinement would follow and encouraged the field practitioners to stay with the process.

At this important juncture of moving from Generative Skills to Content Standards, EFF was relying on specialists of various sorts, an inner developmental team, as well as the field testers. This field testing represented a critical aspect in the process. Its purpose was to enable EFF developers to gain as much information as possible about the educational value of the standards "before . . . bring[ing] the technical experts back in to clean-up and refine the standards." The field testers were asked to participate in the effort as full partners "in figuring this out . . . to help push our collective thinking one step further, to help identify the holes and rough edges" (Stein, NIFL–4EFF, April 14, 1998).

In a more formal statement, Stein emphasized the importance of "mak[ing] the Standards useful tools for teaching and learning as well as [for] assessing progress and success." As she further described the EFF vision:

> The result of all this work will be an accountability framework for the adult literacy and basic literacy skills field that enables us to focus measurement and reporting as well as assessment and instruction on results that matter to adult learners, communities, employers, funders, and policymakers. If the framework makes sense [on pedagogical grounds], then programs will be able to

use it as the basis for their reporting requirements. At that point EFF will move from a framework for teaching, learning, and assessment to one that enables and encourages system reform. (Stein, NIFL–4EFF, March 20, 1998)

This first field-testing phase of the Content Standards ended in May 1998. Additional work included a debriefing meeting in June where framework planners met with "state and program administrators . . . to discuss the 'fit' between EFF and state/program requirements" (Spacone, NIFL–4EFF, July 1, 1998). Field testers highlighted their research, showcasing the ways in which they "utilized the EFF Standards and framework." The meeting provided a format to further flesh out the hard work of refining the Content Standards, including "the performance indicators," which needed the most work. Meeting participants were asked to:

> 1. identify the performance indicators that describe the most essential characteristics of the standard; 2. combine and eliminate as many indicators as necessary; 3. rewrite the priority performance indicators to sharpen their focus and make them simpler; 4. check to make sure that all the essential elements of the standard remain; and 5. check to make sure that the "final" performance indicators are observable, documentable, and verifiable.

After the meeting, Stein headed up a "task center" that "revised," "simplified," and re-wrote the standards. This included their presentation in a "new format" (Levinson, NIFL–EFF, November 15, 1998) that consisted of a chart with two columns for of each standard. One side of the chart listed the performance indicators. This was usually a simple statement, such as "Clearly identifies purpose for speaking and audience," for the standard "Speak So Others Can Understand." The other side of the chart included Types of Evidence, such as "Explains, either verbally or in writing, the purposes for speaking and the characteristics of the audience." The page also contained a brief definition of the corresponding Generative Skill, a box that placed each of the Four Purposes in one of the quadrants, and in the box specific examples of types of activities specific to each standard, such as "make a request," "influence others," or "understand something more fully" (Content Standards for Adult Performance–Revised, November 1, 1998, p. 34). With the delineation of precise performance indicators, which would still require additional, mostly modest revisions, EFF began to lay the basis for the development of measurable standards.

Additional, but less extensive, field testing of the revised Content Standards, followed in late 1998 through early 1999, both to further refine the performance indicators and to "help us think about and develop an EFF performance continuum and EFF assessment system" (Levinson, NIFL–4EFF, November 15, 1998). The second round of field testing was also designed to shed additional insight on the range of classroom usages that the standards might stimulate. Examples were incorporated into the "Blue Book" (Stein, 2000) to illustrate the correlation between effective teaching/learning and the EFF Content Standards.

ADDITIONAL DEVELOPMENTS

The 16 Content Standards were refined for a final time and published in what is referred to as the Blue Book (Stein, 2000). The standard "Read Critically" was changed in the final rendition to "Read with Understanding." "View Critically" was changed to "Observe Critically." Use "Mathematical Concepts and Techniques" took a more functional orientation, redefined as "Use Math to Solve Problems and Communicate." "Solve Problems" gained a more action-oriented dimension in its expansion to "Solve Problems and Make Decisions." In general, these revisions sharpened the application dimension that linked mastery of relevant knowledge to effective action.

Changes in the performance indicators (ultimately referred to as "components of performance") also reflected a tightening of the relation between relevant knowledge and direct applicability. For example, in the first revised version of the standard, "View Critically," the performance indicator "effectively overcomes external and internal barriers to comprehension" (Content Standards–Revised, 1998, p. 37) was removed. In the final rendition, renamed "Observe Critically," a new *component of performance* was added: "Determine the purpose for observation and use strategies appropriate to that purpose" (Stein, 2000, p. 33). Without this focused purpose, overcoming barriers to comprehension was viewed as somewhat less than relevant from the logic of constructivist pedagogy. Other shifts followed suit, as reflected, for example, in the Math Standard. Thus, a new component of performance was added: "Apply knowledge of mathematical concepts and procedures to figure out how to answer a question, solve a problem, make a prediction, or carry out a task that has a mathematical dimension" (p. 35).

The standard, "Research," was shifted from the Decision-Making to the "Life Long Learning Category," redefined as "Learn Through Research." Instead of "identifies the question to be answered or assumption to be tested" (Content Standards–Revised, 1998, p. 40), in the final rendition it is the student's responsibility to "pose a question to be answered or make a prediction about objects or events" (Stein, 2000, p. 53). In removing "develops and implements an appropriate strategy for inquiry" (Content Standards–Revised, 1998, p. 40), in the final version of the standard, students are challenged to "use multiple lines of inquiry to collect information" and to take personal responsibility to "organize, evaluate and interpret findings" (Stein, 2000, p. 53). In short, the learning/teaching scaffolding becomes more internalized, reflective of the shift that Kegan (1994) described as that from "third order" to "fourth-order consciousness" in response to the "mental demands of modern life."

Stein (2000) referred to the "interchangeability of the skills within a category." Any one Content Standard might not be the most important one for any specific learning objective, as the "skills one needs to draw on will vary from situation to situation depending on the task and context" (p. 17). For pedagogical purposes, the Content Standards and their accompanying components of performance are designed to stimulate "adult learners to think about all the skills in a given category as tools they may want to draw on selectively to achieve their purpose more effectively" (p. 18). EFF developers did not deny that students had alternative paths to learning. As expressed in the Levinson (1998) document to the 25 field researchers, "We know [for example,] that many of the adults we work with are quite competent in many facets of their daily life without the ability to read critically." That is because "they compensate for the limitations in reading skills by drawing on other skills that are stronger—good listening skills, for example, or good problem solving skills" (p. 4).

This acknowledgment was central to respecting the importance of "multiliteracies" as characterized both by the advocates of the New Literacy studies such as Merrifield's and those of the participatory literacy/alternative literacy movement like Fingeret, Lytle, McGrail, and Auerbach, who were far from uniform in their thinking. This recognition was also relevant to the more mainstream literature on learning disabilities with its significant focal point on alternative compensatory strategies in meeting life goals (Corley & Taymans, 2001). Nonetheless, the critical point argued by the EFF developers is that the capacity to draw on all the Content Standards better assures "maximum flexibility in carrying out the common activities" within the context the Key Activities within the Role Maps. The assumed result would be adults better able to realize the Four Purposes of Access, Voice, Independent Action, and Bridge to the Future in relation to important aspects of their lives. As summarized by Stein (2000), "*Being able to use all the skills in each category with a high degree of competence maximizes flexibility, giving adults a range of choices for how they can meet daily challenges and opportunities*" (p. 18, italics in original).

Only after the Content Standards and their components of performance were firmly established did it make sense, from the logic out of which EFF framers operated, to begin systematic work on performance levels. The EFF leadership team recognized the importance of establishing performance standards from the project's inception in order to address the fundamental issue of measurability in response to Congress' query posed in 1993. Yet they held back until the Content Standards and components of performance were firmed up.

Once in place, accurate measurability requires "a behavioral-anchoring process that can be used to develop descriptions (and examples) of performance at various levels for each of the EFF standards" (Stites, 2000, p. 2). Performance standards would then need to adhere to *construct validity* in terms of their technical proficiency based on the operative frameworks, which in the case of EFF is a constructivist theory of learning. Yet, as discussed in chapter 6, effective performance standards also require *consequential validity* in terms of reflecting the goals of policy as well as those of other key constituency, including students, instructors, program administrators, and funders. Stites also referred to *face validity*, particularly for a consensus-based national framework in which performance can be described in a commonly agreed-to language that is "meaningful and understandable to all" (p. 2).

As discussed in chapter 6, these divergent aspects of performance measurement are not necessarily synchronized within given accountability systems, although EFF developers had sought assiduously to make them so. Stites acknowledged the difficulty of reconciling performance standards based on these divergent sources of validity and sought to mediate the tensions among them. He identified "the first priority" in the "garnering [of] broad-based support (and involvement) for developing an assessment framework that supports measures of meaningful results in adult learning and establish[ing] reasonable expectations for resources needed to support such results" (p. 4).

Among other factors Stites argued, this would require an alignment of EFF Standards with those of the NRS as well as the broad framework that underlays the NALS in their focus on prose, document, and quantitative literacy. It would also necessitate alignment with frameworks like CASAS and other accountability systems adapted at the state level in order to achieve the public legitimacy required to establish a national consensus. The challenge was to identify the subtle interfaces among seemingly divergent epistemologies where EFF standards might link with these other frameworks in a manner that would legitimize its own constructivist and metacognitive premises. As Stites described it, the need "is to convince policy makers and funding agencies that such evidence [as discerned through ethnographic and qualitative research] is as valid (and reliable) as standardized test results . . . [which] means changing the ways that policy makers think about validity" (p. 5).

Thus, notwithstanding the importance EFF developers placed on linking their framework with current and projected policy orientations, they remained adamant on the need to establish performance standards on the same constructivist framework that informed EFF from its inception. EFF produced an in-house manual that provided a basis for such an approach (Ananda, 2000), although turned more directly for input to the National

Academy of Sciences publication, *How People Learn: Brain, Mind, Experience and School* (Bransford, Brown, & Cockings, 1999). This resulted in a framework for measuring EFF Content Standards based on four dimensions of performance—*knowledge base, fluency, independence,* and *range*—to be organized from "novice to expert" (*EFF Voice,* 2001, pp. 9–10) levels of competency. This framework would be calibrated to each of the components of performance of the 16 EFF Content Standards and would serve as the foundation of the performance-based assessment system that EFF developers sought to develop and legitimize.

Knowledge base includes the storehouse of information students possess on a given topic, as well as the capacity to "organize their knowledge into meaningful patterns around big ideas, basic principles, for easy retrieval" (p. 9). As elaborated by EFF assessment coordinator, Peggy McGuire (2000), "The goal is to assure that as an individual's store of knowledge relative to a particular domain or skill grows, the structure of the knowledge base also develops, becoming increasingly coherent, principled, useful, and goal oriented" in ways that "can be draw[n] upon for effective action in the world" (p. 2).

Fluency is the extent to which "experts can effortlessly and automatically retrieve and apply relevant knowledge in a particular situation" (*EFF Voice,* 2001, p. 10). Effective knowledge users "do not have to search through everything they know in order to find what is relevant" (Bransford, Brown, & Cockings, 1999, p. 43). Rather, experts possess the capacity to scan and select appropriate information in the most expeditious manner. "Automatic and fluent retrieval are important characteristics of expertise" (p. 44). This does not always mean that experts work more quickly than those who possess fewer skills. Because problems are often complex, experts "may take more time, because they are capable of looking at an issue from more angles than those who have less of a knowledge base" (*EFF Voice,* 2001, p. 10). From a Deweyan (1933/1989) inquiry perspective, experts may also be willing to explore the ramifications of a problem longer before taking action. All else being equal, "fluency is important because effortless processing places fewer demands on conscious attention" (Bransford, Brown, & Cockings, 1999, p. 43). This enables a student to focus more on the essentials of a given problem, disregarding what is not important or that which might lead the learner astray.

Independence is the capacity "to function with less guidance and support" in "retriev[ing] and apply[ing] knowledge to specific situations" (*EFF Voice,* 2001, p. 10). It represents the internalization of metacognitive capacity as reflected in Kegan's (1994) fourth-order consciousness in meeting the challenges of modern life, and depending less on "more knowledgeable others" (Vygotsky, 1978) for important realms of knowledge acquisition. The more advanced stages of this dimension do not simply reflect independent mastery of relevant content, although that is critical. They bring out the more fundamental process of learning how to learn and finding the scaffolding support for new learning within one's own internal scheme of resources. The objective here is not simply self-direction. The metacognitive objective is "the goal of fostering the order of consciousness that *enables* [italics in original] self-direction" (Kegan, 1994, p. 274). Even when they require resources from others, independent learners "are better able to determine what kinds of assistance they may need" (*EFF Voice*, 2001, p. 10). The internalization of the scaffold is premised on maximizing what one can do for oneself, while relying on others only to the minimum extent necessary.

Range refers to the ability "to use skills and knowledge in increasingly complex tasks" (p. 10). McGuire (2000) argued that this dimension of performance "gets to the heart of defining how well an individual can use a skill" (p. 3). As put by Bransford, Brown, and Cockings (1999), "Learners do not always relate the knowledge they possess to new tasks, despite its potential relevance." The extent to which individuals can draw on what they know in one situation to resolve an issue in another is the difference "between usable knowledge . . . and less-organized knowledge, which tends to remain 'inert' " (p. 237). In considering range, McGuire (2000) referred to "the degree of familiarity/unfamiliarity of a task or context; the structuredness/unstructuredness of the task; and the complexity of the task" (p. 3). The expert draws on self-knowledge in one area to help master problems in a new area even when the latter is highly complex and unfamiliar.

As of this writing (January 2004), EFF framers are still in the process of refining these dimensions of performance that will eventually apply to all of the components of performance of the 16 Content Standards. In their proposed finished form, these will include a descriptive focus, as well as the creation of a competence range from novice to expert. Concurrent with that work, as discussed in the next two sections, EFF developers have worked closely with the U.S. Department of Education's Division of Adult Education and Literacy (DAEL) to link EFF performance standards with those of the NRS in what is described as a "Win–Win Proposition" (*EFF Voice*, 2001, p. 1).

Currently, a grid is available, identifying provisional characteristics of the dimensions of *Knowledge Base, Performance* (which integrates fluency and independence), and *Range*, along with a rating system from 0–100 that charts levels of competency applicable to any of the Content Standards. The scale 0–60 is designed to correspond to the six NRS levels. Thus, under *Knowledge Base*, characteristics include mastery of relevant vocabulary, content knowledge, and strategies for applying content knowledge (EFF Assessment Consortium, 2002, pp. 49–50). Content knowledge refers both to the *skills* needed to function in the specified area, as well as a mastery of the related subject matter. The rating of 6–10, provisionally corresponding to the proposed NRS Level 1, is defined as "minimal familiarity with content-related facts, operations, concepts, rules, protocols and/or practices" (p. 49). The 16–20 range, tentatively corresponding to the proposed NRS Level 2, is defined as "familiarity with a small store of content-related facts, operations, concepts, rules, protocols, and/or practices" (p. 49). The third NRS equivalency level is defined as "familiarity with a good enough store of facts, operations, concepts, rules, protocols, and/or practices to carry out the task" (p. 49). The fourth and fifth levels currently read the same as the third, indicating that the framework requires further development. The significant difference in the sixth level is the shift from capacity "to carry out the task" to "meet[ing] the demands of the task" (p. 49).

It remains to be determined whether or not these subtle distinctions of performance ultimately designed to intersect with each of the 16 Content Standards bring clarity or exacerbate the proliferation syndrome over measurement. Irrespective, they serve as an additional set of heuristics designed to enhance highly focused context-based learning. As evident in other aspects of the EFF framework, the complexity in seeking comprehensiveness has required some simplification for the purpose of practical implementation. The issue of whether or not the subtle descriptive distinctions of the levels of the components of performance can be calibrated through quantitative symbolization for standardized measurement purposes remains unresolved.

EFF/NRS CONNECTIONS

Merrifield (2000) identified a major tension within EFF "between creating an accountability structure and supporting effective instruction" (p. 39). That tension extends back to the origins of EFF in the desire of NIFL to report in measurable ways on the nation's progress toward achieving National Educational Goal 6. The response of NIFL and the Goals Panel included a critique of the then current 1993 national adult education program, pointing to its fragmentation and lack of specific focus to support a viable assessment/accountability system that could provide Congress with the needed information. Beder (1999) identified a similar lack of system coherency and called for a "comprehensive national longitudinal evaluation that would measure long-term impact" (p. 125). In *Contested Ground*, Merrifield (1998) also advocated for additional research of a comprehensive sort. What is needed, she argued, is a way of satisfying the diversity of somewhat conflicting constituents, which lays out a coherent direction that could establish a broad consensus for the field's directionality. Without such a focus, as argued variously by Beder, Merrifield, Stites, and Stein, the field could only be mired by perpetual fragmentation and conflict.

EFF does not fully measure up to Beder, Merrifield, and Stites' vision of comprehensive research. Nonetheless, it is the most daunting national project ever launched in ABE/adult literacy that has sought to integrate learning, teaching, formal research, assessment, accountability, and social policy. Whether EFF would, in fact, serve as the vehicle for providing the field's direction through the establishment of a national consensus on *its own premises* is another far from fully resolved manner. From the political perspective of 2003, this is at best, a dubious hope. *The Workforce Investment Act of 2003* as introduced in the House, identifies the purpose of NIFL as that of "provid[ing] national leadership in promoting reading research, reading instruction, and professional development in reading based on scientifically based research" (H.R. 1261, 2003, p. 151). Linking scientific-based educational research with reading instruction theory and practice, based on phonemic mastery as an orienting principle, is part of a back-to-basics movement reflective of the Bush administration's promotion of educational conservative ideas and policy. It charts out a different direction for NIFL than that carved out in the 1990s when EFF served as its flagship in the ushering in of system reform based on progressive educational principles. The removal of EFF from NIFL sponsorship in 2004 completes the cycle.

EFF has been invariably caught up with the politics of literacy from which it has sprung from its inception. In this respect, it could not have been *but* influenced by the vicissitudes of shifting U.S. electoral politics. Interpreted from another angle, EFF might be viewed as a visionary effort designed to rise above conflicting perspectives in the quest to integrate the various components of a cohesive intellectual, political, and social framework, but that the politics of literacy and the enduring reality of American pluralism invariably intrude. That does not invalidate the vision, or its efficacy as an educational framework for the many practitioners who have drawn on it. However, it does put into question its practicality as a framework for national reform at least as played out in the politics of adult literacy from 1995 to 2004.

This tension is reflected within two matters that pervaded the politics of literacy in the 1990s. First, notwithstanding EFF's effort to expand National Educational Goal 6 beyond a prevailing interpretation that links adult literacy to the imperatives of the workforce, the domination of this thrust within federal and state sectors throughout the decade has persisted and intensified. Second, despite the desire of EFF planners to establish an assessment/accountability system premised on constructivist standards that might require a metaphor other than quantification to authenticate, this was constrained by federal accountability mandates based on the criteria of standardization, measurability, and quantification that stemmed from positivistic and neopositivistic research traditions (Mertens, 1998). Both of these tendencies came to symbolic fruition in the 1998 passage of the Workforce Investment Act and accompanying National Reporting System. This legislation reinforced an outlook of adult literacy substantially different from the broadly consensual vision and constructivist theory of learning that has characterized the EFF project.

There were obvious strands of connection linking EFF developers to the state directors of adult education and the federal offices of Office of Vocational and Adult Education (OVAE) and Department of Adult Education and Literacy (DAEL) in their mutual quest to establish a coherent national adult education program, between 1994 and 1998. Even so, two significantly different, and largely incompatible, sources of direction originated out of Washington, DC, during those years. On the one hand, the National Coalition for Literacy and the state directors pursued the more immediate path of reality-based interest politics in the effort to influence ABE/adult literacy legislation in Congress throughout the 1990s. As discussed in chapters 1 and 4, their vision extended beyond a workplace focus, but its politics was perpetually circumscribed by what was viewed as policy realism that required a temperament toward compromise in accepting whatever could be reasonably accomplished in any given legislative cycle. Intellectual coherency was less important than the need among the state directors and the NCL leadership for a typically brokered consensus among the major policy players, buttressed by a strong reality focus grounded in the interest politics of Washington, DC.

From its inception, EFF operated out of a different set of premises. Although its developers also sought consensus, its origins emerged out of the moderate progressive wing of the community-based adult literacy sector. This was the case with Stein (1992), who had been a consultant for the Association for Community Based Education, and also with Bell and Merrifield from the Center for Literacy Studies (CLS), who supported the project early on. The progressive Massachusetts staff development agency System for Adult Basic Education Support (SABES) also played an important role early on in EFF, with the Citizen/Community Member Role Map emerging from the collaboration between the CLS and SABES, as well as the Mayor's Commission of Philadelphia. This social progressivism was tempered through the inclusion of more mainstream entities, such as the National Center for Family Literacy (NCFL), which had a major influence on the shaping of the Parent/Family Role Map, as well as the influence of SCANS, O*NET, and the National Skills Standard Board on the Worker Role Map. Thus, the more conservative-leaning NCFL and the globalization focus that shaped the Worker Role Map modulated the progressive social vision that influenced the early founding of EFF and the Citizen/Community Member Role Map.

To add to the complexity, before coming to NIFL, Stein was not only a director of education for a community-based organization for women in

Massachusetts. She was also chief education planner for the state employ-ment and training agency and was deputy director of the technocratic-leaning, New Democrat, Governor Michael Dukakis' Commonwealth Lit-eracy Campaign. Stein was simultaneously influenced by an imagery of efficiency, streamlining, and "reinventing government," characteristic of the early Clinton–Gore era, while remaining passionately committed to community activism and progressive education. Thus, diverse ideological strands at the sociopolitical level were operating within EFF. In the mutual quest to construct a national consensus, there were some linkages between the policy thrusts of the NCL and state directors and the EFF leadership. However, the two Washington, DC–based movements that sought to redi-rect federal policy never cohered into a common program and plan of ac-tion in the 1990s.

Whatever basis for potential collaboration may have existed at a socio-political level through the aegis of NIFL, the long-term focus of EFF and its intellectual precepts in constructivism made it highly incompatible with the pragmatic and more pressing needs of the more overt policy sector. How-ever much EFF developers worked to construct a viable consensus, without a close link with the ABE policy leadership, a substantial gap persisted, a fis-sure that intensified with the passage of the WIA/NRS and the culture wars that it unleashed throughout the adult literacy sector.

With the passage of this legislation in 1998, NIFL was in crisis and had to swiftly act to try to bring together the two Washington, DC–based sectors, without which the very survival of the agency would be in jeopardy, to say nothing of EFF, which had no standing in Congress. Neither did it have much legitimacy in the Clinton administration with its narrow focus on workforce readiness and welfare reform. These pressures required EFF de-velopers to establish significant linkages with the NRS, notwithstanding the substantially different philosophical and political premises that gave shape to the two.

This linkage was telegraphed to the field in a 1999 joint letter between Andrew Hartman, then director of NIFL, and Ronald Pugsley, then direc-tor of DAEL, which describes some ways in which the NRS and EFF "can complement one another." The letter acknowledged a critical distinction in that NRS focused "on performance standards" or levels, "while EFF has developed content standards." Also different is the nature of what each fo-cuses on. The NRS is designed to provide information "on the core indica-tor areas defined by the Workforce Investment Act": learning gains via lev-els, numbers of students who have attained high school completion, and entry into jobs. EFF is designed to identify "the skills and knowledge adults need in order to carry out their roles as parents, citizens, and workers."

Notwithstanding these differences, Hartman and Pugsley characterized the NRS and EFF as "clearly related." The linkage was that certain NRS "core indicators" were compatible with certain of "the skills EFF has identified as essential content knowledge" particularly in the Communication Standards and Worker Role Map. The letter noted the correlation between the 12 NRS levels in reading, ESL, and math, and EFF's intent to "develop a performance continuum," for the Content Standards most closely proximate to the NRS core indicators. The letter also suggested that all of the EFF standards might "ultimately . . . prove useful to NRS." At the very least, the directors reasoned, "the projects' paths cross[ed]" and the two agencies that they headed would need to nurture these potential linkages "in sensible, mutually beneficial ways."

The directors identified three ways in which the NRS and EFF could collaborate. The first was to develop compatibility between "defining and measuring performance for NRS core indicators and EFF's content standards." This would allow EFF performance indicators to count as "NRS reporting requirements," without which federal funding could not be allocated. The directors pointed to another area of commonality, where both frameworks sought to make their "standards more inclusive of those with disabilities" (Hartman–Pugsley Letter, October 12, 1999). Program improvement represented the third area of commonality, although for the purposes of this discussion, the most important was the focus on performance standards.

The EFF–NRS connection, characterized as "A Win–Win Proposition," was further discussed in the winter 2001 edition of the *EFF Voice*, in the lead article written by Hartman. The NIFL director pointed to the importance of EFF building "on state-of-the art knowledge about how people learn and how to measure learning," which would enable teachers to base "instruction in response to learner needs." Yet, what most "excite[ed]" Hartman was "the partnership" with DAEL and the "willingness" of that agency and NIFL "to collaborate on issues critical to strengthening adult education" (*EFF Voice*, 2001, p. 1). Hartman informed the readership that this collaboration was reflected in the National Literacy Summit of 2000 that firmed up "a broad, customer-driven consensus that . . . instruction should focus on real-life skills that make a difference in people's daily lives." NIFL's partnership with DAEL "enables us to begin another important task called for by the Summit—reconciling the goals of EFF and NRS" (p. 2). The newsletter also included a message from Pugsley, who stated that as a result of the "joint effort . . . of defining a continuum of performance," DAEL "will be able to include EFF results into the National Reporting System" (p. 1).

What Pugsley and Hartman did not comment on was the firestorm of criticism of the NRS on the NLA, which began brewing in September 1999 and intensified when Pugsley joined the list as a guest in November. Also not discussed were the substantial philosophical differences in the underlying epistemologies and politics of literacy on which the NRS and EFF were based. Tensions related to the EFF–NRS connection were highlighted in several NIFL–4EFF messages posted in April 2001 between Brenda Bell, an EFF Field Research and Development Coordinator, Kathleen Olsen, a recipient of a NIFL fellowship charged with the task of linking EFF with NRS, and myself.

CRITICAL DIALOGUE ON THE EFF–NRS CONNECTION

In response to the *EFF Voice* publication, Demetrion raised several issues, particularly "the challenge of linking the highly constructivist EFF standards with the behaviorist assumptions that ground NRS 'levels' . . . that do not adequately or accurately reflect the rich experience of learning." Demetrion acknowledged the experimental nature of the EFF–NRS connection. He was aware as well of the political realities forcing NIFL's hand, and pointed to the need both to give this effort "wide girth," but also to maintain a "critical" posture on the viability of this linkage. The issue, as he stated it, was whether the EFF developers would sufficiently influence the next generation of NRS to " 'complexify' them so that they more appropriately emulate the constructivist standards . . . upon which EFF standards are based," or whether the positivist and behaviorist assumptions inherent within the NRS would influence the evolution of the EFF performance standards. He questioned, in particular, whether the "empiricist" framework of the NRS in its valorization of " 'standardization,' 'uniformity,' and 'measurability' " would force an undue reliance on "rubrics" (Demetrion, NIFL–4EFF, April 16, 2001) to the neglect of more qualitative measures of assessment. More subtle assessment than reliance on a number would be required, Demetrion intimated, to discern the impact of the components of performance, as students sought to work through particular *literacy events* within various life contexts to which they might be attending.

Demetrion wondered, for example, if the component of performance, "analyze the information and reflect on its underlying meaning" (Stein, 2000, p. 25) under the standard "Read with Understanding," could be accurately subsumed within a standardized rubric. The very nature of what might be viewed as "reflection" to say nothing of the even more subjective phrase, "underlying meaning," literally makes no sense from a strict positivistic perspective, particularly in the elusive quest for objectivity and certainty that underlays the quantitative metaphor even as an operative ideal. "Whether or not the paradigms are *inherently* incompatible or whether a convergence is possible on *intellectual* [italics in original] coherence is a matter to be seen and a worthy experiment" (Demetrion, NIFL–4EFF, April 16, 2001). Although understated, Demetrion intimated that unless such a convergence did take place, EFF was in danger of sacrificing the philosophical ground on which the project was premised from its inception.

Demetrion also wondered whether "the emerging model of measurement [will] be based upon the process-oriented Standards, which stress, in effect, learning how to learn, and are highly constructivist, or will the focus of measurement emanate from the contextual role maps which are more easily discernable through behaviorist paradigms of instrumentality and measurement." Both the content of what will be measured and the methods of assessment that become viewed as legitimate spoke to the tensions implicit within the EFF–NRS connections, which were not raised in the EFF newsletter. While acknowledging that these difficult issues required resolution in a process that was in an early stage of development, the message was intended to sharply raise a set of issues belied by the "Win–Win" rhetoric reflected in the EFF publication (Demetrion, NIFL–4EFF, April 16, 2001).

Olsen argued that EFF and NRS were potentially compatible through the development of well-constructed rubrics. In the manner of giving and following directions, for example, a numerical metaphor could be used to track the progression of student mastery. "At each level the complexity of the task increases from simple one-step directions at level 1 to complex multi-step directions at level 6." This rubric could be developed, Olsen reasoned, from "authentic performance-based tasks which can be used to" calibrate the levels. Regardless of the specific goal, Olsen argued that well-constructed rubrics could provide a means of linking qualitative and quantitative assessment measures, and thereby meet the needs both of the NRS and EFF. Referring this time to the EFF framework, Olsen made the point that "care must be taken . . . that all the components of performance for a particular standard are incorporated at the same time." For example, to assess writing, the rubric scoring designers would need to take into account all of the following: "the student determining the purpose, taking care with mechanics, organizing well and revising or editing" (Olsen, NIFL–4EFF, April 17, 2001).

Whether the metaphorical container of a quantitative symbol could hold the qualitative complexity that would go into a measurement formula that seeks to give due consideration to all of the components of each Content Standard is a questionable matter. Olsen made a substantial point that in principle well-constructed rubrics provide a basis for anchoring qualitative and quantitative data. Nonetheless, the extent to which rubrics can adequately account for the rich scope of the EFF Standards remained largely unexamined.

In response to Demetrion's query, Bell identified the Content Standards and not the Role Maps as the focus of "EFF's Assessment Framework." This included eventually "creating performance tasks . . . [for] all of the components" of each standard, including their analysis and "rat[ing] along the four dimensions" of *knowledge base, fluency, independence,* and *range*, and setting standards for levels of progress ranging from novice to expert for each component.

Bell pointed out that the immediate task was on the development of measurement scales of the components of performance for those Content Standards supported by the NRS. Details, at that time remained vague "since we don't know yet what the continua will look like and where levels will be, [and, therefore,] we can't say much about the specifics of the linkage to the NRS."

It was clear that the purpose of the NIFL–DAEL collaboration was "to provide research-based performance descriptors for each NRS level" that, in turn, would result in "identify[ing] a range of performance tasks that benchmark transition points from level to level for both ABE and ESL." With that linkage firmed up, "programs [would be able] to report both what students know and what they can do at each level" (Bell, NIFL–4EFF, April 19, 2001). As a result of the influence of EFF, the second generation of NRS would more likely connect its "levels" to actual student performance on an array of contexts relevant to the lives of students. In short, EFF would continue to refine performance measurements for the 16 Content Standards for a multiplicity of assessment purposes, while working with DAEL in broadening the scope of the NRS next time around to better align the instruments of measurability with more of the specific content and contexts of student learning. The ongoing work of developing performance measurements to reflect EFF Content Standards would continue, even as political reality intruded in the need to establish a strong linkage between the EFF Standards and the NRS regardless of philosophical tension in the underlying assumptions within the two frameworks.

Demetrion pressed the need to clarify the tension between devising an accountability system reportable to federal and state government ultimately on "all 16 standards," while also measuring "learner outcomes related to the roles of parent/family member, citizen/community member and worker" (*EFF Voice*, 2001, p. 4). He referred to the difference between the "process-oriented standards" and the "role maps [which] are the most directly product-based portions of the framework" and therefore, more susceptible to directly "measurable outcomes and perhaps most easily reportable through the behaviorist, linear, . . . and standardized model [of reporting as characteristic of] the current generation of NRS." Demetrion agreed that there was nothing intrinsically wrong with reporting on the outcome areas identified in the Role Maps. Rather, "the problem is in how they are reported and the various intents reflecting both the overt and 'hidden' curriculum of the meaning and purpose of adult basic education implicit within them."

Accepting at face value the assumption that the "specific direction of the second generation . . . remain[ed] open," Demetrion encouraged EFF developers to explore with DAEL the feasibility of reconstructing a national reporting system that would be based in part on "sampling and obtaining multi-measures on fewer students. This would help the federal government to gain a fuller understanding on how, what, and why students have learned" (Demetrion, NIFL–4EFF, April 21, 2001). His core concern was that without an alteration in underlying presuppositions that gives shape to a federal assessment/accountability system, the philosophical premises on which EFF are based would be invariably compromised. As he put it in describing the operating assumptions of system reform that he proposed:

> Such a system would be based on qualitative as well as quantitative information, but not privileging the latter as the "primary" measure. Both qualitative and standardized information are useful and relevant. It is only the privileging of one philosophical research tradition (positivism, empiricism, behaviorism) over others (phenomenology, critical theory, ethnography, constructivism) that makes it seem that one is "objective" and the other is "subjective."

Demetrion argued, "If consensus is going to emerge amidst contested ground, subtle and sustained mediation of the issues which do conflict need to take place." As he intimated, these could not be easily resolved through EFF–NRS, "Win–Win Proposition" rhetoric.

How these political, pedagogical, and epistemological issues would work themselves out remained unclear at the time of this interchange, as well of the more specific relation of EFF to the then to-be-determined second generation of the NRS. According to the EFF/NRS *Interim Report*, published a little over a year later, various iterations and refinements of EFF/NRS Level descriptors would take place with the hope of shaping the WIA reauthorization act. These would include the development of rubrics as the primary mechanism to coordinate the constructivist-driven EFF Standards with the linear-based NRS requirements for the purpose of establishing "benchmarks for use in state assessment systems" (EFF Assessment Consortium, 2002, p. 33). As a result of the joint project, an array of tools and products for teachers, such as "handbooks and technical assistance resources" (p. 34) to integrate the Content Standards with instruction, would also be developed.

Even in the next generation of the NRS there would only be a limited opportunity to utilize EFF Standards as the basis for assessment within states. As described somewhat euphemistically in the *Interim Report*, the joint EFF/NRS "project would work with states that had chosen not to use an existing standardized instrument to report progress on the NRS." That would make this option practically open only to a few states that drew on "standardized *alternative assessments*" (p. 5, italics added). The EFF–NRS connection preserved the *principle* that EFF could be aligned with the second generation of the NRS. Yet, the chances of its framework laying the basis for a national consensus become increasingly doubtful, given the unlikelihood of most states utilizing a standardized alternative assessment. A state mandate based on EFF Content Standards, moreover, would require a level of compulsion that could imperil EFF's heuristic framework and grounding in constructivist pedagogy.

The substantial tensions within EFF are at least threefold. The first is whether or not behaviorist or constructivist intellectual premises will ground the accountability system on which "results that matter" are measured. The second is whether or not (and to what extent) a more comprehensive framework other than human capital development will shape the operative assumptions of ABE/adult literacy federal policy. The third is the extent to which EFF can serve as the framework to establish a national consensus on the direction and purpose of the field. As of this writing, none of the prospects that would support the more expansive aspects of the EFF vision seem likely. That prospect is even dimmer with NIFL's removal of EFF sponsorship.

SUMMARY REFLECTION

From the point of view of the EFF leadership team, the primary purpose of the Content Standards is less their heuristic value than their role in establishing an assessment/accountability system. Still, EFF developers do emphasize that the efficacy of the Content Standards for instructional purposes is determined by the extent to which they enable students to progressively move toward self-identified learning goals (Stein, 2000). The achievement of a concrete objective, such as obtaining a driver's license, may seem like a simple example, but even here what a student views as an acceptable outcome (which, from a student-centered viewpoint, should be the object of measurement) is not always clear.

Students may not have passed the test, yet improved on their ability to study for it the next time around. This enhanced capacity as an essential clearing ground for passing the test in the future may be viewed by the student as a worthy attainment in its own right. Then again, the student may be so fraught with a sense of disappointment as to not be able to see beyond the problem of not passing the test. Determining the level of satisfaction gained through learning, hence its significance as defined from a student-centered perspective, may be discerned through "thick description" and critical "triangular" analysis. There is something invariably interpretive about the value individuals attribute to certain results, whether in achieving particular outcomes or in the form of changed beliefs and attitudes. Hence, without a discriminating analysis of the data of student perception, it is difficult if not impossible to evaluate what is learned.

Largely missing in performance-based accountability assessment is subtle attention to what Dewey referred to as the "means–ends continuum" in the continuous interaction between "ends-in-view" and various phases of attainment throughout a learning process. As Dewey (1938/1963) argued:

> Every experience is a moving force. Its value can be judged only on the ground of what it moves toward and into. . . . It is . . . the business of the educator to see in what direction an experience is heading [and to monitor it moment-by-moment]. . . . Failure to take the moving force into account so as to judge and direct it on the ground of what it is moving into means disloyalty to the principle of experience itself. (p. 38)

On Dewey's epistemology, it is only by paying close attention to the propulsive dynamic that stimulates learning and motivation within the larger process of progressively working through the resolution of some problem or issue that the most efficacious growth takes place. In the fanciful example, the "moving force" might be a change in perspective through self-reflection, dialogue, or some other means that enables the individual to interpret the "failure" as an essential aspect of moving toward the goal. Given the interactive dynamic between processes and outcomes, some measurement of growth in learning should be an important aspect of a comprehensive approach to assessment.

The heuristic value of the EFF standards, as well as the other dimensions of the framework, is based on the capacity to exploit something of the rich potential in each teaching moment throughout the "means–ends continuum" within the context of any learning situation. This Deweyan dynamic is premised on the assumption that "the mind at every stage of growth has its own logic" (Dewey, 1933/1989, p. 181). Such a Deweyan impulse is *implicit* in the EFF constructivist framework, although *underdeveloped* because of the concentrated effort among framers to focus on the highly significant work of creating a consensus-driven performance-based assessment system that reflects externally derived, agreed on standards through which to evaluate student learning.

Viewed from the operative assumptions of EFF, progress is not determined by calibrating the heuristic dynamic of "growth," as resident, in part, in the propulsive space identified in Vygotsky's (1978) zone of proximal development, between what the learner can accomplish independently, and what is learned through scaffolding support. In EFF's performance-based assessment system, progress is discerned in terms of proximity or distance from the objective standard based on a "widely acknowledged definition of what is of value; a definition that then can be used by any of us and all of us as a comparison point" (Stein, 1997, p. 10). From a policy orientation, EFF Content Standards would serve as the measurement benchmark of the proposed national framework by providing "a mechanism for communicating what customers and stakeholders in that [reformed] system [proposed by EFF] can expect" (p. 11). The ideal result would be an overcoming of the perceived fragmentation, diffusion, marginality, and perceived ineffectiveness of the current ABE system.

I do not question the value of such an effort, but only point out certain unresolved tensions between the policy goals of EFF and the pedagogical and epistemological assumptions of its constructivist premises. A grappling with these tensions is essential in order to legitimize the propulsive dynamic of creative learning within the difficult-to-capture learning/teaching processes in particular instructional settings that is stimulated in an EFF pedagogical climate.

As described by many practitioners on the NIFL–EFF listserv, as well as in NIFL's major publication, *Equipped for the Future Content Standards: What Adults Need to Know and Be Able to Do in the 21st Century* (Stein, 2000), proponents of EFF maintain that the relation between the Content Standards and pedagogy is iterative and synergistic. The Blue Book obviously gives substantial attention to policy and system issues of building a national consensus. Yet, it also illustrates the potential of EFF in stimulating significant learning beyond what may seem readily evident through naturalistic methods of student-centered and participatory-based methodologies. As put by Caroline Beverstock in support of the EFF framework:

> Even though I've felt that I was reasonably good at helping students to articulate their goals, I found the structure of the roles made visible on paper helped students to say more, and, I suspect, set more significant goals. For example, a young mother of two volunteered that she had never registered [to vote] and that she'd like to do that and prepare to vote. I doubt that would have come out in past, less focused conversations. (Stein, 2000, p. 95)

For more than a few practitioners, the somewhat structured EFF framework has opened a viable pathway to creative instruction in better linking self-directed learning with highly specific student goals and interests.

Even still, if from a pedagogical perspective the primary value of EFF lies in its heuristic capacity, then it also needs to be acknowledged that it is a framework only, although one quite comprehensive that students and instructors may or may not find particularly effective in any given learning context. Other means and other approaches may be equally—or more—effective within particular instructional situations and settings. The enduring tension within EFF is between its pedagogical potentialities and its function as an objective measurement system based on the progressive mastery of external standards.

This tension within EFF is creative for some, but for others it is not. From the perspective of heuristics, it does not matter whether one draws on the entire framework, only from elements, or not at all from it. From an educational perspective, it can be creatively adapted to a range of content areas and methodologies, while not necessarily providing the centerpiece to an instructional program, although it could, logically, also play that role. However, from a *systems* outlook, such a limited or partial utilization may be viewed as a symptom of incoherence, and, therefore, inadequate as a mechanism through which to establish a national consensus about the purpose and direction of ABE.

Given this predicament, adding a Deweyan supplement to a framework many already view as overly complicated may simply overburden EFF and lead to the deconstruction of its *system* based on its own constructivist premises. Yet, from an educational slant, failure to formally factor in the creative dynamic of subtle learning processes may very well result in the failure to consider that which is most critical in particular educational settings. It is this tension that is enduring within EFF, which is further intensified as developers have sought ways to merge their constructivist and highly process-oriented framework within that of the linear-based National Reporting System (NRS).

The tension is even more heightened in the current period, based on the operative assumptions of the U.S. Department of Education under the Bush administration, which tends to view the concept *constructivism* pejoratively as an educational "ideology," in contrast to the more "objective" empiricism of hard science (U.S. Department of Education, 2002). Whether the constructivist precepts that underlie the EFF project can pass muster on the principles of science that have become embedded into law is an empirical question that remains to be determined. In any event, given the redefinition of the purpose of NIFL as described in H.R. 1261 and the removal of EFF from the agency's sponsorship, it is difficult to be sanguine about likely prospects that EFF, as conceived by its framers, will achieve the system reform envisioned throughout much of the 1990s.

The potential role of EFF as part of a broader *field-driven* revitalization movement is another matter. The latent, never thoroughly developed contribution of EFF to such a movement is its linkage to the articulation of a coherent public philosophy. This implicit EFF vision is based on the imagery of the active citizen contributing to the reconstruction of mediating institutions and social structures as a pathway of enhancing a more viable political culture based on democratic principles of public participation. Whether or not, or the extent to which, the National Institute for Literacy can serve as the vehicle for such an articulation of a public philosophy based on the "middle ground" premises identified by Dewey, Bellah and his colleagues,

Barber, Habermas, Rawls, Hart, and Novak, as argued for in this study in the current neoconservative era, is another matter.

Regardless, it is argued that some such reconstruction of the U.S. politics of literacy is essential to establish the value system that would underlie the type of assessment/accountability system required to support the constructivist pedagogical vision of EFF and the intellectual presuppositions of the New Literacy Studies. The extent to which EFF can flourish outside its embedment within NIFL and have sustained national influence through its interstate group of partners and the Center for Literacy Studies, its current research and development center, remains an open question.

Given the current emphasis on "American values," perhaps as an ironic (from a progressive slant) intent of the Bush educational policy, a profound revitalization of the U.S. democratic tradition, which could also lead to the renewal of public and policy support for adult literacy, will emerge. There are aspects of neoconservative political thought on which to draw for such a project in its support of the mediating role of the volunteer sector and the call for corporate responsibility. However, short of a neoconservative hegemony on the interpretation of U.S. democratic political culture, any broad-based civic education will raise a plurality of perspectives that could intensify ideological differences, exacerbating an already pervasive polarized political discourse. The issue is whether and/or the extent to which the proponents of neoconservative ideology pervasive within the current U.S. Department of Education (circa 2004) will encourage or participate in such an open discussion within the contexts of the nation's history and civics classrooms and across the nation's public airwaves. Similarly, whether print and TV journalism would support such discussion by providing balanced scope for a diversity of perspectives will raise more than a little skepticism among critical observers.

Also questionable is the extent to which the progressive left would accept the U.S. constitutional and democratic traditions as a groundwork for ongoing political and cultural discussions even while maintaining a sharp critical analysis of any current embodiment in pointing to the importance of its greater realization (Barber, 1998). In short, there is more than a little suspicion among the liberal and progressive camps that "American values," as defined by the Bush administration, serve merely as a form of political rhetoric. For many critics, this standpoint functions as a "hidden curriculum" to mask other ideological forces that would place current power arrangements and corporate interests ahead of the strengthening of the democratic vitality of the republic that neoconservative political philosophers, from their own interpretive grids, are attempting so much to reinvigorate. For coherent national discussion to advance, progressives and liberals of various ideological strands would need to enjoin the neoconservatives in this discussion of American democracy, particularly in pressing forward the call toward perpetually establishing "a more perfect union" within the United States as this nation's most idealistic telos (Jackson & Watkins, 2001).

The project for which I am advocating would require a rejection of an uncritical pietistic embrace of the founding fathers as heroes that neoconservatives love so dearly. It would also call for a repudiation of any cynical deconstruction of the intent of the founders or of what they actually accomplished in the construction of the Constitution and the partial embodiment of democratic ideals in the midst of difficult historical challenges that brooked no easy solutions. Perhaps a working through of these political tensions will reveal an underappreciated middle ground, which could lead to a substantial political and cultural revitalization of an inclusive U.S. democratic tradition enacted through various forms of sustained political discourse. This would not lead to facile agreement on all the particulars of what constitutes a democratic culture and society, but it would help to provide a coherent frame of reference to ground public discussion about the trajectory of national political life.

Such a democratic discourse could also provide the basis for the revitalization of adult literacy defined as a form of national treasure in enabling those without privilege to enjoy the fruits of, and to participate in, the invigoration of a more vital political culture through their appropriation of a public education broadly defined. A coherent public philosophy giving shape to a politics of literacy grounded in "American values" is currently lacking. Its articulation could inform a national vision not only about its own worth, but about its potential role in helping (however modestly) to revitalize a democratic political culture—hence, the contribution, at least potentially, of adult literacy education to the public good.

Leadership in enacting such a vision would logically have belonged to the National Institute of Literacy via the vehicle of the EFF project in providing the resources for lifelong learning and civic and cultural renewal through the efficacy of active citizens reinvigorating the primary institutions and organizations of local life as well as personal selves. However, the creative energy for such a national revitalization would likely now need to stem from grassroots sources in an effort to gain greater legitimacy through coalition building and advocacy.

Whether the potential democratic resources resident in the nation's political culture or the forces of the marketplace, mass media, and the legacy of limited civic engagement would prevail in any such scenario is a matter to be determined through ongoing historical investigation. There is more than a little reason to doubt whether a sufficient critical mass among a broad specter of neoconservative, liberal, and progressive educators would be willing to embrace the U.S. democratic ethos, however variously defined, as a methodological grounding point for framing a national dialogue and debate on the purposes and values of adult literacy education. What I raise here is the prospect that such a revitalization of the nation's political culture is resident within the plausibility structure of the U.S. democratic tradition. Such potentiality does not necessarily lead to corresponding action. Neither does it rule it out. It does provide a possible resource for a construction of the politics of literacy based on "American values," however variously defined. This topic is further discussed in chapter 11.

Research Traditions: Problems, Paradigms, and Polemics

Unlike medicine, agriculture, and industrial production, the field of education operates largely on the basis of ideology and professional consensus. As such, it is subjected to fads and is incapable of cumulative progress that follows from the application of the scientific method and from the systematic collection and use of objective information in policy making. We will change education to make it an evidence-based field.
—U.S. Department of Education Strategic Plan (2002–2007, p. 48)

In some studies . . . "purity" has taken precedence over theoretical meaningfulness. This could easily lead to methodological fetishism when the direction of research is dictated nether by theory nor by the subject of inquiry, but by the methods that guarantee the reliable reproduction of data.
—Kozulin (1990, p. 230)

When highlighted in the polarized fashion as reflected in the two quotes, there is more than a degree of skepticism that divergent theories of knowing will result in widely agreed on working frameworks to orient research on adult literacy education. Given the tensions between what Mertens (1998) characterized as *positivist/postpositivist, interpretive/constructivist,* and *emancipatory* paradigms of social science research, this conflict has no easy resolution. It is not that these divergent approaches through which Mertens structured *Research Methods in Education and Psychology* are inherently contradictory. Yet, when their respective logics are vigorously pursued, substantially different pathways of research and theory construction open up.

The issue is compounded by the political process in the determination of which discourses are privileged, and what consequences follow in terms of what gets attended to and what remains neglected or marginalized (Lagemann, 2000). For example, the government (through the National Institute for Literacy) had undertaken a great deal of research in the Equipped for the Future project. In Mertens' terminology, the EFF project is based on the interpretive/constructivist research paradigm. Viewed from this perspective, the construction of meaning making of both the researchers and the participants of an educational study critically impact on what is discovered in the process of investigation. What emerges, proponents argue, is not the singularity of objective truth. It is, rather, a plausible interpretation based on relevant evidence, subject to critical scrutiny that seeks to make sense of the available information. This includes the need to take into account such subjective factors as human consciousness and the socio-cultural matrices in which behavior and perception are situated.

EFF's operative assumptions, based on the "softer" sciences of constructivism and ethnography (with an important role to boot for practitioner-based research), are rendered suspect under educational policy of the administration of George W. Bush. This is so because the qualitatively focused assumptions that have grounded the EFF project fail to pass muster in the neopositivistic environment that gives shape to current governmental criteria as to what constitutes valid educational research. Its emphasis on exacting scientific methodologies in quest of direct causal attribution discounts much that qualitative research methodologies illuminate.

These tensions between conflicting educational research traditions have been marked in the United States throughout the 20th century (Lagemann, 2000). They are particularly heightened at this time, given the sharp ideological focus of the current Bush administration. In accordance with its prevailing neoconservative educational philosophy, this administration, in conjunction with a supportive Congress, has elevated scientific-based educational research to a level of policy legitimacy never previously achieved by the federal government, in clarity of vision and singularity of purpose. The educational progressivism that underlies the operative assumptions of both the interpretive/constructivist and emancipatory research paradigms is under a sophisticated political attack by an administration that is rewriting educational policy and establishing its research institutions on neoconservative premises that have been operative since the Reagan era.

The administration's goals in the area of educational research are laid out in the *U.S. Department of Education Strategic Plan 2002–2007*. A key component is the enforcement of "rigorous" standards in the analysis of fundable research projects that "will match those applied by the most respected research journals and scientific research agencies." The *Strategic Plan* calls for a stringent peer review process "enlisting only qualified scientists who have high levels of methodological and substantive expertise pertinent to the projects being reviewed." The desired result is publications that "meet the highest standards of scientific rigor" (p. 52). Those favored journals would not likely include progressive leaning ones like *Educational Theory* or *Adult Educational Quarterly*.

In order to accomplish its objective, the *Strategic Plan* points to the need for "flexibility" in the reauthorization of statutes that were intended to support the Office of Educational Research and Improvement (OERI) (p. 55). The draft version of the strategic plan (February 2002) may have gotten closer to the department's intent in calling for "sweeping [legislative] changes" in order to implement its far-reaching vision (p. 49). With the passage of the Education Sciences Reform Act, OERI was eliminated and replaced with an Academy of Education Sciences designed "to insulate our federal research, evaluation, and statistics activities from partisan or undue political control" (Viadero, 2002, p. 1).

It is a contestable claim on whether politics can be eliminated by funding only "scientifically valid" research (p. 2). As stated by Representative Michel N. Castle, the bill's sponsor, "I want quality education research not fads or anecdotes to inform educators' decisions on the best way to improve student learning and narrow achievement gaps" (p. 1). It is this pitting of calls for rigorous scientific methodology juxtaposed against rhetorical caricatures of other types of educational scholarship, which dominate current neoconservative educational, qua political, discourse. This rhetorical strategy renders problematic the viability of a working synthesis or framework between and among the research traditions that Mertens (1998) described that could inform studies on adult literacy education. This political issue is noted, although largely bypassed in this chapter. Rather, the focus here is on definitional assumptions and critical epistemological divergences among key research traditions.

OVERVIEW OF MERTENS' THREE RESEARCH TRADITIONS

In *Research Methods in Education and Psychology*, Mertens (1998) systematically reviewed theoretical frameworks, or "paradigms," that shape social science research. She did not infer that there is no convergence among the paradigms. Still, she did make the case that they represent substantially different modes of research with significant consequences in terms of questions asked, topics explored, and conclusions drawn. Mertens identified the three broad categories of research in her constructed typology through the realms of *ontology* (perceptions of the nature of reality), *epistemology* (the nature of knowledge and the relationship between the knower and the known), and *methodology*. Through this grid, she examined an extensive range of topics related to each research tradition. Mertens worked through her model in broad philosophical terms and in highly intricate methodological detail, highlighting the strengths and limitations of each paradigm. Her discussion included an impressive body of cited research that she skillfully laced throughout her narrative.

Crucial for *Conflicting Paradigms in Adult Literacy* are the broad affinities between Mertens' research paradigms and the three schools of adult literacy education identified in the earlier chapters. The emancipatory paradigm in its embodiment in critical pedagogy and practitioner-based inquiry is closely linked to the school of participatory literacy education. The positivist/postpositivist perspective has the preponderant influence in the federal government's policy on adult basic education, especially in its most recent incarnation in the form of "evidence-based research." The interpretive/constructivist paradigm underlies the New Literacy Studies in its ethnographic sensibility and qualitative and case study research focus.

Mertens acknowledged that there is a certain selectivity in her choice of research traditions, which follows along similar lines as discussed by Carr and Kemmis (1986). Cherryholmes (1988) had a similar, although slightly different, categorization. Mertens' work also shared an affinity with Polkinghorne's (1983) *Methodology for the Human Sciences*, which examines various research traditions, including early and mid-20th-century positivism, pragmatism, human action, and existentialism, phenomenology, and hermeneutics. In terms of social science research in general, Polkinghorne spoke of "an unresolved tension between the requirements of producing indubitable truths and the requirements of addressing the most significant questions about the human realm" (p. 2). This tension invariably intrudes into the contestable arena of values, a conflict that Mertens acknowledged by the nature of her paradigmatic typology.

Mertens (1998) noted how her three broad categories can be drawn on to include related disciplines, intellectual movements, and methodologies. Under positivism/postpositivism (hereafter neopositivism, as the term postpositivism is used by Phillips & Burbules, 2000, for example, in a contrasting way to the positivist research tradition), she listed experimental, quasi-experimental, correlational, causal comparative, and quantitative research. This paradigm draws its working model from the hard sciences based on the ideal of the neutral investigator in search of objective truth. Researchers operating out of the interpretive/constructivist paradigm seek to illuminate internal representations of consciousness and social interaction as situated contexts of human embedment. Mertens placed naturalistic, phenomenological, hermeneutic, symbolic interaction, ethnographic, and qualitative research within this framework, which takes into account the subjectivity of the researcher. Within the emancipatory paradigm, she listed critical theory, and research based on neo-Marxist, feminist, Freirian, participatory, and transformative perspectives (p. 7). The focus here is on the role of power in its influence on the construction of knowledge in terms of which discourses are privileged or marginalized in any given historical context. There is also within this paradigm an emancipatory hope that personal, societal, political, and cultural reform can lead to a more just and equitable society, particularly for oppressed social groups.

Mertens noted, but did not discuss, the fourth paradigm of postmodernism. This, in many respects, is an extension of modernism in its rejection of metanarrative foundational truths in highlighting the centrality of perspectivism (Antonio, 1998). Although this chapter does not formally address it, it draws on a tempered postmodern sensibility in the belief that truth related to human experience is historically situated rather than grounded in foundational verities hovering "above" or outside history in some "God's eye" perspective. This leaves considerable room for an informed pluralism of methods and ideas based on the quest for a best-fit interpretation consistent with the data (Rescher, 2001). Such an informed pluralism, which I link to philosophical pragmatism, takes into account the influence of theory construction and preliminary hypothesis formation in the shaping of which sets of facts and corresponding methodologies are deemed most relevant in any research project (Pawson & Tilley, 1997).

According to Mertens' central argument, "researchers make methodological choices based on their assumptions about reality and the nature of knowledge that are either implicitly present or explicitly acknowledged" (p. xiv). Rather than residing above the fray of human interpretation in some value-free arena, Mertens argued that ontology, epistemology, and methodology are inherently dependent on mental constructs that stem from particular worldviews. Building on Kuhn (1970), Mertens accepted as a foundational principle the centrality of paradigms in the construction of social science knowledge. Her goals are summative and broadly eclectic. She sought to clarify, but not to trump, any particular paradigm with another in her discussion of research traditions.

POSITIVIST/NEOPOSITIVIST PARADIGM

Whether social science research locates its intellectual home within the natural sciences or in the "softer" realms of cultural anthropology, history, and social philosophy, or in some critical blending, is a debate that has challenged scholars throughout the 20th century (Lagemann, 2000). At the center of the controversy is the role of positivism, a "rationalistic, empiricist philosophy" (Mertens, 1998, p. 7) grounded in a natural science model of investigation in quest of direct causal explanation of phenomenon based on a combination of inductive experimentation and deductive reasoning.

As Mertens and others noted, positivism has gone through various stages of evolution throughout the 19th and 20th centuries. Contemporary definitions are more nuanced and sophisticated than earlier variants in accepting the inevitable gap between finite human knowledge and objective truth. Neopositivists still view the latter as an ideal, based on the ontological assumption that observable truths, at least in principle, exist within the context of social experience.

Mertens drew out the core precepts of neopositivism in the realms of ontology, epistemology, and methodology. In the domain of ontology, early 20th-century positivist thinking held "that one reality exists and that it is the researchers job to discover that reality" (p. 8). Neopositivists likewise accept the existence of an objective reality, which, however, "can be known only imperfectly because of the researchers human limitations" (p. 9). From this vantage point, the aim is to get as close as possible to the objective truth, to discover " 'reality' within a certain realm of probability" (p. 9). In the classical positivist research tradition, there is a radical separation between the researcher and the subject of the research. Whereas neopositivists acknowledge that the researcher influences the subject of the research, they maintain, in principle, that the researcher should remain neutral in the quest for objectivity by following "prescribed procedures rigorously."

Neopositivists analyze qualitative information through a methodology that depends on "a fixed-response format." The goal of such research is to discern general patterns that can be evaluated through aggregate quantitative analysis. Neopositivists note that "many of the assumptions required for rigorous application of the scientific method," such as random sampling, are not always applicable for social science research. For that reason, they rely more on "quasi-experimental" processes that are less rigorous than purer experimental design in order to apply the "methods of the natural sciences . . . to people" (p. 10). Neopositivists make an important adjustment in accounting for the human factor, according to Mertens. Even still, an underlying belief system links the neopositivists with their positivist predecessors in the quest for exactness, direct causal attribution, and application of rigorous methodology in the search for objective knowledge about social phenomena.

INTERPRETIVE/CONSTRUCTIVIST PARADIGM

Those operating out of the positivist tradition seek to disclose observable, sense-derived information about some phenomenon. In its various manifestations reflected in the scholarly traditions of phenomenology, ethnography, hermeneutics, and philosophical pragmatism, the interpretive/constructivist paradigm seeks to provide qualitative descriptions of individuals and local communities, particularly the construction of meaning and its impact on behavior. The model of scholarship drawn on is not that of the hard sciences, at least in its pre-Einsteinian and pre-Darwinian phases. This second paradigm draws on the fields of cultural anthropology, cognitive psychology, history, literary analysis, and social philosophy, as well as the "harder" social sciences.

Accepting the inherent subjectivity of the data of human consciousness and the variability of social interaction, scholars drawing on these traditions seek a rich representation of some significant dimension of human experience, which is inherently pluralistic in interpretation and meaning. Sharing a close affinity with Dewey's (1929/1958) *Experience and Nature,* Searle (1994) referred to " 'biological naturalism' " in which "mental events and processes are as much a part of biological natural history as digestion, mitosis, meiosis, or enzyme secretion" (p. 1). Searle acknowledged the "third-person character of . . . epistemology" on which traditional science depends. Yet, he also pointed to the irreducibility of the "ontology of mental states" as "a "first person ontology" (p. 16). If subjective human consciousness is part of the data, then methodologies and modes of inquiry are needed to probe into its realm. In its "thick" qualitative descriptive and analytic depth, this is the province of the interpretive/constructivist paradigm, which draws on aesthetic, historical, and scientific modes of investigation. As Searle described the challenge:

> The question "*How* is the existence of the phenomena to be verified?" should not be confused with the question "*What* is the nature of the phenomena whose existence is verified?" The crucial question is not "Under what conditions would we *attribute* mental states to other people?" but rather, "What is it that people *actually have* when they have mental states?" "What are the mental phenomena" as distinct from "How do we find out about them and how do they function causally in the life of the organism?" (p. 23, italics in original)

Searle acknowledged the difficulty of this task. Still, he pressed the point that given the irreducibility of first person consciousness, its quest is an unavoidable challenge if the goal of social science research is to unearth important aspects of human experience as defined by historical actors. Dewey (1929/1958) expressed it this way: "Genuine empirical method sets out from the actual subject matter of primary experience, recognizes that reflection discriminates a new factor in it . . . , makes an object of that, and then uses that new object . . . to regulate, when needed, further experiences of the subject matter already contained in primary experience" (p. 18).

As a baseline for investigation, Searle and Dewey pointed to the irreducibility of human experience and consciousness and the problems that emerge from them. It is this starting point, they argued, that systematic social science research needs to illuminate. Cochran-Smith and Lytle (1993) argued similarly in their study of teacher research, in their linking of "systematic and intentional inquiry" (p. 7) to "an intellectual process of posing and exploring problems identified by teachers themselves" (p. 9). Legitimate research takes place, the authors of *Inside/Outside* maintained, by whatever methodologies yield greater insight into the issue at hand. With Dewey, overcoming perplexity is also a driving force in teacher research. Notwithstanding this subjective grounding, effective communication of the results of any teacher research project requires the capacity to persuade others, particularly other teacher researchers, of the soundness of the case that is made, even in the call for additional research.

With Searle (1994), the authors of *Inside/Outside* would argue that effective inquiry draws on the "universal" methodology—"any tool or weapon that comes into hand" (p. 23) that leads to a proximate and progressive resolution of a problem or a question toward enhanced clarity and understanding. This is precisely Dewey's (1938/1991) argument in *Logic: The Theory of Inquiry* in which he provided a sophisticated road map from problems identified to "warranted assertions" through the rugged path of "controlled inquiry" (p. 29).

In their various ways, Searle, Dewey, and Cochran-Smith and Lytle provided support for the interpretive/constructivist paradigm in supplying rationales and methodologies for systematic inquiries into first person human experience. For them, the realm of consciousness represents core datum, the importance of which depends on the specific focus of the research project. The attainment of relevant knowledge designed to bring a particular line of investigation to a satisfactory conclusion still requires "competent inquiries" (Phillips & Burbules, 2000, p. 4). Employing appropriate methodologies, as the case requires, is a key instrument in its progressive achievement.

In providing a sophisticated view of neopositivism, Mertens (1998) noted that researchers in this tradition acknowledge that "facts are theory laden" (p. 11). Still, their reliance on a "hard" scientific epistemology is congruent with a broad-based perspective that runs consistently through 20th-century positivist discourse. A common critique of the interpretive/constructivist paradigm from this vantage point is that it relativizes objective reality. This, according to critics, derails the possibility of attaining usable information that can cohere into a cumulative body of knowledge. As with the positivist tradition, there are graduations and refinements. Nonetheless, Mertens (1998) pointed to broad commonalities within this paradigm in the belief in the multiplicity of meaning, the importance of the social construction of knowledge, the irreducibility of consciousness, and the inevitability of human interpretation. Empirical data is accounted for within the interpretive framework of a given qualitative study.

In terms of ontology, this second research paradigm is based on the belief that "reality is socially constructed" as it applies to human beings, without denying the objectivity of facts. It is the significance of any particular fact or set of facts that is the issue, as well as what sets of observations different perceptions open to human investigation. Meanings, even of the same or similar phenomena, are viewed as inherently pluralistic. Such "multiple mental constructions . . . may be in conflict with each other," even as they may be equally real in their representation within human consciousness within the context of particular cultural and social interactions. The object of research in this mode is to present as cogently as possible something of the complexity and nuance of the various perceptions of the historical actors in a given study, while eschewing "the notion that there is an objective reality [of a singular nature when it comes to human meaning] that can be known." Rather, "the researcher's goal is to understand the multiple social constructions of meaning and knowledge" (p. 11) as applied to any line of investigation. This requires narrative contextuality at a high level of coherence in a manner that sufficiently grapples with the empirical evidence, subject to critical analytical scrutiny.

In terms of epistemology, scholars working out of the interpretive/constructivist paradigm acknowledge that "the researcher [rather than the 'fixed-response format' of prescribed methodologies is] . . . the instrument for data collection" (p. 175). The subjective factors of beliefs and assumptions, including empathy or antipathy to the subject of a given study, invariably color the results. In this sense, this research paradigm more closely resembles the academic disciplines of the liberal arts as well as the "softer" social science of cultural anthropology. Instead of what proponents view as the elusive quest for a singularly clear objectivity, the goal of such research is "confirmability" wherein "data can be tracked to its sources, and the logic used to assemble interpretations can be made explicit in the narrative" (p. 11). In addition to the criteria of confirmability, Imel, Kerka, and Wonacott (2002) added the categories of credibility, transferability, dependability, and authenticity (p. 4). Rather than the ideal of certainty, the object of research from this paradigm is to present a convincing description that merges theory and primary evidence in a manner that is both narratively coherent and critically competent. Such research takes into account both the data and the context within a particular interpretive framework. This includes attunement to an aesthetic grasping of the situation, as well as a need for grounding in "controlled inquiry."

Methodology follows in the quest to achieve critical analysis through what Geertz referred to as "thick description." Mertens (1998) pointed out the standard tools of qualitative research: direct observation, interviews, surveys, and collection and analysis of primary documentation. Seeking credibility, confirmability, and "coherence with the data" (Rescher, 2001), authenticity rather than certainty is achievable through the triangulation of evidence combined with the persuasiveness of the description and the logic and scholarship that underlies it. Through this methodology, different types of evidence are placed in juxtaposition to each other following the model of critical historical investigation. The researcher plays a crucial role not only as the instrument of data collection, but in the construction of the account that seeks to be convincing rather than definitively conclusive. This requires an explanation of the facts. Yet, it leaves broader scope for interpretive analysis than in the positivist/neopositivist paradigm with its ideal of a surer objectivity and search for tight attributions between cause and effect.

EMANCIPATORY PARADIGM

Researchers operating out of the positivist/neopositivist paradigm critique the interpretive/constructivist framework for its lack of scientific rigor and its proclivity toward relativism (Phillips & Burbules, 2000). Those who work out of what Mertens (1998) referred to as the emancipatory paradigm base their critique on the failure of the interpretive/constructivist framework to come to terms with the reality of the way knowledge is constructed through the exercise of epistemic and political power (Carr & Kemmis, 1986). Mertens (1998) gave thought to labeling this paradigm "critical theory," but decided against that because of its historical association with Marxist political and economic theory (p. 15). In settling for a broader framework, Mertens was able to incorporate a wide range of research that includes critical theory and neo-Marxism, as well as contemporary scholarship in critical pedagogy, feminist theory, and Afro-centrist studies. Within the emancipatory paradigm, Mertens included participatory and transformative approaches such as practitioner-based inquiry. The literature of these various types of research is vast, and differences among specific schools of thought within this paradigm are significant, although Mertens highlighted the broad similarities.

The power–knowledge nexus is a central feature of the emancipatory paradigm. The phrase comes from the work of French social philosopher Michel Foucault based on his articulation of "regimes of truth" as historically constructed through discourses of power (Rabinow, 1984). The concept has roots in Marxist premises wherein the economic forces of capitalism serve as the superstructure that gives shape to the social, political, and economic institutions of Western middle-class states as well as to their cultural formations, including the construction of personal identity. Standing Hegel on his head, Marx (Marx & Engels, 1959) argued that ideals "are nothing else than the material world reflected by the human mind and translated into forms of thought" (p. 145), hence, his concept of ideology wherein ideas mask the power of capital to underlie all aspects social, cultural, and political reality in the bourgeois state.

Thus, in a Marxian worldview, "ideology" operates through "false consciousness" in the shaping of thought and behavior of individuals in their various self-perceptions and group and institutional affiliations, typically against their own best interests. For adherents, this is a pervasive factor in capitalistic identity formation. Freire (1970), who drew extensively, although not exclusively, from Marxian premises, depicted the invader from within (capitalist ideology) in its intrusion into the "inauthentic" consciousness of the oppressed, which a liberated pedagogy is designed to critique and gradually overcome.

The development and refinement of Marxian and neo-Marxian thought throughout the 20th century, including the influence of the Frankfurt School of critical theory, is beyond the scope of this overview. The significant point for our purposes is the importance of Marxian social criticism in underlying a certain stream of social science research in emphasizing how knowledge formation is constructed through the influence of power. The broad impact of Marxian social thought extends beyond economic motivation, although that, in varied nuanced forms, continues to underlie a great deal of current critical social theory. It is the illumination of power, itself as a sociocultural and political reality, which has had a substantial influence in the arena of critical social science research. This focus has extended into the areas of cultural identity formation, wherein categories of gender, race, ethnic, and sexual orientation are viewed just as importantly as class in the construction of social reality.

In *Poverty, Racism and Literacy*, Corley (2003) illuminated some of the key features of Marxian/post-Marxian social science research, which has informed educational studies. Pointing to the widespread persistence of poverty in African American and Hispanic populations in the United States, Corley challenged traditional interpretations of literacy as an independent variable leading to employment, self-sufficiency, and general life enhancement. The "assumption that there are jobs for the poor who are able to improve their literacy skills" (p. 1) is the basis of functional literacy doctrine that gives support to what Auerbach (1992a) and others referred to as the "literacy myth," emphasized in the policy and prescriptive literature.

The problem, Corley (2003) noted, is that sufficient jobs for poorer, minority groups do not exist in sufficient numbers "that pay sufficiently well to create pathways out of poverty" (p. 1). The consequence, according to Auerbach (1992a), is that the "literacy myth" serves an ideological function that masks the gap between the poor and other groups, which perpetuates the fable of equality, hence, the viability of democracy itself, as it pertains to social and economic opportunity. Those informed by this critical sensibility point to a "hidden curriculum" that builds on the mythos of equality of opportunity as a means of legitimizing social and economic stratification (Corley, 2003, p. 1).

Based on these realities, Corley argued that "adult literacy education cannot divorce itself from the defined power relationships that are practiced within social institutions" (p. 1). Building on Freire (1970), Giroux (1983), and others, Auerbach and Corley maintained that an understanding of how power is mediated through such categories as class, race, ethnicity, and gender represents a critical baseline of social science research on the formation of such constructs as adult literacy education. This is also a central thesis in Mertens' (1998) description of the emancipatory paradigm, a "far from unified body of work" (p. 17) that nonetheless has the construction of knowledge through the aegis of power as one of its underlying common attributes.

The other feature is the emancipatory potential of a participatory and transformative research focus and corresponding pedagogy. The concept, extending back to the Marxian notion of not merely understanding, but of changing the world, is the major praxeological focus of this school of research. This viewpoint is also exemplified in the pragmatic research tradition wherein "the refined objects of reflection" achieve their justification to the extent to which "they solve perplexities" within human experience that results in an "enlarged use of enjoyment of ordinary things" (Dewey, 1929/1958, p. 7).

Similarly, Freire (1970) spoke of "a pedagogy which must be forged *with* [italics in original] not for, the oppressed . . . in the incessant struggle to regain their humanity" (p. 33). Aronowitz and Giroux (1993) discussed the critical role of teachers as "transformative intellectuals" in assuming the responsibility of working with other groups in the struggle to establish "schools as democratic spheres" (p. 49). Corley (2003) stressed the importance of "ensur[ing] that instructional methods and processes center on shared power and responsibility between teacher and learners" (p. 2), whereas Auerbach (1992a) pointed to a "fourth pedagogical tendency [which] aims to integrate the voices and experiences of learners with critical social analysis." As she further described it:

> It focuses on transforming both the content and the processes of literacy education in order to challenge inequities in the broader society. In terms of content, this means centering instruction on the lived realities of learners as it relates to the broader social context (so that issues of power and inequity become the subject matter itself). In terms of processes, it means problematizing reality as the basis for dialogue, critical analysis, the collaborative construction of knowledge, and action outside the classroom. (p. 79)

For Auerbach and others, ignoring these realities of social, cultural, political, and economic impact is to disregard the data of lived experience. As

Mertens (1998) summarized the operative assumptions of the emancipatory paradigm, "Researchers must focus on how oppressed groups' lives are constrained by the action of the oppressors, individually and collectively, and on the strategies that oppressed groups use to resist, challenge, and subvert" (p. 18). The purpose of such research is not simply to gain critical insight, but to provide the knowledge base among participants to resolve particular problems that they identify through critical reflection.

In its critical and emancipatory manifestations, this third paradigm has embodied a wide array of educational scholarship. This gives shape to its *ontology*, which combines the emphasis on "multiple realities" with a strong focus on the social and political construction of reality, and an interactive *epistemology* between the researcher and researched. *Methodologies* include both quantitative and qualitative approaches, with the focal point on the illumination of power as well as the emancipatory potential of a "liberatory" praxis (pp. 20–21).

As a textbook, *Research Methods in Education and Psychology* does not provide in-depth probing of the philosophical frameworks of each position. It somewhat skirts the issue as to whether the paradigms provide alternative windows of perception or are simply incommensurable in the contradictions among them, without much prospect of mediating potential. In her reflection, Mertens "suggest[ed] the possibility of developing a new paradigm *in the future* [italics in original] that looks to everything as a matter of degree rather than dualistically" (p. 28). In this she took a guardedly optimistic stance on the potential commensurability of the research paradigms she laid out in her text. It might be assumed by the operating logic that underlies her book that she shared in Bernstein's (1983) pragmatic vision that divergent research traditions reflect "differences of emphasis rather than absolute cleavages" (p. 59). From this hopeful perspective, they shed alternative insight among communities of investigators seeking illumination over particularly obtuse problems. The issue, however, may not be merely a matter of epistemology, even in its multifaceted complexity. The more enduring problematic may be the inescapable influence of political power in the determination of which knowledge discourses are privileged or marginalized within particular political cultures.

SCIENTIFIC RESEARCH IN EDUCATION: OVERVIEW

In its *Strategic Plan 2002–2007*, the U.S. Department of Education advocates for "revolutionary change" (p. 1) in the nation's schools and teacher training institutions "from a culture of compliance and susceptibility to fads to a culture of achievement, professionalism, and results" (p. 2). The need to ground educational research on a scientific basis is a critical piece of this vision. Supportive legislation followed the issuance of the *Strategic Plan* in the *Leave No Child Behind Act* (2001) and the *Educational Sciences Reform Act* (2002).

In taking advantage of the "rising enthusiasm for evidence-based educational policy and practice" (p. 1), Shavelson and Towne (2002), the authors of an influential National Research Council's (NCR) publication, sought to establish a sophisticated approach to scientific-based educational research. In this, the authors of *Scientific Research in Education* would like to move beyond the polemics of political partisanship even as Shavelson and Towne took into account the inevitability of policy informing research agendas. Notwithstanding the inherent tensions between the partisanship of politics and the disinterestedness of science, the authors discerned a peculiarly apt time in the current political environment for education-based scientific research to play a substantial role in revitalizing the nation's schools. They called on the research community to take full advantage of the moment, lest they squander the opportunity the receptive climate has afforded them.

Although not wedded to any single epistemology or methodology, the authors work predominantly out of the neopositivist paradigm. *Scientific Research in Education* includes passages that are not well integrated with the main focus of the text, which point to a broader understanding of science than that embedded in the neopositivist paradigm. Shavelson and Towne, for example, did not propose even a proximate resolution of the different paradigmatic perceptions of research as articulated by Mertens (1998). They did not discount its importance, but their main objective was to incorporate highly selective insight into other frameworks as a means of enhancing the credibility of the neopositivist paradigm. The authors also noted in passing an appreciation for a wider realm of educational scholarship than that which falls under the category of scientific research, the implications of which they failed to develop. In short, there is an unresolved tension in *Scientific Research in Education* between these broader issues and the desire to flesh out a sharply defined scientific research agenda for education that can be accepted within current policy circles based on neopositivist assumptions.

Shavelson and Towne maintained that whether of the physical, biological, or social sciences, "at its core, scientific inquiry is the same in all fields." As a basic definition, scientific research "is a continuous process of rigorous reasoning supported by a dynamic interplay among methods, theories, and findings." The result is "models or theories that can be tested," which are supported by "self-regulating norms of the scientific community over time." It is this which grounds scientific-based research, rather than a "mechanistic application of a particular scientific method to a static set of questions" (p. 2). In short, scientific thinking is a habit of mind based on disciplined reasoning, close examination of the evidence, and careful theory construction as applied to specific sets of problems.

The object, in Dewey's (1938/1991) terminology (which the authors appropriate, but not the pragmatic epistemology that underlies it), is the "control of inquiry so that it may yield warranted assertions" (p. 11). The authors of the NRC study noted, with Dewey, that it is these well-formulated warranted assertions rather than a purer quest for certainty that drives scientific investigation. However, contra Dewey, they eliminated the realm of values as a proper arena for scientific investigation. Shavelson and Towne identified six principles congruent with the neopositivist paradigm, four of which are discussed below, as core methodological criteria that enable scientific investigation to come as close as possible to achieving the ideal of objective truth in the quest for reliable, cumulative knowledge.

POSE SIGNIFICANT QUESTIONS THAT CAN BE INVESTIGATED EMPIRICALLY

Shavelson and Towne's (2002) first principle is the posing of significant questions that can be investigated empirically. Whereas there is a subjective factor in the determination of what is an important problem, as an applied field, scientists working on educational research draw on the expressed needs of practitioners as well as the policy sector in helping to determine the focus of their work. Whatever the topic, there is usually "an effort to fill a gap in existing knowledge or to seek new knowledge, to better understand the identification of the cause or causes of some phenomena, or to formally test a hypothesis" (p. 3). This requires the exercise of creative imagination in sharpening "the quality of the question posed" and in the careful work of "moving from hunch to conceptualization and specification of a worthwhile question" (p. 55). Within certain policy and practical constraints, there is wide latitude for scientific researchers to help define specific problems on which to focus their research.

Qualities of "testability and refutability" are critical to valid investigation, as is "a solid understanding of the relevant theoretical, methodological, and empirical work that has come before" (p. 55). In taking a strong neopositivist stance, the authors underscored the centrality of objectivity in contrast to value-based questions, "which cannot be submitted to empirical investigation and thus cannot be examined scientifically" (p. 59).

In the denial of value-related questions as a proper field of domain for scientific investigation, the authors assumed a sharp divergence with other modes of research, particularly the emancipatory paradigm in which the quest to grasp and progressively resolve perceived sources of injustice drive the purpose of research. In Dewey's (1929/1988) terms, "Thinking [and here he meant the types of inquiry that an investigation requires, as well as resulting postulations] is objectively discoverable as that mode of serial re-

sponsive behavior to a problematic situation in which transition to the relatively settled and clear is effected" (p. 181). For Dewey, values, as a natural
aspect of human experience, give shape to the formation of a research project, the modes of its investigation throughout the means–ends continuum,
and its "ends-in-view" in the quest for a more desirable outcome. The NRC
report is certainly driven by values. The authors acknowledged as much in
the promotion of scientific rigor as a means to enhance educational research. Yet, *Scientific Research in Education* skirts around a fuller coming to
terms with the relation between values and research, a topic Mertens
probed through her typology, as well as in the pragmatic epistemology that
drives Dewey's (1938/1991) *Logic: The Theory of Inquiry.*

LINK RESEARCH TO RELEVANT THEORY

Linking research to relevant theory is the second scientific principle identified by the authors of the NRC study. The relation between data and theory
flows in both directions. An overarching theory can guide the focus of research, data collection, analysis, and logical reasoning and can lead to the
formation of empirically supported theories. In this, scientific theory construction as described by Shavelson and Towne shares a family resemblance
with various research traditions as identified by Mertens (1998). A primary
difference in the neopositivist paradigm is the rigor by which it seeks to explain direct causality. In seeking to establish a secure knowledge base
wherein data and theory construction are tightly integrated, the goal is the
"generat[ion of] cumulative knowledge" that includes, where warranted,
"occasionally replacing theoretical understanding" (Shavelson & Towne,
2002, p. 3).

Noting that research in the social sciences "is qualitatively more complex
than inquiry in the natural sciences," the authors acknowledged that "scientific understanding often requires an integration of knowledge across a rich
array of paradigms, schools of thought, and approaches" (p. 48). This is an
important insight. Yet, it is a sensibility that is underdeveloped in *Scientific
Research in Education.* Reflecting its dominant neopositivist bias, as Mertens
defined the term, the authors held that theory construction needs to follow
a rigorous analysis of the evidence that requires the strictest of deductive
reasoning from the data, susceptible to "falsification," wherein a singular
case to the contrary can prove the hypothesis or theory false. It is on this basis of investigation that the authors lay their hope for the emergence of cumulative knowledge in particular areas of research such as testing and assessment, and phonological awareness, which they summarized in chapter
2. However, in doing so, Shavelson and Towne did not take into account
disconfirming evidence based on other research traditions than those they

tracked in following the historical trajectory of research in these areas. That is, they did not address the Kuhnian notion that research progresses at least in part as a result of different paradigms than that of "normal science," which may open up novel understanding beyond a given framework.

In neopositivist research, theory construction is tightly linked to the data based on the ideal of causality discerned empirically, combined with rigorous analytical reasoning. Although all research paradigms take account of the data and depend on logical reasoning, they do so from different premises. In constructivist and postmodern research projects, theory does not aim at the attainment of an undisputed objective truth, even as an ideal. Rather, given the assumption that realities are multiple, even as some evidentiary-based perceptions are deemed better or worse, divergent theories serve as a plausible explanatory accounting that opens up insight into a range of social, cultural, and psychological experience that might not otherwise be given an accounting.

Except in extreme cases, this broadening of what is viewed as legitimate research in the social sciences does not lead to an uncritical relativism. It does call for a close analysis of context, with the acknowledgment that interpretation, however plausible, remains a *construct*—otherwise put, a hypothesis. Researchers working out of interpretive/constructivist and emancipatory frameworks maintain that in the human and social sciences, meaning making is typically a contestable process, where an accounting of the facts may occur in different ways that are nonetheless coherent within particular research traditions in which they are embedded. Notwithstanding the haunting specter of relativism, canons of research and disciplinary traditions provide a measure of stability. These help to modify such tendencies, where subjectivity and imaginative engagement remain an inherent part of the process of critical investigation in the movement toward clarity, coherence with the data, and dialogical encounter (Cherryholmes, 1988; Rescher, 2001).

In the emancipatory paradigm, theory construction takes into account an analysis of power, along with the potential efficacy of human action in the transformation of experience. Building on Freire's (1970) assumption that "humanization . . . is man's vocation" (p. 28), Aronowitz and Giroux (1993) constructed a theoretical project to probe the issue of how to "develop a radical pedagogy that makes schools meaningful so as to make them critical and . . . to make them critical so as to make them emancipatory" (p. 103). The grounding point of their work is the tradition of scholarship on education stemming from Marxian social, cultural, and psychological "reproduction" theory that posits schooling as a substratum of capitalist identity formation linked to the oppression of marginalized social groups. In their articulation of *resistance theory*, the authors both build on and move beyond various neo-Marxian interpretations as developed throughout the

20th century. Specifically, Aronowitz and Giroux sought to use the concept of resistance as a lever "for understanding the complex ways that subordinate groups experience educational failure" (p. 98). This insight, in turn, serves a greater purpose of refining a school of thought, *critical pedagogy*, that takes seriously its emancipatory reconstructive potential that filters into a critical analysis on how oppression operates within schooling and throughout society and culture.

In contrast, the neopositivist paradigm posits a radical separation between political ideology and science wherein values cannot intrude into the realm of legitimate investigation. Theory, generally of a "mid-range" (Shavelson & Towne, 2002, p. 60) type, emerges only through an exacting analysis of causal relations based on rigorously logical inferences of observable data. In the emancipatory paradigm, political power, broadly defined, is the centerpiece of its interpretive focus. Theory provides both analysis of existing power relations and resources for the reconstruction of a more desirable future as defined by those subscribing to this point of view. The emancipatory research paradigm draws on hard data, particularly statistical information on the distribution of wealth and privilege, based on factors of class, race, gender, and ethnicity. Its theory construction is more of an intellectual process wherein the social facts are woven into interpretive refinements stemming from, but moving beyond, Marxist and neo-Marxist categories of social analysis that have the reality of power as its primary referent. Those operating out of this paradigm typically acknowledge its value-laden intent and claim that all research paradigms are similarly so oriented.

USE METHODS THAT PERMIT DIRECT INVESTIGATION OF THE QUESTION

The third scientific principle identified by Shavelson and Towne (2002) is the role that methods play in scientific research. The authors made two points: First, exacting methods are important in scientific research and, second, the utilization of specific methods depends on the nature and scope of the research question. All things being equal, a research project is enhanced if it "can withstand scrutiny by multiple methods" (p. 64).

Internal validity refers to whether and the extent to which a particular factor, or set of factors, causes a specific behavior. As Mertens (1998) pointed out, this is an important aspect of neopositivist research methodology, confirmed in Shavelson and Towne (2002). Another is *external validity*, which points to the extent to which a finding in one case generalizes to others. Underlying both is the need to discern causal relationships, which experimental design is devised to address. In neopositivist research, causation requires a precise analysis of independent variables, those factors that can be clearly distinguished from others in their contribution to the observed behavior.

External validity or making sound generalizations based on analysis of sample studies depends on the quality of its randomness in faithfully representing the population or the factors under analysis. In neopositivist research, *experimental design* represents the ideal of a true sample where researchers "can be assured that groups are truly comparable and that observed differences in outcomes are not the result of extraneous factors or pre-existing differences" (Gribbons & Herman, 1997, p. 3). *Quasi-experimental design* is relied on when obtaining a random sample is not feasible or appropriate for the purposes of a particular investigation.

Although a purer experimental design is more effective in demonstrating causal attribution, problems remain where its laboratory model "may not be feasible to implement in the 'real-life' practice of educational settings" (p. 114). Nor may it be an accurate reflection of them. As Gribbons and Herman (1997) noted, "With complex educational programs, rarely can we control all the important variables . . . even with the best experimental design" (p. 4). In pointing to the value of "randomized field trials" for scientific-based educational research, Shavelson and Towne (2002) acknowledged the relevance of studies that use "other methods" (p. 125). The authors included in the repertoire "in-depth qualitative approaches that can illuminate important nuances, identify potential counterhypotheses, and provide additional sources of evidence for supporting causal claims in complex educational settings" (pp. 125–126).

In linking methodology to questions pursued, Shavelson and Towne noted that in research projects where "concepts or variables are poorly specified or inadequately measured, even the best methods will not be able to support strong scientific inferences" (p. 66). The authors pointed out that the type of precision inherent in independent factor analysis of causal attribution is easier to undertake in the natural rather than in the social sciences. Pointing to the limitations of applying such rigor to an applied field like education, Shavelson and Towne observed that "measurement reliability and validity is particularly challenging" (p. 66). At issue as well, and not addressed by the authors, is the Kuhnian hypothesis pointing to "the impossibility of full translation between rival paradigms" in which "different methodological standards have nonidentical sets of cognitive values" (Malhotra, 1994, p. 5).

There is considerable subtlety in *Scientific Research in Education* in the call for multimethods, in their acceptance of qualitative/quantitative complementariness, and the acknowledgment of the legitimacy of other research tradition than scientific-based educational research. Still, the broader ontological, epistemological, and methodological implications of the divergent research traditions that invariably impact on the range and types of investigations deemed plausible are not significantly addressed by the NRC report.

PROVIDE A COHERENT AND EXPLICIT CHAIN OF REASONING

Neopositivism

Shavelson and Towne identified "inferential reasoning" as a core principle of scientific research. What is required, they noted, is a type of logical analysis that is "coherent, shareable, and persuasive to the skeptical reader" (p. 4). They also pointed out the importance of establishing a "chain of reasoning . . . that another researcher could replicate" (p. 67). In addition, scientific analysis requires "rigorous reasoning that systematically and logically links empirical observations with the underlying theory" it seeks to explain. To the extent that findings are generalizable, their relevance in the building of cumulative, usable knowledge is thereby enhanced.

These neopositivist assumptions are based on two presuppositions. First, inferential reasoning leading to hypothesis construction and theory formation needs to be carefully linked to the empirical evidence. Second, methodological rigor leads to an accurate as possible analysis of the relation between cause and effect. The fewer factors requiring control, the more likely the accuracy of the causal attribution. As an example, in the field of adult literacy education, experimental and quasi-experimental research might focus on a comparison study that seeks to discern how students at different reading levels within a given program process such variables as the alphabet principle, sight-word memorization, and context clues within an academic year.

Such a research agenda has actually been recommended. An interdisciplinary panel meeting of experts was called together in 2000 to give advice to several federal adult and childhood education agencies to identify priority areas for adult and family literacy programs. Noted was the lack of "instructional effectiveness" in adult and family literacy and the need to "know about the timing and mode of delivery of reading instruction" (NICHHD, 2000, p. 1) as a baseline for improving reading ability. Because of the limited "scientific study of literacy interventions with adult learners," there is a paucity of information "about causal relationships between instructional methods or approaches and literacy outcomes" (p. 2). The panel charted out examples of viable research projects, as quoted here, that could rectify the information gap:

- What role do phonemic awareness, the alphabetic principle, and phonics play in literacy learning and adult instruction, and how does this role vary with different groups?
- What are the optimal instructional methods to increase vocabulary in adult literacy learners, and how can these methods be optimally integrated with other components of reading?
- Do vocabulary gains in specific areas . . . improve reading ability?
- Does comprehension strategy instruction differ for adults vs. school-age learners, and how can this information be used to develop optimal instructional methods for adults?
- What is the impact of increased vocabulary on reading fluency and on reading comprehension? (p. 7)

Research projects designed to delineate the various factors of causal attribution to answer these questions would require some combination of formal testing at several intervals, detailed observation, and rigorous control over teaching methodologies, instructional materials, and instructional time. Interviews with students and teachers would help to further discern the impact of various methodologies in a given program, but the problem of "response bias" would need to be carefully controlled. Such a research project would be attempting to control for *internal validity* in the elucidation of and degree to which various factors contributed to enhanced reading ability.

Attaining *external validity* would require additional numbers of students and programs to achieve sufficient comparison based on a random sample (or as close to a random sample as possible) that could be statistically generalizable to a broader population. The information gleaned through such research might provide "evidence-based" criteria on which to make reasoned hypotheses about the emergence of phonemic awareness within adult literacy students at various reading ability levels. Various other factors related to research rigor and sufficient contextuality would need to be taken into account in order to gain a fuller picture. However, the more aspects of the reading process brought in, the more difficult it becomes to isolate causal attribution at a statistically salient level of generalization. The fewer factors considered, the less attention is paid to the many contextual factors that influence specific reading programs.

Highly pointed research projects like these may be enhanced by neo-positivist research methodologies and derivative logical analysis in the search to assign causal attribution. Although useful in adding insight into highly particular questions like the influence of the alphabet principle, as the authors of *Scientific Research in Education* noted, there are limitations in these types of studies. In the specific example provided, considerations like motivation and the relevance of student interest and knowledge of the content of the reading material would need to be factored in as intervening variables (Sticht, 1997b). Moreover, as Shavelson and Towne (2002) pointed out, the social sciences and educational research in particular are not as amenable to neopositivist methodologies as are the natural sciences, due to the greater instability of the data and the increased variances of the human factor.

The field of adult literacy poses additional problems. Its research base is considerably more limited than K–12 education. In addition, basic definitions and purposes attributed to adult literacy education are not only currently unresolved, but contestable. The very definition of literacy on whether it is synonymous with reading and writing or metaphorically linked to learning and knowledge, hence to "reading the world," remains unresolved. So is the matter of federal policy on the appropriate role of adult literacy, whether its primary purpose is its contribution to economic development or the enhancement of civic polity, or if both, in what manner. In varied ways, these contextualizing factors subtly intersect in the shaping of specific adult literacy programs.

Even in the current climate, neopositivist research has much to contribute, but the conflicting issue of the definition of literacy and policy orientation requires a broader frame of reference than an intellectual tradition that eschews values as a legitimate field of investigation. Considerable clarification would be needed, for example, before subjecting the following question to scientific investigation in the neopositivist vein, which may not be amenable to causal analysis at a high level of generality: "To what extent does motivation affect literacy and how does motivation interact with instruction and content to affect literacy? How does culture alter both how motivation is defined and how it might be measured? What is the relative role of motivation in various groups of adult learners?" (NICHHD, 2000, p. 9).

In the chain of reasoning argued for in the neopositivist paradigm, the concept of *rigor* carries considerable weight. It represents a vision metaphorically connected to an imagery of laboratory-like control and precision as an ideal, notwithstanding a more complex reality acknowledged by those operating out of this framework. Mertens (1998) identified five stages in neopositivist research methodology that provide the links to the logical chains of reasoning that underlie it. The first is the identification of "an appropriate problem." The second is the identification of "the variables to be included in the study." The next step is the need "to identify [the] appropriate persons" and groups to investigate. The fourth is the collection of "quantifiable data." The last step is "to analyze the data and interpret the results" (pp. 95–97). The critical factor remains the extent to which causal attribution can be made to a high level of certainty and generality in assessing impacts of independent variables that underlie the neopositivist imagery of precision, exactness, and data control.

Qualitative Research Tradition

An example of the interpretive/constructivist paradigm is *qualitative research,* an umbrella term for a variety of types of studies that seek to illuminate something of descriptive human experience as perceived by contemporary or historical actors. Studies in this mode seek to grasp significant aspects of the *"meaning people have constructed"* (Merriam, 2001, p. 6, italics in original) about their lives. Qualitative research projects take into account such things as the different play of language meaning in various contexts and situations, the interface between consciousness and social interaction, intra- and intergroup behavior, and the various interactive influences of institutions on personal and community life. The focus of such research is on how subjects of a study interpret their own lived experience rather than third person analysis, even as the presence of the interpreter is inevitably present.

Rather than generalizability and replicability even as an ideal, the purpose of qualitative research is to provide "thick description" of a particular case or environment. The object is to illuminate something of the complexity of the relation of human consciousness and social behavior within a situated context. If compellingly described and well researched, it is argued that qualitative studies can have applicability beyond the immediacy of their particular focus, even as they typically lack replicability in a strict scientific sense.

Corresponding methodologies and chains of reasoning are grounded in the academic disciplines of cultural anthropology and such fields as history, cognitive psychology, and literary analysis that require tools of research that are more imaginative and supple than strictly rigorous as reflected in neopositivist design. Based on the maxim that methodologies are determined by the purposes that shape the research questions, coherence and chains of reasoning follow different pathways in studies based on the interpretive/constructivist paradigm than those grounded in neopositivist precepts. They are inherently qualitative in the effort to describe a complex interplay of psychological, social, and cultural factors as played out in specific contexts and situations. Scientific logic as articulated in the NRC report is not ignored or given canonical status. It is selectively drawn on as appropriate in any given study even as the assumption that values have no place in educational research is rejected.

At the core of the qualitative research tradition is the central role of the researcher as "the primary instrument for data collection and analysis" (p.

7, original italics removed). Based on the variability of the research project, studies in this mode provide a wide range for choice where interpretation cannot be radically separated from the process of data selection, collection, and analysis. The inevitable result is that the investigator imposes coherency through the basic focus of the research design and the theoretical presuppositions that underlay the study, the types of data collected, and in the rhetorical style as well as the substance of the constructed narrative. Somewhat skeptically, Pawson and Tilley (1997) noted that "the researcher's account of such an open-ended reality must therefore be selective and rest upon his or her preferred assumptions, pet theories, [and] cherished values." The authors went on to observe that "since, on this view there is no single objectivity to report upon, hermeneutical dialectical circles . . . go round in circles, rather than constituting a linear advance on the truth" (p. 21). Notwithstanding this critique, given the indubitableness of multiple realities, the effort to describe human complexity remains a compelling challenge that may require critical hermeneutical probing.

Whereas subjectivity is a presupposition of the qualitative research tradition (congruent, advocates insist, with the nature of human experience itself), academic discipline is achieved, in part, by grounding the research in the scholarly literature of the particular topic at hand. This includes "pointing out the exact nature of the contribution" (Merriam, 2001, p. 51) of the ways in which the specific research topic interfaces with the existing scholarly literature. More than a literature review, this requires a critical drawing on the scholarship as part of the broader work of making a well-constructed argument. Coherency is achieved in part by the value judgment of the community of scholars who determine how well the current study is placed within the given literature and the extent to which they and other readers judge its contribution in refining, shifting, or in some other way, expanding the knowledge base of the topic under investigation.

Academic discipline is also achieved by competent data analysis and theory construction consistent with the objectives of qualitative research. Analysis draws on "inductive and deductive reasoning" in the moving back and forth "between description and interpretation" (p. 178). The process involves "category construction" that reflects the corresponding levels of analysis of the data. As discussed in the previous chapters on the EFF project, this requires a combination of intuition and a systematic sifting of the available evidence. The creation of "categories and subcategories" emerges through a "constant comparative method of data analysis" (p. 179). This includes informed hypothesis construction that extends beyond the data, but is congruent with it.

Theory development emerges as an extension of this inductive and deductive reasoning process in the navigation "from concrete description . . . to a somewhat more abstract level . . . using concepts to describe phenomena" (p. 187). In the working with and through the data and emerging categorizations, advanced hypothesis formation takes on a functional role, as the researcher senses that the evolving "category scheme does not tell the whole story" (p. 188). Formal theory may emerge in the very quest for greater clarity that pushes the researcher toward increased abstraction as part of the process of further sifting through the interrelations between the data, emerging interpretive categories, and the secondary scholarship in which the topic at hand is embedded.

Theory based on qualitative research requires *parsimony,* or simplicity, in its interpretive power and scope in its applicability to a wide array of situations. Although not related primarily to qualitative research as depicted in Merriam's *Qualitative Research and Case Study Applications in Education,* Marxist social theory is an example that fits both of these categories. Its core thesis of economic determinism underlies its analysis of capitalism. At the same time, its scope is broad in application to a wide range of spheres in the realms of culture, politics, society, economics, and individual psychology. In my own research, I have drawn on Dewey's (1916, 1938/1963) concept of *growth* defined as the *enhancement* of experience through critical reflection and thoughtful action. As expressed by Dewey (1938/1963), "Growth in judgment and understanding is essentially growth in ability to form purposes and to select and arrange means for their realization" (p. 84). I have drawn on this concept as a broad explanatory heuristic to explore many facets of adult literacy education (Demetrion, 2000b, 2001b, 2002).

In addition to its explanatory power in going beyond the data, the value of theory is its relative endurance in providing a degree of canonical stability within academic research. Mezirow's "perspective transformation," Dewey's concept of "growth," Gardner's notion of "multiple intelligences," Vygotsky's social interaction theory, and Kegan's work in developmental psychology are examples of theoretical constructs that have been incorporated into qualitative research projects that have spawned a wide array of studies. In neopositivist, as well as qualitative research, "values like the dedication of the pursuit of truth, openness to counter evidence, receptiveness to criticism, accuracy of measurement and observation, honesty and openness in reporting results" (Phillips & Burbules, 2000, p. 54) are equally important. These approaches differ in how these values are sifted through divergent ontological and epistemological assumptions and investigative methodologies that shape underlying assumptions of various research traditions.

For example, in qualitative research, the terms *dependability* or *consistency* are used instead of the concept *reliability,* which is too closely associated with the positivist goal of replicability. What is referred to as research *dependability* is achieved through the use of "multiple investigators, multiple sources of data, or multiple methods" (Merriam, 2001, p. 204). In qualitative research, no singular source of evidence is typically viewed as definitive.

More critical is the extent to which different data sources confirm or disconfirm a particular argument or conclusion. What is important is how events and circumstances are interpreted within the context of their embedded situation, including the invariably openness of qualitative research design to multiple (but not infinite) perspectives. In general, the richer and more complex the triangularity of sources and methods, the more dependable the findings will be, although the "proof" is in the overall coherence of the argument as mediated by significant interpretative communities. When well executed, qualitative research is coherent. Its investigative process requires an explicit chain of reasoning grounded in the ontological, epistemological, and methodological premises that underlie its logic.

Those critical of qualitative research point to its "militant agnosticism on [the concept of] *truth*" (Pawson & Tilley, 2000, p. 22). Critics also point to the failure of researchers in this tradition to make *independent* judgments beyond the task of probing the subtleties of description (pp. 22, 23), although Maxwell (2004) argued that "the ability of qualitative methods to directly investigate causal processes [in single cases] is a major contribution that this approach can make to scientific inquiry in education" (p. 6). Critics from the emancipatory paradigm argue that qualitative studies are often exceedingly thin on their description of how power is mediated through the categories of class, gender, race, ethnicity, and historical traditions.

Critical Pedagogy

Overview. "A coherent and explicit chain of reasoning" (Shavelson & Towne, 2002) is also discernable in the *critical pedagogy* that underlies *Education Still Under Siege* (Aronowitz & Giroux, 1993, pp. 65–109). The authors' discussion of the evolution of reproduction and resistance theories, leading toward their own "theory of resistance," is systematically developed and intellectually cogent. Based on the criteria identified by Shavelson and Towne (2002), the argument of Aronowitz and Giroux is "coherent" and "sharable," although not likely "persuasive to the skeptical reader" (p. 4).

Indeed, Shavelson and Towne (2002) would view suspiciously, the "meta-theory" that grounds critical pedagogy. In their second scientific principle, they highlighted a more "modest" "mid-range" theory construction "that [in] account[ing] for some aspect of the world" (p. 6) is based on a logical and tightly correlated deduction process stemming from data gleaned through direct observation, supportive methodologies, and tentative hypothesis formation. Critical pedagogy does not eschew logic, empirical evidence, or methodological rigor. Its core premise, emerging from neo-Marxist political philosophy, has a basic grounding in demographic patterns of wealth and power distribution that can be illustrated through quantitative and qualitative means. The scholarship that supports critical pedagogy provides an alternative lens on social and cultural experience than that typically accessible in normative educational discourse.

Aronowitz and Giroux (1993, chap. 4) focused on the task of reconciling the relation between personal agency and social structure. In chapter 4, they sought enhanced space for emancipatory theory construction as the basis for establishing an informed praxis even in constrained social environments where the distribution of cultural and political power between marginalized social groups and those at the center of institutional authority is far from equal. This tension is teased out in this chapter as part of these authors' larger purpose of working out a coherent intellectual framework that is simultaneously critical and transformative.

Thus, for Aronowitz and Giroux, theory construction is driven by the praxis of linking critical pedagogy to "emancipatory interests," a potential that the authors noted is only latent within the reproduction and resistance theory that they trace. This underdeveloped tendency needs to become more overt in order to "become the object of debate and political analysis" (p. 102), and consequently, a lived possibility. The purpose of what follows is neither to defend nor to critique critical pedagogy. It is, rather, to demonstrate something of the logic and chain of reasoning through which Aronowitz and Giroux (1993) constructed their argument.

Reproduction Theory.   In neo-Marxist thought, *reproduction theory* refers to the ways in which the economic system and the social, political, and cultural institutions and mores of modern life interact to produce a "normalized" capitalistic worldview that becomes *reified* in individuals, groups, and the broader collective consciousness of a society. The normalized world order is the product of a "dominant ideology" and corresponding "forms of knowledge" that result in "the distribution of the skills needed to reproduce the social division of labor" (p. 65) required for the functioning of the economic system. This reproduction theory is an indispensable feature of neo-Marxist thought in its critical power to expose the *created* reality of capitalism. Through ideology critique, its purpose is to interrogate the "false consciousness" of the social world within capitalism, particularly its linkage to a natural-like human evolution, almost akin to a state of nature (Hayek, 1960).

Aronowitz and Giroux's (1993) discussion of reproduction theory consists of a systematic overview of three of its main typologies as described in various neo-Marxian educational studies. To summarize the *economic-reproductive model*, Aronowitz and Giroux drew on *Capitalist Schooling in America* (Bowles & Gintis, 1976). The authors of *Education Still Under Siege* noted a "correspondence theory" at the center of Bowles and Gintis' analysis, which "posits that the hierarchically structured patterns of values, norms, and skills that characterize the workforce and the dynamics of class interaction are mirrored in the social dynamics of the daily classroom encounter" (p. 70). The result is a "grim" determinism at the center of schooling in the United States.

Aronowitz and Giroux argued that the *cultural-reproductive model* is equally deterministic. This cultural influence is subtler in that it opens up space for personal assent. Still, it remains unduly pessimistic in the limited opportunity available for construction of identities outside the boundaries of given norms. The authors drew on French sociologist Pierre Bourdieu, particularly his concepts of the *habitat* (positionality) and *habitus* (psychological dispositions). Bourdieu linked the first with the mores of the historically constructed institutional and material world, and the second "to a set of internalized competencies and structured needs, an internalized style of knowing and relating to the world that is grounded in the body itself" (p. 77). In Bourdieu's analysis, "culture becomes the mediating link between ruling class interests and everyday life" (p. 75). As with *Capitalist Schooling in America*, so with Bourdieu, the social world within schooling and throughout the broader sociocultural realm is one that is highly constrained.

The third embodiment is the *hegemonic-state reproductive model* in which the authors drew on the work of the Italian communist intellectual Antonio Gramsci. In this typology, the state enforces the "hegemony" of "the dominant classes" through "an ever-changing combination of force and assent" (p. 83). Through formal power and the more subtle influence of ideology, "the common sense view" of citizens becomes conformed to the interests of the "dominant classes." Within the state, there is scope for competing interests that emerges amidst the "conflicts among different factions of the ruling class." However, Aronowitz and Giroux were quick to note that notwithstanding the "relative autonomy of the state," the literature stresses the importance of "what various factions of the ruling class have in common." Consequently, "the structured silences regarding the underlying basis of capitalist society" (p. 85) remain intact.

The strength of reproduction theory, according to the authors, is the multitextured critical analysis of 20th-century capitalism. The authors of *Education Still Under Siege* agreed that critical pedagogy needs to be analytically rigorous in identifying sources of what they defined as oppression. Even so, they are concerned about how reproduction theory overly emphasizes the ways in which the social world acts on individuals "behind their backs," as it were, which impedes the emergence of an emancipatory vision. What is needed, and the answer to which their theory construction points, is a "language of critique [that] unites with the language of possibility" (p. 46).

Resistance Theory. The theoretical formulation that Aronowitz and Giroux constructed at the end of chapter 4 is a refinement on *resistance theory*, a more recent development in neo-Marxist critical theory than reproduction theory. The core value that the authors attribute to resistance theory is that it spotlights the ways in which individuals and various groups complexly *defy* normative pressures to internalize the hegemonic order. The authors noted that research based on resistance theory illustrates something of the "internal working of the school" largely ignored in reproduction theory that opens up conceptual space to better bring out "how human agency accommodates, mediates, and resists the logic of capital and its dominating social practices." Schooling, on this account, "not only serves the interests of domination but also" draws out "emancipatory possibilities" (p. 91) for progressive change. In short, the conceptual insights that resistance theory opens up breaks the logjam of "the theoretical cemetery of Orwellian pessimism" (p. 99) that Aronowitz and Giroux found all-too-pervasive in neo-Marxist studies like *Capitalist Schooling in America.*

The authors provided a nuanced discussion of resistance theory. Its common denominator is the subtle interplay between the efficacy of human agency and the force of structural determinism. In this tension, the authors drew out the complex "dialectic" between the "ideological constraints embedded in capitalist social relationships . . . [and] the process of self-formation within the working class" (p. 92). It is this insight that the authors build on in the development of a critical pedagogy that is simultaneously critical and potentially transformative.

Notwithstanding its strengths, Aronowitz and Giroux pointed out several problems in the dominant strands of resistance theory they analyze. One problem is the failure to distinguish between the different types "of oppositional behaviors" (p. 94), not all of which points in the direction of resistance to the dominant order. Clearly, some oppositional behavior reflects this sharp political orientation, if even only implicitly. Yet, other manifestations may simply be forms of rebellion, and in some cases even downright reactionary prejudice in the guise of racism or sexism. The authors also noted that resistance theory fails to sharply distinguish between "forms of ideological domination" that intrude on the consciousness of the oppressed and the more direct impact of overtly "repressive institutions" (p. 95) that does not gain an inner assent.

In addition to these factors, Aronowitz and Giroux cited resistance theory for failing to sufficiently note the subtle differences in the ways in which students resist, a range that extends from "overt acts" to more "quiet subversive" (p. 96) action. Simply put, "when resistance theory is discussed, its contradictory nature is usually not analyzed seriously, nor is the contradictory consciousness of the students and teachers treated dialectically" (p. 96). These fine distinctions are important, the authors noted, in contributing to the creation of a pedagogy that is both critical and utopian. The vision unleashed is designed to simultaneously account for the inevitable constraints imposed by the dominant order as well as to reflect the openness of the range of possibilities that a productive appro-priation of power by various oppressed groups can unleash. This ongoing critical project of tempered hope is essential, the authors argue, to break the logjam of despair reinforced by the blatant determinism of reproduc-tion theory and the more subtle pessimism of resistance theory based on neo-Marxian premises.

Thus, there is a need for a critical pedagogy as dynamically attuned as possible to the subtle interplay between structural constraints and agency-driven possibilities, acknowledging "student resistance in all of its forms" as an expression "of struggle and solidarity that, in their incompleteness, both challenge and confirm capitalist hegemony" (p. 102). On the interpreta-tion of Aronowitz and Giroux, a critical pedagogy aimed toward an emanci-patory potential requires disciplined theory construction and on-the-ground praxeological activity. It is in the former that *Education Still Under Siege* provides a sophisticated analysis that is coherent and exhibits a logical chain of reasoning based on the premises that give shape to the authors' vi-sion of critical pedagogy. Needless to say, the role of theory construction takes on a quite different appearance in the emancipatory than in the posi-tivist/neopositivist paradigm, although both provide a "coherent and ex-plicit chain of reasoning" based on their respective premises. Equally evi-dent is the susceptibility of critical pedagogy to a wide array of criticisms among scholars and practitioners who do not accept its orienting principles of political analysis and its utopian philosophical grounding.

CONCLUDING REMARKS

This chapter has drawn on Mertens' (1998) *Research Methods in Education and Psychology* for its organizing framework in the laying out of three distinc-tive approaches to social science research. As noted, these typologies are based on substantially different assumptions that closely parallel the distinc-tive schools of adult literacy education discussed throughout this book. The extent to which the paradigms that Mertens drew out are commensurable or incommensurable is unresolved in her text and in this chapter. It is clear that their differences are substantial in the arenas of ontology, epistemol-ogy, and methodology, and derivative implications for educational scholar-ship. It is through the sensibility of Mertens' paradigmatic typology that this chapter examines core principles of scientific investigation as summarized in *Scientific Research in Education* (Shavelson & Towne, 2002).

In addition to their differences in orientation and scope, also evident is the interminable nature of the conflicting perspectives resident within these research paradigms. Dascal (1997) argued that philosophical conflict has the capacity to "clear the way for the emergence of *radical innovation*" (italics in original) because reasoned intellectual disagreements "invite the appearance of non conventional ideas, methods, techniques and interpretations" (p. 12). Instead of leading to interminable quarrels, "the pressure exerted by criticism" stemming from an inquisitive stance among the research traditions can lead to the "elimin[ation] of theories that have been refuted" and "for the appearance of new ones" (p. 17). The need, Dascal argued, is for "the possibility of a dynamical and dialectical interaction between openness and closure, which connects (rather than *dis*connects) the components of relative stability ('closure') and instability ('openness') in the evolution of science" (p. 23).

As the controversies are political as well as epistemological in scope, as applied to adult literacy education, the prospect for resolution is unlikely, stemming from the respective intrinsic logics of the research paradigms identified by Mertens (1998). Resolution would require mediation at a very high level of symbolic communication at the interstices of scholarship and political culture. Dascal (1997) called for a pragmatic resolution at the level of semantic discourse in the seeking out of an "instrumental rationality" that speaks "coherently and clearly" to the issues at hand. The dialogical encounter of the better argument is the "non-arbitrary ideal" at the center of this pragmatic effort. Even so, "pragmatic norms" are also "contingent" because "the very idea of instrumentality is interpretable in different ways in different contexts" (p. 26).

What is needed for a more operatively consensual approach is a loosening of the paradigmatic logic of the three typologies of research described by Mertens as part of an exploratory search for the kind of innovative breakthroughs discussed by Dascal (1997). This is an indispensable ideal in pursuit of realization, in which an effort is made in the next chapter through an application of Dewey's (1938/1991) theory of logic to his educational concept as growth. It is this linkage of Dewey's mode of experiential inquiry (the basis of his logic) to his educational philosophy that holds one prospect of giving shape to a middle ground pedagogy of literacy that in principle could mediate the prevalent paradigms that characterize the field. The following chapter provides an overview of such a framework at a theoretical level. A detailed roadmap and a systematic working through of the various conflicts that divide would be an important critical project that moves well beyond the purposes of this book.

Toward a Mediating Pedagogy of Adult Literacy Via Dewey's Model of Inquiry and His Accompanying Metaphor of Growth

> *Inquiry is a* continuing *process in every field with which it is engaged. The settlement of a particular "situation" by a particular inquiry is no guarantee that that settled conclusion will always remain settled. The attainment of settled beliefs is a progressive matter; there is no belief so settled as not to be exposed to further inquiry. It is the convergent and cumulative effect of continued inquiry that defines knowledge in its general meaning. In scientific inquiry, the criterion of what is taken to be settled, or to be knowledge, is being so [italics in original] settled that it is available as a resource in further inquiry; not being settled in such a way as not to be subject to revision in further inquiry.*
>
> —Dewey (1938/1991, p. 16)

> *It . . . becomes the office of the educator to select those things within the range of existing experience that have the promise and potentiality of presenting new problems which by stimulating new ways of observation and judgment will expand the areas of further experience. He must constantly guard what is already won not as a fixed position but as an agency and instrumentality for opening new fields which make new demands upon existing powers of observation and of intelligent use of memory. Connectedness in growth must be his constant watchword.*
>
> —Dewey (1938/1963, p. 75)

The preceding chapter linked the three schools of adult literacy reviewed in this book with the distinctive paradigms of research traditions identified by Mertens (1998). Such a schematic typology oversimplifies both the complexities of the research traditions and the schools of thought. Still, they provide a clarifying function that helps to tease out important issues of definition and values that are central to a grappling with the pedagogy and politics of adult literacy. In addition, in focusing primarily on the various rationales underlying each of the three frameworks laid out by Mertens, my objective was to open up a field of space for a more exploratory research agenda than that for which a rigorous adherence to the typologies might allow.

In order to move toward praxis, although in what can only be a limited way, this chapter bypasses the effort to resolve the controversies over research traditions. I seek instead a framework in adult literacy research that, in principle, could mediate scientific inquiry to the complex nuances of social contextuality and human contingency. Specifically, I seek to open up a creative space through an appropriation of Dewey's (1938/1991) key text, *Logic: The Theory of Inquiry,* and his related work on inquiry as an exploratory map through which to examine his concept of *growth* as applied to adult literacy education. Other mediating reference points could be drawn on, such as feminist epistemology or Popper's critical rationalism. I focus here on Deweyan pragmatism, in which my research is most grounded, while making links from it to the New Literacy Studies.

One of the advantages of this angle is that Dewey's "experimentalist philosophy" (Burke, Hester, & Talisse, 2002, p. xii) resides metaphorically between the research traditions described by Mertens. It is participatory-oriented rather than spectator-based in its focus on progressively resolving problems, as perceived in direct experience. In this respect, Dewey shared a strong affinity with the epistemological and moral assumptions that underlay practitioner-based inquiry (Demetrion, 2000b). His logic is sharply in-tuned with the operative assumptions of 20th-century scientific methodology, but the span of his "laboratory" roams wide along the landscape of "lived" human experience, including the specific field of education, as well as that of political culture and aesthetics. Through an integrative philosophical vision, Dewey sought to draw compelling continuities between common experience and formal scientific investigation while noting important differences in scope. That link is a methodological one. It is the quest to establish "logical forms" in the pursuit of inquiry in the process of progressively working through an "indeterminate situation" (Dewey, 1938/1991, p. 3) toward one that is increasingly unified and determinate that emerges with the resolution of the problem at hand, the "ends-in-view."

Dewey pointed to the ubiquity of inquiry as a pervasive human experience and the search for problem resolution strategies wherever perplexing situations arise. Inquiry is endemic as long as problematic situations that require searching exist. In a well-constructed inquiry project, according to Dewey's hypothesis, logical forms "accrue" as extensions from the situation in which they are aroused. Rather than preexisting forms based on certain general theories or epistemological presuppositions, the structures of logic about teaching adults how to read, for example, will grow out of successful inquiries that seek to resolve this question. In Dewey's terms, "the forms *originate* [italics in original] in operations of inquiry" (p. 11) that can only prove themselves in the actual work that they accomplish. That is in the resolution of a given problem, without which "no amount of theoretical plausibility is of avail" to justify them.

Dewey accepted the importance of generalizations and abstractions to the extent to which they are functionally relevant to the particular inquiry under investigation. What he rejected are a priori assumptions that are then imposed on situations that skew potential modes of inquiry that might otherwise arise from the situation itself. Thus, in terms of teaching adults to read, phonemic-based, whole language, and interactive or balanced reading theories provide a broad array of general, although often conflicting, explanations. As cumulated ideas of reading theory, little of which has been specifically focused on *adult* literacy, these different perspectives provide a wealth of information, which, on Dewey's inquiry-based experimental model, represent important conceptual tools to be factored in as relevant to the focus of the specific research project at hand.

What is required is an instrumental methodology of hypothesis formation, data analysis, and controlled experimentation. The central focal point is the grappling with a defined problem in which the resolution emerges through the process of a specific inquiry (pp. 105–122). The logical forms that lead to greater generalization will, accordingly, follow. Methodologies and theories play a subordinate or functional role to this scientific process of linking logical forms to the inquiry project at hand. That is Dewey's thesis.

Dewey's inquiry mode of logic, broadly defined as *pragmatic*, both parallels and opens up avenues for assessing the viability of the partially elusive concept of *literacy as growth* that I propose as a middle ground pedagogy of adult literacy in the United States. This notion of growth is discussed in detail in later sections of the chapter. For now, let it suffice to define it as the progressive movement from means to ends in working from problems identified to problems temporally resolved within particular situations in which they arise and in which they are changed. This viewpoint takes reality as defined by actors themselves as an experiential grounding point in the working toward a more satisfactory experience of some definable sort, achieved through inquiry, and sometimes, artistic creation and cultural transformation.

As an interpretive metaphor, definitive-like proof of the viability of Dewey's Darwinian-based concept of growth may move beyond the ground of the evidence through hard scientific investigation. That is not ruled out, but it is beyond the work of this chapter to resolve. It may be more feasible to provide a data-supported description of the various components of this concept. On that supposition, experiments could be set up that test, refine, modify, or raise profoundly skeptical problems with the concept. In principle, therefore, the concept may be falsifiable, but not in the narrow way that Popper (1953/1974, cited in Miller, 1985) rejected, based on "a single counterinstance" (p. 110). This caveat is important for competent investigation in the hard sciences, but particularly so for the human sciences where ideas, multiple interpretations, and observable data conjoin in the formation of hypotheses leading to various explanations of human behavior.

The fruit of such competent investigation is the progressive movement toward decisive explanation based on fresh insight that becomes available as a heuristic, which in turn focalizes additional research. This process of ever-deepening inquiry of data analysis and hypothesis formation into more intricate calibrations continues until a problem is progressively solved. That is, "through a series of intermediate meanings, a meaning is finally reached which is more clearly *relevant* [italics in original] to the problem in hand than the originally suggested idea" (Dewey, 1938/1991). This new formulation may result in novel ways of perceiving experience that would otherwise not be injected into the ongoing construction of human reality. This more refined hypothesis, in turn, requires "operations which can be performed to [further] test its applicability" (p. 115).

The testing of the various components of the literacy as growth hypothesis is more plausible, and the effort, in any event, is essential. It is equally important to describe how the specific parts relate within a coherent system of explanation (Rescher, 2001). This task is more difficult in that the literacy as growth concept merges into a cultural explanatory framework invariably linked to the realm of values and even mythical constructs that nonetheless requires competent empirical explanation of the data at hand. That effort, therefore, may draw from the disciplines of literary theory, philosophy, and history, as much as from social science. That there is data to examine is an empirical given. *What* the data at hand may be and how it may be evaluated is an issue of considerable contestation that cannot be easily resolved given the nature of the human sciences. I draw on Dewey's mode of inquiry as an operative framework to advance my thesis as much as feasible in a single chapter. It remains an open issue on the extent to which the concept of literacy as growth will come to rely more on a cultural than scientific explanation. A broader issue is the extent that scholars and practitioners determine that the concept merits a close examination in the first place.

I am not presenting Dewey's axial concept of growth as a fully blown theory. It is examined here as a potentially fruitful hypothesis that requires additional testing and development from its own operating premises even before all the evidence in support of this construct is in, which is an impossible task in any event.

Utilizing theory as an operational hypothesis, the object of this chapter is to construct and refine one definition of and rationale for adult literacy that builds on existing research. In this chapter and throughout this study, I draw in particular on the collective scholarship of the past 20 years, particularly Auerbach (1989, 1992a, 1992b, 1993), Beder and Valentine (1990), Lytle (1991), Quigley (1997), Fingeret and Drennon (1997), Merrifield et al. (1997), and Sticht (1997a). The neo-Vygotskian research of Heath (1983), Street (1988), Scribner (1988), and Barton (1994a) provide the underlying framework for the New Literacy Studies on which those studying adult literacy in the United States from the "social and cultural practices" (Fingeret, 1992, p. 6) model draw. As noted, the founding work of Freire's (1970) *Pedagogy of the Oppressed* is the key text that underlies the school of participatory literacy.

The singular factor that all of this scholarship has in common is the assumption that literacy is a mediated sign system where print and oral language is internalized as an embodiment and fulfillment of a complex array of societal and cultural values. In short, literacy is both a function and a result of meaning making between the individual, reference groups of various sorts, and the broader macroenvironment. The influence, at least in principle, is dynamically transactional, and sifted through an analysis of the unequal distribution of power, as noted in a good portion of this literature. From this ecological perspective (Barton, 1994a), the proponents of the New Literacy Studies and participatory literacy education maintain that the various meanings and functions of literacy cannot be grasped outside of the multiplicity of contexts in which they are embedded. My work on literacy as growth is planted on these assumptions and seeks to extend and build on this broader stream of research.

As commented on in previous chapters, there are important differences in this emergent scholarship. Auerbach and Sticht, in particular, may be viewed as reflecting sharp divergences in perspective, given the association of the former with the critical pedagogy of Paulo Freire, and Sticht's embrace of functional literacy that informs his early work on workplace and military literacy (Demetrion, 2001a). Like Auerbach, in *Rethinking Literacy Education*, Quigley (1997) was empathetic to critical literacy, particularly in his hard-hitting analysis of federal policy and in his criticism of the ways in which programs fail to adequately meet the needs, interests, and aspirations of many potential students who "resist" active participation in them. At the same time, Quigley was enough of a realist so that in his constructive proposals he identified "working philosophies" that would appeal to programs across a wide perspective of political ideology and educational philosophy.

The other writers previously identified are aware of both the poles of functional and critical literacy. However, they placed their main attention in a fleshing out of the "social and cultural practices" (Fingeret, 1992, p. 6) that define literacy and the environments in which text is embedded as a mediated sign system. It is this perspective that informs the U.S. wing of the New Literacy Studies in its collective understanding of adult literacy as a complex form of personal assimilation within the mores and institutions of the prevailing social order. As part of being broadly in line with prevailing cultural values, the U.S. proponents seek space for a modestly reformist politics and a focus on personal student growth as an ongoing engine of educational practice (Demetrion, 1998, 2001b, 2002; Fingeret & Drennon, 1997; Merrifield et al., 1997; Stein, 2000). The context in which literacy practices are manifest includes the literacy program, as well as various environments in community, home, and work settings. Summarized by Merrifield et al. (1997), "Literacy practices are mediated by social context: where people live, what their jobs are, what is happening in their communities. They are also influenced by personal factors: how people grew up, what their expectations are, what their family's expectations of them are" (p. 182).

Fingeret and Drennon (1997) added specificity through a model of an emergent literacy identity based on what the authors referred to as a "spiral of change." Demetrion (1998, 2001a, 2001b, 2002) linked a "middle ground" pedagogy and politics of adult literacy education to the pragmatic concept of growth articulated by Dewey (1916, 1938/1963), which shares close affinities to Fingeret and Drennon's (1997) vision of *Literacy for Life.* As described in chapter 2, and in chapters 8 and 9 on the EFF project, all of these sets of authors provided case study descriptive analysis to illustrate their various theories that share a strong family resemblance within the literacy as a social and cultural practices framework.

In this chapter, the operative assumptions of the New Literacy Studies are further examined through Barton's (1994a) *Literacy: An Introduction to the Ecology of Written Language,* with comparisons made to the literacy as growth thesis. A more detailed discussion follows on the concept of education as growth as articulated by Dewey (1916, 1938/1963) and Garrison (1997, 1998) and appropriated to adult literacy in my various articles and reports.

LITERACY AS AN ECOLOGICAL SIGN SYSTEM

The focus of Barton's (1994a) *Literacy: An Introduction to the Ecology of Written Language* is the situated nature of the relation between "people's everyday lives and how they make use of reading and writing" (p. 3). This topic has been discussed in *Conflicting Paradigms of Adult Literacy Education*, but Barton's ecological vision adds theoretical specificity that provides important hooks in grasping the core assumptions of the New Literacy Studies.

A central concept in the New Literacy Studies is the importance of "multiliteracies" that give shape to the various metaphors of literacy on which the critical matter of definition hangs. The fact that literacy is perceived as a metaphor for various types of knowledge (Barton identified computer, visual, political, and cultural literacy, p. 13), rather than with the "autonomous" acts of reading and writing, is a significant definitional act. Stressing the "constructed" nature of human language, Barton tied the importance of metaphors to broader sociocultural influences that "hang together and form a discourse." Metaphors, then, "bring whole theories [of language and use] with them" and contribute to the formation "of **organizing ideas**" (p. 18, bold in original).

Drawing on the neo-Vygotskian research that shaped the founding work of the New Literacy Studies, Barton took the root metaphor of an ecological system as a basis to define literacy. Naturally empathetic to social definitions of literacy, Barton looked for a way to include psychological processes in a dynamic system of interaction. As he further explained his use of this metaphor, "an ecological approach aims to understand how literacy is embedded in other human activity," including "social life and in thought," and "its position[ality] in history, language, and learning" (p. 32).

In summing up, Barton provided the following rationale that links the ecological metaphor to the definition of literacy practices that inform the New Literacy Studies: "Instead of studying the separate skills which underlie reading and writing, it [the ecological metaphor] involves a shift to studying *literacy* [italics in original] a set of social practices associated with particular symbol systems and their related technologies. To be literate is to be active; it is to be confident with these practices" (p. 32).

It is clear throughout *Literacy: An Introduction to the Ecology of Writing Language* that Barton was taking a stance as well as being descriptive. For him, pedagogy and politics were invariably linked. The ecological view of literacy depends on, but also contributes to, the flourishing of a reformist political culture. It is the ecological interaction of individual development and intra- and intergroup collaboration as a *transactional* dynamic within culture that makes constructive change of both individuals and the broader society possible.

In his third chapter, titled "The Social Basis of Literacy," Barton provided a more finely tuned description of the New Literacy Studies in which he tried to integrate "the social, the psychological, and the historical" (p. 33) dimensions of literacy as a mediated symbolic sign system. The following discussion draws on four of Barton's assumptions to which I draw references to the literacy as growth thesis. Barton's third assumption—that "people's literacy practices are situated in broader social relations" (p. 41)—is assumed in the following discussion.

Assumption 1

Barton's first assumption is that "literacy is a social activity that can best be described in terms of the *literacy practices* which people draw upon in *literacy events*" (p. 36, italics added). These terms were discussed in chapter 2. As Barton explained it, *literacy events* are specific activities such as reading the newspaper, the Bible, or children's literature that reflect "how literacy is actually used in people's everyday lives" (p. 36). In my own research, the focus is largely on literacy as experienced within the adult literacy program. In this context, both the choral and round robin reading by individual students in our small group tutoring sessions, as illustrated in the case study later in this chapter, are examples of literacy events. Barton argued that a substantial understanding of literacy requires a subtle, ethnographic analysis of specific literacy events. On his interpretation, literacy cannot be reduced to a "variable." Rather, it is a complex social process that has cognitive, affective, and aesthetic, as well as social dimensions, as a meaning-making symbol system that resides within individuals, specific groups of people, communities, and in the broader macrostructure. Any multifaceted analysis of the thesis of literacy as growth that I am proposing would include a need to sift the theory through an in-depth critical descriptive analysis of these small group reading sessions in demonstrating how learning is enhanced or perhaps impeded through them (Demetrion, 1999b).

Barton (1994a) defined *literacy practices* as "the common patterns in using reading and writing in a particular situation." This includes bringing "cultural knowledge to an activity" (p. 37) through behaviors, attitudes, and social discourses that may reflect various systems of communication and power relationships. Barton provided the example of two men writing a letter to the local newspaper. That would be the literacy event. Making decisions about which of the two would write what aspects of the letter, and how its specific focus and style would be determined comprise the literacy practices that give the letter its texture and meaning (p. 37). In my program, whereas the choral and round robin reading would be representations of literacy events, the manner of interaction among the students, between the students and the tutor, and the role of the instructional content in facilitating transactional learning would be among the key literacy practices of the small group instructional setting (Demetrion, 1999b). A careful examination of these interactions and embedded meaning systems would add important evidence to the literacy as growth thesis I am proposing in this chapter, which I attempt to illustrate in the case study example.

Assumption 2

Barton's second assumption is that "people have different literacies which they make use of, in association with different domains of life" (p. 38). As discussed in chapter 1, *domains* refer to the major social roles or situations in which literacy practices are embedded. Examples are work, school, home, church, the neighborhood, and the larger community. It is in the various domains in which the notion of multiliteracies, not simply as reading and writing, but as knowledge and learning, is particularly germane. "Literacies" in the different domains "are not equally valued." Moreover, some are chosen whereas others are imposed. Barton (1994a) referred to "*dominant* literacies" and "*vernacular* literacies" (p. 39, italics in original) reflective of the power relations of the various domains. The diverse literacies and domains are invariably linked to the different functions of the social self supported through various "ecological niches which sustain and nurture [or marginalize] particular forms of literacy" (p. 39).

The literacy program from which my research stems largely takes a school-based approach. For the most part, the life domains are interiorized within its contextually driven curriculum, which draws on instructional material linked to home, work, and community settings. These materials consist of a range of topics on health, consumerism, culture, contemporary social issues, and history, and a broad array of human interest stories. Instructional texts include student narratives from ours and other programs. The program's primary resource collection of anthologies of student essays, oral histories, and learning interviews contains a profusion of commentary by students of a broad range of literacy practices within different domains within and outside of the literacy program. In addition to instructional purposes, I have drawn on these sources liberally to tease out a concept of literacy based on Dewey's metaphor of growth.

As useful as this information is, insight gleaned from a critical reading of self-reported experience is not the same as in-depth ethnographic observation of workplace, community, and home environments in which emerging adult readers interface with a broad array of written text. Efforts at strengthening the literacy as growth thesis in its linkage to the New Literacy Studies would need to include sophisticated observations of some of the key ways in which school-based education intersects with learning and knowledge acquisition in the major social environments outside the program that shape the lives of students. That interface is the quintessence of Deweyan pedagogy in the interpenetration of "the school and society," the title of Dewey's (1990) first major educational publication.

As an emergent concept, a pedagogical metaphor based on Dewey's concept of growth would actively *strengthen* those connections through which learning becomes a dynamic form of living in the multiplicity of contexts that shape and influence the lives of adult literacy learners. In the context of the program described, schooling would provide a special place to probe into a broad array of life-driving issues supported by a curriculum focused on the intersection of aesthetics, culture, functional competency, and cognitive development. The formal pedagogical environment would help to stimulate an enhanced learning mode as adults engage the range of social contexts critical to their lives, while bringing back to the school issues and print artifacts they encounter in those environments. The EFF project provides many of the components that can activate such a pedagogical scheme that a focus on the dynamics of growth could further enhance.

Assumption 4

Barton's (1994a) fourth assumption is that "literacy is based upon a system of symbols." As he further stated it, literacy "is a symbol system used for communication and as such exists in relationship to other systems of information exchange." In short, literacy "is a way of representing the world to others" (p. 43). Here Barton concentrated on the relation between written and spoken language, which are both different and complexly entwined. Noting that writing is more than " 'speech . . . written down,' " Barton pointed out its central role in the creation of durable and reproducible texts (p. 43). On this, writing "extends the function of language, and enables you to do different things." Moreover, writing is not merely a neutral technology. It is "part of a theory of language," a conceptual notion, the value of which needs to be discerned in order to grasp something of the socioculturally derived symbol system that it both reflects and embeds. While noting that "writing is based on speech in some very real ways," Barton stressed the distinctiveness of writing, which "has a life of its own" (p. 44) as an important technology in "the production and reproduction of shared meaning or knowledge" (p. 45).

In the program in which my primary research has been based, student writing has played a significant role. Although I have liberally drawn on student texts to illustrate various aspects about adult literacy education, a systematic study of student writing designed to examine the literacy as growth thesis, would require an analysis of the many phases of the writing process in their various cognitive and social dimensions. This would include a study of how and what topics are selected, an analysis of the composition process, the progression of writing quality measured over time, its role in reading, comprehension, and vocabulary development, and the various meanings to which students attribute to writing as a function of their literacy development.

Research would be needed to examine both the influence of and the extent of any writing beyond the literacy program into the various life domains, and its influence in the broader negotiation of the social world. The purpose of such an investigation would not be merely to *evaluate* an operative hypothesis, although such work is essential. Of similar importance is the utilization of the findings to establish a more effective *praxis* of student writing that links the technology of production to the symbolization of meaning making in the creation of particular texts and modes of expression. The viability of the concept of growth in moving progressively from problem identification to resolution in facilitating the writing process would need to be closely scrutinized at the level of educational practice.

Even still, as noted, the literacy as growth metaphor is subtly influenced by the opportunity structures available in the culture and society. It is at this level, ultimately, that the concept of literacy as growth as a hypothesis and a fruitful metaphor would need to prove its mettle in any process of becoming settled as a workable theory in the mediation of the pedagogy and politics of adult literacy education in the United States.

Assumption 5

According to Barton's fifth assumption, the last one considered here, "literacy is a symbol system used for representing the world to ourselves" (p. 45) that consists of "both a cognitive and cultural basis" that "contributes to the mind and to thinking." Drawing on Vygotsky, Barton viewed the mind as "socially constructed within the physical constraints of being human" (p. 45). Although self-representation is the obverse side to "representing the world to others" (p. 43) in the mediated sign and symbol system in which Barton situates literacy, the primary factor is their dynamic interaction. The critical point is that "all thought is socially constructed, and it is the social practices around literacy, not literacy itself, which shape[s] consciousness" (p. 47).

In the formation of a research project that would be designed to assess the literacy as growth thesis, an analysis of student internal representation in the progressive formation of a literacy identity would play an important role (Fingeret & Drennon, 1997). In particular, this would need to be sifted through the "literacy myth" as an embodiment of the broader cultural myth of the "American Dream" of equality and opportunity for all on the extent to which these open and sustain scope for personal development. This is critical because the issue of growth involves more than concrete development of reading and writing skills and the utilization of classroom learning to effectively engage print-based environments outside the program, although it surely does include this. As the case studies presented in *Literacy for Life* document, the stability of the students' reconstructed literacy identities depended on the degree to which they were viewed by self and others as reasonably satisfactory, despite the continuation of negative self-perceptions. As we leave the case studies in *Literacy for Life*, the predominant feeling is of lives subtly influenced through literacy, but still on the way toward ongoing construction. The longer term impact remains to be negotiated through the interstices of the lifecycle of the individuals in their transactions with the sociocultural contexts of the opportunity structures within New York City where they lived.

Elsewhere, I have made a similar argument drawing on Dewey's concept of growth to underlie a case study report of three adult literacy students in the program I operated in the 1990s (Demetrion, 2001b). With the authors of *Literacy for Life*, I also sought to make the case that "growth" depends on what happens to students inside and outside the program. The ways in which diverse environments subtly interact and how events, perceptions, and values that students connect to adult literacy education are interpreted by self and significant others are crucial, as is the broader sociocultural matrix on personality formation. In short, the literacy as growth thesis draws richly from the New Literacy Studies and contributes to its deepening. Its refinement will require critical ethnographic and historical studies of students' lives inside and outside the program, along with careful analysis of its theoretical dimensions and modes of application as gleaned through observation, continuous idea formation, and the setting up of careful experiments, what Dewey (1938/1991) referred to as "controlled inquiry" (p. 19).

CONCEPTUAL OVERVIEW

> Growth depends upon the presence of a difficulty to be overcome by the exercise of intelligence. . . . It is part of the educator's responsibility to see equally to two things: First, that the problem grows out of the conditions of the experience being had in the present, and that it is within the range of the capacities of students; and secondly, that it is such that it arouses in the learner an active quest for information and for production of new ideas. The new facts and the new ideas become the ground for further experiences in which new problems are presented. The process is a continuous cycle. (Dewey, 1938/1963, p. 79)

Dewey (1916) defined "growth" as the "cumulative movement of action toward a later result" (p. 41), the ends-in-view. In Dewey's (1938/1963) progressive vision, "every experience should do something to prepare a person for later experiences of a deeper and more expansive quality" (p. 47). Continuity within experience is a critical component of this movement in which "every experience enacted and undergone modifies the one who acts and undergoes, while this modification affects, whether we wish it or not, the quality of subsequent experiences" (p. 35).

In the "cumulative movement of action toward a later result" (Dewey, 1916, p. 41), there is a continuous process from identification of needs to resolution in which the desired state (even if not fully grasped or formed) is embedded within each continuous step toward the final objective leading toward the resolution of a particular problem. "An active process [of reflective thought and critical practice] is strung out temporarily, but there is a deposit [a holographic residue] at each stage and point entering cumulatively and constitutively into the outcome" (Dewey, 1929/1958, p. 368). Dewey (1938/1963) referred to the underlying motor of the means–ends continuum as "the moving force" (p. 38) or "guiding idea" (Dewey, 1933/ 1989, p. 203). Ends, in turn, are not finalities, but *ends-in-view*. They become "redirecting pivots *in* [italics in original] action" that serve as new materials in the identification or the working out of new problems and challenges opened up through the process of learning and resolving earlier problems (Dewey, 1922/1988, p. 155). As Dewey (1939, cited in Archambault, 1964) further explained, "In the continuous temporal process of organizing activities into a co-ordinated and co-ordinating unity, a constituent activity is both an end and a means: an end, in so far as it is temporally and relatively a close; a means, in so far as it provides a condition to be taken into account in further activity" (p. 106). Temporal ends become means to new goals in the ongoing process of enriching experience through critical thought, reflective practice, and aesthetic sensibilities as "a fulfillment [in time] that reaches to the depth of our being" (Dewey, 1934/1989, p. 23).

In Dewey's pedagogical vision, it is the special work of the educator to maximize student growth throughout all the stages of a learning cycle. This requires subtle scaffolding, including a close attunement to what is of "*significance*" (Dewey, 1938/1963, p. 68, italics in original) in each moment in a problem-solving or aesthetic process of creation. This discerning capacity is critical in the hard work of achieving purposes from original impulses that initiate a quest for change through "a plan and method of acting based on foresight of the consequences of acting under given observed conditions in a certain way" (p. 69). On his view in 1938, with conservative forces looming, Dewey viewed the failure of educators to diligently guide students through the means–ends continuum in any learning process as an inadequacy in progressive education that inhibited the realization of its vision. Advocates who have not lost their nerve, Dewey argued, needed to take a "next step." That step was to shape the experiential learning process "into a fuller and richer and also more organized form" (pp. 73–74). What was missing and acutely needed was the strong hand of internal discipline in order to establish an "intellectual organization . . . on the grounds of experience" (p. 85), without which progressive education could not evolve on its own terms and secondarily, meet the challenges posed by competing pedagogical perspectives.

Dewey argued that this next step required a much more rigorous aligning of the various relevant factors (e.g., student knowledge, motive, aptitude, and the subject matter) as mediated through a culturally expansive curriculum that, ideally, should frame schooling—notably, an appreciation of the challenges of democratic living in the contemporary setting. As Dewey (1916) expressed it some two decades earlier, "A curriculum which acknowledges the social responsibilities of education must present situations where problems are relevant to the problems of living together, and where observation and information are calculated to develop social insight and interest" (p. 192). Dewey never relented on this purpose, but he did insist on a sharpening of pedagogical rigor linked to the intellectual organization of experience if progressive education was to meet the reconstructive challenges of its own potentiality.

In Dewey's mediating pedagogy, the teacher plays a critically important role as bridge builder in mediating the space between the student and the curriculum, and the school and the society. The process, according to Dewey, can only take place in a manner that honors the moving force of experiential learning, ideally, at every stage throughout the means–ends continuum. This requires input from students and material from the curriculum, both of which provide important pieces of the puzzle in the progressive goal of working toward personal, intellectual, and culturally worthy achievements. It is the artistry, the critical acumen, and the social sensibility of the teacher where the prime responsibility lies, according to Dewey (1938/1963), in bringing the progressive vision of education to fruition. The challenge for the teacher is "to be able to judge what attitudes are actually conducive to growth and what are detrimental" at each stage of the learning process. This requires that teachers possess wide knowledge of subject matter flexibly drawn on as the situation demands, combined with a solid "idea of what is actually going on in the minds of those who are learning" (p. 39).

In addition to continuity, a pedagogy based on growth is a transactional affair among individual learners, the teacher, the text, the curriculum, and the broader sociocultural matrix that informs it. As Dewey put it, "Experience does not go on simply inside the head of a person" (p. 39). What is important is not merely the consciousness of individuals, but the "situation" or environment embodied by individuals that account for both "objective and internal conditions" (p. 42). For Dewey, individual consciousness is an environmental sign that individuals embody as a focal point, stimulated by an *ecological* disturbance that requires a new fit not merely for the person in isolation, but within the context of the sociocultural setting in which personal being is situated. As Dewey put it, "An experience is always what it is because of a transaction taking place between an individual and what, at that time, constitutes his environment" (p. 43).

Problems burst forth within the consciousness of individuals through the ecological contexts they embody. Growth or development takes place within the same, similar, or changing environments, whereas ends-in-view are realized through reconstructed relations between self, society, and culture. Individuals "live in a world" through a "series of situations" (p. 43) and are required to negotiate and sometimes reconstruct the social and cultural context, or at the least, their relation to it. This creative work involves individualism of a high order in the discernment of the various phases of a problem and its application to the self. It is also a social responsibility of mutual engagement in the sharing of resources and the pooling of collective knowledge for the challenges of working together in the creation and strengthening of common purposes.

Establishing such a vision of education and cultural democracy requires a profound shift in dominant tendencies, yet must be based on what Dewey perceived as the foremost ideals of the U.S. political culture. It is on such a vision that Dewey staked his identity. These ideals, in turn, however far from fully realized in concrete historical experience, serve as a vital force in the potent but indeterminate role of shaping the culture through the possibilities they unleash in the stream of a perpetually forming present. Dewey banked his identity on the assumption that the progressive working out of this reconstructive vision is a real possibility rather than an illusion or what is referred to in neo-Marxian social theory as "false consciousness."

Whether focusing on the individual or the broader culture, central to Dewey was his unrelenting commitment to growth in the transforming of potentialities into actualities. Figuratively put, this requires "extracting at each present time the full meaning of each present experience" (p. 49) in the pressing toward the most viable ends-in-view through discriminating reason and judicious discernment. It is this that Eldridge (1998) referred to as "transforming experience," a vision based not only on logic, but also on an aesthetic sensibility and a sociocultural anticipation of democracy as a way of life.

That there is a utopian element to Dewey's educational vision and broader philosophy is evident, although clearly in the "American Grain." The issue is the extent to which it stimulates a progressive realization toward the ideal into the ongoing flow of experience, whether of individual or broader culture reconstruction—in short, the extent to which the ideal is a "live option" in bringing out valued potentialities, or is primarily an illusion. The matter cannot be settled on the grounds of philosophical speculation alone, but requires working out within the stream of the nation's cultural experience. Dewey's concept of growth and broader pragmatic vision of the potentiality of realizing a more enriched life based on creative intelligence through "conjoint action" has much to offer as an operating pedagogy of adult literacy education. Nonetheless, it requires both extensive experimentation in determining its viability and active commitment to its core principles in the effort to establish the conditions where it can be more fully realized. As is argued here and later, there is much with which to work even as problems remain.

TEACHING AS INQUIRY: IMPLICATIONS
FOR ADULT LITERACY EDUCATION

In the previous section, I sought to distill Dewey's concept of growth into something of its theoretical essence, focusing on the core qualities of continuity, interaction, and progressive development toward the ends-in-view, a reconstructed experience on a more desirable plane. That section also emphasized the critical role of the teacher in mediating the dynamics of the learning process. Dewey's concept of growth in learning parallels his description of inquiry in which problems are progressively resolved on route toward "warranted assertabilities." As Dewey put it (1916), "All thinking is research, and all research is native, original with him who carries it on" (p. 148). This is the case in a classroom environment in which Dewey intended it in *Democracy and Education* as well as in a formal scientific investigation. In other work, I have examined core Deweyan precepts in light of case study descriptions of adult literacy students. I have also linked Dewey's notion of growth to the dynamics of the organizational development of the program I operated, as sifted through my own relation to it. The relation between Dewey's concept of growth to that of political culture is a topic that I have discussed elsewhere (Demetrion, 2001a, 2000b, 2001c).

In all of this work I have taken lived experience as a starting point (acknowledging its constructed nature) and the problems and challenges therein as the basis for progressively moving forward toward more desirable ends. This is what Dewey formally referred to as the intellectual organization of experience through the "moving force" of the means–ends continuum. Although more of a regulative ideal than an exact correspondence to reality, something like the "impulsion" of the moving force in the stimulation of potentiality at each moment of learning is a critical factor in the progression toward an achieved ends-in-view. In any comprehensive accounting of the literacy as growth concept, all of this previous research needs to be considered as part of the broader theory I seek to further refine here in a necessarily sketchy way that nonetheless may be useful in moving research on adult literacy education forward within the broad scope of the New Literacy Studies.

The limited focus of this section is to shed concrete light on those prem-ises that underlie Dewey's theory of growth and inquiry. I do so through a case study example of a tutoring episode with a small group of beginning level adult literacy students at one of our community-based centers in the predominantly African American and Caribbean North Hartford. With Dewey (1916), I took what I discerned as "the present powers of the pu-pil[s] . . . [as] the initial stage" in the objective of achieving a more "remote limit," an enhanced learning experience that built on what students knew that in turn could lead into further learning. "Between the two [their expe-rience and goals, as well as mine] lie *means* [italics in original]—that is, mid-dle conditions: acts to be performed; difficulties to be overcome; appli-ances [e.g., the white board] to be used" (p. 127). The process of moving from means to ends is narrated on a two-class session based on the follow-ing poem:

Black Man

Stop black man take a look at yourself
Leave those drugs on the shelf
If you are caught your face is on TV
For the whole world to see.
When the white man is caught he has no face
Just a small write up taking up space.
Emancipation said we were free
That's not the way it seems to me
We're making slaves of ourselves.
So stop black man leave those drugs on the shelves.
Drugs show you what you really want to see
Stop black man that's not Reality.
If you really want to play it cool,
Get an Education go back to school.
Prove to yourself you're no man's fool
Stop black man set yourself free
Drugs are not what they seem to be. (Author unknown, 1997, p. 33) Reprinted
with permission of Peppercorn Books & Press (www.peppercornbooks.com)

The group consisted of men and women of varying ages, including a man in his mid-80s. A few of the students had participated in the program for several years and had only marginally shown improvement on the pre-level CASAS test in which all of their scores were in the 190s range, in effect a "pre-reading" level. Not a single student would have been able to read any portion of the poem independently or would have identified more than a few words by themselves. They did possess rudimentary phonemic aware-ness capacity of varying minimal levels that required thick scaffolding to stimulate.

With concentrated tutor assistance, they could work with texts like I used for these two sessions and participate in an engaging learning process, focusing simultaneously on the content of the reading passage and basic skill development. Throughout the lesson, our objective (mine more overt, which, in turn, I sought to stimulate with the group) was "to use judgment: to hunt for connections in things dealt with" (Dewey, 1916, p. 144) in linking the thinking of both the students and myself to the ongoing project of working through the text. As defined by the flowing logic of our learning–teaching process, we would focus on one letter, one sound, one word, one line, one sentence, one paragraph at a time, or on various points in the poem that came up for discussion.

There were a "plurality of alternatives" (Dewey, 1938/1991, p. 500) available in possible directions to pursue, although in a well-constructed Deweyan design "leading principles" (p. 19) guide the investigative process. Each moment of choice by both the students and myself as to what to do next was an experiment in the ongoing sifting of ideas and data analysis in progressively working toward our desired goal of achieving a satisfactory learning outcome. This process was not simply random, but one shaped by "a guiding idea, a working hypothesis" (Dewey, 1933/1989, p. 203), however emergent and experimental, operative throughout our investigative/learning project. The significant point is not the specific path selected at any given moment, as alternative directions were plausible within the constraints set by the goal, although each decision required an informed judgment call. What was important were the cumulative paths chosen throughout the two sessions in contributing to the broader objective at hand and the role of each decision in building toward that which we sought to achieve. More formally:

> The intellectual question is what sort of action the *situation* [italics in original] demands in order that it may receive a satisfactory objective reconstruction. This question can be answered only . . . by operations of observation, collection of data and of inference, which are directed by ideas whose material is examined through operations of ideational comparison and organization. (Dewey, 1938/1991, p. 163)

The fullness of such a judgment requires retrospective analysis at the completion of a successful operation. Each effort during the process of investigation or construction, in this case of a satisfactory learning experience, remains an experiment, although ideally, increasingly controlled, until the objective is achieved. "As one part [of the means–ends continuum] leads to another and as one part carries on what went before, each gains distinctness in itself." The end result is "an enduring whole [that] is diversified by successive phases that are emphases of its varied colors" (Dewey, 1934/

1989, p. 43). The ends (satisfactory learning) are holographically embedded in the means throughout all the phases of building climactically toward the desired attainment. This is an aesthetic achievement, which can only be experienced, although signs can be pointed to.

The gap between the ongoing quest and the ends-in-view spurs the learning process on. This is the case, Dewey maintained, whether the focus is on growth in experience, inquiry in resolving a problematic situation, or the aesthetic impulse propelling a work of creation. The common denominator is the desire to transform a problematic or incomplete situation into a unified whole through the working out of the means–ends continuum. These core Deweyan precepts characterized my operating principles as I taught the group. How did this informal experiment in Deweyan pedagogy and inquiry progress?

First Session

I introduced this text through an assisted reading methodology, in which the instructor initially reads a few lines with students following along, at first subvocalizing and gradually taking over the reading process in successive readings. This allows beginning-level readers to work with connected and interesting texts and to simulate the process of fluent reading well before independent mastery (which may never be achieved) is attained. This approach is based on the assumption that learning to read takes place through a combination of unconscious assimilation over time through practice, along with specific teaching techniques utilized to build up basic skill mastery. In the assisted reading methodology, explicit word mastery activities (whether phonics or sight-word memorization) are limited to those words that persistently stump students even after three or four readings. This methodology does not imply a rejection of systematic phonemic work at other places in the lesson. It functions to open instructional space for students at this basic level to work with connected text, to simulate a fluent reading process, and to introduce meaningful narratives among those with extremely limited reading capacity.

Students at this level typically do not complete the program with independent reading mastery, although some progress more than others. Regardless of increase in reading ability, students who stay with the process for a multiyear interval may gain a great deal of knowledge that they deem important. This may include greater facility with the world of print, along with enhanced personal insight, and increased knowledge through which to access community resources and social networks. The limited ethnographic literature on adult literacy available documents impact of this multidimensional type. More focused longitudinal research is still needed in order to gain a more thorough understanding of the short, intermediate, and long-range influences among a broad range of students in diverse settings and context.

The tutor who regularly teaches this group was not available, so as the site manager, I took her place. I had tutored this group before and had observed it on a regular basis. The poem, published by Literacy South, was included in a collection of student narratives that I had put together from various programs located in the South and in New England. Over the previous year and more, the group had worked with many student narratives and had created some of their own. I thought they would appreciate this text (my first working hypothesis), but I wondered about the propriety of me, a White, middle-class male from the suburbs, injecting this poem into the session. What did I know about either the experience of the poet—or for that matter, that of the students—in terms of their lives outside of the program? Beyond that, the poem could be interpreted as a stereotypical depiction of the Black, male urban experience. Also, it provided little to account for what various social commentators view as the enduring presence of racism and poverty as a broad-based social, cultural, economic, and political phenomenon of the contemporary urban landscape.

Still, I selected it, as it was an example of a student narrative that had an aesthetic quality to it that I sensed the students would find engaging. I made a presumption that the narrator was Black and would be able to speak to the group through and across the text. Besides, I had to select something and this poem, which I placed in the manual of student narratives in the first place as part of our program's recommended curriculum, seemed an apt vehicle to engage the students in a stimulating learning experience. It also connected with my experienced sense of what would provide an effective instrument for me to stimulate a high quality learning experience among the students, while acknowledging that that could be accomplished as well by other instructional materials. That is, it is less the materials, per se, than the learning that takes place through them as a result of the symbolic role or "middleman" (Dewey, 1916, p. 188) function they play both for the students and the instructor.

There is much in the way that I worked with this group that conformed to the operating assumptions of the New Literacy Studies and to the precepts of participatory literacy education. In that, Dewey's concept of growth represents an elaboration rather than a sharp difference from these perspectives. Thus, I chose a reading selection that linked a personal reflection to broader sociocultural themes that I anticipated the students would find absorbing. Throughout the lesson, I blended holistic and skill-based approaches, and included discussion as an important part of the work. Dewey's concept of growth provides additional nuances, of which I focus on here.

To begin the first session, I asked the students to read and comment on the title in order to set the stage for interaction with the text. The older man from Jamaica called it a "headline." There was some discussion at that point, but not what I viewed as sufficient interest to spend much time on. In our learning climate, *pre-reading* strategies are generally less motivating than *during-reading* activities. That is so because of the crucial importance students place on the actual act of reading as the symbol itself for literacy, wherein preliminary discussions are often viewed as extraneous to the more pressing matters at hand. The initial probe, which was modestly successful, was worth the time, I reasoned, in order to get conversation started, and more importantly, to set a climate of engagement from the very beginning. Another tutor might have pushed this effort further with more success. I assessed the situation from my capacities and objectives, knew I had a lot to work with, and pressed forward. In short, I operationalized a "working hypothesis" that both engagement and working directly with the text were important and moved on, realizing there would be ample opportunity for interaction as the lesson progressed.

Much of our focus in the first session was on working through the first four lines through the assisted reading approach. My goal throughout was to insure as thorough of a learning process as possible, in part, by enabling students to experience the simulation of fluent reading, which I wanted to plant into their organic hardwiring. Although not possible within the context of a short teaching period, the broader purpose of such a methodology is to help students develop an innate habit of fluency that is partially stimulated by this approach. As we progressed, individual students haltingly read one line at a time while others helped out. I wrote the text on the white board one line at a time. The board, too, served as an instrument in enabling the group to work together more effectively as a unit. We did some choral reading. Mostly I asked individuals to read while others followed along. I helped out as needed, only intervening for the purpose of maintaining relative fluidity of reading.

In the midst of this activity, we interspersed conversation about the poem. One discussion focused on the attempt to identify the narrator. There was diversity of opinion, but it was more or less taken for granted that the narrator was African American. What was not so clear was whether it was a man, speaking perhaps of his own experience on what he had learned in leaving the world of drugs, or whether it was a woman taking a position from a moral standpoint, speaking to her community on the need for Black men to get their lives together. We probed that a bit, but did not try to come to closure. It was an interesting question in the given moment, but not a burning issue as the "moving force" of the lesson pushed me on toward the main goal, which was for each student to read a portion of the poem as independently as they could, while also taking into account something of its content.

I wrote down common words from the poem like "man," "at," "a," "the," "you," and "see" on the board—words that would often come up in other texts the students would read. We compared the words "on" and "no," which needed some attention as some of the students mixed them up. Where needed, I focused on helping students to make the sight–sound connection. For example, one student had difficulty with the word "if." I stressed the continuous "f" sound as in "fff" and asked the others not to say anything until that student recognized that word on her own. My goal there was both to assess and experiment with that student's capacity to master the sounds in the word without context clues. The students wrote the words down as I drilled them throughout the lesson. My objective was to have them experience reading those words automatically even if that capacity did not hold beyond the lesson. An exercise like this, I reasoned, would leave patterns of learning and memory traces that would depend on much additional work for reinforcement of both a fluent and a structured type.

I asked the most advanced student to come to the board and lead the group in the reading of the first four lines. I focused on encouraging fluent reading, helping out with words with as little intrusion as possible. Each of the other students followed suit. I took time with this. I wanted each student to experience that sense of successfully reading the lines on the board. All the students continued to have problems with certain words, although they had progressively improved from our initial efforts to the time they each got to the board.

We continued the same sequence for the next 6 lines, which included a discussion of the couplet:

> When the white man is caught he has no face
> Just a small write up taking up space.

The students had difficulty making an inference, so I suggested that it meant that if a White person were arrested on drugs there would be little publicity in the newspaper or television, but the opposite was the case for Black people. The group acknowledged my interpretation, but it was not clear to me that it was significantly important to them at the time. We continued with our general game plan—reading fluent text, identifying sight words, and breaking words down phonetically. The working through of the first 10 lines with only limited discussion on the content of the poem ended the first day's session.

Second Session

The original students came back for the second session, along with two who had not attended the first day. One student shared the poem with some men she knew and her son, who was entering seventh grade. He also joined our tutoring session. He said he liked the poem. I asked him what stood out. He pointed to the line of "making slaves of ourselves" through drugs. He took additional copies of the poem to give to others. The mother of the boy taped the poem to her refrigerator and asked for additional copies. One student who was not at the first session wanted a copy for her brother.

We spent most of the session reviewing the first 10 lines of the poem in a manner similar to that already described. Seeking to build continuity in the progression of the students' learning, I asked those who attended the first class to initiate the reading of the first 4 lines. Then I asked the two additional students to follow suit. I worked on words with which students had difficulty, either through phonemic methodologies or through sight-word memorization.

One student could not identify the word "caught." She initially said "face." That was an impulsive response. She was one of the more advanced readers of the group. I encouraged her to slow down and concentrate on the sounds of the letters. With my helping her to focus, she got the "c" and "t" sounds. I also helped her with the "au" phoneme, but she was unable to put the word together. A member of the group enacted out "caught" and the word came to her. In listing the common words on the board again, this time I added "caught." Every time it was this student's turn, I asked her to read that word and to resist impulsive guessing. With some deliberation, at the third try, she was able to identify the word without the use of context clues.

The difference between how Blacks and Whites that get arrested for drugs are depicted by the media was more extensively discussed in the second session. Because there were additional group members, including the seventh grader at the second session, I felt there was more of an interest in exploring that topic than in the first session. That was an inference on which I acted. I dramatized the situation as described by the poet where a Black male from Hartford arrested for drugs might be depicted on page 1 of *The Hartford Courant* accompanied by a photo. By way of contrast, a story about a White male from suburban Avon arrested on a similar charge might be found in a small box on page 47. I used the white board to illustrate these scenarios, exaggerating the difference to drive home the point. This time there was more engagement in the topic.

We continued with our work. Many students were able to read and understand the word "emancipation." One student substituted the word "little" for "small." Time was rapidly fading, so we worked more quickly on the last seven lines. I continued to assist students with word recognition, while also providing minimal scaffolding in helping them to read portions of the poem whole.

Because of the limited reading level of the students, I concentrated more on basic skill development than on content, but as discussed, the poem had done its work without much explicit focus on it. If I had a third session, then I might have centered on language experience reflections by the students. Their own texts, in turn, would have provided the basis for additional reading material, in which we would have continued to focus on skill-building mastery and content exploration. The regular tutor was on site for the second session. With a little prodding from me, one of the students told the tutor that she would like to start the next fall session with that poem. Another student asked for additional material like that. As I perceived it, within the context of our two sessions, students attained their aims of undergoing a satisfying learning experience that built on then current abilities, interests, and imaginative possibilities. Those sessions, which built on earlier lessons that the students had with their regular tutor, opened the possibility of further development.

REFLECTION

In short, there was continuity with the group's earlier work, where I focused on helping students to build on areas of interest, styles of learning, and the knowledge base they had developed with their tutor. I sought to engage them in a teacher-guided interactive learning climate at the periphery between their abilities and what they could come to know with supportive assistance provided at the right time and amount. Searching for and working out of that permeable boundary was the underlying dynamic out of which I operated, a discerning process that requires continuous observation, hypothesis formation, and data analysis in the midst of the learning/teaching cycle.

Pushing such learning to the hilt was the "guiding idea" that I sought to activate throughout the entire effort. This was not a controlled experiment, a formal inquiry process as Dewey (1938/1991, pp. 105–122, 415–436) described in *Logic*. It was a fluid teaching assignment where I drew on my implicit appropriation of Dewey's concepts through a commonsense methodology of "extracting at each present time [something like] the full meaning of each present experience" (Dewey, 1938/1963, p. 49). To state this in more precise terms, I drew on what I perceived as student potentiality all the way through the sessions. That "moving force" required continuous inference making and judgment formation by both the students and myself in our mutual quest to achieve a satisfying learning experience. As described, the process was interactive. Yet, in rejecting an "Either–Or philosophy" (p. 21) of teaching, it was I who was responsible for setting and largely sustaining the direction. The following passage from Dewey's (1933/1989) *How We Think* provides an apt description of the role of the teacher that I sought to approximate in our particular situation:

> The practical problem of the teacher is to preserve a balance between so little showing and telling as to fail to stimulate reflection and so much as to choke thought. Provided the student is genuinely engaged in a topic, and provided the teacher is willing to give the student a good deal of leeway as to what he assimilates and retains (not requiring rigidly that everything be grasped or reproduced) there is comparatively little danger that one who is himself enthusiastic will communicate too much concerning a topic. If a genuine community spirit pervades the group, if the atmosphere is that of free communication in a developing exchange of experiences and suggestions, it is absurd to debar the teacher from the privilege and responsibility granted to the young [in our case, the students], that of contributing his share. The only warning is that the teacher should not forestall the contributions of pupils, but should enter especially at critical junctures where the experience of pupils is too limited to supply just the materials needed. (p. 334)

As Dewey (1938/1963) more pithily stated it, "Development occurs through reciprocal give-and-take, the teacher taking, but not afraid to give" (p. 72).

The critical factor is the centrality of the working toward the intellectual organization of experience, which was a hallmark of Deweyan (1990) pedagogy as early as 1900, as depicted in *The School and Society* and *The Child and the Curriculum*. Based on his interactive pedagogy, the key to grasping the significance of formal subject matter "is a question of interpreting them as outgrowths of forces operating in the child's life, and of discovering steps that intervene between the child's present experience and richer [educational] maturity" (p. 189). Whether in education or in formal inquiry-based logic, this process of "interaction and adjustment" (p. 188) in systematically searching for finer attunement in the working out of a problem, has remained a consistent hallmark of Dewey's philosophy. In terms of education, and certainly in adult literacy, one of the core challenges remains linking the routines of daily teaching to longer term curriculum foci.

My purpose in describing the details of this particular teaching episode is to illustrate something of the convergence of Dewey's theory of logic and concept of growth in a concrete situation applied to adult literacy education. The key to both is the emphasis on the progressive intellectual organization of experience for the purpose of resolving particular problems of smaller or larger scope as experienced by participants within a situation in which a problem or a question applies. In planning for these two sessions, the immediate challenge that I set out was to develop a sufficiently invigorating learning environment in which students would be engaged and probing through their individual efforts and group participation. Recognizing this challenge was the "disturbance" that provoked the search for the instruments to accomplish my aim.

The point here is not that the quality of our work together actually reached any epitome of maximum student potential, a literally impossible state of achievement. Even still, for what reasonably could be accomplished in two sessions, student learning seemed significant as far as I could tell, but additional research and other observational perspectives would have added much refinement to this general assessment. Other teachers would have taken the group in different directions with perhaps equal or more success than I. Other, more skillful teachers could have improved on the specific actions and methods that I drew on. It is less the specifics that I am stressing than their connection to the operative assumptions about learning and inquiry that I draw on in this chapter. These core components of Dewey's theory of education are, namely, building continuity stemming from previous student knowledge and areas of interest, stimulating informed interaction throughout a learning process, and working at the student's learning edge between what they can not do on their own, but is within reach, with assistance. The additional key element is the need for both the students and the teacher to make reasoned inferences all the way through a learning cycle via progressively refined hypotheses formation and data analysis in the deliberate work of moving closer to the objective at hand.

In short, the goal is growth, which Dewey (1938/1963) defined at its most fundamental base as the "desire to go on learning" (p. 48). Furthermore, growth means "continuity, reconstruction of experience" in which, ideally, "every experience should do something to prepare a person for later experiences of a deeper and more expansive quality" (p. 47). For Dewey, as with the advocates of the New Literacy Studies, learning is not merely a classroom phenomenon, but life application linked to fundamental issues that matter to students. The sessions based on the poem *Black Man* gravitated in this direction, although continuity in learning in fleshing this assumption out would require much more than what could possibly be accomplished in the short time that we worked together on this poem. Among other things, it would require a broader curricular focus, including sustained attention both to basic skill development and thematic content focus.

Other than a listing of its core components, a further discussion of Dewey's fruitful concept of growth, which would require much additional research, cannot be taken on here. Each one of the following core concepts may be viewed as approximating a "middle-range" hypothesis, more amenable, in principle, to testing and verification. Such research would logically contribute much to a refinement, a modification, or even a rejection of the concept of literacy as growth, which as a metaphor may overshoot the evidence ascertained to "prove" the hypothesis. That research would be an important undertaking. So is the need to view the concept of growth ecologically as a signpost, the meaning of which has its ultimate reference in a cultural context as a metaphorical referent for life-enhancing knowledge. With these caveats stated, the following are among the core components of Dewey's concept of growth that beg further analysis:

1. Learning is an intermediary process toward the resolution of a problem in the movement toward reconstruction in desirable ends-in-view established through the inquiry process.
2. Knowledge acquisition is a progressive affair of moving gradually from what is known to what is not known, with effective learning processes built throughout the means–ends continuum.
3. Each moment of a learning process in the move from means to ends has its own internal integrity, what Dewey described as a qualitative whole.
4. What is experienced throughout the learning process, a qualitative whole, is a blending of emotion, social experience, and cognition, mediated by a situation that is culturally constructed. Symbolization is at the core of this phenomenon.
5. It is the integrity of working through the process via an increasingly refined recursive cycle of hypothesis formation, data analysis, observation, and experimentation stimulated by "guiding ideals" or "leading principles," that leads to the ends-in-view.
6. Making reasoned inferences throughout all the stages of working through the means–ends continuum is an essential factor in the work of hypothesis formation, data analysis, and in the determination of what it is that is observed and focused on.
7. Instructional materials are tools that help to facilitate and focus learning. Their value is the extent to which they connect the subject matter with some question, issue, or problem with which the students are concerned that in some way advances learning as discerned, in the final analysis, by the students.
8. "A curriculum which acknowledges the social responsibilities of education must present situations where problems are relevant to the problems of living together, and where observation and information are calculated to develop social insight and interest" (Dewey, 1916, p. 372).

CONCLUSIONS

In seeking to make a reasoned argument for the validity of Dewey's concept of growth and his corresponding theory of inquiry as a way of situating a working epistemology and mediating pedagogy of adult literacy education, the reach of this chapter extends beyond what I would *like* to grasp. Popper set the standard that I do not achieve as follows: "Propose theories which can be criticized. Think about possible decisive falsifying experiments—crucial experiments. But do not give up your theories too easily—not, at any rate, before you have examined your criticism" (Popper, 1974, cited in Miller, 1985, pp. 126–127).

In this chapter, I have sought to demonstrate the plausible application of Dewey's conceptually polished philosophy of logic and learning to adult literacy. This is a viewpoint that I do not intend to too easily give up, as I have been honing in on the thesis of literacy as growth in published formats and in practice for over a decade. Following Popper, the theory I propose certainly can be criticized, but I focus here on developing the core idea and do not examine potential criticism in this chapter. Elements of the literacy as growth thesis may be susceptible to falsification, although not necessarily the concept as a whole, at least not by rigorous scientific methods because the idea moves into the realm of a cultural metaphor, not different in principle from Freire's "pedagogy of the oppressed" or the rhetorical counter-image of "functional literacy." These three concepts of adult literacy can be supported through corroborating empirical data, but the metaphorical language that they each embody may well overshoot the capacity for scientific verification via a rigorous falsification principle as articulated particularly in the positivist/postpositivist paradigm (Mertens, 1998). In this respect, the concept of literacy as growth moves beyond more boundary-defined "middle-range theories," which are sufficiently limited, so that, in principle, "testing" can serve as the means for determining their validity (Pawson & Tilley, 1997; P. J. Stanovich & K. E. Stanovich, 2003).

No doubt, this is a problem. Yet, if language itself is inherently metaphorical, then there is an element in thinking that seeks to find words to convey ideas as they are forming and coming into shape. In this respect, science might also be viewed metaphorically as that symbol of exacting precision designed to gain control over some portion of the world. With Dewey, it is not science per se, but the scientific methodology of disciplined thought and controlled experimentation that is viewed as the most viable means of tackling and progressively resolving human problems. Dewey is hopeful, but not overly sanguine as the tension between science and culture is particularly sharp in his experientially based philosophy, notwithstanding his quest to fuse them. Situating logic in the "existential matrix of

culture," Dewey (1938/1991) acknowledged that "the subject matter of social problems is existential" (p. 481). Although there are generalities in
logic, "practical inquiry" into human affairs is situational, contextual, historical, value-laden, and symbol-driven as defined by the problem at hand
and the various means of their resolution. As with the natural sciences, so in
human affairs, "competent inquiry" via the scientific methodology is still
one of the most viable means available to achieve such ends. Nonetheless,
Dewey's discussion of science as applied to the cultural realm is a highly
nuanced and tensively laden qualified one.

This tension pervades Dewey's penultimate chapter in *Logic*, "Social Inquiry" (pp. 481–505). Thus, he noted in the opening paragraph that there is
no sense that humanly complex cultural disciplines like anthropology and
history can be directly shaped into a science, particularly like physics.
Dewey's working hypothesis focuses on whether "the development of methods, which, *as far as they go* [italics added], satisfy the logical conditions that
have to be satisfied in other branches of inquiry," first and foremost that of
physics and mathematics. Notwithstanding this qualification, Dewey sounds
an optimistic refrain, noting that "the very backwardness of social inquiry
may serve . . . to test the general logical conceptions that have been reached"
(p. 481) in science. Thus, despite the reservations, Dewey posited considerable faith in his hypothesis, noting, however, that his proposal remains subject to rigorous examination.

With these caveats, Dewey proceeded to lay out the cultural matrix of
social inquiry in which "the ultimate ground of every valid proposition
and warranted judgment [of logic] consists in some existential reconstruction ultimately effected" (p. 483). The methodology as with the natural sciences remains the same—inference making, problem identification, hypothesis formation, data analysis, testing, and observation in the
"correlivity of fact and ideas" (p. 485). However, on Dewey's hypothesis,
the accrual of logical forms that emerges in the process will depend on
the nature of particular inquiries that cannot be determined outside of
them in some a priori principles of universal logic or theoretical principles that govern a particular body of study. At best, these serve a hypothetical function that needs to be scrutinized in its applicability to the particular investigation at hand.

With an investigation under way, it then becomes feasible to sharpen the
focus of the inquiry "out of the complex welter and existential and potentially observable and recordable material" available. Specifically, the " 'facts
of the case,' " the problem set up, and early idea formation shape the focus
of the inquiry that helps determine what becomes viewed as significant for
the question at hand. Data analysis, observation, hypothesis refinement,
and experimentation follow from the trajectory of the probe unleashed until a "warranted conclusion" (p. 491), for that particular problem, emerges.

In short, logical forms in the shape of considered judgments that bring an inquiry to an informed close are discovered through the process of an effective search. That is Dewey's hypothesis. The result, furthermore, is an "objectively unified situation" (p. 493) that terminates a given inquiry as determined by those participating in it—a close that opens the gateway to other problems and investigations in a continuous process of adjustment and reconstruction to new needs and situations.

Stuhr (2002) made an important argument in highlighting the tensions in Dewey between his openness to culture and the variegation of human experience and his "single, abstract pattern of inquiry" based on the scientific methodology. Stuhr pointed to two problems. The first is the need for a better accounting of cultural and epistemological pluralism that "require multiple genealogies of particular inquiries." Given this postmodern sensibility, the second is the viability of Dewey's emphasis on "determinant unified situations." Stuhr was empathetic to Dewey's melioristic quest and argued that if these problems are addressed, then Dewey's open mode of inquiry can be reconstructed to better account for a "more fully pluralistic universe" (p. 284).

Stuhr's points are well taken. When one looks beyond a strictly scientific interpretation of social and cultural experience, many subtle factors in the diversity of how knowledge is constructed come into play that cannot be simply mediated even by the subtlety of Dewey's experientially based logic. As part of the situation that needs to be addressed, a pragmatic sensibility would have to take into account the pervasive tensions in the realm of social inquiry, as related in this book to the pedagogy and politics of adult literacy education. As it stands, enduring and substantial tensions inhibit the surfacing of a broad-based national vision, without which a coherent federal policy is unlikely to emerge. Given this problem, Dewey's effort to instill methodological rigor within the social, cultural, and political spheres might be viewed in another, more empathetic symbolic light in which his theory of inquiry can come to serve as a fruitful heuristic to move human knowledge and social science research forward. Dewey was not unaware of this interpretation. In his words, just "because social phenomena do not permit the controlled variation of sets of conditions in a one-by-one series of operations . . . the [assumption that the] experimental method has no application at all, stands in the way of taking advantage of the experimental method to the extent that is practicable" (Dewey, 1938/1991, p. 502).

The conflict to which Stuhr pointed can at least be mitigated by paying close attention to the range of relevant situations that might give shape to an inquiry project that are not necessarily circumscribed by science, strictly speaking. The quality and type of any complex human problem might come into play, which requires an intelligent and thorough search. These would include those that are more historically or culturally based, such as problems related to public education and political culture, which subsumed Dewey throughout his adult life. As noted in *Logic*, the cultural matrix is inescapable. Those working out of the pragmatic philosophical tradition would do well to press hard on the implications of the many "existential" factors that give shape to a problem, while simultaneously infusing research with the highly focused intellectual and empirical rigor that are the hallmarks of Dewey's most formal thinking.

It is this ineradicable fusion of culture and science that *Logic: The Theory of Inquiry* seeks to bring together even if Dewey's reach through his rigorous conceptualizations cannot account for the full range of complexities that he seeks to address through his quest for unified thought. In this respect, *Logic* is a symbol of that for which Dewey would like to achieve as the pinnacle of his lifelong quest to unify experience, thought, culture, and science. So it may be with Dewey's parallel concept of learning as growth. Its validity as applied to adult literacy education may depend as much on values at the level of political culture as that of science, as a potent symbolization of possibilities for personal and cultural renewal in an American context. This is my working hypothesis that requires additional analysis, clarification, and elaboration.

In Quest of a More Perfect Union Through a Double-Vision Perspective of Hope and Skepticism

> *Faith in the power to imagine a future which is the projection of the desirable in the present and to invent the instrumentalities for its realization, is our salvation. And it is a faith that must be nurtured and made articulate. (Dewey, 1917, p. 71)*

> *A free market system must be set within a framework of political and legal institutions that adjust the long term trend of economic forces so as to prevent excessive concentrations of property and wealth, especially those likely to lead to political domination. Society must also establish, among other things, equal opportunities of education for all regardless of family income. (Rawls, 2001, p. 44)*

The previous two chapters focused on divergent epistemologies on the assumption that clarity over research traditions is critical in addressing the intellectual undergirding of the pedagogy of adult literacy. The mediation that I propose is that of a middle ground pedagogy based on a flexible appropriation of the New Literacy Studies, informed by Dewey's theory of inquiry and educational philosophy. On this I accept the premise that literacy is a metaphor for knowledge that includes the skills of reading and writing, but is defined by the symbols and sign systems operative in a given sociocultural setting. As suggested in chapters 7 and 8, an expansion of the EFF project as a means of establishing a pedagogical and political framework congruent with core precepts of the U.S. founding political culture may provide a valuable grounding point in situating such an effort.

It is the formulation of a coherent public philosophy that is currently missing in policy discussions on adult literacy. This is a problematic gap that brooks no simplistic solutions, but one that may be essential to grap-

ple with in any effort to move adult literacy from the margins to the mainstream in the policy sector and in the broader public culture. This chapter
presents what Rawls (1993) referred to as a "realistic utopia," grounded in
the liberal, democratic, republican, and constitutional principles of the
U.S. political tradition as a potentially viable basis through which to construct a public philosophy of adult literacy education. I present this as a serious possibility in the Jamesian sense of a "live option" without minimiz-
ing the difficulties of this pathway.

   In focusing on the articulation of this public philosophy, the praxeological work of moving from the contemporary setting to the ideal needs to
extend beyond what this book can address, but I am not without hope that
what is written here can influence that effort. What I emphasize in this
chapter are some of its core precepts. As discussed in chapter 1, I seek to
weave together a fluid philosophy of American liberalism that incorporates
the civic republican vision of the public good, and related strands of democratic politics and constitutional theory. This I take on notwithstanding the
studied objection of Diggins (2000), who pointed to Lockean liberalism as
the singular basis to ground a national consensus, as reflected in Lincoln's
appropriation of the Declaration of Independence. I do so in order to
point to something of its imaginative dynamic in the possibility of establishing a middle ground politics of literacy based on the diversity of influences
that gave shape to the founding political culture of the United States. In
this, sharp demarcations between liberalism, republicanism, democracy,
and constitutionalism are attenuated in a manner that accounts for the diversity of discourses that have shaped this political tradition throughout the
nation's history (Macedo, 1990).

DEWEY'S DILEMMA AND OURS

There is no easy route toward the formation of a viable public philosophy of
adult literacy education in the U.S. contemporary setting. The political culture is particularly polarized in the current period, with a neoconservative
ascendancy challenging the fundamental precepts of both the New Literacy
Studies and a somewhat desiccated participatory literacy movement. In
moving substantially to the Right, the National Institute for Literacy
(NIFL), which had acted throughout the 1990s as a mediating broker in an
effort to bring about a moderately liberal consensus, especially through its
flagship, EFF, is no longer in a position to play that role.

   The merger between Literacy Volunteers of America and Laubach Literacy Action launched the new agency, ProLiteracy Worldwide in October
2002. Potentially, this organization could take on that leadership function.
However, among other things, it would have to clearly identify its priorities

in relation to both its core constituency and the broader field, particularly between the adult education system and the adult literacy sector. There is currently little evidence pointing to the viability of a singular source of leadership that is likely to emerge, whether through the National Coalition for Literacy (NCL), the adult student movement Voice for Adult United Literacy Education (VALUE), the State Directors of Adult Education, or Pro-Literacy Worldwide.

With NIFL's political shift to the Right, the ground is more contested than ever, with no public philosophy of adult literacy education on the horizon to provide an underlying sense of coherency that might underpin the activities of a working coalition. With EFF, there is a latent public philosophy implicit in the core dynamics of a civic liberal political culture, yet with little impetus in the current setting to stimulate its appropriation within the adult literacy field. In this chapter, I seek to build on what is implicit in the politics that underlies EFF in the effort to tease out something of a viable political philosophy in grounding a national effort, while noting the invariable difficulties in any call for coherency in a pluralistic system marked by considerable contentiousness.

In his key text, *The Public and Its Problems*, Dewey (1927) sought to confront a similar dilemma. Dewey was both plagued and challenged by the underlying struggle to reconstruct a vital democratic ethos where both he and the more skeptical Lippmann (1922/1997) pointed to its eclipse in the era of modernity of the early decades of the 20th century. What Dewey (1927) meant by a public was an organized constituency that has the capacity to effect governmental policy and the public culture as defined by its own grounding values and purposes, rather than those of special interests or administrative elites. In an era where a singular public was no longer viable (if it ever was), the challenge that Dewey laid out as the basis for sustaining a vibrant democratic political culture was in finding the "political means" by which "the interests of the governors" could be conjoined "with those of the governed" (p. 93).

For Dewey as for Lippmann, the problems, which are still with us, are several-fold. A key feature to which both pointed was the breakdown of coherent centers of localized power as symbolized in the democracy of the small town meeting and frontier setting. Factors contributing to this demise included the explosive growth of big business and the rise of the mass production factory system, the immigration of millions of eastern and southern Europeans and Chinese into the nation's urban centers, and the exponential growth of mass communications through the telegraph, telephone, radio, cinema, and "yellow" journalism. Other forces included the expansive influence of political lobbyists, administrative functionaries, and the rise of the expert in virtually all fields, including that of journalism. According to Dewey and Lippmann, these influences eroded the capacity of common citizens to adequately understand and grapple with the complex issues of the day. The cumulative impact of these changes fundamentally altered the 20th-century social, political, and cultural landscape of the United States from any vestiges of its idealized past of a citizenry-based liberal democratic republic.

As Dewey described it, "The invasion of the community by the new and the relatively impersonal and mechanical modes of combined human behavior is the outstanding fact of modern life" (p. 98). The result, according to Dewey and Lippmann, was the further erosion of the viability of democracy traditionally conceived through the ethos of the rugged individual and the idealized small town. From the vantage point of 1927, Dewey wondered whether that individual was turning "ragged." In its stead, he called for a new individualism based on "the new social corporateness that is coming into being" (Dewey, 1930, p. 83). This "new individualism" required a richly cooperative ethos in which personal aspirations become increasingly defined through vital social intercourse within the contexts of multiple publics and a broad array of social networks.

It was democracy that was central to Dewey's (1930) vision, "the ideal of equality and opportunity and freedom for all without regard to birth and status." This ideal, grounded in the promise of 1776, was what Dewey viewed as "our essential Americanism . . . prized as the new note of a new world" (p. 17). It was this grounding that Dewey pointed to as the basis of the nation's core political value system, even as the promise has remained elusive throughout much of the nation's history. On his interpretation, this could only *but* take the inevitable organizing principles of the contemporary era into account for even the prospect of establishing a revitalized democratic ethos in the new climate of the third decade of the 20th century. This required a cultural and intellectual embrace of a new individualism equipped to deal with the associational challenges of the time.

Dewey's (1927) key question was whether under the circumstances of modern life, in which "there are too many publics for conjoint actions" (p. 137) of an enduring sustainable sort, any coherent notion of a viable public was possible. To this momentous problem, to which Lippmann could only supply a prognosis of skepticism, the question that Dewey posed— but only partially answered—was: "By what means shall its inchoate and amorphous estate be organized into effective political action relevant to present social needs and opportunities?" (p. 125). His brief answer, which he did not view as on the horizon short of the transformation of what he referred to as the Great Society into an idealized Great Community, was free and open communication of the vital issues of the day as the very basis and bedrock of democracy. The core challenge, the very ethos of the political tradition on which Dewey staked both his vision and identity was in finding "the conditions under which the inchoate public now extant may function democratically." In "its generic social sense," democracy as a way of life as he elsewhere put it, is synonymous with the free-flowing impetus of open communication and diligent inquiry sustained throughout the political culture.

Dewey's vision of the Great Community was an ideal, which by its very nature, was perpetually beyond the horizon of realization. However, the search for it as a utopian strain based on the ideal of America, as embodied in the spirit of 1776, had untold practical influence in the work of progressively moving toward it in the creation of a more humane culture in the present. It was the possibility of this nurturing as a viable cultural product that Dewey viewed as an indispensable prerequisite for the progressive discovery of "the means by which a scattered, mobile and manifold public may so recognize and define and express its [real] interest" (p. 146).

Description was one thing. A detailed roadmap was another—one that Dewey did not supply. As he acknowledged, the sketch of a revitalized public that he proposed was only a "hypothetical one." He had no assured sense that the political reconstruction that he sought would occur. He focused instead on the negative claim that without its progressive realization, democracy itself could only be impaired (p. 157). Sill, he did provide more than a bare outline in identifying something of substance of the ideal even without a detailed means–ends analysis.

Central to this was vital community engagement through a variety of mediating structures. In this, at least in its ideal construct, "the pulls and responses of different groups reinforce one another" with the result that "their values accord" (p. 148). This sense of vital communities was the organizing ideal to Dewey's notion of the "associated life." Hence, it is through "conjoint activity" where "the idea of democracy" most thoroughly pertains (Dewey, 1939/1993). As a cultural resource, its flourishing requires embodiment "in all the incidents and relations of daily life." It is this foundation of democracy based on the "faith in the potentialities of human nature as that nature is exhibited in every human being irrespective of race, color, sex, birth, and family" (p. 242) that Dewey viewed as the cultural analogue to the Declaration of Independence.

On this cultural definition, "liberty is that secure release and fulfillment of personal potentialities which take place only in rich and manifold association with others." This Dewey (1927) further defined as "the power to be an individualized self making a distinctive contribution and enjoying in its own ways the fruits of association" (p. 150). This was his vision of the United States in its finest utopian potential as a living experiment in democracy and liberty through the convergence of personal fulfillment and cultural reconstruction. Nothing short of the continued viability of this legacy was at stake, Dewey argued, in the resolution of the public and its problems in the early decades of the 20th century.

Similar problems face the U.S. adult literacy sector in the first decade of the 21st century. Its public is scattered and eclipsed despite the potency of literacy as a symbol of democratic possibility in the progressive realization of human potentiality and cultural reconstruction through adult basic education. The diffusion of the network itself is a major problem in the difficulty of galvanizing a coherent public response, although that has always been the case with this sector even with the centripetal force that NIFL provided in the 1990s. An equally pressing problem may be the lack of a unifying public philosophy in which adult literacy is linked with the core values of the nation's political culture as latently embedded in the EFF project and as discussed throughout this chapter.

Given the sharp conflicts that have marked recent history, there is more than a little reason for skepticism. Even still, following Dewey, I issue the negative rejoinder that unless something like a coherent public philosophy of adult literacy education emerges, the current state of fragmentation and contested ground is only likely to continue. Beyond that, "it is sheer defeatism to assume in advance of actual trial that democratic political institutions are incapable of either further development or of constructive social application" (Dewey, 1935/2000, p. 86). Unless the effort is made, it will not be known if the experiment in democratic reconstruction as applied to this field is possible. At the same time, the prospect is only viable if some notion of an American realistic utopia is something that can be believed in and worked toward as a live option of committed practice. That, too, remains uncertain. I can only articulate the hypothesis at this point, noting that the failure to give it due consideration also constructs reality within the channels of certain pathways. Regardless of the choices that are made, consequences follow.

A DOUBLE-VISIONED PERSPECTIVE

In NLA discussions spanning several years, it is primarily Catherine King and I that have discussed the relation between the U.S. political ethos and adult literacy with some consistent depth. Drawing both on the historical lineage of the U.S. constitutional tradition and Dewey's concept of a reconstructed public through the revitalization of mediating structures and institutions, King and I situate the politics of literacy within a reformed impetus within capitalism that seeks to realize the fuller potential of the nation's democratic political culture. I have also made this argument in a series of articles in situating this form of democratic politics of literacy as a "symbolic midway point between structural-functional views of literacy linked to the stabilization of the status quo and more radical Freirian variants that seek substantial transformation of the social order" (Demetrion, 2002, p. 34).

The working hypothesis of this chapter is that situating the politics of literacy within this mediating framework can help to establish a consensual value system based on core American principles. This ground, in turn, would link federal policy to an enhanced appreciation of the many contexts wherein adult literacy education contributes to the public good. Such a reconstruction would represent a substantial expansion in values from the predominant model of human capital development that underlies federal policy. A democratic focal point would far from eliminate the economic rationale, but would contextualize it as a key dimension within this broader framework. For this project, I mostly build on Dewey (1927, 1930, 1935/ 2000), Bellah, Madsen, Sullivan, Swindler, and Tipton (1992, 1996), and Rawls (1993, 2001), who provided substantive content for such a politics from somewhat different, although related, angles.

On an optimistic note, it is argued here that this democratic lineage holds the potential to undergird a coherent political culture through which to situate the politics of adult literacy in the United States that is currently lacking. For this shift in values, I draw heavily on Rawls' (1993, 2001) concept of *justice as fairness*, which provides some of the political and constitutional interstices to buttress Dewey and Bellah et al.'s more cultural interpretation of democracy and civic responsibility. Whereas this democratic vision has often been belied by reality, the ideals expressed in the nation's founding documents—namely, the Declaration of Independence, the U.S. Constitution, and Bill of Rights—speak to enduring, although far from fully realized, values within the American political culture. The ideals also resonate within much of the main focus of adult literacy education, and particularly EFF, in helping individuals to become more connected to the U.S. mainstream in work, family, and community settings while maintaining their own sense of individual identity (Demetrion, 1998; Fingeret & Drennon, 1997).

The gap between the ideal and reality has often bred a sense of skepticism, if not outright cynicism. This also is an important aspect of the nation's political consciousness often overlooked by those seeking consensus and common values in the quest for a workable praxis. Moreover, an unswerving critical stance remains vital as an essential dimension of the political landscape. With Villa (2001), this book accepts the important role of critic in the exercise of "a corrosive intellectual honesty" (p. 20) that seeks to puncture holes in comprehensive and largely utopian efforts of social/ political reconstruction. As Villa put it, the position of skeptic requires a certain "estrangement of thought from politics, from the incessant demands of active citizenship" for the purpose of elevating independent thinking through the vocation of "dissident citizenship" (p. 30). For this, Villa offered the skepticism of the Socratic gadfly. In raising issues and questions that those invested only in building the city cannot or dare not ask, Villa argued that this critical posture is essential to becoming a "philo-sophical citizen" (p. 36). In Villa's vision, the most profound political "thinking does not take place in the public realm," but "through a space and form of discourse of its own" (p. 38), in which Pericles and Socrates are sharply contrasted.

What Villa sought to subject to a powerful Socratic dissolvent is any no-tion "that citizens are in need of something like a shared political faith or a strong sense of common values if they are to rise above the anomie and in-difference which characterizes so much of contemporary political life" (p. 56). He was less concerned about such alienation that haunts the writing, particularly of Bellah et al. (1992, 1996), who attempted to construct the "good society" through what Villa would view as the aegis of a nostalgic civic republican tradition reconstructed for the modern era through an ideal-ized engagement of the active citizen. According to Bellah et al. (1996), "The erosion of meaning and coherence in our lives is not something Americans desire" (p. 282), although the authors viewed its reality as a per-vasive tendency of modernization. In their call for a republican reconstruc-tion of the U.S. political culture, the authors did not long to embrace "a neotraditionalism that would return us to the past." Rather, they sought cul-tural resources resident, although largely latent, within core national values that "might lead to a recovery of a genuine tradition, one that is always self-revising and in a state of development." It is this hermeneutical retrieval of the civic republican tradition that the authors seek to draw on to "help us find again the coherence we have almost lost" (p. 283).

In agreement with Diggins (2000), Bellah et al. (1992) acknowledged that "Lockean individualism" is, in many respects, the nation's "central value system." However, with Barber (1998), they argued that this is funda-mentally flawed in its one-sided emphasis on rights to the greater neglect of constructing a viable democratic polity based on the broader public good on which certain political theorists argue, the vitality of the American ex-periment in democracy depends. "Institutional change," for which the au-thors of *The Good Society* advocate in the public realms of government, law, business, economics, education, and religion, "involve(s) changing the value system . . . through drawing on alternative ones that already have some standing in the society," notably the underdeveloped, but potentially viable, "civic republican tradition" (Bellah et al., 1992, p. 288). The public good, which the authors defined as that "which benefits society as a whole," consists of "everything from adequate public facilities to the trust and civic friendship that makes public life something to be enjoyed rather than feared." In short, the civic republican tradition "presupposes that the citi-zens of the republic are motivated by civic virtue as well as self-interest. It views public participation as a form of moral education and sees its purposes as the attainment of *justice* and the *public good*" (Bellah et al., 1996, p. 335, italics in original).

This chapter draws selectively on this tradition, which shares close affinities with Dewey's cultural vision of democracy through a revitalized public and Barber's (1998) image of "strong democracy." Rawls' (1993) concept of *justice as fairness* sifted through his text *Political Liberalism*, which also influences this chapter, draws on another set of presuppositions than the "comprehensive" (Rawls' term) belief in civic republican ideology, which nonetheless, shares important similarities to it. This reconstructive project to tease out these more expansive aspects of the U.S. political tradition is tinged with more than a little critical skepticism. Yet, it does not do so to the extent of dousing the tempered hope that grounds the reform impetus inherent in the nation's political culture, which has risen to the surface at specific critical times.

Villa (2001) was more skeptical. What troubled him is less the assumed anomie and fragmentation as expressed by Bellah et al., Barber, and Dewey. Rather, it is the concern that the common "social life and [received] public opinion are constantly generating shared beliefs, passions and rarely examined convictions . . . [that] has the character of a feverish dream since it is driven by misguided certainties about wherein virtue exists and who is and is not virtuous" (p. 57). Instead of "the will to believe" (p. 56) that some claim is needed to sustain the good society, critical Socratic questioning "gives us something [else] to aspire to: a disillusioned and hence and more authentic brand of moral citizenship" (p. 58). This is a view shared by Diggins (1994), who in his sustained attack against the pragmatic philosophical tradition places "gnawing suspicion . . . [as] the critic's highest obligation" (p. 431).

Notwithstanding his skepticism, Villa (2001) acknowledged both the role of Pericles and Socrates in maintaining the vitality of Athenian democracy so that city building and critical reflection go hand-in-hand, even as they have sharply distinctive functions. Given this important context where "Athens' constitution makes democratic individualism possible" (p. 49), Socratic skepticism serves as a continuous reminder that any effort at political reconstruction not only remains incomplete and fragmentary. It is also potentially dangerous in its fulfilled state in the Tocquevillian specter of the tyranny of the majority run amok that can brook no significant countervoice in the public square.

However, there is little prospect of that in the civic republican tradition, which remains at most a muted, although potentially viable, subtext to more dominant trends pervasive within the contemporary U.S. political culture. This chapter goes forward in democratic theory construction in search of the good society, with the specter of Villa's Socratic gaze sharply in mind even if the critical voice at times seems understated in the work of pressing in on the effort to draw out something of its fuller potential.

Whatever the limitations, and they are substantial, as promise has occasionally moved closer to reality—whether in the women's, labor, or civil rights movements of the 19th and 20th centuries—the founding democratic vision has served an important leverage point at critical historical junctures. As put by Rawls (1993), "I think it a matter of understanding what earlier principles require under changed circumstances and insisting that they now be honored in existing institutions" (p. xxxi). As similarly expressed by Macedo (1990), "The founding era . . . must be seen not as a completed act of liberal statecraft, but as the initiation of an ongoing project of publicly interpreting, questioning, debating, and reshaping . . . in the struggle to complete the unfinished business of liberal construction" (p. 76). Macedo characterized the U.S. Constitution as "an aspirational document that provides not only institutions to argue within, but ideals to strive for and argue about . . . like basic human equality" (p. 76). It is on this vision of "a more prefect union" that this chapter seeks to establish the telos for a renewed politics of literacy within the context of U.S. political culture.

At certain times, this democratic vision has enabled marginalized groups to claim the right of inclusiveness based on the values expressed in those founding documents, specifically, the rights to freedom, liberty, and equal opportunity, the sine qua non of the American creed of justice. It is the priority of these rights that grounds Rawls' (1993) vision of justice as fairness in a call for "reciprocity" in the quest for "social cooperation between citizens" in a social and political culture marked by "reasonable pluralism" (pp. 3–4). For Rawls, this profound minimalism on core constitutional values is "the most reasonable basis of social unity available to citizens in a modern democratic society" (p. xli). In varying ways, Dewey, Bellah and his colleagues, Rawls, and Hart (2002) drew on the taproot of the democratic constitutional ethos, whether in more literal or more symbolic manifestations, as in Dewey's expansive vision of democracy as a way of life in the fulfillment of human potential. At times, this political framework has resulted in law that has given such claims further sources of legitimacy, an enactment, it is argued, that is critical to its fuller embodiment (Habermas, 1998). Through his lyrical refrains, Lincoln characterizes the political tradition of U.S. democracy as something "constantly looked to, constantly labored for, and even, though never perfectly attained, constantly approximated, and thereby constantly spreading and deepening its influence and augmenting the happiness and value of life to all people, of all colors, everywhere" (cited in Macedo, 1990, p. 76).

As put by Diggins (2000), "Always Lincoln returns to the meaning and significance of the Revolution." On this, Diggins was no gnawing skeptic. As he explained:

> As in the Revolution, so too in the Civil War Lincoln is less interested in politi-
> cal explanations than in moral convictions about America's historical founda-
> tions. He seeks to bring the past into a meditative association with the pres-
> ent. The meaning and purpose of American history for Lincoln is to make its
> political ideals a vital part of the contemporary national culture—and culture
> is not only what a country has accomplished but also what it has chosen to re-
> member about itself. (p. 181)

It was this exact vision that Martin Luther King Jr. drew on 100 years later in his "I Have a Dream" speech, where he wedded the civil rights movement of the 1960s to the nation's founding vision in the Declaration of Independence, as well as to the "aspirational" language of the Preamble to the U.S. Constitution.

The challenge for adult literacy is whether or not, and/or the extent to which, a similar level of legitimacy for a constitutionally based "aspirational" democracy as a grounding value can be attained at the dawn of the 21st century. Without such a linkage, it is argued the field is likely to remain limited in its capacity to find a substantial voice within the political culture. This is so because other political discourses, notably those stemming from human capital development and related cost–benefit utilitarian precepts, will tend to continue to circumscribe the realm of what becomes defined as political legitimacy.

There are compelling reasons why such a coherent political framework is unlikely to come to pass in such a marginalized field as adult literacy. The force of the current thinking to dominate political reality is pervasive. So also are the difficulties of sustained coalition grassroots mobilization to effect significant change at the federal level. The capacity of the field to ground such politics within a coherent conceptual framework of democratic theory is also a matter of no minor account in assessing the viability of an accompanying democratic praxis. The challenges are formidable with the effort perpetually haunted by the knowledge/power specter of Foucault's critical gaze.

Given the influence of the past to shape the present and foreseeable future, there are good grounds to remain skeptical, but one wonders what impact such a "realistic" stance has in moving forward or forestalling democratic *praxis*; in short, what alternatives are available instead of pursuing this vision of adult literacy education? To discount the difficulties is to place a utopian gloss on natty political details that have perplexed the field since at least the early 1990s. Yet, to assume that it will fail is to prematurely close the door on the constrained, but open experiment of U.S. democracy (Schlesinger, 1986). It is to the specifics that we now turn. For that we draw on the NLA postings of King and myself and incorporate more formal scholarship on political culture to further broaden the discussion.

A DEMOCRATIC COMMONWEALTH VISION

While noting its value for students, Doingo-Ingersoll (NLA, May 18, 1999) questioned the relevance of Catherine King's claim of building "democratic community" and providing for "a social meeting place" as a "sufficient program objective" in securing funding support for adult education programs. King responded that such purposes are valid "combined with other objectives" of a more specific educational focus. King further maintained that social facilitation "is an implicit mandate of a democratic society who wants to remain civilized and therefore democratic." This argument was premised on the assumption that "all educational programs have a social dimension," even while acknowledging that some are more focused on specific educational objectives like "reading and doing computer work." The balance between the two differs with the specific focus of programs. Pointing to social facilitation as an important function of culture, King argued that if this subtle influence were downplayed in adult education, the intrinsic value of "a civilization" itself could "slowly erode."

Extending her argument, King pointed to what she viewed as the "corrosive force" and "short-sightedness of fiscal policy that still defines education in positivist terms [where q]uality is defined as quantity." From this premise, King argued, "education merely means getting a job; [which supports the notion that] if human performance is not robotic, it's inadequate; and everything is for something else and never for itself" (King, NLA, May 19, 1999). Against this, King contrasted the relaxed informality "of a social meeting place and the facilitation of community" (Doingo-Ingersoll, NLA, May 18, 1999) that allows for a broader exchange of ideas than might be accessible through a functional focus of learning in the more restrictive sense. Elaborating on this idea, King elsewhere noted:

> *If* [italics in original] we are really a democracy, education is an adult right and a policy makers' first-priority democratic duty. Funding continuing adult education is central to creating and maintaining a vibrant civil society, a strong productive and creative infrastructure-matrix, and is essential to anyone's idea of what it means to be involved in a "commonwealth," as in [a] "Common" "Wealth?" (King, NLA, June 10, 2001)

If the cultivation of such a learning environment is not a policy objective, then it should be, King argued, both for the sake of the participating students and for the vitality of the culture in the effort to better realize the nation's founding ideals of a democratic polity stemming from citizenry education in the wide sense. In short, King embodied a Jeffersonian vision of participatory and locally based democracy where citizens come together to discuss significant issues and sometimes to act on them.

King further discussed the connection between democracy and collaborative associations in another message. Drawing on DeTocqueville's *Democracy in America* as a reference point, King noted that "a single voice in a democracy carries little weight." It is for the purpose of enhancing democracy, she argued, that "in America voices are grouped together in associations and groups" (King, NLA, November 8, 1999). The democratic communities that comprise the adult education learning centers provide an apt model, a concept taken up by Hart (2002) in his discussion of ward republics. In contrast to " 'third world' countries" that often consist of "oppressive regimes," in the United States, King argued, the challenge is not to create new forms of government, but to more truly live out the principles inherent within the nation's core political traditions. For this reason, there is no need within the United States "to develop a new political system from the ground up. Our problem . . . is for the people here to rediscover and recognize the value of what they already have, and take the necessary steps to keep it" (King, NLA, November 8, 1999). Such principles have less to do with the machinery of government per se, that is, the structure of democratic institutions, although these are critically important. It is, rather, in fully living out of a democratic value system in no small measure through the voluntary associations and institutions like public libraries, which strengthen community and knowledge building in local and neighborhood settings.

In a more critical vein, King questioned the wisdom of the current thrust of federal policy on adult literacy as "woefully ignorant of the intimate relationship between general education and the civilizing factors that are crucial to a developing democratic culture" (King, NLA, November 11, 1999). The failure to substantially support adult education in its linkage to the ethos of democracy not only bodes ill for individual students but also impairs the republic. As Hart (2002) put it, "Education for Jefferson was both the most important function of democratic government and the means of its survival." The influence was mutually reinforcing. "Democratic citizens required education to enable them to participate in government, and educated citizens needed to participate in government to preserve and promote democracy" (p. 135). Lincoln (2000) expressed it this way:

> Upon the subject of education, not presuming to dictate any plan or system respecting it, I can only say that I view it as the most important subject which we as a people can be engaged in. That every man receive at least a moderate education, and thereby be enabled to read the histories of his own and other countries, by which he may duly appreciate the free value of our institutions, appears to be an object of vital importance, even on this account alone, to say nothing of the advantages and satisfaction to be derived from all being able to read the Scriptures, and other works both of a religious and moral nature, for themselves. (p. 223)

Lack of attention to this grounding point of cultural citizenship as a basis to support adult education should cause policymakers to be vitally concerned, King argued. As she rhetorically asked, who "will carry the civilizing vision if those in power don't?" (King, NLA, November 11, 1999).

King pointed to the wide gap between the need for adult education based on the commonwealth vision of the virtuous republic and current government policy. In her view, the problem was confirmed and compounded based on statistics of those served and the professed need, as defined by the National Adult Literacy Survey (NALS), in identifying 90 million Americans bereft of adequate skills to function proficiently in society. Based on these "realities," King questioned what she viewed as the highly reductionist response of a federal policy focused on "trying to collapse programs together to save money, or merely focusing on short-term 'jobs,' or worrying obsessively about accountability issues at the expense of everything else." In an argument reminiscent of Dewey's in linking education broadly conceived as part and parcel of a common humanizing quest to enrich both individual lives and the common body politic, King drew specific connections between this expansive view of adult education and the republican values of the constitutional ethos of the United States. In her words, "The inalienable rights of 'life, liberty, and the pursuit of happiness' are no cliché, and are not unrelated here. If 'happiness' means 'a good life,' and a good life means to discover, understand, and pursue one's own potential, then a continued general education is where living minds and hearts go to open up our potential and 'pursue happiness.'"

On this understanding, "literacy is the first door to this 'liberty.' It is not a gift of government. It's a mandate issued from the Constitution" (King, NLA, November 11, 1999). Elsewhere expressed, "Once legislators recover a notion of adult education as a civic duty, funding adult education . . . will take on another hue" (King, NLA, December 28, 2000).

NLA list moderator, David Rosen (NLA, April 8, 2001), challenged King to "explain to us where in the U.S. Constitution this right and promise is, or where state legislative and administrative bodies have made the specific promise that all adults are entitled to free general education, regardless of age." In questioning the very capacity of adults who were unable to read to participate in the civil discourse, King argued that literacy "is absolutely essential to a participatory democracy." King also pointed to the Preamble to the Constitution that called for "a more perfect union" and "the Blessings of Liberty to ourselves and our posterity" (NLA, April 8, 2001) and wondered what the value of such " 'blessings' " could be "if no one understands them." Pointing to the First Amendment, King wondered that "without literacy and education [how] adults [are] supposed to be 'free' to do these very things that the First Amendment is supposed to secure for us, like read the 'press,' or 'speak' intelligently . . . or to 'petition the Government for a redress of grievances.' " Echoing Jefferson, she insisted that it is "education [that] rests at the basis of the whole project."

King concluded in a Jeffersonian/Deweyan refrain by linking democracy to education broadly defined in which the two mutually reinforce each other:

> Our Constitution is a generalized document written precisely that way so that human consciousness—thoughtful human beings—can then mediate the general into the ever-changing particular. I believe that the situation of Literacy and Adult Education is on the cusp of a crisis in our democracy, where the particular situation is straining against the underlying tenets of the Constitution that already assume, as the First Amendment clearly shows, commonwealth principles and a fundamentally literate and educated polity. (King, NLA, April 8, 2001)

King further elaborated on her views in a discussion with Tom Smith, where she agreed that adult literacy needs to be "tied to a broader agenda of empowering and mobilizing the marginalized." However, she disputed the notion that this consists of traditional leftist politics in terms of "organizing for unions, health care, livable wages, civil rights, etc." King identified a prior set of values, a "political agenda *already extant* [italics in original] in all education and teaching." This is "the potential release that invites the students to follow their own questions and develop their own selves."

The more fundamental objective, therefore, is in "releas[ing] in our students the critical exigence that *would* [italics in original] question such things as oppressive work and family situations, and the political threads that connect these situations to themselves and their situations, e.g., their individual and group power inherent in voices raised around their own issues." Based on these assumptions, overt "political participation is but a probable response to this prior release and awareness" that will follow as students expand their capacity to analyze the complex set of issues that variously impact their lives. What is needed, King argued, is a polity that supports and legitimizes policy justification for adult literacy on the premise that the "foundational . . . connection between democracy and adult education" (King, NLA, June 11, 2001) serves the national interest in the broadest sense of perpetually revitalizing the democratic roots of the U.S. political culture. Going beyond the argument that adult literacy education is merely a right, King elsewhere maintained that the more fundamental matter is the political solvency of the nation's constitutionally rooted political culture. In a comment rhetorically intended for policymakers, King argued: "You have a responsibility to the whole idea of a democracy you live in to take all possible and reasonable steps to ensure literacy and education for our adult population—the polity who are the substance of our political culture" (King, NLA, July 30, 2001).

Based on King's commonwealth vision, "adult continuing education is not a gift from taxpayers." Neither "does it require a proximate return on investment" in the narrow or literal sense. It represents, rather, a critical baseline "of a vibrant and healthy democracy." Accepting job skill development training as one essential aspect of adult literacy education, King insisted that the more primary matter is to "maintain the power balance between corporate and Commonwealth interests." Balancing such social interests is the "political responsibility" of the government as an essential feature of "educat[ing] our citizens to understand their own voices in a democratic-commonwealth culture" (NLA, July 30, 2001).

King identified additional ways that "adult education and democracy are connected." The first is the importance of teaching adult literacy students more "*about* [italics in original] democracy" (NLA, July 30, 2001). A reasonable inference from King's messages is that the content of an adult education civics curriculum would include an exploration of the underlying dynamics and persisting tensions in the unfolding drama of the U.S. "experiment" in democracy, with a sharp focus on stimulating among students the capacity to think critically about them.

King also identified the importance of expanding the knowledge base of adults through a broad array of topic areas and projects. The result of such public knowledge acquisition from her commonwealth perspective is that the intellectual capital of the polity would be expanded. Given the increasing knowledge demands and multifaceted information flows of the early 21st century, King maintained that it is more important than ever to nurture through adult education "the vibrant ground of general reflection and dialogue, and the development of the People [an obvious constitutional image] who make up our culture" (King, NLA, March 6, 2002). For King, this represented a primary responsibility of sustaining a democratic polity that provides the political rationale on which to situate and clarify the literacy practices identified by the proponents of the New Literacy Studies, embedded in EFF, and in Dewey's concept of democracy and education. In short, "the more complex the world is, the more crucial is the ongoing education of our adults" (King, 2002, p. 28).

King's understanding of democracy is radical in the Deweyan (1935/2000) sense "as perception of need for radical change" regardless of how gradual and partial such change may be in fact. Although the "educational task [of informing democratic citizenship] cannot be accomplished merely by working on men's minds without action that effects actual change in institutions," what Dewey referred to as "resolute thought, is the first step in the change of action that will itself carry further the needed change in patterns of mind and character" (p. 66). Without such a belief as an operative ideal that has undetermined consequences in real-world settings, Dewey argued that any impetus toward the vision of democracy as a way of life is invariably limited and artificially restricted by more "realistic" mind-sets that often serve the purpose of creating self-fulfilling and self-sealing prophecies. It is this vision of democracy as a way of life, wedded to the literacy myth as promise of fulfillment of the American idealism of radical inclusiveness, that King and Demetrion (below) argued could serve as the outer perimeter of a reconstructed politics of literacy congruent within the basic tenets of the U.S. political culture.

THE CONTRIBUTION OF ADULT LITERACY TO THE PUBLIC GOOD

Following King's lead, Demetrion (NLA, February 10, 2001) joined the discussion through a call for "a policy reconstruction [that included] a broadening of what is viewed as the public good." This required "shifting the perceived value of adult literacy from an economic argument to that of enhancing the democracy, which includes the former, but does not place it as the central policy *raison d'être* for the field's justification." As Demetrion argued, the EFF focus on the three social roles of family member, community member, and worker, along with an expanded role of the self, could provide the basis for an underlying public philosophy of adult literacy. What would need to be more deliberately spelled out is the role of the participatory citizen engaged in enhancing the viability of mediating institutions.

Demetrion pointed to "three major contributions of adult literacy to the public good; hence, to the democratic republic of the United States of America." Drawing on the EFF project, Demetrion identified the first potent source as the increased impact adult literacy learners could have in various local institutions and social networks. Such impact is often circuitous, as the distinction between literacy and what Sternberg (1997) referred to as *practical intelligence* applied to various social contexts is not always direct nor easily discernable. One of the major contributory influences for the strengthening of a democratic culture is that "such enhanced mediating institutions and social networks . . . help to create better bridges between the autonomous individual and large social forces [that] . . . strengthen the body politic in its varied manifestations" (Demetrion, NLA, February 10, 2001). That is at least their potential.

Bellah et al. (1996) called such engagement the enhancement of "social capital" in response to the pervasive impact of "pressures to disengage from the larger society" (p. xi). The authors linked the notion of *social capital* to "the confident sense of selfhood that comes from membership in a society . . . where [members] both trust and feel trusted, and to which [members] . . . securely belong" (p. xi). It is the public confidence in this connection that the authors believe is in jeopardy and needs to be reconstituted for the preservation and enhancement of the public good and as a basis of renewal for U.S. democracy.

The authors of *Habits of the Heart* did not maintain that the strengthening of mediating institutions alone would resolve the many social and economic problems that perplex the United States. These require broader societal and economic reform "to overcome institutional difficulties that cannot be directly addressed by voluntary [or local] associations alone." Still, the authors did identify mediating institutions and associations as powerful points of contact where individuals can have sustained impact within the immediacy of the contexts to which they are or could be engaged. Hence, "over the long haul [they can] increase our social capital and thus add to the resources we can bring to bear on our problems" (p. xxiii).

In addition to the strengthening of mediating institutions, Demetrion identified a second contribution of adult literacy to the public good in the prospect of creating a profusion of print and video-based texts based on the voices and experiences of adult literacy learners. Such texts would become incorporated into "all levels of schooling, public forums, and other venues" (Demetrion, NLA, February 10, 2001) to stimulate fruitful social and cultural interchange. More broadly, such a resource could contribute to a flourishing of a more comprehensive range of "pluralistic perspectives which characterize our national life" that would "expand upon who has the right to speak and be heard within a public context" through a public articulation of voices from "the bottom-up." Demetrion maintained that this expansion of public discourse "would enhance the entire culture" and thereby strengthen the ethos of democracy, as expressed in Dewey's (1939/1993) felicitous phrase as "a way of life" (p. 241).

The third contribution of a revitalized adult literacy education to the public good that Demetrion envisioned is the field's potential influence in expanding a more general understanding of the educational process that could impact on schooling at any level. Demetrion based this claim on the assumption that, given its experimental and community-based focus in a wide array of social environments supported by a range of divergent pedagogies, "adult literacy education [potentially] . . . is one of the most creative forms of education that exist[s]." Following this logic, Demetrion maintained that "a well-supported system would better enable the field to push its creative edge further." This would not only enhance the quality of adult literacy programs, but would "make a contribution to practice, research, and theory throughout the field of education and, most certainly, throughout the sub-field of adult education within its many branches" (Demetrion, NLA, February 10, 2001).

In drawing on Barber (1998) in another message, Demetrion contrasted democracy in the weak and strong sense and located current policy in the former and his and King's position on literacy and democracy in the latter.

As he put it, on the surface, few would disagree on linking democracy and adult literacy to what King referred to as "a new mainstream foundation for adult education and literacy in the United States" (cited in Demetrion, NLA, March 17, 2001):

> On the face of it in the democratic, though capitalistically driven republic of the United States of America, who would disagree? But the nub of the matter, and this is really critical, is whether democracy in the strong sense represents the foundational value system of the nation's political culture to which the economic system is subordinate, or whether the economic system is primary, to which the political system is subordinate. On the latter reading, democracy in the weak sense might better serve the requirements and logic of capital, than democracy in the strong sense. . . . This is particularly so if democracy in the strong sense also requires a vibrant civic culture premised on the notion of the public good, defined in terms of human flourishing, a more egalitarian realization of distributive justice, and the strengthening of our mediating institutions. The latter includes the workplace, but also our civic institutions and local communities. As Catherine [King], David Heath, and others have argued, literacy, at all levels of society is an important mediating factor in the expansion of democracy and the establishment of a more humane society.

In pushing this argument, Demetrion noted the substantial gap between given "realities" and the ideal, as he and King had variously articulated it. Although this gap should never be ignored or dismissed, what was required, Demetrion argued, was less attention to "measuring the distance, which remains vast, but moving toward it, however likely piecemeal and partial . . . [through] dynamic linkage between advocacy from below (the field) with what ultimately becomes instituted into law." This necessitated a "We the People" sensibility of sustained participatory advocacy in order to move beyond the current political focus "which perhaps represents a lot of specialized interests, particularly corporate" (Demetrion, NLA, June 30, 2001). This was an ethos of democracy in the strong sense as outlined by Barber (1998), which "employs a language of citizenship, community, fraternity, responsibility, obligation, and self-realization" (p. 129), a viewpoint considerably distant from current practice.

This somewhat expansive notion of democracy would not negate the language of rights as well as that of "interest, privacy, contract, and representation," which as an exclusive focus, Barber connected to democracy in the weak sense. Barber's broader intent is to "ground [this rights-based language] . . . in the actual conditions of interdependency and sociability that constitute the real social and economic environment of politics" (p. 129). For Barber, this means pushing the more visionary streams of U.S. constitutional and democratic thought in a manner that leads to "a change in emphasis rather than a radical remaking of the American system of government" (p. 130). King and Demetrion similarly advocated for this tempered position.

Even still, the matter of moving viably toward this ideal remains problematic. On Demetrion's argument this requires subtle discernment on identifying focal points of plausibility in negotiating the space between current realities and future prospects. Focusing on the gap, Demetrion (NLA, July 30, 2001) acknowledged that the image of democracy for which he and King advocated, supported in the literature of Barber, Dewey, Bellah et al., and Rawls "is always going to outpace the reality." Still, the vision remains critical as a frame of reference to focalize field direction and advocacy based on premises that he elsewhere identified as "the outer perimeter of the idealism of American society and culture based on its founding [political] myths" (Demetrion, 2002, p. 54).

This was an embrace of the "liberal tradition" in a reconstructive mode "in the quest to progressively humanize it." This space is grounded in "political meliorism," a "pragmatic trajectory" of moving, sometimes imperceptibly, other times more dramatically, "from the given to the potential" (p. 55) within the highly specific context of U.S. democratic and constitutional thought and practice. Notwithstanding the invariable gap between the reality and ideal, Demetrion called for "some inspiring middle ground . . . [in order] for the moderate left and the enlightened mainstream to come together to pursue the long-term work at hand." This would require working "across the spectrum of [political] ideology [in a way] . . . that respects both pluralism and the need to move forward with a coherent and inclusive vision of the future." With an admixture of hope and skepticism, Demetrion (NLA, June 30, 2001) referred to such a vision as "worthy of this nation's best efforts" and wondered whether there was "the collective will and political courage to pursue it with unswerving vigor and critical acumen."

Demetrion continued in a follow-up message to draw out some of its problematic aspects, while continuing to look both with hope and skepticism through an exercise of political culture making, rather than accepting, the given as a permanent reality. Pushing the duality of hope and skepticism, he wondered from where, if not in these founding ideals, viable "values [would] arise to establish an underlying framework for a political culture of adult literacy education for a long-term national vision." Extending the query, he acknowledged that the vision he and King proposed might be "too all-embracing and encompassing for the more 'pragmatic' and piecemeal work that needs to take place." This was less an admission than a potential point of public probing in the seeking of coherent ground through which to establish a politics of literacy viable at the national level.

While acknowledging the doubts and searching for open discussion, Demetrion maintained the negative "that unless something more enduring/more coherent grounds the process, then the field is not likely to get off the dime of interest politics." That being the case, Demetrion speculated that policy would continue to be "defined by whatever climate governs DC politics at whatever time policy is pursued." If the field were going to take "a more determinate role in shaping its own destiny," then it would need to engage "the political culture through a combination of grassroots and top-down initiatives via a more coordinated and inclusive field effort." This would require, in turn, a "common value system respectful both of pluralism and diversity, which characterizes our field and U.S. culture . . . [that] yet provides a platform for a commonality of action and belief." This, he argued, could most comprehensively stem from a "reconstruction of the U.S. democratic tradition" (Demetrion, NLA, July 1, 2001).

Notwithstanding this tempered hope, critical questions remained. "Can the field mobilize the internal resources to put together a viable consensus to build its house for the long haul? . . . Would such an effort result in the desired impact? Would the work be worth the effort?" (Demetrion, NLA, July 14, 2001). In turn, what was the price to be paid for not pursuing the vision? Demetrion "neither dismiss(ed) the prospect or assume(d) necessarily that it is or will be easy." Rather, he held to the negative ground by emphasizing that, short of a "core connection between sound practice and sound scholarship to that of policy, only fragmentation and dissention and/or a lot of resignation/withdrawal would be the probable end result." However difficult or improbable, "given the current policy focus on economics, there is not another public philosophy" other than democracy to offset the impact of capitalism to shape the field's political value structure. While admitting his own doubts, Demetrion argued that the position for which he and King contended was "both substantial and largely neglected, though premised on core values of the U.S. political culture (even amidst the contradictions)." Needed were "forums where this argument can be meaningfully fleshed out" (NLA, August 2, 2001) to help in the very determination of whether or not the effort to pursue this was viable. As he argued, the experiment had yet to take place.

In an NLA message titled "Meeting Adult Needs: Reality vs. Rhetoric," Sticht (NLA, February 17, 2002) referred to research (Sum, Kirsch, & Taggart, 2002) pointing to the nation's "mediocrity and inequality" in "accepting in fact, if not in rhetoric, 'a basic skills underclass.' " Demetrion noted that "from a certain structural view in terms of maintaining current power arrangements . . . such an underclass may be viewed as functional." From this perspective, rhetoric on democracy could be interpreted as a manifestation of the "hidden curriculum" designed to reinforce given socioeconomic arrangements. Still, in pointing to the priority placed on "American values" in the U.S. Department of Education (USDoE) under the Bush administration, Demetrion argued that this emphasis had the ironic potential of stimulating "a thorough and critically profound analysis of the US democratic tradition." That, in turn, "could also lead to the re-newal of public and policy support for adult literacy."

In drawing out this problematic, although plausible, prospect, Deme-trion noted that any such "vigorous national debate . . . will raise a plurality of perspectives and . . . inevitably veer into the realm of ideology." Whether the conservative-leaning USDoE would "foster such an open discussion within the contexts of our classrooms and U.S. history and civics curricu-lums" remained problematic. Challenging also was whether "the progres-sive left . . . [could] take seriously the . . . U.S. constitutional and demo-cratic traditions as an important framing perspective . . . even while maintaining a sharp critical analysis of any current embodiment . . . in pointing to its greater realization." Hence, whether there was "a collective will" across the ideological spectrum to pursue any such national discussion able to take "democracy . . . however variously defined as a methodological grounding point," remained a troubling matter (Demetrion, NLA, Febru-ary 18, 2002).

Demetrion's probe was intended to exploit largely untapped possibili-ties, based on the call to embrace patriotism and "American values," in or-der to subject those tenets to a critical public discussion of their various meanings. This mediating space based on the U.S. constitutional and dem-ocratic ethos would "not necessarily lead to easy agreement on all the par-ticulars about what constitutes a democratic culture and society. However, it would help to provide a coherent frame of reference to ground public discussion about the trajectory of national life" wherein to situate the poli-tics of adult literacy education.

In seeking to walk a tightrope between hope and suspicion, Demetrion stressed the need to maintain a methodological open mind as essential to the search for a viable politics of literacy within the context of the U.S. polit-ical culture. As he put it in another message, "it is imperative not to cede the imperfect U.S. constitutional and democratic tradition to the neo-con-servatives, but with [Jessie] Jackson [Jr.] and others, to contest with and against them on the meaning of this 'more perfect union' and how it be-comes enacted in the life of this nation" (Demetrion, NLA, March 2, 2002).

JUSTICE AS FAIRNESS AS A PRINCIPLED
MINIMALISM FOR A PUBLIC PHILOSOPHY
OF ADULT LITERACY EDUCATION

In acknowledging the difficulties inherent in identifying a "broad-based in-clusive consensus," Demetrion (NLA, March 5, 2002) argued for a method-ological minimalism based on Rawls' concept of "justice as fairness." Rawls based this notion on the enduring reality of the pluralism of modern U.S.

society. From this vantage point, it is not plausible to establish collective unity on comprehensive principles such as a retrieval of the civic republican tradition as called for by Bellah et al. (1996), or the Freirian-based "pedagogy of the oppressed" in its largely wholesale critique of the given U.S. political structure. "The issue is whether there is a coordinating principle or perspective, a profound minimalism [within the context of the main tenets of U.S. political culture] that can evoke widespread agreement, notwithstanding the notable differences in comprehensive doctrines" (Demetrion, NLA, March 5, 2002) across the body politic.

What is needed, Rawls (1993) argued, is an "overlapping consensus" on core principles, which, for such nations as the United States, stems from its basic constitutional ethos. In drawing on core constitutional principles, the pragmatic social consensus "is based on something substantive and not merely [on] what arises amongst the community of participants themselves" (Demetrion, NLA, March 5, 2002). This is in contrast to the Habermasian ideal of intersubjective communication, which is implicit in Merrifield's (1998) call for dialogue as a possible way of resolving the field's contested ground. It is also a point of divergence from "a somewhat narrow interest politics, which unwittingly or not, reinforces a cost-benefit, utilitarian mind-set" (Demetrion, NLA, March 5, 2002) characteristic of the politics of the National Coalition of Literacy and state directors of adult education.

Rawls (2001) situated his position of constitutional democracy on two basic principles. At the most primary level is the axiomatic assumption that "each person has the same indefeasible claim to a fully adequate scheme of basic liberties, which scheme is compatible for all." Based on this prior assumption, "social and economic equalities are to satisfy two conditions: first, they are to be attached to conditions of fair equality to all under conditions of fair equality of opportunity; and second, they are to be the greatest benefit of the least advantaged members of society" (pp. 42–43). Notwithstanding acute differences in interpreting what equality of opportunity means in concrete situations, Rawls' political vision contains a strong distributive theory of justice for the purpose of enabling all citizens to exercise their basic liberties. This, in turn, stems from the "original position" (p. 14) based on the political culture of a constitutional democracy of "free and equal citizens engaged in cooperation, and made in view of what they regard as their reciprocal advantage or good" (p. 15).

This principled position is Rawls' axiomatic starting point for the grounding of his admittedly idealized political philosophy, the most reasonable basis that he can discern for situating a degree of social unity amidst the ineradicable pluralism of modern life. Given the reality of "reasonable pluralism" "what better alternative is there than an agreement among citizens themselves reached under conditions that are fair for all"

(p. 15), he argued, based on the core assumptions resident in the nation's founding political documents? In providing a clearing ground stemming from these most basic premises of constitutional democracy, Rawls chipped away "an uncluttered view" (p. 8) in the construction of a coherent political framework on the foundational principles of liberty, equality, and opportunity for all citizens.

From this staring point, Rawls identified "primary goods" that "citizens need as free and equal persons living a complete life" in a constitutional democracy. "They are not things it is simply rational to want or desire, or to prefer or even to crave." Rather, Rawls pinpointed the primary goods as a "political conception" (p. 58) of those things that most contribute to the two principles on which justice as fairness is established: the right to liberty and equality of opportunity. These include the basic rights of free speech articulated in the 1st Amendment. Primary goods also refers to aspects of the social realm, such as "freedom of movement and freedom of choice against a background of diverse opportunities, which opportunities allow the pursuit of a variety of ends and give effect to decisions to revise and alter them" (p. 58). In addition, primary goods address issues of "income and wealth . . . generally needed to achieve a wide-range of ends, whatever they may be" (pp. 58–59). They also refer to more subtle matters like "the social basis of self-respect, understood as those aspects of basic institutions normally essential if citizens are to have a lively sense of worth as persons and be able to advance their ends with self-confidence" (p. 59).

Rawls based his concept of political justice on a limited rather than comprehensive framework, like those stemming from Marxism, biblical theology, the civic republican tradition, or critical pedagogy. Nonetheless, his swathe cuts wide in identifying the factors that contribute to the notion of radical equality and basic liberties deemed essential to ground the concept of citizenship in a constitutional democracy. For example, based on Rawls' argument, "background institutions must work to keep property and wealth evenly *enough* [italics added] shared over time to preserve the fair value of the political liberties and fair equality of opportunity over generations" (p. 51). This needs specificity, and is subject to argumentation, as Rawls acknowledged. Notwithstanding this important consideration, it is precisely in these primary goods that he established the basis for justice as fairness measured in terms of social reciprocity. This claim, in turn, stems from core constitutional premises, which give clarity to his concept of distributive justice. Among these primary goods, Rawls held a high place for education that advocates of adult literacy could build on to more sharply define the literacy practices identified by Merrifield, Barton, and others. These, then, can be linked with the concept of justice as fairness as an axiomatic grounding point for a politics of literacy and provide a degree of coherency currently lacking congruence within the political culture of the United States.

Justice as fairness represents a different grounding point to situate the politics of literacy beyond that of human capital development, while drawing on a set of assumptions that are plausible from the perspective of the main tenets of the U.S. democratic and constitutional political culture. Rawls identified this position not as a foundational stance based on precepts of universal justice. He viewed it, rather, as "realistically utopian . . . [in] probing the limits of practical possibility" (p. 4) within the specific political culture of the United States. It serves as a coordinating principle to ground a degree of social unity amidst a highly pluralistic society. In short, justice as fairness, is a political concept in

> seek[ing] to moderate divisive political conflicts and to specify the conditions of fair social cooperation between citizens. To realize this aim, we try to work up, from the fundamental ideas implicit in the political culture, a public basis of justification that all citizens as reasonable and rational can endorse from within their own comprehensive doctrines. If this is achieved, we have an overlapping consensus of reasonable doctrines, and with it, the political conception affirmed in reflective equilibrium. It is this last condition of reasoned reflection that, among other things, distinguishes public justification from mere agreement. (p. 29)

Like Bellah et al., Rawls was concerned about what may be viewed as the undue fragmentation of the nation's social life and political culture. Given the enduring reality of pluralism in contemporary U.S. life, Rawls looked for a more restrictive framework through an "overlapping consensus," where those of diverse persuasions agree on core constitutional principles. Rawls' political vision is based on a prior assumption of "what . . . a just society [would] be like under reasonably favorable but still possible historical conditions, conditions allowed by the [i.e., *this*] social world" (p. 4). While sharing a broad affinity with Barber, Dewey, and Bellah et al. in the quest to proximately fulfill the utopian vision of U.S. democracy, he added considerable specificity in pursuing the logic inherent in what he interpreted as fundamental constitutional principles.

Rawls based his political philosophy on the notion of a "well-ordered society," an essential precondition needed to establish "reciprocity" throughout the body politic. Without this, he argued, it would be impossible to "adjudicate . . . claims of political right" (p. 9) that stem from agreed on principles based on his constitutional vision of justice as fairness. Rawls acknowledged that such a society does not pertain in the actual practice in politics of the United States. Rather, it remains "hypothetical, since we ask what the parties . . . could, or would, agree to, not to what they have agreed to." He also conceded that his proposal is "nonhistorical, since we do not suppose the agreement has ever, or indeed ever could actually be entered into" (pp. 16–17).

The importance of the ideal for Rawls "lies in the fact that it is a devise of representation or, alternatively a thought-experiment for the purpose of public- and self-clarification." That is, "it models what we regard—here and now—as fair conditions under which the representatives of citizens, viewed solely as free and equal persons, are to agree to" (p. 17) based on constitutional principles *if* a well-ordered society did exist. Through this ideal (what Rawls might refer to as the underlying telos of the U.S. political culture), the principle of reciprocity comes into play in mediating justice as fairness throughout the civic and social polity. In this respect, justice as fairness is similar to any ideal. What Rawls claimed as unique is its finely attuned calibration to the intricacies of constitutional democracy stemming from foundational principles, working outward. Still, he acknowledged that the gap between the ideal and the actual is incredibly distant, if not perpetually elusive. As Rawls concluded:

> We try to show that the well-ordered democratic society of justice as fairness is possible, and if so, how its possibility is consistent with human nature and the requirements of workable political institutions. We try to show that the well-ordered society of justice as fairness is indeed possible according to our own nature and those requirements. This endeavor belongs to political philosophy as reconciliation; for seeing that the conditions of a social world at least allow for that possibility affects our view of the world itself and our attitude toward it. No longer need it seem hopelessly hostile, a world in which the will to dominate and oppressive cruelties, abetted by prejudice and folly, must inevitably prevail. None of this may ease our loss, situated as we may be in a corrupt society. But we may reflect that the world is not in itself inhospitable to political justice and its good. Our social world might have been different and there is hope for those at another time and place. (pp. 37–38)

This may seem improbable. Skepticism is more than warranted. Yet, the counter problem of grappling with the implications of not pursuing something akin to this vision also requires consideration in any substantial evaluation of Rawls' theory of justice as applied to a reconstructed U.S. politics of literacy.

SUMMARY ANALYSIS

This chapter poses no easy solutions in the quest to establish a democratic politics of literacy congruent with the founding ideals of the political culture of the United States. Skepticism abounds on a variety of perspectives, from the enduring pluralism and contestability of the field's constituency, to the suspicion that constitutional democracy itself in the strong sense—as variously advocated by Barber, Dewey, Bellah et al., and Rawls—can provide the needed framework. Whether from the literacy mainstream of the NCL and state directors of adult education, the advocates of participatory and critical pedagogy, or the neoconservative intellectuals and policymakers of the current USDoE, there is little present inclination to embrace the U.S. democratic and constitutional ethos to situate the politics of adult literacy in the construction of a federal or national vision. Neither does Dewey's more expansive notion of democracy and education provide any self-evident organizing synthesis. Such skepticism does not negate the viability of the project outlined herein. However, it does raise the most critical of issues as to the place of any visionary ideal as well as this particular one as played out in the realpolitic of DC interest politics and the enduring pluralism of contemporary social life.

We proceed, first, by rearticulating the problem, the field's marginality in the body politic. The NCL and state directors have called for an operational consensus, which is echoed in Merrifield's *Contested Ground* (1998) and other quarters. With the singular exception of EFF, and there only partially so, the basis, the value system, the political context, and the pedagogical framework to ground such an accord have not been laid out. Merrifield and Stites, in particular, highlighted the sharply contestable positions of various major constituents when underlying issues are pressed. Merrifield's call for dialogue is vital. Yet, this Habermasean quest for consensually driven communicative reasoning in the disinterested search for the better argument, does not resolve the potent issue of coming to terms with values in a divisive political culture.

Whether the deliberate articulation of the ethos of the U.S. democratic and constitutional tradition in quest for "a more perfect union" can provide a basis in values to give shape to a coherent politics of literacy has not been tested. It is less to revisit the problems at this stage than to discerningly probe into this prospect in order to flesh out something of the fuller potential of what it may offer and then to consider continuing problems. Particularly valuable is the prospect of establishing a political philosophy grounded in the founding political culture of the United States. This vision has reverberated at times, throughout the nation's history, to usher in political, cultural, and social reform by tapping into the primary values of equality, liberty, opportunity, and social justice for all. As an American birthright, these values point to the very consequence of citizenship that grounds the doctrine of popular sovereignty.

Stated in the negative, what is at stake in not embracing this value system as a foundation for the reconstruction of the politics of literacy is the very basis of this democratic and constitutional ethos. In the baldest terms, it either does in fact represent the political value system underlying the nation's political culture, or it is a chimera, sometimes embraced as rhetoric to mask something considerably less, notably the interest politics of those groups and sectors that possess the most power and influence within and over the federal government. What is at risk, then, is not merely surrendering the illusion of idealism. Rather, it is any notion of democracy in the strong sense as a fundamental political value, *in fact*, of the nation's political culture. As argued, this political grounding point, although often muted, has the capacity at critical junctures to tap into the nation's most idealistic, what Rawls named "realistically utopian" beliefs, as a leading source of democratic reform. The critical issue, in the language of William James, is whether democracy as discussed in this chapter represents a "live option" congruent with the nation's most realistically idealistic political values. Remaining with the negative, the question then becomes what it means, in fact, not to embrace the quest for "a more prefect union" at the very least, as a realistically utopian national project in providing the long-term coherency in situating the politics of literacy in the United States.

It is hypothesized here that if adult literacy can find its public voice within and through this democratic ethos, it will be tapping into the most potentially dynamic energies of the American political culture. That does not guarantee success as the experiment in self-government continues. The concern is that unless the field of adult literacy can develop a politics of literacy congruent with the more dynamic ideals of the political culture in which it is situated, it is likely to be subsumed by forces that define the field from without. If democracy as articulated in this study does not provide the core political identity for adult literacy in the quest to move from the margins to the mainstream, then one wonders what sources of value and influence will come to define the politics of literacy.

The hypothesis formulated in this chapter builds on an assumption of gradualism. This would include an expansion of investment language, focusing more on long-term impact, as part of a broader paradigmatic shift from human capital development toward democracy as the underlying public rationale in support of adult literacy education. This expanded notion of investment language would be wedded to the constitutional premise of adult basic education as, in Chisman's (2002) words, an "inalienable right," based on the foundational premises of popular sovereignty and participatory democracy. The larger objective is to establish a discourse "where images of 'investment' in literacy can imperceptibly merge with broader rationales linked to the strengthening of the public good" (Demetrion, NLA, December 31, 2001). As similarly put by Chisman (2002), whereas it is imperative for adult literacy to base its public rationale "on the highest national principle," such idealism needs to be wedded to "the muse of self-interest." Given the ethos of democratic capitalism at the core of the political culture, the only viable near-term framework for a reconstruction of the politics of literacy in the United States is to show how "self-interest and principle intersect" (p. 13). Even still, the issue of values priority cannot be easily avoided, lest the long pull of a cost–benefits utilitarian rationale continues to dominate and constrain the realm of what is viewed as the possible.

A viable praxis that seeks to stimulate a shift in values would need to include the critical work of negotiating with the current political system, along with maintaining investment language as a critical pillar of public justification. This would also require realistic appraisals of the constraints imposed by any current legislative cycle. It is difficult not to fathom the need for political realism of the most sophisticated sort if the field is to maintain even the tenuous public legitimacy it currently posses, a far cry from any shift "from the margins to the mainstream" proposed by Sticht and others. The outstanding issue is whether such interest politics, including a more expansive notion of investment language, should characterize the long-term policy as the *singular major rationale* of the field, or whether a more comprehensive values reorientation based on an intentional embrace of democracy would be needed to undergird this effort.

There are notable risks in any field embrace of a fundamental realignment that seeks to move beyond cost–benefits utilitarianism (self-interest) to that of democracy as an underlying political framework to situate the politics of literacy. Obviously, there are no guarantees of success. Yet, and this is no small matter, by drawing on this political vision, the field has an additional resource in tapping into the political process itself by calling the government to account on its own professed value system. This may be particularly germane in the current Bush administration, with the USDoE's emphasis on "American values," patriotism, and civic virtue. On the argument of this chapter, the field would enjoin this discussion by basing its value system on the substance of these terms and calling any administration or congress to account that utilizes such language as a form of rhetoric to mask other interests. Legitimate disagreement on the meaning of U.S. democracy will remain, and they are substantial (Barber, 1998; Novak, 1991). Yet, the field itself would have a potent vehicle to keep the discussion on adult literacy grounded within an overarching political framework stemming from the founding discourses of the U.S. republic. One viable result would be a likely contribution to the civic education of the nation by more fully publicizing the nation's founding political vision, in its embedment, however partially, in any given historical period.

Any such shift would not likely come from the grassroots level alone, but would require some giving way among key political leaders of the "politics of interest" (Bellah et al., 1996, p. 200) to that of a "politics of the nation" (p. 202). It would require, metaphorically speaking, a meeting halfway of engaged citizens working with mediating institutions at the grassroots and local levels with those within larger institutions of government, law, business, and education willing to draw on the more idealistic strands of the nation's founding political vision for the common work of reconstructing the quality of public life. For Bellah et al., the fuller potential of this civic vision can only come to play when the top leadership of a Washingtonian or Lincolnian quality matches the impassioned commitment to the public good at the local level among organized constituencies. As expressed in the *Good Society* (Bellah et al., 1992), "to renew the endowment of our political institutions we must simultaneously reinvigorate an active citizenry and develop organizational forms [at the broader national level] in which their participation can be meaningful" (p. 133). Without this, the large institutions of national life that invariably intrude on what Habermas referred to as the "lifeworld" cannot but deleteriously effect the quality of life at the local level, such as the operation and the values orientations of local adult literacy and ABE programs.

Whether Rawls' profound minimalism can provide an operative framework for a reconstructive politics of literacy is an open issue and there are good reasons to doubt it. On the other hand, without something like this as a way of providing a semblance of coherency within a pluralistic society, stemming from the nation's foremost political ideal, the quest for a "more perfect union," it is quite plausible that the consensus called for will simply not be able to gel. Still, any embrace of this vision is a precarious affair requiring compelling motivation combined with the intentional behavior of a wide collection of groups and social networks that would lead something akin to a social contract between them.

Whether or not, or the extent to which, such a move would be productive to the long-term viability of the field, or even plausible, remains an open question. In the final analysis, there may be nothing more available than what Popper (1957) called "piecemeal social engineering," which he contrasted to the "utopian engineering" that may be an apt depiction of even of Rawls' restrained vision. Yet even that, which on Popperian terms is a hypothesis, does not discount the role of ideals in facilitating reform. The matter merits further scrutiny in terms of possibilities open to the field of adult literacy and as a reflection of the vibrancy of the nation's political culture.

References

Academic Innovations. (2000). *The SCANS skills and competencies: An overview.* Retrieved January 2, 2004, from http://www.academicinnovations.com/report.html

Adult Education and Family Literacy Act: Program year 2000–2001. Report to Congress on State Performance. Washington, DC: Office of Vocational and Adult Education.

Akinnaso, F. N. (1991). Literacy and individual consciousness. In E. M. Jennings & A. C. Purves (Eds.), *Literacy systems and individual lives: Perspectives on schooling* (pp. 73–94). Albany, NY: State University of New York Press.

Ananda, S. (2000). *Equipped for the Future assessment report: How instructors can support adult learners through performance-based assessment.* Washington, DC: National Institute for Literacy.

Antonio, R. J. (1998). Mapping postmodern social theory. In A. Sica (Ed.), *What is social theory? The philosophical debates* (pp. 22–75). Oxford, England: Blackwell.

Archambault, R. D. (Ed.). (1964). *John Dewey on education.* Chicago: University of Chicago Press.

Aronowitz, S., & Giroux, H. A. (1993). *Education still under siege* (2nd ed.). Westport, CT: Bergin & Garvey.

Auerbach, E. R. (1989). Toward a social-contextual approach to family literacy. *Harvard Educational Review, 59*(2), 165–180.

Auerbach, E. R. (1992a). Literacy and ideology. *Annual Review of Applied Linguistics, 12,* 71–85.

Auerbach, E. R. (1992b). *Making meaning, making change: Participatory curriculum development for adult ESL literacy.* McHenry, IL: Center for Applied Linguistics and Delta Systems.

Auerbach, E. R. (1993). Putting the p back in participatory. *TESOL Quarterly, 27*(3), 543–545.

Auerbach, E. R., & Wallerstein, N. (1987). *ESL for action: Problem posing at work.* Reading, MA: Addison-Wesley.

Author unknown. (1995). *National skills standards for high performance manufacturing.* Washington, DC: National Coalition for Advanced Manufacturing.

Author unknown. (1997). *Not by myself: Creating communities of new writers in the south.* Durham, NC: Literacy South.

Barber, B. (1998). *A passion for democracy: American essays.* Princeton, NJ: Princeton University Press.

Barton, D. (1994a). *Literacy: An introduction to the ecology of written language.* Malden, MA: Blackwell.

Barton, D. (1994b). Preface: Literacy events and literacy practices. In M. Hamilton, D. Barton, & R. Ivanic (Eds.), *Worlds of literacy* (pp. vii–x). Clevendon, Avon: Multilingual Matters.

Beder, H. (1991). *Adult literacy education: Issues for policy and practice.* Malabar, FL: Krieger.

Beder, H. (1999). *The outcomes and impacts of adult literacy education in the United States.* Cambridge, MA: National Center for the Study of Adult Learning and Literacy.

Beder, H. W., & Valentine, T. (1990). Motivational profiles of adult basic education students. *Adult Education Quarterly, 40,* 78–94.

Bednar, A. K., Cunningham, D., Duffy, T. M., & Perry, J. D. (1992). Theory into practice: How do we link? In T. M. Duffey & D. H. Jonassen (Eds.), *Constructivism and the technology of instruction: A conversation* (pp. 17–34). Hillsdale, NJ: Lawrence Erlbaum Associates.

Bell, D. (1967). Notes on the post-industrial society. *The Public Interest,* No. 6, pp. 24–35, and No. 7, pp. 102–118.

Bell, D. (1973). *The coming of the post-industrial society.* New York: Basic Books.

Bellah, R. N., Madsen, R., Sullivan, W. M., Swindler, A., & Tipton, S. M. (1992). *The good society.* New York: Vintage.

Bellah, R. N., Madsen, R., Sullivan, W. M., Swindler, A., & Tipton, S. M. (1996). *Habits of the heart: Individualism and commitment in American life.* Berkeley: University of California Press.

Bernstein, R. J. (1983). *Between objectivism and relativism.* Philadelphia: University of Pennsylvania Press.

Bernstein, R. J. (1986). *Philosophical profiles: Essays in a pragmatic mode.* Philadelphia: University of Pennsylvania Press.

Bingman, B. (2000). *Action research on documenting learner outcomes: Can we move beyond the Workforce Investment Act?* 2000 AERC Proceedings. Retrieved January 2, 2004, from http://www.edst.educ.ubc.ca/aerc/2000/bingmanm1-final.PDF

Bossort, P., Cottingham, B., & Gardner, L. (1994). *Learning to learn: Impacts of the adult basic education experience on the lives of participants.* British Columbia, Canada: Adult Basic Association of British Columbia. Retrieved August 12, 2004, from http://www.nald.ca/fulltext/pat/L2L/cover.htm

Bowles, S., & Gintis, H. (1976). *Schooling in capitalist America: Educational reform and the contradictions of economic life.* New York: Basic Books.

Bransford, J. D., Brown, A. L., & Cockings, R. R. (1999). *How people learn: Brain, mind, experience, and school.* Washington, DC: National Academy Press.

Burke, F. T., Hester, D. M., & Talisse, R. B. (Eds.). (2002). *Dewey's logical theory: New studies and interpretations.* Nashville: Vanderbilt University Press.

Burke, T. (1994). *Dewey's new logic: A reply to Russell.* Chicago: University of Chicago Press.

Carabell, J. (1999). Confessions of a reluctant standard-bearer. *Focus on Basics, 3*(Issue C), 15–18.

Carnevale, A. (1991). *America and the new economy.* Washington, DC: American Society for Training and Development/U.S. Department of Labor and the U.S. Department of Education.

Carnevale, A. P., Gainer, L., & Meltzer, A. (1990). *Workplace basics: The essential skills employers want.* San Francisco: Jossey-Bass.

Carr, W., & Kemmis, S. (1986). *Becoming critical.* London: Falmer Press.

Cheatham, J. B., Colvin, R. J., & Laminack, L. L. (1993). *Tutor: A collaborative approach to literacy instruction.* Syracuse, NY: Literacy Volunteers of America.

Cherryholmes, C. C. (1988). *Power and criticism: Poststructural investigations in education.* New York: Teachers College Press.

Cherryholmes, C. C. (1999). *Reading pragmatism.* New York: Teachers College Press.

Chisman, F. P. (1989). *Jump start: The federal role in adult literacy.* Southport, CT: Southport Institute for Policy Analysis.

Chisman, F. P. (2002). *Adult literacy and the American dream.* Council for Advancement of Adult Literacy. Retrieved January 2, 2004, from http://www.caalusa.org/caaloccasionalpaper1. pdf

Chisman, F. P., & Associates. (1990). *Leadership for literacy: The agenda for the 1990s.* San Francisco: Jossey-Bass.

Cochran-Smith, M., & Lytle, S. L. (1993). *Inside/outside: Teacher research and knowledge.* New York: Teachers College Press.

Comings, J. (1992). Keeping assessment out of program accountability. In L. McGrail & L. Purdom (Eds.), *Adventures in assessment. Volume 3: Looking back, starting again* (pp. 43–44). Boston: System for Adult Basic Education Support.

Condelli, L. (1996). *Evaluation systems in the adult education program: The role of quality indicators.* Washington, DC: Pelavin Research Institute.

Condelli, L., & Kutner, M. (1997). *Developing a national outcomes reporting system for the adult education program.* Washington, DC: U.S. Department of Education Office of Vocational and Adult Education and Literacy.

Content Standards for Adult Performance—Revised. (1998, November). National Institute for Literacy.

Cook, W. (1977). *Adult literacy education in the United States.* Newark, DE: International Reading Association.

Corley, M. A. (2003). *Poverty, racism, and literacy* (ERIC Clearinghouse on Adult, Career, and Vocational Development No. 243 EDO-CE-02-243). Retrieved January 2, 2004, from http://www.ericfacility.net/databases/ERIC_Digests/ed475392.html

Corley, M., & Taymans, J. M. (2001). Adults with learning disabilities and the role of self-determination: Implications for literacy programs. *Canadian Journal for the Study of Adult Education,* November, 149–167.

Covey, S. R. (1995). *The seven habits of highly effective families.* New York: Covey Leadership Center.

CT's Annual Performance Report 2001. (2002, March 8). Handout at meeting with local ABE directors.

Custer, R. L. (2000). Authentic assessment—Basic definitions and perspectives. In R. L. Custer, J. W. Schell, B. McAlister, J. L. Scott, & M. Hoepfl, *Using authentic assessment in vocational education* (pp. 1–5). Columbus, OH: ERIC Clearinghouse on Adult, Career, and Vocational Education Center on Training for Employment.

Custer, R. L., Schell, J. W., McAlister, B., Scott, J. L., & Hoepfl, M. (2000). *Using authentic assessment in vocational education.* Columbus, OH: ERIC Clearinghouse on Adult, Career, and Vocational Education Center on Training for Employment.

D'Amico, D. (1997). *Adult education and welfare to work initiatives: A review of research, practice and policy.* Washington, DC: National Institute for Literacy.

D'Amico, D. (1999). *Politics, policy, practice, and personal responsibility: Adult education in an era of welfare reform.* Cambridge, MA: National Center for the Study of Adult Learning and Literacy.

Dascal, M. (1997). *Epistemology, controversies, and pragmatics.* Online paper presented at Conference After Postmodernism. University of Chicago. November 14–16, 1997. Retrieved January 2, 2004, from http://www.focusing.org/apm_papers/dascal2.html

Demetrion, G. (1995). *Welcome to our world: A book of writings by and for students and their tutors. Volume II.* Hartford, CT: Literacy Volunteers of Greater Hartford.

Demetrion, G. (1996). Book review. Peter M. Senge. *The fifth discipline: The art and practice of the learning organization.* New York: Doubleday Currency. *Adult Basic Education, 6*(2), 105–111.

Demetrion, G. (1997a). Adult literacy and the American political culture. In D. R. Walling (Ed.), *Under construction: The role of the arts and humanities in postmodern schooling* (pp. 169–192). Bloomington, IN: Phi Delta Kappa Educational Foundation.

Demetrion, G. (1997b). Student goals and public outcomes: The contribution of adult literacy education to the public good. *Adult Basic Education, 7*(3), 145–164.

Demetrion, G. (1998). A critical pedagogy of the mainstream. *Adult Basic Education, 8*(2), 68–89.

Demetrion, G. (1999a). The postindustrial future and the origins of competency-based adult education in Connecticut: A critical perspective. *Adult Basic Education, 9*(3), 123–148.

Demetrion, G. (1999b). A scaffolding paradigm: Small group tutoring at the Bob Steele Reading Center 1990–1999. *Adult Basic Education, 9*(1), 46–66.

Demetrion, G. (2000a). *Crossing critical thresholds at the Bob Steele Reading Center: Transforming potentiality into actuality.* Retrieved January 2, 2004, from http://www.nald.ca/fulltext/ George/crossing/page1.htm

Demetrion, G. (2000b). Practitioner-based inquiry: Theoretical probings. *Adult Basic Education, 10*(3), 119–146.

Demetrion, G. (2000c). *Reflecting on culture wars in adult literacy education: Exploring critical issues in "Contested Ground."* National Adult Literacy Data Base. Retrieved January 2, 2004, from http://www.nald.ca/fulltext/cultrwar/cover.htm

Demetrion, G. (2001a). Discerning the contexts of adult literacy education. *Canadian Journal for the Study of Adult Education, 15*(2), 104–127.

Demetrion, G. (2001b). Motivation and the adult new reader: Student profiles in a Deweyan vein. *Adult Basic Education, 11*(2), 80–108.

Demetrion, G. (2001c). Reading Giroux through a Deweyan lens: Pushing utopia to the outer edge. *Educational Philosophy and Theory, 33*(1), 57–76.

Demetrion, G. (2002). Exploring the middle ground: Literacy as growth. *Adult Basic Education, 12*(1).

Demetrion, G., & Gruner, A. (1995). *Dialogues in literacy.* Hartford, CT: Literacy Volunteers of Greater Hartford.

Dewey, J. (1916). *Democracy and education.* New York: The Free Press.

Dewey, J. (1917). The need for a recovery of philosophy. In L. Hickman & T. Alexander (Eds.), *The essential Dewey: Vol. 1. Pragmatism, education, democracy* (pp. 46–69). Bloomington: Indiana University Press.

Dewey, J. (1927). *The public and its problems.* Athens, OH: Shallow Press.

Dewey, J. (1930). *Individualism old and new.* New York: Minton, Balch & Company.

Dewey, J. (1958). *Experience and nature.* New York: Dover. (Original work published 1929)

Dewey, J. (1963). *Experience and education.* New York: Collier Macmillan. (Original work published 1938)

Dewey, J. (1988). *Human nature and conduct.* Carbondale: Southern Illinois University Press. (Original work published 1922)

Dewey, J. (1988). *The quest for certainty.* Carbondale: Southern Illinois University Press. (Original work published 1929)

Dewey, J. (1989). *How we think* (rev. ed.). Carbondale: Southern Illinois University Press. (Original work published 1933)

Dewey, J. (1989). *Art as experience.* Carbondale: Southern Illinois University Press. (Original work published 1934)

Dewey, J. (1989). *Essays and how we think, revised edition.* Carbondale and Edwardsville, IL: Southern Illinois University Press. (Original work published 1933)

Dewey, J. (1990). *The school and society and the child and the curriculum. An expanded edition with a new introduction by Philip W. Jackson.* Chicago: University of Chicago Press.

Dewey, J. (1991). *Logic: The theory of inquiry.* Carbondale, IL: Southern Illinois University Press. (Original work published 1938)

Dewey, J. (1991). *How we think.* Buffalo, NY: Prometheus Books. (Original work published 1910)

Dewey, J. (1993). Democracy—the task before us. In D. Morris & I. Shapiro (Eds.), *John Dewey: The political writings* (pp. 240–248). Indianapolis: Hackett Publishing. (Original work published 1939)

Dewey, J. (2000). *Liberalism and social action.* Amherst, NY: Prometheus Books. (Original work published 1935)

Diggins, J. P. (1994). *The promise of pragmatism: Modernism and the crisis of knowledge and authority.* Chicago: University of Chicago Press.

Diggins, J. P. (2000). *On hallowed ground: Abraham Lincoln and the foundations of American history.* New Haven, CT: Yale University Press.

Dreyfus, H. L., & Rabinow, P. (1983). *Michael Foucault: Beyond structuralism and hermeneutics* (2nd ed.). Chicago: University of Chicago Press.

Drucker, P. (1969). *The age of discontinuity.* New York: Pan Books.

Duffey, T. M., & Jonassen, D. H. (Eds.). (1992). *Constructivism and the technology of instruction: A conversation.* Hillsdale, NJ: Lawrence Erlbaum Associates.

EFF Voice. (2001). *2*(1).

EFF Assessment Consortium. (2002). EFF/NRS Data Collection Project, 2000–2001. *An Interim Report on the Development of the EFF Assessment Framework.* University of Tennessee: Center for Literacy Studies, SRI International.

Eldridge, M. (1998). *Transforming experience: John Dewey's cultural instrumentalism.* Nashville: Vanderbilt University Press.

Engel, M. (2000). *The struggle for control of public education: Market ideology vs. democratic values.* Philadelphia: Temple University Press.

Fingeret, A. (1989). The social and historical context of participatory literacy education. In A. Fingeret & P. Jurmo (Eds.), *Participatory literacy education* (pp. 5–15). San Francisco: Jossey-Bass.

Fingeret, A., & Jurmo, P. (Eds.). (1989). *Participatory literacy education.* San Francisco: Jossey-Bass.

Fingeret, H. A. (1992). *Adult literacy education: Current and future directions an update.* Columbus, OH: ERIC Clearinghouse on Adult, Career, and Vocational Education.

Fingeret, H. A., & Drennon, C. (1997). *Literacy for life: Adult learners, new practices.* New York: Teachers College Press.

Fosnot, C. T. (Ed.). (1996). *Constructivism: Theory, perspectives, and practice.* New York: Teachers College Press.

Freire, P. (1970). *Pedagogy of the oppressed.* New York: Seabury Press.

Freire, P. (1985). *The politics of education: Culture, power, and liberation.* Granby, MA: Bergin & Garvey.

Foucault, M. (1972). *The archeology of knowledge and the discourse on language.* New York: Pantheon.

Gadamar, H. H. (2002). *Truth and method* (2nd rev. ed.). New York: Continuum Publishing.

Garrison, J. W. (1997). *Dewey and Eros: Wisdom and desire in the art of teaching.* New York: Teachers College Press.

Garrison, J. W. (1998). John Dewey's philosophy as education. In L. A. Hickman (Ed.), *Reading Dewey: Interpretations for a postmodern generation* (pp. 63–81). Bloomington: Indiana University Press.

Gee, P. (1986). Orality and literacy: From the savage mind to ways with words. *TESOL Quarterly, 20,* 719–748.

Gillespie, M. K. (2002a). *EFF research principle: A contextualized approach to curriculum and instruction.* Washington, DC: National Institute for Literacy.

Gillespie, M. K. (2002b). *EFF research principle: An approach to teaching and learning that builds expertise.* Washington, DC: National Institute for Literacy.

Giroux, H. A. (1983). *Theory and resistance in education: A pedagogy of the opposition.* South Hadley, MA: Bergin & Garvey.

Giroux, H. A. (1995). *Pedagogy and the politics of hope: Theory, culture, and schooling (a critical reader).* Boulder, CO: Westview Press.

Glasser, B. G., & Strauss, A. L. (1967). *The discovery of grounded theory: Strategies for grounded theory*. London: Weidfenfeld & Nicolson.

Graff, H. (1979). *The literacy myth: Literacy and the social structure in the nineteenth-century city*. New York: Academic Press.

Graff, H. (1987). *The labyrinths of history: Reflections on literacy past and present*. London: Falmer Press.

Gribbons, B., & Herman, J. (1997). *Practical assessment: Research & evaluation*. Accessed online at http://ericae.net/paregetvn.asp?v=5&n=14

Gunn, G. (1987). *The culture of criticism and the criticism of culture*. New York: Oxford University Press.

Habermas, J. (1973). *Legitimation crisis*. Boston: Beacon.

Habermas, J. (1998). *Between facts and norms: Contributions to a discourse theory of law and democracy*. Cambridge, MA: MIT Press.

Hart, G. (2002). *Restoration of the republic: The Jeffersonian ideal in 21st century America*. New York: Oxford University Press.

Hayek, F. A. (1960). *The constitution of liberty*. Chicago: University of Chicago Press.

Heath, S. B. (1983). *Ways with words*. Cambridge, England: Cambridge University Press.

Herman, A. (1998). *Message from the Secretary of Labor: Implementing the Workforce Investment Act of 1998*. Retrieved January 2, 2004, from http://www.doleta.gov/usworkforce/documents/misc/wpaper3.cfm

Hirsch, E. D., Jr. (1997, April 10). Mathematically correct: Address to California State Board of Education. Retrieved April 10, 2004, from http://ourworld.compuserve.com/homepages/mathman/edh2cal.htm\

H.R. 1261. (2003). *Workforce Reinvestment and Adult Education Act of 2003 (Introduced in the House)*. Retrieved January 2, 2004, from http://edworkforce.house.gov/markups/108th/21st/hr1261/320srb.pdf

Hunter, S. St. J., & Harman, D. (1985). *Adult illiteracy in the United States*. New York: McGraw-Hill.

Imel, S., Kerka, S., & Wonacott, M. E. (2002). *Qualitative research in adult, career, and career-technical education* (ED 472366). ERIC Clearinghouse on Adult, Career, and Vocational Education. Abstract summary retrieved January 2, 2004, from http://wdcrobcolp01.ed.gov/CFAPPS/ERIC/resumes/records.cfm?ericnum=ED472366

International Reading Association and National Council of Teachers of English. (1994). *Standards for the assessment of reading and writing*. Newark, DE & Urbana, IL: International Reading Association and National Council of Teachers of English.

Jackson, J. Jr., & Watkins, F. (contributor). (2001). *A more perfect union: Advancing new American rights*. New York: Welcome Rain Publishers.

Johnson, H., & Broder, D. S. (1997). *The system: The American way of politics at the breaking point*. Boston: Little, Brown.

Johnston, W. B., & Packer, A. E. (1987). *Workforce 2000: Work and workers for the twenty-first century*. Indianapolis, IN: Hudson Institute.

Jurmo, P. (1989). What needs to be done to build participatory alternatives. In A. Fingeret & P. Jurmo (Eds.), *Participatory literacy education* (pp. 81–91). San Francisco: Jossey-Bass.

Kegan, R. (1994). *In over our heads: The mental demands of modern life*. Cambridge, MA: Harvard University Press.

King, C. B. (2002). The relationship of education to democracies. In G. Spangenberg (Ed.), *Making the case: Adult education & literacy: Key to America's future* (pp. 27–28). Council for Advancement of Adult Literacy. Retrieved January 2, 2004, from http://www.caalusa.org/makingthecase.pdf

Kirsch, I. S., Jungleblut, A., Jenkins, L., & Kolstad, A. (1993). *Adult literacy in America: A first look at the results of the National Adult Literacy Survey*. Washington, DC: Education Testing Service, for the Office of Educational Research and Improvement, U.S. Department of Education.

Kliebard, H. M. (1995). *The struggle for the American curriculum 1893–1958* (2nd ed.). New York: Routledge.

Kozulin, A. (1990). *Vygotsky's psychology: A biography of ideas.* Cambridge, MA: Harvard University Press.

Kuhn, T. (1970). *The structure of scientific revolutions* (2nd ed., enlarged). Chicago: University of Chicago Press.

Kumar, K. (1978). *Prophecy and progress: The sociology of industrial and post-industrial society.* Middlesex, England: Penguin.

Kumar, K. (1995). *From post-industrial to post-modern society: New theories of the contemporary world.* Malden, MA: Blackwell.

Lagemann, E. C. (2000). *An elusive science: The troubling history of educational research.* Chicago: University of Chicago Press.

Lankshear, C. (1993). Functional literacy from a Freirian point of view. In P. McLaren & P. Leonard (Eds.), *Paulo Freire: A critical encounter* (pp. 90–118). London: Routledge.

Lappe, F. M., & Dubois, P. M. (1994). *Quickening of America: Rebuilding our nation, rethinking our lives.* San Francisco: Jossey-Bass.

Lestz, M., Demetrion, G., & Smith, S. W. (1994). *"Reading the world:" Life narratives by adult new readers. Volumes I and II.* Hartford, CT: Literacy Volunteers of Greater Hartford.

Levine, K. (1982). Functional literacy: Fond illusions and false economies. *Harvard Educational Review, 52*(3), 249–266.

Levinson, L. (1998). *Guidelines for field research.* Washington, DC: NIFL.

Lewis, T. (1998). *Toward the 21st century: Retrospect, prospect for American vocationalism.* Columbus, OH: ERIC Clearinghouse on Adult, Career, and Vocational Education.

Lincoln, A. (2000). *The life and writings of Abraham Lincoln* (P. Van Doren Stone, Ed.). New York: Modern Library.

Lippmann, W. (1997). *Public opinion.* New York: The Free Press. (Original work published 1922)

Lukes, A. (1999). *Theory and practice in critical discourse analysis.* University of Queensland, Australia, for L. Sara (Ed.). International Encyclopedia of the Sociology of Education, Elsevier Science, Ltd. Retrieved January 2, 2004, from http://www.gseis.ucla.edu/courses/ed253a/Luke/SAHA6.html

Lytle, S. L. (1991). Living literacy: Rethinking development in adulthood. *Linguistics and Education, 3,* 109–138.

Lytle, S. L., & Wolfe, M. (1989). *Adult literacy education: Program evaluation and learner assessment.* Columbus, OH: ERIC Clearinghouse on Adult, Career, and Vocational Education Center on Education and Training for Employment.

Macedo, S. (1990). *Liberal virtues: Citizenship, virtue, and community in liberal constitutionalism.* New York: Oxford University Press.

Malhotra, Y. (1994). Role of science in knowledge creation: A philosophy of science perspective. Brint Institute. Retrieved January 2, 2004, from http://www.brint.com/papers/science.htm

Manno, B. V. (1994). Outcome-based education: Miracle cure or plague? Hudson Institute, Inc. Retrieved January 2, 2004, from http://www.educationreport.org/article.asp?ID=240

Marx, K., & Engels, F. (1959). *Marx and Engels: Basic writings on politics and philosophy* (L. S. Feuer, Ed.). Garden City, NY: Anchor Books.

Maxwell, J. A. (2004). Causal explanation, qualitative research, and scientific inquiry in education. *Educational Researcher, 33*(2), 3–11.

McGrail, L. (Ed.). (1991–1994). *Adventures in assessment: Learner-centered approaches to assessment and evaluation in adult literacy* (Vols. 1–6). Boston: System for Adult Basic Education Support.

McGuire, P. (2000). Performance standards for teaching and learning with the Equipped for the Future (EFF) Content Standards [Electronic version]. In *Adventures in assessment* (pp. 1–14). Boston: SABES/World Education.

McLaren, P., & Leonard, P. (Eds.). (1993). *Paulo Freire: A critical encounter.* London: Routledge.

Merriam, S. B. (1988). *Case study research in education: A qualitative approach.* San Francisco: Jossey-Bass.

Merriam, S. B. (2001). *Qualitative research and case study application in education. Revised and expanded from case study research in education.* San Francisco: Jossey-Bass.

Merrifield, J. (1998). *Contested ground: Performance accountability in adult basic education.* Cambridge, MA: National Center for the Study of Adult Learning and Literacy.

Merrifield, J. (2000). *Equipped for the future research report: Building the framework, 1993–1997.* Washington, DC: National Institute for Literacy.

Merrifield, J., Bingman, M. B., Hemphill, D., & Bennett deMarrais, K. P. (1997). *Literacy, language, and technology in everyday life.* New York: Teachers College Press.

Mertens, D. M. (1998). *Research methods in education and psychology: Integrating diversity with qualitative and quantitative approaches.* Thousand Oaks, CA: Sage.

Mezirow, J. (1996). Contemporary paradigms of learning. *Adult Education Quarterly, 46*(3), 158–172.

Miller, D. (Ed.). (1985). *Popper selections.* Princeton, NJ: Princeton University Press.

Mislevy, R. J., & Knowles, K. T. (2002). *Performance assessments for adult education: Exploring measurement issues: Report of a workshop.* The National Academies Press. Retrieved April 10, 2004, from http://books.nap.edu/books/0309084539/html/R1.html

(n.a.). (1988). *Bottom line: Basic skills in the workplace.* Washington, DC: U.S. Department of Labor and U.S. Department of Education.

(n.a.). (1991). *Business Council for Effective Literacy: Newsletter for the Business and Literacy Communities.* No. 28 July 1991.

(n.a.). (2001). *The National Reporting System Implementation Guidelines.* Washington, DC: U.S. Department of Education.

(n.a). (2001). *Workforce Investment Act: Better guidance needed to address concerns over new requirements.* Washington, DC: United States General Accounting Office, October 2001.

(n.a.). (2001). *Measure and methods for the National Reporting System for Adult Education: Implementation guidelines.* Washington, DC: Division of Adult Education and Literacy Office of Vocational and Adult Education, U.S. Department of Education.

Naisbitt, J. (1984). *Megatrends.* New York: Warner Books.

Nash, A., Carson, A., Rhum, M., McGrail, L., & Gomez-Sanford, R. (1992). *Talking shop: A curriculum sourcebook for participatory adult ESL.* McHenry, IL: Center for Applied Linguistics and Delta Systems, Inc.

National Commission on Excellence in Education (NCE). (1983). *A nation at risk: The imperative for educational reform.* Retrieved January 2, 2004, from http://www.goalline.org/Goal%20Line/NatAtRisk.html#anchor791390

National Educational Goals Panel. (n.d.). *National Educational Goals Panel: Building a nation of learners.* Washington, DC. Retrieved January 2, 2004, from http://www.negp.gov/page1-7.htm

National Institute of Child Health and Human Development. (2000). *Adult and family literacy: Current research and future directions—A workshop summary.* Retrieved January 2, 2004, from http://www.nichd.nih.gov/crmc/cdb/AFL_workshop.htm

National Institute for Literacy-Equipped for the Future Discussion List. (1997–2004). Retrieved January 2, 2004, from http://literacy.nifl.gov/lincs/discussions/nifl-4eff/equipped_for_future.html

National Institute for Literacy (NIFL). (1998, September 21). Policy update. *Workforce Investment Act offers opportunities for adult and family literacy.* Washington, DC: National Institute for Literacy.

National Institute for Literacy (NIFL). (1998, November 18). Policy update. *States seek input in implementing new literacy law.* Washington, DC: National Institute for Literacy.

National Literacy Act of 1991. Public Law 102-73, H.R. 751.

National Literacy Advocacy Listserv (NLA). (1997–2003). Retrieved January 2, 2004, from http://lists.literacytent.org/pipermail/nla-nifl-archive/

Northcutt, N. (1975). *Adult functional competency: A summary.* Austin, TX: Texas University.

Novak, M. (1991). *The spirit of democratic capitalism.* New York: Madison Books.

Ohio State Literacy Resource Center (OLRC) Legislative Alerts. (1995–1997). Specific documents cited:

- Economic opportunity for adults, 12-19-94 (p. 155)
- The Way We Were: Policy Directives and Call to Action, 2-95 (p. 156)
- To LLA Councils, State Organizations, and Friends, 5-25-95 (pp. 150 and 159)
- From Congressman Tom Sawyer, 3-16-95 (p. 158)

Pawson, R., & Tilley, N. (1997). *Realistic evaluation.* London: Sage.

Phillips, D. C., & Burbules, N. C. (2000). *Postpositivism and educational research.* Lanham, MD: Roman & Littlefield.

Polkinghorne, D. (1983). *Methodology for the human sciences: Systems of inquiry.* Albany, NY: State University of New York Press.

Popper, K. R. (1957). *The poverty of historicism.* London: Routledge.

Popper, K. (1985). The growth of scientific knowledge. In D. Miller (Ed.), *Popper selections* (pp. 171–180). Princeton, NJ: Princeton University Press. (Original work published 1960)

Quigley, B. A. (1997). *Rethinking literacy education: The critical need for practice-based research.* San Francisco: Jossey-Bass.

Rabinow, M. (1984). *Foucault: Reader.* New York: Pantheon.

Rawls, J. (1993). *Political liberalism.* New York: Columbia University Press.

Rawls, J. (2001). *Justice as fairness: A restatement.* Cambridge, MA: Harvard University Press.

Rescher, N. (2001). *Philosophical reasoning: A study in the methodology of philosophizing.* Malden, MA: Blackwell.

Royce, S., & Gacka, R. (2001). A longitudinal study of Pennsylvania's adult education success stories. Pennsylvania Department of Education Bureau of ABLE Leadership Grant 98-00-0007. Retrieved July 31, 2004, from http://www.able.state.pa.us/able/lib/able/Learning ForLife.pdf.

Sandel, M. (1996). *Democracy's discontent. America in search of a public philosophy.* Cambridge, MA: The Belknap Press of Harvard University.

Sarup, M. (1993). *An introductory guide to post-structuralism and postmodernism* (2nd ed.). Athens, GA: University of Georgia Press.

Savner, S. (1999). *Key implementation decisions affecting low-income adults under the Workforce Investment Act.* Center for Law and Social Policy.

SCANS. (1991). *What work requires of schools: A SCANS report for America 2000.* Washington, DC: U.S. Department of Labor.

Scribner, S. (1988). Literacy in three metaphors. In E. R. Kingten, B. M. Kroll, & M. Rose (Eds.), *Perspectives on literacy* (pp. 71–81). Carbondale, IL: Southern Illinois University Press. (Reprinted from *American Journal of Education, 93,* 6–21)

Scribner, S., & Cole, M. (1981). *The psychology of literacy.* Cambridge, MA: Harvard University Press.

Searle, J. R. (1994). *The rediscovery of the mind.* Cambridge, MA: MIT Press.

Secretary's Commission on Achieving Necessary Skills (SCANS). (1992). *Learning a living: A blueprint for high performance. A SCANS report for America 2000.* Washington, DC: U.S. Department of Labor.

Senge, P. (1990). *The fifth discipline: The art and practice of the learning organization.* New York: Doubleday Currency.

Schlesinger, A. M., Jr. (1986). *The cycles of American history.* Boston: Houghton Mifflin.

Schneider, M., & Clarke, M. (1999). *Dimensions of change: An authentic assessment guidebook.* Greensboro, NC: Peppercorn Books.

Shavelson, R. J., & Towne, L. (2002). *Scientific research in education.* Washington, DC: National Academy Press.

Sica, A. (Ed.). (1998). *What is social theory? The philosophical debates.* Malden, MA: Blackwell.

Smith, S. W., Ball, E., Demetrion, G., & Michelson, G. (Eds.). (1993). *Life stories for new readers.* Hartford, CT: Literacy Volunteers of Greater Hartford.

Spangenberg, G. (Ed.). (2002). *Making the case: Adult education & literacy: Key to America's future.* Council for Advancement of Adult Literacy.

Stanovich, P. J., & Stanovich, K. E. (2003). *Using research and reason in education. How teachers can use scientifically based research to make curricular and instructional decisions.* Washington, DC: The Partnership for Reading: National Institute for Literacy, National Institute of Child Health and Human Development, U.S. Department of Education, U.S. Department of Health and Human Services.

Stein, S. G. (1992). A new framework for assessing program quality: Meeting the challenge of the National Literacy Act of 1991. In M. A. Corley, D. Lane, K. Smith, M. Williams, X. Eichorn, I. Mansoor, & S. Stein (Eds.), *Program and provider perspectives on developing indicators of program quality for adult education programs* (pp. 73–92). Washington, DC: Pelavin Associates.

Stein, S. G. (1995). *Equipped for the future: A customer-driven vision for adult literacy and lifelong learning.* Washington, DC: National Institute for Literacy.

Stein, S. G. (1997). *Equipped for the future: A reform agenda for adult literacy learning.* Washington, DC: National Institute for Literacy.

Stein, S. (2000). *Equipped for the future content standards: What adults need to know and be able to do in the 21st century.* Washington, DC: National Institute for Literacy.

Steinfels, P. (1980). *Neoconservatives: The men who are changing American politics.* New York: Simon & Schuster.

Sternberg, R. J. (1997). *Successful intelligence: How practical and creative intelligence determine success in life.* New York: Penguin Putnam.

Sticht, T. G. (1990). *Testing and assessment in adult basic education and English as a second language.* San Diego, CA: Applied Behavioral & Cognitive Sciences.

Sticht, T. G. (1997a). *Functional context education: Making knowledge relevant.* San Diego, CA: Consortium for Workforce Education and Lifelong Learning.

Sticht, S. T. (1997b). The theory behind content-based instruction. *Focus on Basics, 1*(Issue D), 6–9.

Sticht, T. G. (2000). *The adult education and literacy system (AELS) in the United States: Moving from the margins to the mainstream.* El Cajon, CA: Author.

Sticht, T. G. (2001). The International Adult Literacy Survey: How well does it represent the literacy abilities of adults? *Canadian Journal for the Study of Adult Education, 15*(2), 19–36.

Sticht, T. G., & Armstrong, W. B. (1994). *Adult literacy in the United States: A compendium of quantitative data and interpretive comments.* San Diego, CA: San Diego Community College.

Sticht, T. G., Erickson, P. R., & Armstrong, W. B. (1996). *Content standards for adult basic education: Part One. Moving toward draft standards & a vision for system reform (CONSABE): Voices from the community.* San Diego: Consortium for Workforce Education and Lifelong Learning.

Stites, R. (1999). A user's guide to standard-based educational reform: From theory to practice. *Focus on Basics, 3*(Issue C), 3–7.

Stites, R. (2000). *Regie Stites's responses to questions from the NIFL Equipped for the Future discussion list.* Washington, DC: National Institute for Literacy. Retrieved January 2, 2004, from http://www.nifl.gov/lincs/discussions/nifl-4eff/guest_stites.html

Stites, R., Foley, E., & Wagner, D. (1995). *Standards for adult literacy: Focal points for debate.* Philadelphia: National Center on Adult Literacy.

Street, B. V. (1988). *Literacy in theory and practice.* Cambridge, England: Cambridge University Press.

Stuhr, J. (2002). Power/inquiry: The logic of pragmatism. In F. T. Burke, D. M. Hester, & R. B. Talisse (Eds.), *Dewey's logical theory: New studies and interpretations* (pp. 275–285). Nashville: Vanderbilt University Press.

Sum, A., Kirsch, I. S., & Taggart, R. (2002). *The twin challenges of mediocrity and inequality: Literacy in the U.S. from an international perspective.* Educational Testing Services. Retrieved January 2, 2004, from http://www.ets.org/research/pic/twinchall.pdf

Taylor, D. (Ed.). (1997). *Many families, many literacies: An international declaration of principles.* Portsmouth, NH: Heinemann Trade.

Toffler, A. (1970). *Future shock.* New York: Random House.

Toffler, A. (1981). *The third wave.* New York: Bantam Books.

U.S. Department of Education. (2001). *Measures and methods for the National Reporting System.* Washington, DC: Division of Adult Education & Literacy Office of Vocational & Adult Education, U.S. Department of Education.

U.S. Department of Education. (2002, February 7). *Strategic Plan 2002–2007 Draft.* Washington, DC: U.S. Department of Education.

U.S. Department of Education. (2002, March). *Strategic Plan 2002–2007.* Washington, DC: U.S. Department of Education.

Venezky, R. L. (1990). Definitions of literacy. In R. L. Venezky, D. A. Wagner, & B. S. Ciliberti (Eds.), *Toward defining literacy* (pp. 2–16). Newark, DE: International Reading Association.

Viadero, D. (2002). Bill would remake OERI into education sciences' academy. *Education Week,* March 6. Retrieved January 2, 2004, from http://www.edweek.org/ew/newstory.cfm?slug=25oeri.h21

Villa, D. (2001). *Socratic citizenship.* Princeton, NJ: Princeton University Press.

Vygotsky, L. S. (1978). *Mind and society: The development of higher psychological processes.* Cambridge, MA: Harvard University Press.

Wagner, D. A. (1991). Literacy as culture: Emic and etic perspectives. In E. M. Jennings (Eds.), *Literacy systems and individual lives: Perspectives on schooling* (pp. 11–19). Albany, NY: State University of New York Press.

White, H. (1987). *The content of the form: Narrative discourse and historical representation.* Baltimore: Johns Hopkins University Press.

Wilson, W. J. (1996). *When work disappears: The world of the new urban poor.* New York: Vintage.

Workforce Investment Act—Title II. (1998). Nashville, TN: Department of Labor & Workforce Development Home Center.

Younkins, E. W. (1999). Michael Novak's portrait of democratic capitalism. *Market & Morality,* 2(1), 1–24. Retrieved January 2, 2004, from http://www.acton.org/publicat/m_and_m/1999_spr/younkins.html

Author Index

Subject Index